Design of Multithreaded Software

DESIGN OF MULTITHREADED SOFTWARE

The Entity-Life Modeling Approach

Bo I. Sandén

A John Wiley & Sons, Inc., Publication

Copyright © 2011 by the IEEE Computer Society

Published by John Wiley & Sons, Inc., Hoboken, New Jersey. All rights reserved

Published simultaneously in Canada

For general information on our other products and services or for technical support, please contact our Customer Care Department within the United States at (800) 762-2974, outside the United States at (317) 572-3993 or fax (317) 572-4002.

Wiley also publishes its books in a variety of electronic formats. Some content that appears in print may not be available in electronic formats. For more information about Wiley products, visit our web site at www.wiley.com.

Library of Congress Cataloging-in-Publication Data is available.

ISBN 978-0470-87659-6

Printed in Singapore

oBook ISBN: 978-0470-90491-6
ePDF ISBN: 978-0470-90490-9

10 9 8 7 6 5 4 3 2 1

Contents

III Background and Discussion

8 Real-Time Software Architectures and Data-Flow Design Approaches   231

Foreword

As computer-based systems become ever more ambitious and ever more complex, it is vital to keep a firm grasp of the fundamental ideas of their conception and design. This book focuses on one of the most fundamental ideas of all. The world we inhabit, and our experiences in it, have an inescapable time dimension. To deal properly with the world and to satisfy the functional requirements of the systems we build, we must master the intrinsic complexities of this time dimension. Many sequential processes progress in parallel in the world, interacting wherever events in two processes involve the same entity. The computer software must mirror, respect, and exploit this sequentiality and concurrency, and also add its own interacting processes to implement the additional behaviour and control necessary to satisfy the requirements.

Bo Sandén has written a splendid book that should be read by every developer of systems that interact with the real world. The multithreading theme that gives the book its title treats the identification and design of individual threads—that is, of concurrent processes—and the synchronisation and control of their interactions at common entities. The book succeeds excellently in this difficult area, expounding patterns of thread interaction that clarify both the problems they address and the solutions they offer.

The developer of a system of this kind must give explicit consideration both to the real world and to the world inside the computer and must recognise clearly that these are distinct, though interrelated, worlds. In some development approaches these distinct worlds are subtly confused, especially where the software itself embodies a model—that is, a surrogate or simulation—of the real world. Some writers on object-oriented development take too little thought for the distinction between a software object and the real-world entity it models. Their readers are then disinclined to pay enough attention to the real world, and the resulting systems are not quite fit for purpose. In this book, Sandén has taken care to make a clear and explicit distinction between *event threads* in the real world and the related *control threads* in the software: He gives both the real world and the software world the attention that is their due. This is a book for designers and programmers who want to align their software faithfully to the real-world requirements that they are striving to satisfy.

The central justification of a focus on threads and concurrency is the fundamental role of time in the world and in the computer, but it has another virtue too. The thread structure—capturing the role of each thread and its interactions with other threads—forms an excellent basis for the software architecture. An object structure alone cannot inform an architecture. Sandén points out that a thread structure can embody the key idea of a software architecture, clearly exposing the concept and underlying principle of the system design. This notion chimes well with the notion of the *operational principle* of a machine expounded by the physical chemist and philosopher Michael Polanyi. The operational principle of a machine specifies "how its characteristic parts—its organs—fulfill their special function in combining to an overall operation which achieves the purpose of the machine. It describes how each organ acts on another organ within this context." An object structure alone cannot reveal the operational principle of a system, but the thread structure, where threads are associated either with objects or with execution of system functions, can reveal it clearly and memorably. The book has several problem examples that illustrate architectural choice by presenting alternative thread structures embodying alternative operational principles.

MICHAEL A. JACKSON

London
October 2010

Preface

Where I am not understood, it shall be concluded that something very useful and profound is couched underneath.

JONATHAN SWIFT

This book is an introduction to the **entity-life modeling** (ELM) design approach for certain kinds of multithreaded software. ELM focuses on *reactive systems*, which continuously interact with the problem environment. They include embedded systems as well as such interactive systems as cruise controllers and automated teller machines. ELM is also useful for process interaction simulation software.

ELM is a systematic approach to threading. It doesn't attempt to make multithreading look easy but uses its full power. My goal has been to present it clearly and precisely. Not everyone in the information technology trade must understand threading. Few even venture beyond scripting and mark-up languages to traditional programming. Even with all the multiprocessors we now have, it's enough if a few understand concurrency and set up a project infrastructure that takes advantage of multiprocessing. Others can work within such a structure.

Part I covers two fundamentals: program language thread support and state diagramming. These are necessary for understanding ELM and are there chiefly as references. If you have never used threads, then a language text in Ada, C#, or Java may be the best starting point. The book is based on the following major papers on ELM:

J. R. Carter and B. I. Sandén, "Practical uses of Ada-95 concurrency features," *IEEE Concurrency*, vol. 6 no. 4, pp. 47–56, Oct./Dec. 1998.

A. Q. Dinh, "A development method for real-time software in a parallel environment." Ph.D. thesis, George Mason University, Fairfax, VA, 1994.

B. I. Sandén, "An entity-life modeling approach to the design of concurrent software," *CACM*, vol. 32, no. 3, pp. 330–343, Mar. 1989a.

B. I. Sandén, "Entity-life modeling and structured analysis in real-time software design—A comparison," *CACM*, vol. 32, no. 12, pp. 1458–1466, Dec. 1989b.

B. I. Sandén, "Modeling concurrent software," *IEEE Software*, pp. 93–100, Sept. 1997.

B. I. Sandén, "A design pattern for state machines and concurrent activities," *in Proc. 6th International Conference on Reliable Software Technologies—Ada-Europe 2001, Leuven, Belgium, May 14–18, 2001*, D. Craeynest and A. Strohmeier, Eds., Lecture Notes in Computer Science, vol. 2043, Springer-Verlag, 2001, pp. 203–214.

B. I. Sandén, "Entity-life modeling: Modeling a thread architecture on the problem environment," *IEEE Software*, pp. 70–78, July/Aug. 2003.

B. I. Sandén and J. Zalewski, "Designing state-based systems with entity-life modeling," *Journal of Systems and Software*, vol. 79, no. 1, pp. 69–78, Jan. 2006.

For me, the book in progress has served as a mind tool that let me penetrate all aspects of ELM, much more so than individual papers where a single case study must often suffice.

ACKNOWLEDGMENTS

Among those who have supported and encouraged the work on ELM in various ways over the years or otherwise have been helpful to the book project are Ben Brosgol, Anhtuan Dinh, Stephen Ferg, John Harbaugh, Jan Hext, John McCormick, Melvin Neville, Tony Robertiello, Jim Rogers, Alexander Romanovsky, Ray Schneider, Rob Scott, Alfred Strohmeier, Janusz Zalewski, and many excellent students in the graduate programs at George Mason University and Colorado Technical University and in external courses and tutorials.

In particular, Jeff Carter gave detailed feedback on the ELM chapters. Jörg Kienzle's and Janusz Zalewski's feedback greatly improved Chapters 4, 5, and 8. I also appreciate the many constructive and encouraging comments from anonymous paper reviewers.

I have quoted several works by Michael Jackson, who wrote the Foreword to this book. His recent books have also led me on to other readings. David Rine pointed me to Blum's definitive work, *Software Engineering*. Fred Brooks's *The Mythical Man-month* led me to such unlikely yet inspiring sources as Sayers's *The Mind of the Maker* and Glegg's *The Design of Design*.

Jessica Pierson helped me with line editing and found many imprecise turns of phrase. We went back and forth over some sentences and paragraphs, which was a great learning experience for me. If something still appears unclear, I must have added it afterward. She also took on the index as her personal project. Together with Martha Hall and Janusz Zalewski, she also helped me track down the sources of many quotes.

The quote that opens Section 2.2 is from Mezz Mezzrow and Bernard Wolfe, *Really the Blues*. Copyright © Mezz Mezzrow and Bernard Wolfe. Reprinted by arrangement with Citadel Press/Kensington Publishing Corp. www.kensingtonbooks.com

The quote that opens Section 9.2.1 is from Neal Stephenson, *SNOW CRASH*. Penguin Books 1993. Copyright © Neal Stephenson, 1992. Reproduced by permission of Penguin Books, Ltd.

PROGRAM EXCERPTS

Those program excerpts that are included are mostly in Ada, which may appear biased since ELM is language independent. The reason is that I no longer make a point of implementing all examples as I did when I wrote my previous book *Software Construction*. Readers are invited to implement each example in their language of choice as an invigorating exercise.

HEADINGS AND REFERENCES

Headings of sections that belong in a certain chapter but are unnecessary for basic understanding are marked with an asterisk.

Comments and suggestions are welcome at bsanden@acm.org. My current examples are mostly limited to traditional, soft real time and include various control systems. Examples illustrating other applications of multithreading would be useful.

EXERCISES

Most chapters are followed by exercises, which range from simple illustrations of central concepts from the chapter to realistic examples. Some of the latter are quite open ended and may require some research. They are based on real applications, and full specifications would be unwieldy.

Bo I. Sandén

Colorado Springs, Colorado
December 2010

FOUNDATIONS

Introduction

1

"Begin at the beginning," the King said gravely, *"and go on till you come to the end; then stop."*

Lewis Carroll, Alice's Adventures in Wonderland, 1865

"Begin at the middle," Mason said.

Erle Stanley Gardner, The Case of the Fugitive Nurse, 1954[1]

1.1 ENTITY-LIFE MODELING

At first sight, the idea of any rules or principles being superimposed on the creative mind seems more likely to hinder than to help, but this is quite untrue in practice. Disciplined thinking focuses inspiration rather than blinkers it.

Glegg, 1969

Much threaded software deals with events occurring either in the real world or in some simulated world. Such problem environments are commonly rich in structures on which we can build the software. This book shows what structures to look for. It introduces **entity-life modeling** (**ELM**), an approach for designing dynamically scheduled, multithreaded software.

With ELM, we pattern the threads in the software on ***event threads*** found in the problem domain and a ***thread architecture*** on an ***event-thread model*** of the domain. An event thread often represents the life history of some ***entity*** in the domain, whence the term entity-life modeling. Here are its main properties:

- ELM bases multithreading on a simple, intuitive principle in the manner of object orientation where we model classes in the software as well as their relationships on domain objects and their relationships. ELM puts thread structuring on par with class structuring.

---

[1]Reprinted by permission of the Estate of Erle Stanley Gardner.

- ELM is practical. It proposes no new definition of concurrency but builds on threading concepts that programmers have used for decades. Such classic multithreading involves two kinds of participants:

  1. *Threads*, such as those in Java or C#, Pthreads, or Ada tasks.[2]
  2. *Shared objects* that are "thread safe." This means that each object enforces mutual exclusion on the threads that attempt to call its operations. In Java, such objects are called *synchronized*; in Ada, *protected*. I shall use the neutral term **safe objects**.

Classic multithreading is directly implementable, which is important in real-time and systems programming. It's also flexible; indeed, it lets us write "wildly nondeterministic" programs (Lee, 2006). The guard against that is design discipline:

- To rein in the untrammeled nondeterminism, ELM requires that all threads be part of a *thread architecture*, which is a defined structure of threads and safe objects. ELM helps designers quickly identify the major candidate thread architectures for a given problem. Choosing the right architecture can make a critical difference: One architecture may require a much greater programming effort than another and may incur much greater runtime overhead.

- ELM is a constructive approach to threading. Classic multithreading isn't as tractable formally as other concurrency models where, for instance, deadlock can be detected analytically. With ELM, we deal with deadlock as a practical issue and construct the thread architecture to be deadlock free.

- ELM is a design principle, not a stepwise method. It bases thread architectures directly on the problem domain. You don't have to take on faith that some long procession of steps will lead to a workable solution.

Because object orientation is now widely accepted, I assume in parts of the book that control threads operate on instances of classes. But ELM isn't limited to object-oriented software; you can use it just as well in C or even an assembly language as long as threads and mutual exclusion are supported. Safe objects needn't be instances of classes but can be singleton modules, as in some of the Ada examples. ELM doesn't rely on such potentially costly, object-oriented features as dynamic binding—but doesn't preclude them either.

ELM threads capture a dynamic aspect of the problem domain that objects don't handle well. It makes thread modeling into a conceptual tool that differs from and complements object orientation. It attempts to make threading a practical, working abstraction that is as productive and expressive, if not as ubiquitous, as objects. Like object orientation, ELM promotes conceptual continuity from problem analysis through implementation: Event threads in the problem domain become control threads in the software.

---

[2]When necessary, I shall use the term **control** *threads* for such software threads to distinguish them from *event* threads.

ELM frees threading from such technical constraints of the day as limited processing capacity. This leaves such inherent concurrency issues as deadlock prevention and the general desire to make the architecture tractable.

1.1.1 Reactive Systems

ELM targets *reactive* systems. According to Harel, certain systems exhibit a "*reactive* behavior, whereby the system is not adequately described by specifying the output that results from a set of inputs but, rather, requires specifying the relationship of inputs and outputs over time. Typically, such descriptions involve complex sequences of events, actions, conditions, and information flow, often with explicit timing constraints, that combine to form the system's overall behavior" (Harel and Pnueli, 1985; Harel et al., 1990, p. 403)

Such a sequence of events is an event thread and can be described by a state machine together with the actions. Many actions impact the world outside the software. Unlike computations, they are often irreversible.

Reactive systems include those that operate in real time in the widest sense, such as embedded control systems as well as telephone switches; interactive systems from automated teller machines and gas pumps to travel reservation systems (Wieringa, 2003); and *event-processing* systems (Sommerville, 2007) such as many games. ELM also applies to discrete-event simulation based on the *process interaction* worldview.[3] In other words, ELM finds multithreaded solutions in problem environments that are inherently concurrent.

1.2 OVERVIEW OF THIS BOOK

The book has three main parts: *foundations, the ELM way,* and *background and discussion.* Part I has three chapters:

- Chapter 1 positions ELM within the field of software engineering. Section 1.6 ends the chapter by introducing relevant parts of the Unified Modeling Language (UML).

- Chapter 2 covers the threading support in Ada and Java (including real-time Java) and discusses Pthreads briefly. Because ELM is tailored to how threads actually work, this is an important point of reference: In order to understand ELM and compare it with other design approaches, we must comprehend threading in some depth.

- Chapter 3 deals with state modeling. Although a fair number of books cover it, I often find the treatment lacking. Many books make little distinction between a state diagram and a flowchart or a UML activity diagram.

Part II consists of four chapters, each focused on an aspect of ELM itself:

- Chapter 4 introduces ELM, its rationale, and background.

- Chapter 5 shows how to design software based on event threads and introduces the *sequential-activities* and *concurrent-activities* design patterns.

---

[3]With ELM, a simulation model of some entity and a control system for the entity tend to have much the same architecture.

- Chapter 6 introduces two event-thread patterns for resource sharing: the *resource-user-thread* and *resource-guard-thread* patterns. When we analyze a problem with shared domain resources, we can often choose one pattern or the other.

- Chapter 7 extends the discussion of resource sharing to the case where an entity has simultaneous exclusive access to multiple resources. The focus is on deadlock prevention.

Part III has two chapters:

- Chapter 8 discusses real-time software design and multithreading in general.

- Chapter 9 traces the origins of ELM and is for those interested in methodology evolution. It gets a little personal as I relate the professional experiences that led me to develop ELM.

I try to contain most preaching and speculation in Chapters 1, 8, and 9 and keep the other chapters matter-of-fact. Yet I also want to convey the creative joy of software design and suggest possibilities that go beyond my examples. No doubt, ELM seems much more dry and forbidding in theory than in its application.

Should you consider reading the book cover to cover, be warned that Part I—particularly the massive Chapter 2—is quite comprehensive and included mostly for reference. Not all the information about threading in various languages is necessary for understanding the rest of the book.

For an overview of ELM, go straight to Part II, Chapter 4. Part II and Chapter 4 in particular define the terminology we need to discuss ELM. They give many examples of the realities from which the abstractions are drawn. Not all solutions are mine, but I put them in a systematic framework. Programmers like to design by analogy or by tweaking existing software. Some of the examples may be close enough to the reader's own problems for such reuse by reediting.

1.3 MULTITHREADING

As multiprocessors[4] are becoming widespread, more programmers are confronted with threading. Many have easy access to Java, whose thread support works for many simple applications. Threads let us benefit from multiprocessors to speed up execution. They are also useful on a uniprocessor where one thread can compute while others may be waiting for external input.

ELM architectures are intended to be hardware independent, benefit from multiprocessing if it's available, and run optimally on a single processor otherwise. They require no particular multiprocessor thread-scheduling policy (Stallings, 2008).

Multiple threads can coexist in one address space, as within one UNIX® process. Context switching between threads is quicker than between processes, and thread interaction is much easier, cheaper, and more flexible than process

---

[4]By "multiprocessing" I always mean **symmetric multiprocessing (SMP)**, where multiple processors access a common memory. I don't exclude other architectures such as nonuniform memory access (NUMA), but I don't target them specifically.

interaction. Threads interact by accessing safe objects in the common address space. To protect the integrity of their data, safe objects enforce *mutual exclusion* on the calling threads. Also known as *exclusion synchronization*, mutual exclusion requires that each operation on a safe object be completed before another can start.[5]

ELM doesn't address directly how to use parallelism to speed up heavy computations in such applications as image processing.[6] The book touches on the issue. In the *concurrent-activities* pattern, for example, multiple computations can progress simultaneously in each state. Having multiple threads computing in parallel is in the spirit of ELM.

*1.3.1 Preemptive and Nonpreemptive Threading

Avoid selecting a tool that's only minimally sufficient for the job.

McConnell, 1996

Threads can be run with or without preemption. In an execution environment with *preemptive* scheduling, a higher priority thread takes over the processor from a lower priority thread whenever it needs it. With *nonpreemptive* scheduling, each thread keeps a processor until it releases it voluntarily. With nonpreemption on a uniprocessor, each thread has exclusive access to all data until it releases the processor; data must be locked[7] only if it must remain under exclusive access even after the thread has relinquished the processor.

Adding threads to a sequential software system can be a big step and nonpreemptive threading a tempting solution—The single processor serves as a lock: While one thread owns it, no other thread can access any data, and a thread owns the processor until it releases it. This makes programming simpler (Gustafsson, 2005).

The disadvantage is that we cannot easily improve the performance of a program based on nonpreemption by adding processors. Even on multiprocessors, the nonpreemptive scheduler must ensure that only one thread runs at a time. Hence, nonpreemptive scheduling won't let a software system grow into multiple processors smoothly.

ELM assumes that the execution environment may be preemptive. This requires that every thread lock any shared data to guarantee exclusive access. The locks protect the data both in case of preemption and in case a thread running simultaneously on another processor tries to access the data. The locking is implemented with safe objects.

1.3.2 Using Threads

Multithread programming deserves respect but shouldn't inspire awe. You can learn how threads operate and how to make them behave. There is no deep, dark mystery. The basic concepts are widely taught, and it's easy enough to get a threaded toy program to work. Threading is no different than other advanced

---

[5]Mutual exclusion can be relaxed for operations that don't change any data. Hence, some synchronization mechanisms give multiple threads at a time *read* access to a safe object.

[6]Compilers for languages such as Fortress try to maximize the use of multiple processors for computations that can be done in parallel (Allen et al., 2008).

[7]Locking is the traditional way of enforcing mutual exclusion. Other mechanisms are possible (Section 2.1.4.1.5).

concepts, such as polymorphism, that software engineers have embraced. *Why* we use threads and what improvements we can expect aren't as well understood. Threads aren't really toys, after all, and can capture the dynamic behavior of entities more important than bouncing balls and dining philosophers.[8]

1.3.2.1 Thread Scheduling

Traditionally, the design of a reactive system has focused heavily on rationing limited processor resources. For this, hard deadlines are identified and the system design is focused on proving that they are all met.[9] Once the design problem is given this form, standard solutions apply. As a result, designers have been known to invent hard deadlines in systems that really have none.

Some computing to hard deadlines may always be necessary, often in response to emergencies. It typically coexists with other computations without deadlines. With multiprocessors, it's not difficult to give processing time to single threads with hard deadlines as long as there are processors to go around: Each such thread can have its own processor until the deadline is met. For these reasons, deadlines aren't ELM's main focus. Instead, it works largely with *dynamically* scheduled threads, which have priorities but *no* specific deadlines. ELM's thread architecture allows for threads with hard deadlines, too, but with ever more multiprocessors, they need no longer be the designer's overshadowing concern.

1.3.2.2 Message Passing

It is also common to let threads communicate by means of message passing. This is necessary with processes but not with threads in a common address space. They can communicate much more directly and simply. ELM takes advantage of this.

In widely taught analysis and design methods for message-based multithreading, modularization comes first, and the modules are then fitted with threads as a means to provide a control structure. Some concurrent object-oriented languages give each object a thread that executes a *live* routine (also known as *body*), services message queues, and invokes the object's operations in response to each message (Caromel, 1993).

Other design approaches focus first on classes and their interactions. In a second step, some objects are given threads and made to communicate via messages. This can be easier than arranging the modules in a single sequential control structure (Sommerville, 2007).

In some message-based designs, a single input is handed from one thread to another to a third, causing a streak of context switches. With this arrangement, threads tend not to preempt each other but run to completion and return to some idle state to wait for the next input. Such a design often affords nothing that we couldn't do more easily and with less overhead in a single-thread program. With ELM, each input is normally handled from beginning to end by a single thread.

---

[8]The dining philosophers is a popular toy problem that illustrates deadlock (Section 7.2.3).
[9]A computation has a hard deadline if it must complete by a certain time to avoid more or less dire consequences (Section 8.2.2.1).

1.3.2.3 A Different Mindset

Some believe that no matter the design, we always end up with the same software when the dust settles. But retrofitting modules with threads isn't the same as designing directly for threading, as with ELM. Instead, it's limiting both conceptually and practically: Conceptually, threading can be more than a pragmatic engineering device. Threads can model aspects that are unique and central to a given problem. They needn't be subordinated to modules. Practically, we can produce more efficient multithreaded software by designing from the start to the strengths (and limitations) of threads.[10]

Any architecture must be closely related to the tools and construction materials at hand. We can expect no technological leap from adopting a new tool or new material merely to prop up existing techniques. For that, we must instead design to the character of the new tool or material (Perry and Wolf, 1992). So it is with threading.

For those accustomed to tying threads to objects or other modules, ELM may require a major shift in mindset. By contrast, those who have already found their own way to ELM-style thread architectures will find support for their view in this book.

1.4 ENGINEERING THE INTANGIBLE

The programmer builds from pure thought-stuff: concepts and very flexible representations thereof.... thought-stuff—which nevertheless exists, moves, and works in a way that word-objects do not.

BROOKS, 1995

What once led me and many others to programming was the opportunity to build elegant mechanisms largely unconstrained by any medium. Putting good software together from what Brooks calls "thought-stuff" isn't as easy and playful as it may sound, however. Where a mechanical designer can study a working prototype, a software designer can only contemplate the mechanism in the mind. It's easy for anyone to tell a graceful machine from an ungainly contraption—not so with software, where any ugliness can be hidden safely out of sight. All the same, observations about mechanical engineering often bear upon software design as well. Alike, software designers and mechanical engineers should avoid cleverness and seek a certain elegance of design (Ferguson, 1994; Glegg, 1969).

Ever since computational antiquity, people have sought to impose some structure on software to make up for the lack of inherent, physical constraints. Some structuring—such as decomposition into self-contained modules—is generic enough to apply to any design. In much administrative and interactive software it may be all we need.

A reactive system, by contrast, deals with developments in the real world as they unfold. So it is for simulation software in a way and for many kinds of animation. That means that static module structures aren't enough; we must also capture the dynamics. That is the focus of this book.

---

[10]These are design issues and don't preclude *implementing* ELM threads by means of classes such as *Thread* and its descendants in Java.

In mature engineering disciplines, most development is done to proven models (Bassett, 1991). This is as it should be in software, too. Architecture evaluations assess the adequacy of software architectures and, for instance, check that they meet required response times and are modifiable (Bass et al., 2003; Kazman and Bass, 2002). Such an evaluation is perhaps not the occasion to question the basic architecture.

At the same time, engineering solutions must evolve toward greater simplicity as technology improves and is better understood. To make this happen in software, developers must challenge the established order from time to time and try new ideas in research projects. For many, ELM is such a new idea.

1.4.1 Software Architecture

Let us change our traditional attitude to the construction of programs. Instead of imagining that our main task is to instruct a computer what to do, let us concentrate rather on explaining to human beings what we want a computer to do.

Knuth, 1992

The *software architecture* of a system is defined as the structure or structures of software elements, their externally visible properties, and their relationships (Bass et al., 2003). A viable architecture is considered a milestone deliverable in software development (Garlan and Perry, 1995).

A *view* of an architecture is "a representation of a coherent set of architectural elements" (Bass et al., 2003). A given architecture can normally be described from several perspectives (Kruchten, 1995; Perry and Wolf, 1992). For example, the concurrency view looks at processes, threads, and synchronization.

We tend to associate the word "architecture" with buildings, so it's easy to conclude that a software architecture is only a static structure of black boxes. For reactive software, a better analogy is the architecture of machinery with interacting, moving parts.

1.4.1.1 Thread Architecture

To develop software is to build a Machine, simply by describing it.

Jackson, 1995

I define thread architecture as the structure of threads and major safe objects in a software system. "ELM architecture" always refers to ELM *thread* architecture. By bringing out the threads, an ELM architecture shows how the software machine is meant to work. For a multithreaded system, an understandable description of its dynamics is an essential deliverable; it's not least important if the architecture is subject to external review (Bass et al., 2003; Kazman et al., 1996; Kazman and Bass, 2002).

When threads exist merely to support some other dominant architectural style, we can often describe the architecture in terms of objects, for example, and simply state that the objects have threads that communicate via messages. Not so with ELM, where at least some threads are fundamental to the whole architecture; we cannot fully describe how the system works if we abstract them away. This doesn't mean that the threads must be at the highest level of the software architecture, however. Each subsystem can have its own thread architecture, and every thread is local to a physical node and to a process.

As Jackson puts it, "the problem is not at the computer interface—it is deeper into the world, further away from the computer" (Jackson, 2001). Such deep structures can be brought out by an ELM architecture. This can help to make the architecture quite evocative and give a mental picture of the software in problem-domain terms. For example, we may have a thread per user, a thread per call in a telephone switch, or a thread per train on a model railroad.

Software architectures in general often erode during development and evolution (Bosch and Lundberg, 2003; Kruchten et al., 2006; Perry and Wolf, 1992; Shaw and Clements, 2006). For example, we may start with a strict layering where every module calls modules in lower layers only. Later, a hurried maintainer corrupts that architecture in order to fix a bug. A robust thread architecture stands a better chance to endure. Once it's in place, everyone works within it to architecture-specific rules and guidelines. It can fade into the infrastructure together with language primitives and the operating system interface (Bass et al., 2003). If it's made into a framework, people will understand that adding a new thread type isn't the thing to do.[11]

1.4.2 Conceptual Integrity

Forms which grow round a substance, if we rightly understand that, will correspond to the real nature and purport of it, will be true, good; forms which are consciously put round a substance, bad.

THOMAS CARLYLE, *ON HEROES AND HERO-WORSHIP*, 1841

An architecture is said to have *conceptual integrity* if all its parts serve one central purpose. Such an architecture appears to spring from a single mind (Brooks, 1995). As Ian Sharp puts it, behind any good piece of software, we will find a designer who "fully understood what he wanted to do and . . . created the shape" (Randell and Buxton, 1970). A close-knit group of "resonant minds" (Brooks, 1995) can also bring about conceptual integrity, but not a committee seeking a compromise. Much more than other software architecture terms, conceptual integrity implies engineering elegance and a creative vision of the whole—the "gestalt" of the system.

The thread architecture must have conceptual integrity even if we achieve it nowhere else. Not many need to be involved in defining the architecture, but it should be understandable to all concerned. It's much easier to remain faithful to an architecture throughout the life cycle if it can be grasped easily in its entirety. For example, a maintainer of a multithreaded program should be able to understand the thread architecture right away. Before we modify a program statement, we must know exactly what threads execute so we can avoid unpredictable consequences. It's helpful that the individual threads remain in the implementation, even at runtime.

[11]One example is Enterprise Java Beans (EJB), which you program on the assumption that the EJB container will allocate a thread to each incoming request (Bass et al., 2003).

1.4.2.1 The *Key Idea* of an Architecture

Nothing can be reasonable or beautiful unless it's made by one central idea, and the idea sets every detail.

AYN RAND, THE FOUNTAINHEAD, 1943¹²

[T]he central idea as a force that provides cohesion at all levels of abstraction can be seen in even simple designs.

TAYLOR, 2000

ELM turns the designer's attention to threads of events occurring in the reality where the software is to function. This helps the designer to visualize how the software will interact with its environment. Such a vision can be expressed as an event-thread model of the problem and be built right into the architecture.

A given problem can have more than one valid event-thread model. ELM finds the major models and candidate thread architectures with little ceremony. In turn, the thread architectures define how each solution will work. Comparing possible solutions is essential to architectural design and to engineering in general (Bass et al., 2003; Garlan and Perry, 1995; Joint Task Force, 2004; Perry and Wolf, 1992).

A *key idea* captures the gist of a particular architecture in a pithy sentence or two. The rest of the architecture follows, not trivially, but logically. This is illustrated by the two architectures for the flexible manufacturing system in Chapter 7. The original solution can be summed up in the key idea "one thread per job." Intuitively, each job pursues its completion. Within the restrictive ELM framework, the phrase defines the architecture. This solution was first suggested by students at the Wang Institute (Sandén, 1994, 2009).

Later, Rob Scott suggested that, instead, the workstations could drive the solution by procuring jobs to work on. (In that solution, workstations have threads and the jobs are passive objects.) It turned out that a workable, alternate architecture could be built on that key idea (Sandén, 2009). Alone, it allowed us to view the complete solution in our minds' eyes and see that it was viable before putting marker to whiteboard (Ferguson, 1994).

An architecture can be sublimated into a key idea only if it has conceptual integrity. It helps that a typical ELM architecture has few thread types and safe classes—scale is achieved by means of instantiation, not by adding new types (Perry and Wolf, 1992).

I know from practical experience that programmers prefer to be guided by a simple design principle than by any stepwise recipe. Most software engineers take well to designs that flow consistently from a key idea and serve a central purpose. When new people come onboard a project, it's a great moment when their eyes light up and they cannot wait to voice the key idea in their own words.

*1.4.3 Analogical Modeling

This is because of a completely general property of systems: the machine is a model of each domain, and vice versa.

JACKSON, 1991

---

¹²Reprinted by permission of the Ayn Rand Institute.

Both object orientation and ELM model the software on the reality. The software becomes an *analogical model*, that is, a model some of whose structures are the analogs of structures in the problem (Section 4.1.2.1). The concept isn't new. Thus wrote Richard Fairley (1985, pp. 3-4):

> In a very real sense, the software engineer creates models of physical situations in software. The mapping between the model and the reality being modeled has been called the intellectual distance between the problem and a computerized solution to the problem. A fundamental principle of software engineering is to design software products that minimize the intellectual distance between problem and solution; however, the variety of approaches to software development is limited only by the creativity and ingenuity of the programmer.

Jackson structured programming (Section 9.3) pioneered the idea of modeling program control structures on the sequential structures found in the input and output data. But even the mainstream structured analysis and design (Section 8.3) view module decomposition in a similar light (Yourdon, and Constantine 1979, pp. 20-21):

> [I]f there is a piece of the application naturally known as A, then there should be a piece of the system which implements the A function. Similarly, if there is a natural relationship between part A of the problem and part D of the problem, there should be a similar relationship between part A of the system and D of the solution—and no other extraneous relationships.

Object orientation introduced more versatile tools for analogical modeling than functional modules. It was invented in the 1960s by simulationists who wanted to create software models of things in the problem domain. The first object-oriented language, Simula 67, was based on Algol and was intended for process interaction simulation (Birthwistle et al., 1979; Dahl and Nygaard, 1966).

1.5 THE DEVELOPMENT PROCESS

A software system should be perfect on every level like a Mozart symphony.

BJARNE DÄCKER, 1996

In the beginning was programming. "Being a programmer by trade, programs are what I am talking about," wrote Edsger Dijkstra in 1972 (Dahl et al., 1972).[13] He observed that programmers must deal with a ladder of abstractions from the architecture down to the individual instruction (Dijkstra, 1989). The "ancients" of computer science moved easily up and down based on solid, practical understanding of the workings of a computer. In that spirit, ELM humbly attempts to trot along.

Such a happy state couldn't long endure, however. This isn't the place to trace the history of software design. But at some point the hands-on makers of software parted ways with those interested in abstraction.

---

[13]Since then, "programming" has come to be seen as a lowly pursuit, but I like it as a description of a whole "system of practice" (Denning and Freeman, 2009). A newer and broader term is *computational thinking* (Wing, 2006).

Artisan programmers still ply their craft quite freely, based on technical expertise (Taylor; 2000; Turkle, 1984; Winograd, 1996). To be sure, the required knowledge increases all the time. Developers fight an uphill battle to keep up with technological innovation and spend much time learning new interfaces and foundation classes (Whittaker and Atkin, 2002). There's little room for abstract designing. The architecture is in their heads and becomes embodied in the software. Artisans expect others to figure it out by reading the program and don't mind leaving those who cannot in the dark. Many "self-taught and peer-taught" artisans have a keen interest in technical excellence and in how things work (Conti, 2005).[14] They're always ready to dive into a program text and may not see a need to document as an aid to others.

At the same time, design has tended to become "an activity totally secluded from actual implementation" (Meyer, 1988, p. xv). You can be a software architect without having studied any actual software and with only vague concepts of programming. Confident in their mastery of models, designers may regard programmers as mired in details and incapable of abstraction.

By contrast, artisan programmers often think of design as a more or less pompous ritual with little bearing on the programming. Should the resulting architecture be unrealistic, the implementers redesign it—discreetly—based on practical engineering wisdom and common sense.

As an engineering discipline we should be content neither with vague, high-level designing nor with the undocumented tradition of the artisans. Only novices need design approaches, some argue; the master hands can take care of themselves. This stunts the evolution of software engineering as a discipline, however. For it to grow and prosper, we must learn how to capture elegant architectures so we can teach, discuss, and critique them.

1.5.1 ELM in the Development Process

First, it is important to recognize that the software process does not involve distinct and separate steps; only the management of the process requires identifiable phases.

BLUM, 1992

I view ELM as a way to blueprint a programming task in which the architects will be personally involved. There is no separate group that tosses the architecture across the cubicle partition. We design to real languages and operating systems—not in a void. Design is merely programming at a certain abstraction. There's no long series of steps. Instead, ELM tells the designer/programmer what to look for in the problem and to consider possible candidate thread architectures early.

That way, an ELM architecture is designed by those who are also responsible for the thread programming and can apply some engineering judgment throughout. I don't envision that large numbers of programmers will ever have the background for this. Not everyone on a project must be a thread programmer. Once an architecture is in place, programming to it and within it is much simpler than free-hand thread programming. For most application designers, the thread architecture can remain safely hidden away.

---

[14]Some are now part of an underground hacker culture (Conti, 2005).

ELM—like object orientation—isn't "design made easy" for novices alone. Seasoned developers work by the same principles, only with more finely honed art. ELM applies to major team efforts with formal milestones and deliverables as well as to the design of a control system for the train set in our basement.

ELM is about engineering optimum multithread mechanisms to solve given problems. I leave it to readers to decide how much documentation and diagramming they need and what process to follow. When we design software that we are to implement alone or in a group, we tend to be less ceremonious than a professional designer. No one requires a complete, massive design document where we may have to "dig for the critical issues within a large mass of noncritical detail" (Boehm, 1998). Instead, the design should focus on areas where a mistake matters the most; that is, it should be risk driven. Routine issues can be dealt with during the programming.

1.5.2 Analysis and Design

Doesn't everyone already do good design? No. My impression is that good design receives more lip service than any other activity in software development and that few developers really do design at all.

McCONNELL, 1996

Textbooks traditionally distinguish between analysis and design. It's sound to begin by describing the problem independently without drifting into design and starting to invent solutions.[15] This analysis can support some major decisions on what parts of the problem should be solved in software, in hardware, and as manual processes.

Object-oriented analysis and ELM alike exist in a twilight zone between analysis and design where we limit the analysis to what can be expressed in software. The object-oriented designer seeks problem-domain entities that map onto implementable classes. ELM applies this to the time dimension: We analyze the problem for event threads that can map onto control threads.

We must always let software considerations inform and rein in the analysis. Doing otherwise assumes that our computer is infinitely malleable and lets us implement anything (Rapanotti et al., 2004). Analysis for its own sake can become an endless hunt for domain relationships, many of which don't even bear on the software design.

1.5.3 Design Upfront

One good idea is worth 1,000 man-hours, and ideas don't cost anything at all.

McKEEMAN, 1989

Every self-respecting software engineering process model includes a design phase early on, but today's software production cycles may not give us time to specify a design in minute detail. "Big upfront design" has a bad name suggesting mechanistic, stepwise methods and obligatory deliverables of dubious value.

Stepwise methods aren't unlike early software tools for mechanical construction: We don't know exactly to what built-in assumptions and constraints

---

[15]Per the *"principle of deferred invention,"* free innovation should be delayed until the description of what is already given has been completed (Jackson, 1995).

we're designing (Ferguson, 1994). The method leads us by the hand through successive, small decisions. We're kept in the dark about the consequences of our choices even as they lock us into the final result. Should it come out too complicated, deciding what to eliminate may not be easy.

Unbeknownst to us, the method rejects or ignores possibly valid alternatives; in fact, stepwise methods rather discourage the comparison of candidate solutions. There's little or no scope for engineering judgment or creativity. If upfront design is like that, no wonder it's avoided by those who are truly interested in the software mechanics.

The specter of big upfront design shouldn't stop us from sketching a few essential diagrams and discussing them with co-workers, though. Design upfront doesn't have to mean stepwise methods. There should be "just enough" design (McConnell, 2004) with a risk-driven focus on issues that may otherwise cause stumbling and backtracking during implementation. Establishing the architecture early has other benefits:

- It helps us to estimate the development effort.
- It can reveal opportunities to reuse existing software (Bass et al., 2003).
- It forces us to give any requirements document or specification a close read where we can uncover and challenge omissions and inconsistencies. The architecture confirms our understanding of the requirements.
- It affords a unique opportunity to consider candidate solutions before too much effort has been invested.
- It lets us air out the architecture and invite diverse viewpoints (Winograd, 1996). In an open environment, there is less risk of holding onto a favorite solution irrationally. Peers not only find our logic errors but may also think of improvements and even radically better alternatives.

Working with a diverse group, the architect must assimilate the input and recognize and incorporate improvements while maintaining the conceptual integrity. Taking differing viewpoints into account is critical to buy-in: Participants with a stake in the architecture are unlikely to abandon it later.

It's not easy, however, to do concrete work at the abstract, architectural level. Keeping one architecture in the mind is hard enough, let alone juggling multiple candidates.

Existing modeling tools and diagram styles aren't ideal for describing architecture. Class and component diagrams capture the statics only, and sequence diagrams tend to drown in minutiae (Section 1.6.2.2). It's particularly difficult to describe the workings of complex, multithreaded software.

Some find the air thin at the heights of abstraction and so prefer to jump right into the hands-on programming. Others may be predisposed for design: Planners-at-heart work out a tidy solution to every little home improvement project before taking tool in hand and tend to construct software in the same fashion. They can usually build it in the mind first as long as the facts are there; it's just "a matter of logically thinking things out" (Glegg, 1969). On the other hand, it may take a different and less systematic sort of person to come up with a radically different and better design.

1.5.3.1 Refactoring

Writing and rewriting are a constant search for what it is one is saying.

John Updike, quoted in Trimble, 1975

Refactoring has brought respectability to redesign at the programming stage. In refactoring, we reorganize a partly or completely finished program by moving attributes and operations between classes, adding and deleting classes, and so on.

Refactoring is one pillar of the *agile* approaches to software development (Douglass, 2009). Agile developers seek the simplest design that solves the immediate problem at hand. If a new case shows up, they amend their first solution. Over time, the changes wear away at the program structure. Refactoring cleans it up (Fowler et al., 1999). Agile approaches rely on test sets to specify a program ("test first"). The same test sets are run to make sure the software still works after refactoring (Beck, 2000).

I'm aware of no guidelines for the safe refactoring of multithreaded programs. Agile developers would start with a rudimentary thread architecture, add and remove threads as they go along, and refactor from time to time. It's much more efficient, I conjecture, to start from a well-thought-out thread architecture. Subtle thread interaction errors typically show up only in uncommon runtime situations, which are difficult to re-create during testing. Thus, we cannot rely on a test set alone to show that a refactored multithreaded program still works.

Once in a while, a major architectural change becomes necessary. For instance, I refactored a resource-user-thread solution for the flexible manufacturing system into a resource-guard-thread solution (Sections 1.4.2.1 and 7.3.2). This proved effective, and I could reuse major parts of the program. But it was a transformation of one clean design into another, not an effort to clean up an architecture running wild. Besides, no one else was affected; no team had to be told of new design rules.

1.6 UNIFIED MODELING LANGUAGE™

[A] good notation has a subtlety and suggestiveness which at times make it seem almost like a live teacher.

Russell, 1922

ELM is no diagrammatic design method. Except for state diagrams, which I recommend as splendid problem-solving tools, it requires no particular diagrams. All the same, ELM practitioners will no doubt want to illustrate architectures graphically. For documentation, it's best to rely on a well-defined diagrammatic language. I use UML in this book to illustrate some thread architectures.

Unfortunately, it can be difficult to capture the workings of a multithreaded system in such formal diagrams. Sometimes, an ad hoc diagram backed up by commentary must do. In fact, even formal diagrams need readable commentary (Raybould, 2006). [Chapter 16 in Bass et al. (2003) is a nice example of text and diagrams combined to describe an architecture with threading elements.]

UML has become the de facto diagramming standard for object-oriented analysis and design. I attempt to follow UML 2.0 (Ambler, 2005; Blaha and Rumbaugh, 2005; Booch et al., 2005; Eriksson et al., 2004; Fowler, 2004; Rumbaugh et al., 2005). UML provides a number of *views* of a system and its problem domain. Each view is an abstraction shown in a number of diagrams. We are here chiefly interested in the *logical view* for analysis and design and, to a lesser degree, in the *use-case view* for requirements elicitation.

Most systems developed with UML or otherwise are administrative in a broad sense and often interactive. For such systems, analysis starts with use-case modeling followed by class diagramming. State diagrams are developed if any class should need one. Sequence diagrams, finally, show how each use case is realized in terms of interacting objects.

Reactive systems often have straightforward class structures and more interesting dynamic behaviors. For this reason, this book pays more attention to state diagramming than UML texts, where it tends to get short shrift. All of Chapter 3 deals with state modeling.

1.6.1 Requirements Elicitation: Use Cases

The requirements will change whether they're allowed to or not.

BERSOFF, 2003

UML provides *use cases* as vehicles for requirements elicitation (Booch et al., 2005; Rumbaugh et al., 2005, Lieberman, 2006, Jorgensen, 2009). A **use case** is a set of usage scenarios tied together by a common goal (Fowler, 2004). It's initiated by an **actor**, which can be anything that exchanges information with the system under study. It can be a category of human users, another system, or a mechanical device. I shall refer to the latter two as *inanimate* actors.[16] The **use-case *flow*** represents the steps taken in a use case. It can be described either in text or in an *activity diagram*, UML's version of the classic flowchart.

An automated teller machine (ATM) is a stock example with a bank customer as the primary actor. The use cases may be *withdraw money, deposit money,* and *view balance. Exceptional* flows cover the cases where the customer's PIN code is invalid, funds are insufficient, or the like.

UML has little to say about use cases (Fowler, 2004). It provides only the rudimentary *use-case diagram,* which associates actors with use cases. Use-case diagrams and textual flow descriptions can help elicit requirements from such stakeholders as bank tellers and supermarket checkers. But often, the complex issue of designing systems for people to use requires prototyping or even ethnography (Sommerville, 2007; Winograd, 1996).

1.6.1.1 Actors and Use Cases in Reactive Systems

The focus on external interfaces is inevitable in a method that asks, "What will the system do for the end user?" as the key question; the answer will tend to emphasize the most external aspects.

MEYER, 1997

Most use-case examples involve interactive systems with human actors.[17] Many reactive systems have interactive aspects, and because use-case modeling is so

---

[16]Dogs, cats, and cattle are actors, too, when they operate some automatic feeding device or the like. They are, of course, nonhuman yet animate actors.

[17]One inanimate actor that you often see is *Time,* shown as a stick figure with a "clockhead." It initiates use cases that are to start automatically at specific times.

popular, it's easy to home in on the human–computer interaction even if almost all complexity lies elsewhere.

It's fine to think of an ATM as interactive, for it deals neatly with one user transaction at a time and does little else. But in other reactive systems a focus on interaction is misleading. Say that we approach a multielevator system with the same mindset—elevators serve customers too, after all. A use-case *travel* with the flow *call elevator, wait, enter, press button, travel, exit* captures the system requirements from a user's point of view. It even lets us express some nonfunctional requirements such as those related to wait times. But it's not traceable into the design. Unlike an ATM, elevator systems don't keep track of individual passengers. This means that the designer cannot build on the use case but must take a different tack altogether.

It's more helpful to think of the elevator cabin as an inanimate actor with a use case that represents a journey from an idle state at the ground floor, up and down one or more times, and back to idleness. Such a use case can capture all the details of the elevator's traveling policy. It also translates into an event thread.

The events in such a thread must be *shared* by the problem domain and the software in the sense that both domains participate in each event or at least notice it (Jackson, 1995). The events *start* and *stop* are such shared phenomena. A traveler's movements in and out of the cabin usually are not.

1.6.1.2 Using State Modeling to Capture Use-Case Flows

The behavior of an elevator actor can be captured to advantage in a state diagram. A single diagram, perhaps no larger than a page, can often capture all the normal and exceptional use-case flows. State diagrams can also capture the use-case flows in such systems as a cruise controller, teller terminal system, or supermarket checkout system.

State modeling is often the best starting point for analyzing any reactive system. There is no need to identify classes first. Quite on the contrary, a state diagram may suggest relevant classes.

1.6.2 UML's Logical View

If it was so, it might be; and if it were so, it would be; but as it isn't, it ain't. That's logic.
LEWIS CARROLL, *THROUGH THE LOOKING-GLASS*, 1872

The logical view of UML describes the structure of the domain and of the system and is the most comprehensive view by far. It lets us express both static relationships and dynamic structures, which capture developments over time. The chief static model is the class diagram while the state diagram (Chapter 3) is the preeminent dynamic notation.

1.6.2.1 Static Structure: Class diagrams

Object Motto: Ask not first what the system does*: Ask what it* does *it* to*!*
MEYER, 1997

A class diagram shows time-invariant relationships between classes. We are interested in classes of objects that the software must (1) *maintain data about,* (2) *interface to,* or (3) *both*. Each class is shown as a box with three compartments: name, attributes, and operations. When attributes and/or operations are irrelevant, each of the latter compartments can be suppressed. Operation calls are expressed in dot notation—*obj.op* (parameters)—to stress that *obj* is not just another parameter but an object whose service is invoked.

The class diagram in Figure 1-1 shows the concrete signal classes *read-card*, *press-open*, and *trip-sensor* as specializations of an abstract signal class *opening-event*. We say that a *press-open* signal **is a kind of** *opening-event*. *<<signal>>* is a *stereotype* that indicates the nature of the classes in the example. This class diagram shows no attributes or operations.

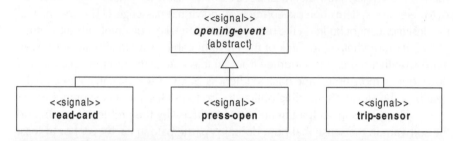

Figure 1-1 UML class diagram. The classes *read-card*, *press-open*, and *trip-sensor* are specializations of the abstract class *opening-event* (Section 3.3.5).

Any concrete class can be instantiated. The classes in this example are events such as a button being pressed. Each instance of *press-open*, for example, is an event occurrence where a specific person presses a certain button at a specific time.

I show no more class diagrams in this book, even though I use communication diagrams to illustrate object interaction. I find that they are understandable without reference to class diagrams.

1.6.2.2 Dynamic Structure: Sequence and Communication Diagrams

Those aspects of a system that are concerned with time and changes are the dynamic model, *in contrast with the static, or object model.*

RUMBAUGH ET AL., 1991

Sequence and *communication diagrams* show how objects cooperate to achieve some goal. A sequence diagram typically shows the implementation of a use case. These diagrams complement the class diagram. The class diagram lists all operations; sequence and communication diagrams explain how the objects interact.

The **sequence diagram** shows a succession of calls between objects (Booch et al., 2005; Fowler, 2004, Jorgensen, 2009). Each object is represented by a vertical, dashed line headed by the object symbol. Time flows from top to bottom.

Sequence diagrams are the chief medium for showing object interaction in use cases of any size and complexity. They can show iterations and selections. Unhappily, they don't support abstraction well and tend to become either too sketchy or too detailed.

Figure 1-2 is a slightly simplified description of a *Job* thread's interactions with various objects, shared or otherwise. It corresponds to the pseudocode in

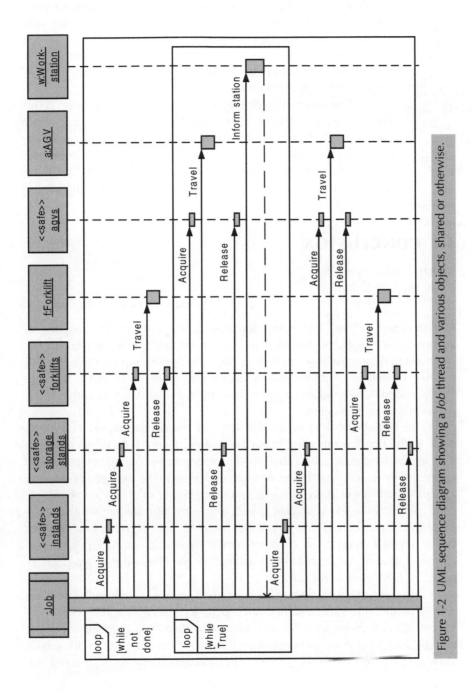

Figure 1-2 UML sequence diagram showing a *Job* thread and various objects, shared or otherwise.

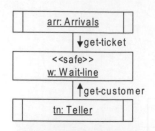

Figure 1-3 UML communication diagram with two thread objects, *arr* of class *Arrivals* and *tn* of class *Teller*, and one passive safe object, *w* of class *Wait-line*.

Section 7.3.2.2. I use a box with double sides[18] as the thread-class and thread-object icon.

In ELM, the concerns of different threads are separated at the safe objects they share. It's best to use a separate diagram for each thread class. The same shared objects may appear in the diagrams of other threads. (In the case of Figure 1-2, the objects are shared between Job threads, so only one diagram is needed.) For the rest of the book, I use pseudocode and excerpts of program text as more compact alternatives to sequence diagrams.

Communication diagrams (Booch et al., 2005; Fowler, 2004) can capture interactions among small groups of objects without specifying the total order of events (as we must in a sequence diagram). The diagram in Figure 1-3 has two thread objects: *arr* of class *Arrivals* and *tn* of class *Teller*, and one safe object, *w* of class *Wait-line*. I use them throughout the book to highlight thread interaction with safe objects.

1.7 CONCLUSION

Utilitas, firmitas, venustas.
Utility, durability, beauty.

VITRUVIUS, DE ARCHITECTURA, CIRCA 25 BC

Multithreading is foreign to many and may appear difficult. It's tempting to assimilate it with something familiar and think of threads as modules, transforms, subroutines, or processes—or to limit ourselves to nonpreemptive threading. All this may be helpful until threading is more widely understood, but in the end, multithreaded design should be geared directly to multiprocessing and not seek to emulate older techniques.

Technology tends to evolve that way. Arc bridges and aqueducts built in stone by the Romans still stand in parts of Europe (Figure 1-4). When steel and reinforced concrete became available, similar structures could be erected more easily. But the crucial realization was that designing to the strengths of the new materials made novel, more efficient, and much bolder solutions possible.

In that spirit, ELM explores threads as construction elements with unique properties. It plays on the full register of threading, but not to the hilt, as might be the way of a clever "cowboy programmer" squeezing out the last bit of performance. That often comes at the price that no one else will ever grasp what's going on. ELM emphasizes clarity.

The idea of basing threads on concurrent series of events in the problem domain exists in the trade, and many an experienced designer will find little new in ELM. After all, giving an entity such as a model train its own thread is intuitive enough. Still, ELM helps to systematize thread-architectural design. It's similar to design patterns that way (Gamma et al., 1995): A pattern is not invented but,

---

[18]The symbol is sometimes used more restrictively to symbolize an *active object* (or its class) (Bass et al., 2003). An active object has a thread (sometimes called a *body*) that serves various request queues and performs the requested operations on the object.

Figure 1-4 The Roman aqueduct at Segovia in central Spain exhibits *firmitas*, *venustas*, and in those parts that still carry water even *utilitas*. (Original ink drawing by N. Sdelnikova.)

rather, discovered in existing systems. By naming it, we make it intellectually accessible so that we can talk about it.

Ray Schneider calls ELM "a point of view," and indeed it prompts the designer to look at the problem from a certain angle. I like to think there's some grandeur in the ELM view and ask the reader to consider it with an open mind. Perhaps someone young and unspoiled will seize on it and take it to places as yet undreamed.

Support for multithreading 2

Concurrent programs are inherently more complex than sequential programs. In many respects, they are to sequential programs what chess is to checkers or bridge is to pinochle: Each is interesting, but the former is more intellectually intriguing than the latter.

ANDREWS, 1991

2.1 INTRODUCTION

Multithreaded programming is more difficult than sequential programming. Much happens behind the scenes and isn't plain to see in the program text. We cannot tell from a set of source statements which threads execute them. Instead, we must form in our minds an idea of how the program works at runtime. This requires a mental effort and some imagination. But it's not as though threads lead secret lives beyond reasonable knowing. With a true mental model, it's all fully understandable.

Once understood, threading is a medium that lets us express the concurrent aspects of a problem domain directly and elegantly, just as an object-oriented language lets us model domain objects and their relationships.

Thread programming requires good understanding at least of the basic concurrency features at our disposal. Our software must be tailored to our programming language; indeed all engineering must be honed to its working materials. Besides, we can often avoid intricate and error-prone programming by putting language features to good use.

Without understanding the threading features, we cannot tell a good architecture from a bad one. Only when we know that threads need stack space and that context switching takes time do we understand why we shouldn't add new threads as freely as we might add subprograms or classes.

This chapter introduces the threading support in Java and Ada. I also discuss Pthreads, which is representative of stand-alone threading packages. The chapter isn't meant as a language primer but chiefly as a reference. It includes some rather uncommon threading features used in the book.

The threading support in such languages as Java and Ada is quite elaborate (Burns and Wellings, 2009). Each language provides it in its own fashion. An Ada programmer works at a certain abstraction, which prevents many errors (Sandén, 2002). Knowing this can be reassuring to such end users as the pilot, astronaut, or nuclear power station operator whose life depends on the correctness of some embedded software. As programming infrastructures go, the threading support in Ada 2005 is both rich and consistent.

A Java thread programmer, by contrast, works hands-on with the nitty-gritty of synchronization. Arguably this is pedagogical: Little is abstracted away so that we deal with much of the synchronization directly, which also means that we can make fatal mistakes.

Pthreads programmers deal in even greater detail with individual, naked semaphores using "programming constructs that are just a thin veneer over the underlying hardware" (Larus and Kozyrakis, 2008). Users of such packages may also tend to view threading as a subordinate device apart from the architecture. Even so, such packages are a way to add threading to programs in languages whose syntax doesn't include it (Hughes and Hughes, 2008).

2.1.1 Basic Multithreading and Synchronization Concepts

Multithreading involves two kinds of participants: (1) the thread and (2) the **safe object**, which enforces mutual exclusion among calling threads. Threads have remained conceptually much the same over the years while the understanding of safe objects is still evolving.

2.1.1.1 Threads

Use threads only where appropriate.

VERMEULEN ET AL., 2000

I use the term "**control thread**" for the kinds of thread provided by a programming language or system to distinguish them from event threads, which is an ELM concept for concurrency in the problem domain. When there is no room for confusion, I use the term "thread" for short. Java, C#, and Pthreads use the term thread that way while Ada calls its control threads **tasks**. On a uniprocessor, only a single thread at a time can actually be running; with multiprocessors, it's one thread per processor.

Each thread has a *stack* and a *program counter*. The stack contains a section (called a *frame*) for each subprogram call from which the thread has yet to return. The frame contains any call parameters and any temporary variables declared by the subprogram. The program counter indicates the next instruction to be executed by the thread.[19] A sequential program works the same and has a single stack and a single program counter. A program with many threads needs much memory space for all the stacks.

Each thread also has a *priority*, which determines the order in which threads access shared resources, including the processors.

---

[19]The place indicated by the program counter is also called the *locus of control* within the thread.

The program counter, stack, and priority are included in the thread's **context.** The operation when a processor stops executing one thread and starts executing another is called a **context switch** because the processor begins working in the new thread's context.

Once created, threads compete for access to the processors. I shall assume that the multiprocessor has a *common global ready queue*; that is, all processors can serve all threads. [In alternative solutions, threads can be bound to individual processors (Stallings, 2008).]

2.1.1.2 Safe Objects and Synchronization

A safe object is a more recent abstraction than threads, but the need to synchronize threads is as old as threading itself. Thus, if multiple threads put items into a buffer and get items from it, each thread must finish its operation before another thread gains access to the buffer. Otherwise, the buffer data structure may be compromised. This is known as *exclusion synchronization* or *mutual exclusion*.

2.1.1.2.1 Semaphores and Critical Sections

Exclusion synchronization lets us define critical sections. A **critical section** is a code sequence that is to be executed by no more than one thread at a time.[20] It's normally protected by a semaphore (Dijkstra, 1968). A **semaphore** is a variable that takes the values *open* and *closed*. A thread that finds the semaphore open closes it and proceeds into the critical section. We say that the thread **acquires** the semaphore. At the end of the critical section, the thread **releases**— opens—the semaphore. A thread that finds the semaphore closed cannot proceed but must keep trying until it finds the semaphore open.[21]

The semaphore concept was obviously borrowed from railroading. Like trains traveling over rail segments, threads are viewed as executing their way through code sections, some of which are shared by multiple threads.

The analogy is imperfect, however, because critical code sections that manipulate the same data form a set that must be protected together: While a thread is executing one section, no other thread is allowed into any section in the set. This is usually implemented by making the critical sections into the operations of one object with a single semaphore. Each operation is bracketed by an acquire call and a release call on the common semaphore. Such an object is called a *monitor* (Section 2.1.1.2.2).

Programmers working in languages without threading support often use packages such as Pthreads (POSIX® threads; Section 2.4). Pthreads provides primitives for defining, acquiring, and releasing semaphores. I shall say that the programmer in this situation works with *naked* semaphores.

---

[20]Some critical sections can be executed by any number of "reader" threads at a time, that is, threads that don't change any data. (See also protected functions; Section 2.3.2.)

[21]Following Edsger Dijkstra, the operations to acquire and release a semaphore, *S,* are often called *P(S)* and *V(S)*. *P* is the first letter of the word *prolagen,* which is formed by combining the Dutch words *proberen* (to try) and *verlagen* (to decrease). *V* is the first letter of the Dutch word *verhogen* (to increase) (Andrews, 1991).

Behind the scenes, there's more to semaphore[22] handling than described above. The *acquire* operation is based on a special hardware instruction called *test and set*,[23] whose operand is the semaphore. This instruction is unique in that it combines a read access *and* a conditional write access: First, it tests a bit at the operand address. If the value is 0, the instruction sets it to 1, thereby closing the semaphore. All this happens *atomically*; the instruction cannot be interrupted. The instruction returns a result code indicating whether the semaphore was found open. The *compare-and-swap* (*CAS*) instruction is slightly more elaborate (Goetz, 2006).

2.1.1.2.2 Monitors and Safe Objects

To avoid working with naked semaphores, we can collect certain shared data and all operations on it within an object. A **monitor**[24] is a safe object with operations, all of which execute under exclusion synchronization with respect to the same semaphore (Hoare, 1974). (A semaphore belonging to a monitor or safe object is also referred to as a *lock variable* or a *lock*, for short).

Before executing any operation on a monitor, a thread first locks the entire monitor. The lock belongs to the monitor and protects all its data. Each operation is a critical section. What's new is the packaging: The operations are encapsulated in the monitor object and use its lock.

A monitor operation can call an operation on another monitor so that the critical sections are logically nested inside each other. With monitors, the sections cannot overlap; a thread always releases first the lock it acquired last. This isn't true for naked semaphores: A thread can acquire semaphore *S*, then semaphore *T*, and then release first *S* and then *T*. This is less neat and more error prone.

Safe objects in Ada, Java, and C# are all variations on the monitor. The code to acquire and release the semaphores is inserted automatically by the compiler. Programming in a language that supports some form of monitors is much easier and safer than working with naked semaphores. I shall refer to the operations on a safe object as **safe operations**.

*2.1.1.2.3 Volatile Data

One special case is where a single data element is shared. The memory hardware ensures that only one processor at a time writes to each memory location. However, copies of a single variable can exist in multiple caches and be updated by different threads concurrently. To avoid this, the programmer can specify certain variables as **volatile**. Every update to a volatile variable is *written through* to memory, and any cached copies are effectively destroyed.

2.1.2 Multithreading in High-Level Languages

At any particular point in time, the features provided by our programming languages reflect our understanding of software and programming.

FAIRLEY, 1985

---

[22]More exactly, a *binary* semaphore. It has two states, represented by 0 and 1 in the hardware. A *counting* semaphore can have more states and might be used to allow up to *n* threads into a critical section.
[23]The assembler instruction name is usually *TSET* or *TAND*, or *TSL* for "test and set lock."
[24]The monitor concept was inspired by the class concept in Simula 67 (Hoare, 1985).

The designers of PL/I made a pioneering but not altogether successful attempt to include threading (Sebesta, 2009).[25] Some versions of Algol and Pascal also support multithreading. Currently, Ada, Java, and C# are some industry-strength languages with built-in threading and monitors. This chapter presents multi-threading in Java and Ada in some detail. To begin, here's a brief overview of each language.

2.1.2.1 Java

Language shapes the way we think, and determines what we can think about.

WHORF, 1956

The Java syntax for threads and synchronized objects (Goetz, 2006; Lea; 2000; Magee and Kramer, 2006; Wellings, 2004) may be familiar to many readers. Threading is integrated with the class structure: A thread class is a descendant of the class *Thread*. Support for mutual exclusion is built into the universal ancestor class *Object*.

Java threading is adequate for its original purpose—windows program-ming, applets, and the like. It's quite flexible for a concurrency expert but makes thread handling in Java almost as error prone as working with naked semaphores. Little protects programmers from the consequences of their own mistakes.

The *Real-Time Specification for Java (RTSJ)* (Bollella et al., 2000; Bollella and Gosling, 2000; Wellings, 2004) is intended to make Java useful for real-time applications. [It does little to render it less error prone (Sandén, 2004).] *RTSJ* circumvents garbage collection and providing interrupt handling. (**Garbage col-lection** is a process that periodically inventories a system and deletes unused[26] objects.) Real-time programmers don't want automatic garbage collection because it makes the timing of the program unpredictable: While the unused objects are being picked out, other processing stops.

2.1.2.2 Ada

A most important, but also a most elusive, aspect of any tool is its influence on the habits of those who train themselves in its use. If the tool is a programming language, this influence is—whether we like it or not—an influence on our thinking habits.

DIJKSTRA, 1976

Java's programming pitfalls lack counterparts in Ada for the most part. Like Java, Ada supports threads and safe objects, but unlike Java, it was intended for safety-critical, real-time applications all along (Barnes, 2006; Burns and Wellings, 2007, 2009; Riehle, 2003). Ada is a much safer alternative for critical systems (Brosgol, 1998; Sandén, 2002). Ada's *tasks* and *protected objects* match Java's threads and synchronized objects conceptually, but their implementa-tion allows much less room for programmer error (Sandén, 2002, 2004). With Ada, a programmer cannot easily make a thread hold an object lock very long

---

[25]The design of PL/I was completed around 1965. Ada ("Ada 83") first appeared in 1983. Java was released in 1994 and C# in 1998.
[26]More precisely, *unreferenced* objects. A **loitering** object is one that is unused but still referenced.

(Section 2.1.4.1). For instance, a protected operation cannot include a `delay` statement (Sections 2.3.1.5 and 2.3.2).

Ada 95 and later versions include support for object orientation but don't extend it to protected objects (Wellings et al., 2000). The latest version is *Ada 2005* (Barnes, 2006; Leroy, 2003). At each point in time, the current version is simply called *Ada*. I shall use "Ada 83," "Ada 95," or "Ada 2005" to tell the versions apart when necessary. (At the time of this writing, the next version is expected to be Ada 2012.)

*2.1.2.2.1 Attitudes Toward Ada

C treats you like a consenting adult. Pascal treats you like a naughty child. Ada treats you like a criminal.

DOUGLASS, 1998

A language that doesn't affect the way you think about programming is not worth knowing.

PERLIS, 1982

Sadly, many programmers came to dislike Ada when it first came out in 1983. The required declarations, some felt, were cumbersome and wordy compared to languages in the C tradition and Fortran. Hackers are said to have found "Ada's exception-handling and inter-process communication features particularly hilarious" (Raymond, 2000). In some ways, Ada was ahead of its time: After those first impressions were formed, its exception handling became the model for both C++ and Java.

The critique of Ada 83's intertask communication features has merit. The makers of Ada 83 departed radically from established practice. They based multitasking not on the traditional separation of threads and safe objects but instead on Hoare's theory for communicating sequential processes (*CSP;* Section 9.4.1) (Hoare, 1985). This led to the *rendezvous* concept (Section 2.3.4), which rests on tasks alone; there is no equivalent of a safe object. For this reason, every shared object needed its own *guardian* task (Sandén, 1994), which enforces exclusive access. Typically, a guardian task executes only while in rendezvous with another task.

Rendezvous-based concurrency does as much as concurrency built on threads and safe objects. But thread programmers accustomed to the traditional ways found the Ada 83 model awkward. Thread programmers have always sought to reduce complexity and overhead by limiting the number of different threads and saw no justification for the guardian tasks. This awkwardness was removed in Ada 95, which introduced `protected` objects.

Ada contains many a "feature designed to make it harder to write bad code" (Raymond, 1993). It aims to protect programmers from their own mistakes even at the cost of limiting somewhat our means of expression. Engineers of safety-critical hardware have subjected themselves to such safeguards for years whereas programming languages seem to curry favor with programmers. Brinch Hansen (1999) said this on the subject in general:

> The 1980s will probably be remembered as the decade in which programmers took a gigantic step backward by switching from secure Pascal-like languages to insecure C-like languages. I have no rational explanation for this trend, but

it seems to me that if computer programmers cannot even agree that security is an essential requirement of any programming language, then we have not yet established a discipline of computing based on commonly accepted principles.

2.1.3 Threads and Processes

Threads are sometimes called *lightweight* processes as opposed to *heavyweight* processes such as those in UNIX®.[27] A heavyweight process defines an address space in which multiple threads can operate. Context switching between threads is normally much faster than between processes. Processes often communicate by means of *messages* which are routed through the operating system. In a distributed system, processes at different nodes can communicate the same way.

Threads in a common address space can communicate more flexibly and efficiently than processes and can exchange data through a variety of safe objects. A message queue is one solution, though rarely the most efficient one. A safe object encapsulating some static data structure may also be safer because the risk of message buffer overflow is eliminated.

Note Some design approaches let threads emulate processes and communicate via messages (Section 8.3). Each thread is artificially confined to a module. It's as though each thread were marooned on an island of code and reduced to waiting for messages from threads on other islands. This view is limiting and ignores the added expressivity when we let threads operate on safe objects.

2.1.4 Exclusion and Condition Synchronization

Exclusion synchronization (also known as *mutual exclusion*) stops multiple threads from calling operations on the same object at the same time, which would jeopardize the integrity of the object's data. Programming languages let us define objects that enforce mutual exclusion. I call them **safe objects**. Ada's *protected* objects and Java's *synchronized* objects are safe objects that come with exclusion synchronization built in.

Exclusion synchronization is usually implemented with semaphores (Section 2.1.1.2.1). The semaphore variable for a safe object is called the object **lock**. A great strength of such languages as Ada and Java is that the programmer need not work with naked semaphores. The compiler generates code that sets and clears the lock for any synchronized operation in Java and any protected operation in Ada.

We say that a thread is *stalled* when it's waiting for an object lock (Brosgol, 2005). A stalled thread is waiting for another thread to complete a computation.

A different mechanism—*condition* synchronization (Section 2.1.4.2)—is necessary when a thread must wait on a condition before performing an operation. We say that a thread *blocks* on a condition. Thus, a thread that attempts to

---

[27]Software *development* processes can also be heavyweight and lightweight. Lightweight development processes are also known as *agile*, and heavyweight processes are often said to have *high ceremony* (Fowler, 2004). By the same token, a UNIX® process may be more ceremonious than a thread in terms of context switching and communication.

retrieve an item from a buffer may block if the buffer is empty. The buffer may remain empty indefinitely.

Exclusion and condition synchronization are intertwined. Take a buffer object with the safe operations *put* and *get,* where a producer thread blocks when the buffer is full and a consumer thread blocks when it's empty. The consumer thread calls *get* and finds the buffer empty. Before blocking, it must release the object lock so that a producer thread can put an item into the buffer.

2.1.4.1 Use of Exclusion Synchronization

Safe operations should always be as short as possible to minimize the time other threads are stalled. A thread shouldn't yield the processor while holding an object locked. Thus, a thread with exclusive access to an object isn't supposed to call *sleep* in Java (Section 2.2.1.1) or `delay` in Ada (Section 2.3.1.5), block on a condition, or be waiting for an external event (Section 2.1.4.2).

If all operations on an object are short, a thread should normally find it unlocked. If not, the wait should be brief. For the same reasons, it's quite unlikely that two threads should attempt to access the same object while a third thread is keeping it locked (Sandén, 2004).

In reactive systems such as in this book, many a safe object is expected to serve as some domain object's software surrogate. Decisions affecting the domain object are based on the surrogate's state so it must reflect the domain object's state faithfully in real time. In that situation, it's particularly important to keep all the safe operations short.

In state modeling, actions are instantaneous; that is, they take no time at all, conceptually. In the real world, we must make sure that the entire space of time—from when the event occurs until the action has been completed—is negligible. We say that the action is *nearly* instantaneous: For practical purposes it takes no time (Sections 3.2.0 and 3.6.4.1).

2.1.4.1.1 Techniques for Exclusion Synchronization

If the wait is always short, we need no orderly queue of threads stalled on an object lock. Let *lo* be a thread that holds the lock of some object, *o*. On multi-processors, other threads can repeatedly attempt access until successful. We say that those threads *spin*. They are not guaranteed first-come–first-served access, but that's usually acceptable on the assumption that a lock is never held long. This can be done without context switching.

On a uniprocessor, a higher priority thread *hi*, running on the *same* processor as *lo*, can preempt *lo,* try to access *o*, and find it locked. In a solution similar to spinning, *hi* yields the processor in the hope of finding *o* unlocked when made running next. If *o* is still locked at that time, *hi* again yields, and so on. (I'll refer to this as *busy waiting*.) In order to give *lo* a chance to execute, *hi* cannot really spin. If *hi*'s priority is much higher, there can be multiple context switches before *lo* releases *o*. This can be avoided with a *priority ceiling* protocol (Section 2.1.4.1.1.1).

2.1.4.1.1.1 Priority Inversion

The situation where a thread—*hi*—is stalled while a lower priority thread—*lo*—runs is called *priority inversion* (Brosgol, 2005; Burns and Wellings,

2007; Douglass, 2009; Goetz, 2006; Lea, 2000; Wellings, 2004).[28] While *lo* holds object *o*'s lock, *hi*, running on the same or a different processor, may also find a need to access *o* exclusively. Unavoidably, *hi* must wait for *lo* to exit the safe operation.

If *lo* continues running at its normal priority after *hi* has stalled on *o*, then a third thread, *bn*, with a priority between those of *hi* and *lo* may preempt *lo*. If *bn* doesn't need access to *o*, it can take over the processor from *lo*. This is sometimes called *push-through* stalling. It's an *avoidable* situation where *hi* is waiting for two lower priority threads: *lo* and *bn*. In turn, *bn* could be preempted, and so forth. As a result, *hi* may wait indefinitely for access to *o*.

We can eliminate push-through stalling by giving *lo* a priority boost in one of two ways:

- Let *lo* *inherit* *hi*'s priority once *hi* has tried to access *o*. That way, *lo* cannot be preempted by *bn*, and *hi*'s wait is limited to the time *lo* takes to complete its safe-operation call.
- Define a *priority ceiling* for *o*. Then all threads run at the priority ceiling while executing safe operations on *o*. The priority ceiling must be the priority of the *highest locker*, defined as the highest priority thread that ever operates on *o*.

Priority inheritance is the more surgical approach, while priority ceiling may be easier to implement. With priority ceiling, a thread operating on a safe object with its priority boosted is never preempted by another thread that needs access to the object. This reduces the overhead.

The priority ceiling protocol is more generous to low-priority threads than priority inheritance: With priority ceiling in effect, *lo* receives a priority boost and operates on *o* at the priority ceiling even if no higher priority thread is stalled on *o*. Especially on a uniprocessor, this generosity is at the expense of any other ready thread, *bn*, with priority between *lo* and the highest locker: Even if *bn* doesn't access *o*, it must wait for *lo* to go back to its normal priority. Thus, the protocol causes a kind of priority inversion in this case. [With multiple processors, *bn* may well find one that's available (Stallings, 2008).]

*2.1.4.1.2 Shared Objects as Bottlenecks
The "bottleneck" device is the one with the highest utilization.

SMITH AND WILLIAMS, 2001

A shared safe object may be accessed so often that it becomes a bottleneck even if each access is brief. The global queue of threads that are ready to run (Section 2.1.1.1) illustrates this (except that the resource users are physical processors rather than threads). Each processor needs exclusive access to the queue in order to pick an eligible thread to run. It matters little which processor gains access to the ready queue next, but the time spent waiting for access is wasted. As the number of processors grows, the queue can become a bottleneck to such a degree that thread scheduling can no longer rely on a single queue. One solution is to have multiple ready queues, each tied to a group of processors.

---

[28]This definition assumes preemptive thread scheduling.

*2.1.4.1.3 Heavy Computation in Critical Sections

As a rule, a thread, t, shouldn't perform a lengthy computation while holding some object, o, locked. Instead, t should perform most of the computation outside o and make only short operation calls on t. This is somewhat more important with multiprocessors than with a uniprocessor. Here's the effect of keeping o locked in each case:

- On a uniprocessor, *higher priority* threads that need o's lock are stalled. No other thread is affected. This is because higher priority threads that don't need the lock can preempt t. Lower priority threads must wait for t to finish the computation and release the processor whether t holds o's lock or not.

- On multiprocessors, *any* other thread that needs o's lock may be affected, regardless of priority. (If t weren't holding o's lock, the other thread could access o using another processor.)

Any object that must be held locked during a lengthy computation must be designed carefully. It's unwise to mix long and short safe operations on the same object because a thread calling a quick operation may be held up for a long time just waiting for the lock.

*2.1.4.1.4 Example: Elevator System

No example in this book has safe operations long enough to make priority inversion an issue, but it might surface in repository systems (Section 6.7). In such problems, some threads post items in a repository, and others analyze and process the items. (They may also be posted by interrupt handlers; Section 2.1.5.) The repository is a shared resource. Posting is typically simple but possibly time critical while the analysis and processing may involve multiple items and be lengthy.

In the elevator problem (Section 6.7.1) the repository holds requests for elevator service. The array of requests from the *up* and *down* floor buttons is in the safe object *External-requests*, which is shared by all elevator threads and sampler threads (Figure 6-10). Sampler threads (or interrupt handlers) call the safe operations on *External-requests* directly.

To impact the entering of new requests as little as possible, an elevator thread first calls the safe object *Servable-requests*. Specifically, it calls *Servable-requests.continue-up* to see if it must continue upward. From within *continue-up* it calls a safe operation on *External-requests* to find any requests from floor buttons higher up. During the call, *External-requests* is locked for samplers and interrupt handlers. *Servable-requests* remains locked (to other elevator threads) throughout the call to *continue-up*, which goes on to see if another elevator has already promised to serve those requests.

*2.1.4.1.5 Lock-Free Exclusion Synchronization

Locking isn't the only way to guard the integrity of data against conflicting updates by different threads. With multiprocessors, more programs are threaded in order to profit from the additional processing capacity. Because locking is considered error prone, other ways of protecting the integrity of shared data are being investigated. The most widely discussed approach is transactional memory

(Adl-Tabatabai et al., 2006; Drepper, 2009; Larus and Kozyrakis, 2008). It can replace locking and be combined with condition synchronization.

Transactional memory builds on concurrency control approaches for database transactions (Coulouris et al., 2005). With database transactions, we control the read and write accesses to the database. With transactional memory, we control the read and write accesses to shared data in memory.

With *lazy versioning*, each transaction stores all writes in a private area until it's ready to commit (Adl-Tabatabai et al., 2006). In order to detect conflicts, each transaction's *read set* and *write set* are tracked. (The read set consists of the addresses from which the transaction has read, and the write set, the addresses to which it has written.)

A typical conflict is where two transactions running at the same time update the same variable. Under *pessimistic conflict detection*, each transaction checks for such conflicts as it goes along. As soon as a conflict is found, one of the conflicting transactions stalls (Adl-Tabatabai et al., 2006). *Optimistic conflict detection* assumes that conflicts are rare and postpones checking until a transaction is ready to commit. If there is a conflict, one or more transactions abort and must start over.

2.1.4.2 Condition Synchronization

Condition synchronization is a device that makes threads wait for a certain condition before they execute a safe operation. It's also known as *barrier synchronization*.[29] In the previously mentioned example, a *Buffer* class has the two operations: *put*, which is called by producer threads, and *get*, called by consumer threads. Producer threads put items into the buffer, and consumer threads retrieve them.

We use condition synchronization if we want to block consumer threads when the buffer is empty and block producer threads when it's full. There is no assumption that these waits will be brief; threads may wait indefinitely. They are typically queued first-in–first-out (FIFO) per priority.

A consumer thread, $c1$, must lock the buffer object in order to see whether it's empty. If $c1$ finds the buffer empty, it blocks until there's data in it. It cannot keep the buffer-object lock during this wait, so before $c1$ blocks, it releases the object lock. After $c1$ is notified that there may be an item in the buffer, it regains the object lock as soon as it's available and again tests whether there is indeed an item.

2.1.4.2.1 Controlling the Access to Shared Resources in the Domain

Condition synchronization is necessary when software controls resource sharing in the problem domain. In an automated factory, for example, jobs on the factory floor vie for access to forklifts (Section 7.3.2) (Carter and Sandén, 1998; Sandén, 1997a). The jobs are represented by *Job* threads in the software, and safe objects represent the forklifts. The *Job* thread is a *resource-user thread* (4.4) and acts as a software surrogate for the physical job: When it calls *acquire* on the software object, the *physical* job gains exclusive access to the *physical* forklift.

In principle, a *Job* thread reserves a forklift for its physical job much the same as it locks a shared data structure: It acquires a semaphore. Still, a forklift operation may continue for several minutes, so exclusion synchronization

---

[29]"Barrier" is also used in the more limited sense of a device that stops parallel activities from proceeding until *all* activities in a set are completed (Andrews, 1991; Goetz, 2006; Wellings, 2004).

won't do. For one thing, we want waiting jobs to form an ordered queue. Besides, when a high-priority job is waiting for a lower priority job to release the forklift, a priority ceiling or priority inheritance protocol is of no help because it's concerned only with processor use. A job probably requires little computing by the manufacturing control system while traveling on a forklift.

A semaphore that protects a domain resource should be encapsulated in a monitor. Yet, *unencapsulated* semaphores are more acceptable in this case than for protecting shared data in memory. I discuss unencapsulated semaphores and monitors in the next sections.

2.1.4.2.1.1 Unencapsulated Semaphores for Domain-Object Access Control

I shall use the term **semaphore safe object** for a safe object with the operations *acquire* and *release*. Let's call it *s*. It includes a Boolean variable, *busy*. The operation *acquire* queues calling threads when *busy* is true. Each critical section is bracketed by calls to *acquire* and *release* on *s* as follows:

```
s.acquire
// critical section where the resource protected by s is used under
exclusive access
s.release
```

Two levels of semaphores and locking are involved here: The object *s*'s hidden lock variable is a hardware semaphore that controls the access to the variable *busy*. In turn, *busy* controls access to the resource. It's a semaphore implemented in software.

The solution extends easily to where *s* controls multiple, equivalent resources. In that situation, *acquire* may return a reference to the resource, *b*, say, that the calling resource-user thread actually acquired. The same reference is sent to *release* as follows:

```
b = s.acquire
// sequence where resource b is used under exclusive access
s.release(b)
```

Unencapsulated semaphore safe objects such as *s* are needed mostly when the critical sections are overlapping rather than nested. In a railway control system, for example, a train may acquire and release track segments in the following kind of pattern:

```
acquire segment n              // Critical section n starts
// The train is on segment n
acquire segment n+1            // Critical section n+1 starts
leave segment n
release segment n              // Critical section n ends
// The train is on segment n+1
leave segment n+1
release segment n+1            // Critical section n+1 ends
```

As in this example, the resource-user-thread's *run* operation contains the critical sections where some resource is used. This looks like a throwback to managing critical sections by means of naked semaphores, but as we have seen, it can be necessary (Carter and Sandén, 1998).

With unencapsulated semaphore safe objects, the programmer is responsible for inserting *release* calls so that the resource is always freed even if an exception is thrown. Failing to do this leads to *"resource leakage,"*[30] which is the situation where a resource is kept locked long after a thread is finished using it, and perhaps forever. For short, I shall refer to the use of unencapsulated semaphore safe objects for the control of access to domain objects as the **semaphore solution**.

2.1.4.2.1.2 Monitors for Domain-Object Access Control

At times we can encapsulate the critical sections where a domain resource is accessed and the semaphore safe object in an other object. I shall call such an object a **monitor** and call this the **monitor solution**. Each critical section is an operation on the monitor object. As a group, they represent all the necessary processing of the shared resource. Having all operations in one place is handy since the programmer must insert the acquire and release calls manually.

*2.1.4.2.2 Don't Use Object Locks to Control Access to Domain Resources!

In some languages (such as Java), nothing stops a programmer from controlling access to domain resources by means of object locks (Sparkman, 2004). **This is not recommended**. Ada effectively makes this kind of misuse impossible by prohibiting "potentially blocking" operations inside a protected operation (Barnes, 2006; Burns and Wellings, 2007).

The object locks may appear to do the job but may not work as intended. This becomes very clear if we replace object locks with some other mechanism for exclusion synchronization. For instance, transactional memory (Section 2.1.4.1.5) is concerned only with memory updates. It takes one of the following two approaches to resolve conflicts:

- Save all updates and apply them after we know that there is no conflict.
- Perform the updates and then undo them when a conflict has been detected.

Other actions that a thread takes (such as giving a train the green light to enter a shared track segment) are side effects with which the transactional-memory mechanism has no way of dealing.

*2.1.4.2.3 Synchronization Terminology

The term "condition synchronization" is all right in the *Buffer* example, where the threads are indeed waiting for a favorable condition to complete their *get* or *put* call. Language designers also use *"state-based* mutual exclusion" for condition synchronization (Brosgol, 2005): The condition defines the state in which the safe object is ready to process a certain kind of call.

---

[30]Compare the more common term *memory leakage*, meaning that memory isn't properly released by some thread or process and so remains unavailable. Eventually, all available memory may leak out, leaving none to be allocated.

Sometimes, the term *competition synchronization* is used for exclusion synchronization, and *cooperation synchronization* for condition synchronization (Sebesta, 2009). The rationale is that the producer and consumer threads must cooperate to manage an empty or full buffer but compete for access to the *get* and *put* operations.

In this book, semaphore safe objects and monitors play an important role for controlling access to problem-domain resources. In such semaphores, condition synchronization is the main feature, and the exclusion synchronization that protects the variable *busy* is an implementation detail–albeit critical. None of the terms really captures this situation. Specifically, the distinction between "competition" and "cooperation" synchronization doesn't hold because the jobs that queue up on the condition are competing for resources. I shall stay with "condition synchronization" for lack of a better alternative.

2.1.5 Interrupt Handling

Software that controls devices in the problem domain must usually deal with interrupts directly. An interrupt signals to the software that a certain event has occurred so that the software may take immediate action. Among other things, the event can be a mouse click, a keystroke, a sensor being tripped, or the completion of a disk input–output (I/O) operation.

Each type of interrupt is typically directed to a specific processor. When the event occurs, a hardware flag is set. Unless interrupts are disabled, the processor checks this interrupt flag essentially after each instruction before it proceeds to the next one. If the flag is set, the processor suspends its execution of the next instruction, disables all interrupts, saves the program counter and other register contents, and executes an *interrupt handler* (also called an *interrupt service routine*, *ISR*). Once the interrupt handler has finished, the flag is reset and interrupts are enabled. At that point, the processor either resumes the interrupted thread or runs the dispatcher to find the most eligible thread to execute. So as not to miss interrupts, the software must handle each one before the next interrupt of the same type is expected; otherwise, the next interrupt may be lost.

An interrupt handler that needs access to a safe object is subject to exclusion synchronization and so may have to wait for a lock to be released. This is one more reason why all safe operations should be short. Of course, interrupt handlers should also be short. (This is quite obvious in Ada where protected procedures can be designated as interrupt handlers; Section 2.3.2.4.)

An interrupt handler mustn't engage in condition synchronization. A practical reason is that there may be no thread that can be queued. In any case, an interrupt must be handled quickly, so the handler mustn't be subject to an indefinite delay.

*2.1.5.1 Interrupt Priorities

As discussed above, interrupt handling is arranged so that the processing of one interrupt cannot itself be interrupted. This simplifies the handling greatly and is practical if interrupts are sufficiently rare compared to the handling time. A more sophisticated hardware design includes groups of interrupts at different priorities where the handling of one interrupt can be preempted by a higher priority interrupt.

*2.1.6 Visualizing Threads

Anyone who deals with threading must create a workable mental image of what's going on below the surface that is the program text. This is because it's difficult to illustrate the workings of a complex, multithreaded program meaningfully in a diagram or otherwise. (Tools based on animation may hold greater promise.) As a result, programmers form their own little theories of threading. Some will say that "code is run in a thread," stressing that it executes in the thread's context (Section 2.1.1.1). By contrast, those who say that an operation "runs as part of a thread" may view the thread as a trace of executed instructions: When a certain operation executes, it produces a portion of the thread's trace.

This book views control threads as active parties that navigate a passive code landscape. In other words, a thread is viewed as an abstract processor.[31] Because processors execute code, we say that a *thread executes* (or *runs*) *code* and that *a thread calls* a safe operation. When we talk about the *caller* of an operation, we're always referring to a control thread. In this view, the threads can be said to drive the execution the same way as a main program drives sequential software (Section 7.4).

2.2 CONCURRENCY IN JAVA™

Gimme a shot of java, nix on the moo-juice.

MEZZ MEZZROW AND BERNARD WOLFE, REALLY THE BLUES, 1946[32]

This section focuses on those syntactical features of Java that are of interest in this book. It's based on Sandén (2004). For further details, the reader is referred to Douglass (1998), Goetz (2006), Gosling et al. (2005), Lea (2000), Magee and Kramer (2006), and Wellings (2004). *RTSJ* is discussed in Section 2.2.5.

2.2.1 Defining and Starting Java Threads

Java provides the abstract class *Thread*, whose operation *run* represents the main logic that a thread performs. A standard way of creating threads is to declare a new class, *T*,[33] say, that extends *Thread* and overrides *run* with some specific processing. Each instance *th* of *T* has its own thread. It's started by the call *th.start*, which can often conveniently be placed in *T*'s constructor. Once started, the thread executes *T*'s *run* operation and has access to *th*'s data.

A different mechanism is necessary for a class, *R*, that needs a thread and already extends another class. For this situation, Java provides the interface *Runnable*, which is where *run* is defined.[34] The programmer lets *R* extend the other

---

[31]ELM takes the threads' perspective and sees the physical processors as resources. We say that the thread *runs on* a processor.

[32]Reprinted by arrangement with Citadel Press/Kensington Publishing Corp.

[33]*T* is not a good class name. Names should be meaningful and typically longer. Because most classes, variables, and the like in this chapter are quite generic, I have opted for brevity.

[34]*Thread* implements *Runnable*.

class and implement *Runnable*. Instantiating *R* creates a *runnable object, ro*, say. To give *ro* a thread, we submit it as a parameter to one of *Thread*'s constructors and then call *start* on the resulting *Thread* instance. This is typically done in a statement such as

```
new Thread(ro).start( );
```

Thread creation and activation can be hidden inside *R*'s constructor in the form

```
new Thread(this).start( );
```

2.2.1.1 The *sleep* Statement

Threads have the fundamental ability to control their own timing by suspending their execution. Concurrent programs may run for hours, days, or even years, and many threads may well be suspended most of the time. Certain threads perform some action on a periodic basis and suspend themselves until it's time to take the action again (Section 4.3.1.2).

A thread suspends itself for *m* milliseconds by calling *sleep*(*m*). After *m* milliseconds, the thread becomes ready and is reactivated as soon as a processor is available. Execution resumes at the statement immediately after the *sleep* statement. The sleep is broken prematurely if an *InterruptedException* is thrown. (Control is then transferred to an exception handler.)

2.2.2 Synchronized Objects in Java

Avoid synchronization.

VERMEULEN ET AL., 2000

In Java, every class has the potential for being a safe class. Every object has a lock variable, which is hidden from the programmer and is sometimes referred to as an *intrinsic* lock (Goetz, 2006). Safe operations in Java are designated as *synchronized* as, for example,

```
void synchronized m(...)...
```

Such a synchronized operation is a critical section: The compiler brackets it with instructions that acquire and release the lock on the object, *o*, on which it's called. That is, a thread calling *o.m* locks *o* as a whole so that no other thread can perform any synchronized operation on *o* (or execute any block synchronized on *o*; Section 2.2.2.1).

This synchronization feature is built in, hence guaranteeing that the lock is always released when a thread leaves a synchronized operation, even if this happens by means of the exception-handling mechanism. I shall refer to any instance of a Java class that has at least one synchronized operation as a *synchronized object*. I shall also call the object *o* synchronized if at least one block exists that is synchronized on *o*.

A Java programmer can choose to make only some operations of a class synchronized. Thus, a read-only operation that returns a single attribute value needn't be synchronized. *The Elements of Java Style* advises the programmer to "avoid synchronization" (Vermeulen et al., 2000). Synchronization carries overhead. In Java, one synchronized operation often calls such another on the same object, incurring the overhead repeatedly.

2.2.2.1 Synchronized Blocks

Do not synchronize an entire method if [it] contains significant operations that do not need synchronization.

VERMEULEN ET AL., 2000

In addition to synchronized operations, Java provides synchronized blocks. Any block in any operation can be synchronized on any object as follows:

```
synchronized (Expression) {/* Block B */}
```

Expression must evaluate to a reference to some object, say *vo* of class *V*. Like a synchronized operation, a synchronized block is a critical section, and the compiler automatically brackets the block with statements to acquire and release the lock on *vo*. Consider first the case where *B* is part of some operation, *m,* on class *V* and is synchronized on the *current object* as follows:

```
class V ... {
  void m( ){
    synchronized (this){
      /* Block B*/
    }
  }
}
```

The above works if not all of *m* requires exclusive access. With only block *B* synchronized, multiple threads can execute the rest of *m* concurrently. In an alternate design, *B* is a separate, synchronized operation.

In the following excerpt, *B* is synchronized on object *wo* of class *W*. This is useful if *m* requires exclusive access to some object—such as *wo*—other than the current one.

```
class V ... {
  void m( ){
    synchronized (wo){
      /* Block B*/
    }
  }
}
```

Arguably, it would be cleaner to make *B* an operation and encapsulate it in the declaration of *W* together with any other operations. All the same, synchronized blocks are useful when many threads perform their own particular operations on a synchronized object. The alternative would be to include many disparate operations in the class declaration.

2.2.2.2 Nested, Critical Sections in Java

Critical sections can be nested in various ways. Here's an example with a synchronized block, B, inside a synchronized operation, m:

```
class V ... {
    synchronized void m( ) {
        synchronized (wo) {
            /* Block B */
        }
    }
}
```

In this excerpt, block B executes with exclusive access to both *wo* and the current instance of V. Other cases of nesting are where a synchronized operation is called from within a synchronized block or operation.

We need nested, synchronized blocks when the updates of two or more objects must be coordinated. Let x and y be two objects controlled by an object z of class Z in the following sense: As part of a synchronized operation, m, on z, it's necessary to update x and y also. We can do this by placing nested blocks, synchronized on x and y, inside m. Within the block C below, the executing thread has exclusive access to x, y, and z all at once:

```
class Z ... {
    synchronized void m( ) {
        synchronized (x) {
        synchronized (y) {
            /* Block C */
        }
        }
    }
}
```

2.2.3 Condition Synchronization in Java

Document synchronization semantics.

Vermeulen et al., 2000

The most common idiom for condition synchronization by far is the statement

```
while (cond) wait( );
```

I shall refer to such a statement as a ***wait loop***. It must be inside a synchronized operation on some object, o, or a block that is synchronized on o. The wait loop stops any calling thread, t, from proceeding as long as the condition *cond* holds. If *cond* is true, t calls *wait*. This is a special operation that makes the calling thread—t in this case—release all its locks on o and place itself in o's *wait set.* When *t* is reactivated from the wait set (Section 2.2.3.2), it continues immediately after *wait( )* with its locks on the object reinstated. It's still inside the wait loop and proceeds to retest *cond*.

It complicates the wait loop syntax that a thread in the wait set may need to be activated to handle an *InterruptedException*. This exception is thrown by one thread and caught by another. Unless the exception is propagated to an enclosing scope, we need a construct such as this:

```
while (cond) try {wait( );}
   catch (InterruptedException e) {/* Take action or ignore exception */}
```

A thread in the wait set that catches an InterruptedException is reactivated, and control is transferred to an exception handler.

2.2.3.1 Placement of the Wait Loop

The wait loop most often appears at the very beginning of a synchronized operation or block and is reached right after a thread locks the object. It can, however, be placed anywhere within a synchronized operation or block. This happens most typically in operations that allocate resources to calling threads. If a thread's request cannot be satisfied with available resources, the thread places itself in the wait set until resources are released. At that time, it continues right after the *wait* call as soon as its locks on the object have been reinstated. If the call to *wait* is inside a correct wait loop, the thread retests the wait condition and reenters the wait set if it's unfavorable.

2.2.3.1.1 Home-Heating Example

A home-heating system (Sections 2.3.2.2.1 and 6.5.2) serves a group of five homes. Due to undersized fuel lines, at most four homes can be heated at a time. As a result, a home must forgo heating in favor of another home once in a while. The system ensures that no home is forcibly without heat for more than 10 minutes at a time. When a home has been without heat for 10 minutes, heating is turned off in the home that has had it the longest.

Each home has a thread of class *Heater* that handles the heating cycle, which takes the furnace of the home through a series of steps when heating is turned on and off. A singleton synchronized object, *tPool*, of class *TokenPool,* models a pool of four heating tokens. Before starting its heater, each *Heater* thread, say *h0*, must obtain a token. It normally does this by calling *tPool.get*. If it cannot obtain a token for 10 minutes, it calls *tPool.insist*. From within *insist*, *h0* calls the *turnOff* operation on the *logicalSwitch* object of the *thread* that has had heat the longest and then waits for that *thread* to turn off its heat. For this, *h0* remains in a wait loop. A thread releases a token by calling *tPool.releaseToken*. Here's class *TokenPool* with a wait loop inside the *insist* operation:

```
class TokenPool {
   int active;                    // Number of active heater tokens
   ...
   synchronized void get( ) ....
   ...
```

```
synchronized void insist( ) throws InterruptedException
{   // Get a heating token
    if (4==active)                          // No token available
    {   // Find the heater h1 that has been on the longest...
        logicalSwitch.turnOff(h1);          // Tell h1 to shut off heat
        while (4==active) wait( );           // Wait loop for h1 to release token
    }
    active++;
}


synchronized releaseToken( )
{   // Release a heating token
    ...
    active--;
    notify( );              // Activate a waiting thread (Section 2.2.3.2)
    }
}
```

In this example, a thread calls *wait* only after it has found that no token is available. The thread then arranges for the heat to be turned off in another home and waits for the heater in that home to shut down.

2.2.3.2 Notifying Waiting Threads

When a thread executes a synchronized operation on an object, *o*, and changes a condition on which one or more threads in *o*'s wait set may be pending, it must *notify* those threads. In standard Java, *o.notify* reactivates *one* randomly chosen thread, *t*, say, in *o*'s wait set. If the *wait* call is correctly placed within a wait loop, *t* reevaluates the condition and either proceeds in the synchronized operation or reenters the wait set. (In *RTSJ*, the most eligible thread is reactivated; Section 2.2.5.)

The call *o.notifyAll* releases *all* threads in *o*'s wait set. This is useful when a condition has been changed so that multiple threads may be able to proceed. But calling *notifyAll* instead of *notify* can be necessary even when we want only a single thread to proceed. In standard Java, this is the only way to be sure that the highest priority thread is activated if there can be more than one thread in the wait set. (It's unneeded in real-time Java; Section 2.2.5.) It's inefficient if the wait set contains many threads, which must all attempt access (Vermeulen et al., 2000).

2.2.3.2.1 Notifying Threads Waiting on Different Conditions

Because each object has a single wait set, *notifyAll* must be called instead of *notify* if the set may include threads waiting on different conditions. When one such condition is changed, *all* the threads must be activated to make sure that any thread waiting on that condition is activated. (With *notify*, a thread waiting on a different condition may be activated instead.) Both *RTSJ* and standard Java require *notifyAll* in this situation.

In the weather buoy (Section 5.4.3.2.1), two or more threads can be blocked at once by different conditions on the same safe object. In general, the *concurrent-activities* pattern (Section 5.4) tends to produce such situations. Except for that, they aren't as common as one might believe. For example, in the *Buffer* class (Section 2.1.4.2), producers are blocked until the buffer is no longer full, and consumers until it's no longer empty; however, the wait set never contains both consumer and producer threads, so we can always call *notify*. (A wait loop is still needed. A producer must call *notify* in case a consumer is waiting and may activate another waiting producer instead.)

In order to call *wait, notify,* or *notifyAll* on some object, *o*, a thread must have *o* locked. The wait set is itself a shared data structure that is protected from conflicting access by the object lock. It has no lock of its own. For this reason, these calls must always be inside an operation or block that is synchronized on *o*.

2.2.3.3 Timing Out the Wait

The operation *wait* takes a time span as an optional parameter. The parameter limits how long the calling thread will wait for the condition to change. If the thread is in the wait set at the end of the time span, it's reactivated. It resumes processing right after the *wait* call just as when reactivated by *notify*. If the call is inside a standard wait loop, the thread proceeds to check the condition and then either continues in the synchronized operation or calls *wait* and returns to the wait set. If we want it to take some other action, we must put in additional logic (Wellings, 2004).

2.2.4 Controlling Access to Shared Domain Resources

As mentioned in Section 2.1.4.2.1, we use condition synchronization to control the sharing of such resources in the problem domain as a forklift truck in the automated factory application. The jobs on the factory floor that may need a forklift are represented by *Job* threads. Depending on the pattern of simultaneous exclusive access, there are two possible solutions: monitors and unencapsulated semaphores.

2.2.4.1 Semaphore Solution

With a semaphore solution, access to the forklift is controlled by a synchronized object, say the instance *f* of class *ForkliftSemaphore*:

```
public class ForkliftSemaphore {
    boolean busy = false;
    public synchronized void acquire() {
        while (busy) wait();        // Wait loop
        busy = true;
    }
    public synchronized void release() {
        busy = false;
        notify();
    }
}
```

A thread, *j*, representing a job that needs the forklift, calls *f.acquire*. Once *j* gets past the wait loop, *acquire* sets *busy* to true, which guarantees the job exclusive access to the forklift. Thread *j* releases the forklift by calling *release*, which sets *busy* to false and notifies any threads in *f*'s wait set. Each statement sequence where the forklift is operated is bracketed by calls to *f.acquire* and *f.release* as follows:

```
f.acquire();
// Critical section where the forklift is used
f.release();
```

While one job is holding the forklift exclusively, other *Job* threads can call *f.acquire* and place themselves in *f*'s wait set. The variable *busy* serves as the lock on the physical forklift while *f*'s hidden lock variable serves only to control the access to the variable *busy* and *f*'s wait set.

2.2.4.2 Monitor Solution

The semaphore solution is somewhat like using a synchronized block for exclusion synchronization. When possible, it's better to collect the critical sections in one place. Here's a monitor for the forklift:

```
public class ForkliftMonitor{
    boolean busy=false;
    private synchronized void acquire(){
        while (busy) wait();        // Wait loop
        busy=true;
    }
    private synchronized void release(){
        busy=false;
        notify();
    }
    public void useForklift(){
        acquire();
        ...                // Critical section: Operate the forklift
        release();
    }
}
```

2.2.5 Real-Time Java (RTSJ)

[I]n fact, almost any garbage-collect-based language would be a poor choice for realtime systems. I wouldn't trust even a model airplane to a system that has to pause at unpredictable times to gather its scattered wits.

JOSEPH KESSELMAN, COMP.LANG.JAVA.TECH, SEPTEMBERS 18, 1998

The *RTSJ* (Bollella et al., 2000; Bollella and Gosling, 2000; Wellings, 2004) is an effort to make Java useful for real-time programming. One of its premises is that a real-time program must be predictable so that the programmer can know ahead of time when certain actions will be taken. This isn't true for standard Java for several reasons. First, the garbage collector, which can interrupt any other processing at any time, adds an element of randomness. Second, standard Java provides for only one scheduling policy. (Scheduling policies such as the rate-monotonic algorithm can let us prove that each thread in a set meets its specified deadline; Section 8.2.2.1.) Third, in standard Java, threads in a wait set are reactivated in arbitrary order, independent of when they attempted access; the wait set isn't an FIFO queue. Here's a summary of *RTSJ* features, some of which have their own sections below:

- *RTSJ* introduces new classes of real-time threads, which are necessary for working around the garbage collector.

- *RTSJ* stipulates that threads in a wait set be kept in FIFO order within priorities. That way, *notify* reactivates the most eligible thread. In fact, *RTSJ* also requires that threads stalled on an object lock be reactivated in FIFO order within priorities.[35]

- *RTSJ* uses priority inheritance as the default policy to mitigate priority inversion. A priority ceiling protocol is also specified (Section 2.1.4.1.1).

- *RTSJ* allows the programmer to specify interrupt handlers.

RTSJ modifies some features of regular Java and introduces some additional ones. In the following, I discuss only those relevant for this book. Other important features of *RTSJ* include various time and clock classes (Bollella et al., 2000; Bollella and Gosling, 2000; Wellings, 2004).

2.2.5.1 RTSJ Thread Classes

RTSJ introduces *RealtimeThread* (*RT*), which is a subclass of *Thread*. *RT* has the subclass *NoHeapRealtimeThread* (*NHRT*).[36] *NHRT* threads have higher priority than the garbage collector and so aren't subject to arbitrary delays caused by it. This places many restrictions on the programmer, however. For example, an *NHRT* thread cannot allocate objects on the heap. Instead, *RTSJ* provides for certain kinds of special memory areas (Section 2.2.5.4).

RT and *NHRT* threads are controlled by the scheduler currently in effect. *RTSJ* requires a fixed-priority, preemptive, base scheduler while others are optional as, for instance, a rate-monotonic scheduler (Section 8.2.2.1).

2.2.5.2 RTSJ Interrupt Handling

Standard Java provides no general way to handle interrupts. *RTSJ* introduces the concrete class *AsyncEvent*, the abstract class *AsyncEventHandler,* and its abstract subclass *BoundAsyncEventHandler* to deal with events such as interrupts. An *AsyncEvent* object, *o*, represents something that can happen, whether it's a *POSIX*® signal (Butenhof, 1997), a hardware interrupt, or a "computed event" created within the software. The object *o* contains references to a set of handlers associated with the event.

---

[35]This may be counterproductive; it may be better to keep exclusion synchronization as simple and fast as possible.
[36]I shall use the term *regular threads* for the instances of such descendants of *Thread* that don't also descend from *RT* or *NHRT*.

When an *asyncEvent o* occurs, *o.fire* is called, and the system schedules the *run* operations of all handlers in *o*. The handlers belong to subclasses of *AsyncEventHandler*.

A handler is schedulable the same as a thread and has either *RT* or *NHRT* characteristics. A *bound* handler (belonging to a subclass of *BoundAsyncEventHandler*) is permanently bound to an *RT* or *NHRT* thread. This affords increased timeliness since there is no need to bind the handler to a thread when it's activated. The price is the memory space the thread takes up. Other handlers share threads; that is, a handler becomes tied to a thread only when activated.

2.2.5.3 Time and Timers in RTSJ

RTSJ provides time classes that allow description of a *point in time* with up-to-nanosecond accuracy and precision. There are *absolute* points in time and times *relative* to some starting point. *Rational time* expresses the number of occurrences per some interval of relative time.

RTSJ also has clock classes. A clock object has a concept of *now*. It can have queued events that fire when their times come. Latency-tolerant events can be queued for a clock that checks its queue less often and thereby off-load the higher frequency clock.

The abstract class *Timer* extends *AsyncEvent*. We can instantiate a timer object that will fire at time *t* according to clock *c* and activate a certain *handler* when fired. It has the operation *disable* that prevents the timer from firing and the operation *enable* that reenables it. A timer won't fire while it's disabled but continues measuring time. If it's enabled by its designated firing time, it will fire then. The operation *start* enables the timer initially and causes it to begin measuring.

The class *OneShotTimer* extends *Timer*. A *OneShotTimer* object fires once, when the clock time reaches time *t*. If *c* has already passed *t*, the timer fires directly. If the timer object was disabled before time *t* and remains disabled, it will never fire. If it was reenabled before time *t* and remains enabled at *t*, it will fire at that time. If it's reenabled after the time *t*, it will fire at once upon being reenabled.

The class *PeriodicTimer* also extends *Timer*. A *PeriodicTimer* object's *fire* operation executes at a rate governed by an interval parameter.

2.2.5.4 RTSJ Memory Areas

In order to be unaffected by garbage collection, an *NHRT* thread cannot reference the heap. Instead, *RTSJ* provides new classes of memory areas where objects can be allocated without being subject to garbage collection. It introduces an abstract class *MemoryArea* with such operations as *enter(Runnable logic)* and *newInstance(Class type)*. The call *m.newInstance(c)* allocates an object of the class *c* in the memory area *m* and returns a reference to *c*. A thread that calls *m.enter(r)* executes *r.run* with the provision that new objects are allocated in *m* by default.

ImmortalMemory is a concrete subclass of *MemoryArea*. Its singleton instance is shared among all threads and contains objects that endure until the program terminates. A subclass of *MemoryArea* called *ScopedMemory* represents memory areas corresponding to syntactic scopes of the program. If *m* is a *ScopedMemory* instance, the call *m.enter(r)* makes *r*'s *run* operation a new scope whose objects are allocated in *m*. More than one thread can allocate objects in a given *ScopedMemory* instance. When the *run* operations of all those threads are complete, the objects in *m* are garbage collected. Scopes can be nested, so the *run* operation of *r* can in turn contain the call *n.enter(s)*, where *n* is another *ScopedMemory* instance and *s* is another runnable. Assignment rules keep longer lived objects from referencing objects in scoped memory.

2.2.5.5 Limiting Priority Inversion in RTSJ

To make execution more predictable, *RTSJ* has the means to limit the effects of priority inversion (Section 2.1.4.1.1). The default policy is *priority inheritance*. *Priority ceiling* is optional in *RTSJ*.

NHRT threads are intended to coexist with regular and *RT* threads and access the same synchronized objects (which must be allocated in memory areas accessible to *NHRT* threads such as immortal memory). But because the garbage collector can preempt a regular or *RT* thread, care must be taken to avoid delaying *NHRT* threads unpredictably. This works differently with priority inheritance and with the priority ceiling protocol.

With priority inheritance, a regular (or *RT*) thread, *l*, may lock a resource, *r*, and then be preempted by the garbage collector. If an *NHRT* thread, *n*, becomes ready, it can preempt the garbage collector but cannot access *r*, which is still locked by *l*. In this situation, *l* inherits *n*'s priority but cannot preempt the garbage collector. Wait-free queues are introduced in *RTSJ* to avoid such situations.

Under the priority ceiling protocol, the anomaly cannot exist where *n* waits for the garbage collector and the collector has preempted *l*. This is because *l* accesses *r* with a priority that is at least as high as *n*'s and thus cannot be preempted by the garbage collector. As soon as *l* is finished with *r*, *n* can access *r*.

2.2.5.6 RTSJ: Wait-Free Queues

To allow cooperation between *NHRT* threads on the one hand and regular and *RT* threads on the other and to avoid inversion situations where an *NHRT* thread would be waiting for the garbage collector, *RTSJ* provides classes of *wait-free* queues. When operating on such a queue, *NHRT* threads call operations that aren't synchronized and don't block while regular and *RT* threads call synchronized, blocking operations. There are two classes, *WaitFreeReadQueue* and *WaitFreeWriteQueue*.

Instances of *WaitFreeReadQueue* allow message traffic *to NHRT* threads *from* other threads. The class has the nonsynchronized operation *read* that returns the next element in the queue. (If the queue is empty, it returns *null*.) The synchronized operation *write* blocks if the queue is full.

Instances of *WaitFreeWriteQueue* are queues of messages *from NHRT* threads *to* other threads. The synchronized operation *read* returns an object from the queue. The nonsynchronized Boolean operation *write(Object object)* inserts an object into the queue. It returns *true* if the insertion is successful and *false* if the queue is full.

*2.2.5.7 Asynchronous Transfer of Control in RTSJ

Asynchronous transfer of control (ATC) lets us abandon an ongoing activity—such as a computation—when an event occurs. (The event is often a time-out.) Suppose we're using rate-monotonic (or some other) scheduling, and a computation exceeds the allotted CPU time. *RTSJ* allows such a computation to be cut short.

An instance of *AsynchronousInterruptedException* (*AIE*) is thrown into the logic that must be asynchronously interrupted. Events other than time can throw an *AIE*. The logic that may be interrupted must be the *run* operation of an object, *I*, that implements *Interruptible*. When the exception is thrown, *I*'s *interruptAction* operation is called. This means that we don't have to catch *AIE* the way we catch other exceptions. (*RTSJ* provides for such low-level handling, too, if the programmer prefers it.)

The class *AIE* extends *InterruptedException* and has the following operations:

- Public Boolean *doInterruptible* (Interruptible *logic*), which executes the *run* operation of *logic* (here called the "*interruptible run*")
- Public synchronized Boolean *fire,* which causes *doInterruptible* to be interrupted
- Public synchronized Boolean *disable*, which marks the start of an ATC-deferred section within an interruptible run
- Public synchronized Boolean *enable*, which marks the end of an ATC-deferred section within an interruptible run

The public interface *Interruptible* has the following operations:

- Public void *run* (AsynchronouslyInterruptedException *exc*), which is the interruptible logic (for an interruptible run)
- Public void *interruptAction* (AsynchronouslyInterruptedException *exc*), which is called if the *run* operation is interrupted

The following example illustrates how these constructs work (Brosgol et al., 2002). For readability, I abbreviate AsynchronouslyInterruptedException to AIE:

```
AIE aie = new AIE( );
aie.doInterruptible(new Interruptible( ) {
// Anonymous, inner class implementing Interruptible:
    public void run(AIE e) throws AIE {
        ...                     // interruptible section
    e.disable( );
        ...                     // optional noninterruptible section
    e.enable( );
```

```
        ...              // optional interruptible section
    }
    public void interruptAction(AIE e) {
    ...                   // Executes if run is interrupted
    }
    });
```

If the thread is in an interruptible section when the exception is raised, it's interrupted at once, and control is transferred to *interruptAction*. If it's in a noninterruptible section, it's interrupted when it reaches the end of the section.

A *sequential-activities* thread contains a sequence of activities each belonging to a different state (Section 5.3). When an event triggers a state transition, the ongoing activity must be stopped and the activity in the new state started. ATC can bring this about. The flexible manufacturing system illustrates a different situation where ATC lets a job thread wait for whichever of two events comes first (Sections 2.3.3.1 and 7.3.2.2).

*2.2.5.7.1 Timing Out an Interruptible Run

The class *Timed* that extends *AIE* can *time out* an interruptible run. Its instances are constructed with the time-out value as a parameter. A common case is a calculation that improves iteratively an approximate result until it converges on a value with a certain precision. (See also Section 2.3.3.) If the calculation doesn't converge within some time limit, a real-time system may need to terminate it and rely on the best approximation available so far. Here is an example of an RT thread containing a calculation that is timed out after 5000 msec (Brosgol et al., 2002):

```
class TimeoutExample extends RealtimeThread {
   public void run( ) {
      new Timed(new RelativeTime(5000,0)).doInterruptible(new
      Interruptible( ) {
         public void run(AIE e) throws AIE {
         ...      // Asynchronously interruptible segment
         }
         public void interruptAction (AIE e) {
         ...      // Executes after timeout
         }
      });
      }
      public static void main(String args[ ]) {
      TimeoutExample te = new TimeoutExample( );
      te.start( );
   }
}
```

With rate-monotonic scheduling, this arrangement can stop a computation that has exhausted its allotted execution time (Section 8.2.2.1).

2.3 CONCURRENCY IN ADA

This section is an overview of important features of the Ada task syntax centering on concepts that come up in later chapters. Refer to an Ada text (Barnes, 2006; Burns and Wellings, 2007, 2009; Riehle, 2003) for a full description of the syntax.

2.3.1 Defining and Starting Tasks

We can declare task types and singleton tasks. An instance of a task type is created either statically or dynamically. I shall refer to declaration and instantiation as task *creation*. It's distinguished from *activation*, which is when a task starts operating as an independent thread of control. The forms of creation and activation are explained in the following sections.

2.3.1.1 Declaration of Single Tasks and Task Types

A task declaration consists of two parts, the *task specification* and the *task body declaration*. The declaration of a task *T* is as follows:

```
task T;         -- Specification of singleton task
task body T is
begin
   loop         -- The logic of the task goes here
   end loop;
end;
```

A task *type* Furnace is specified as follows:

```
task type Furnace (Num : Integer);
```

Num is a *discriminant*, a parameter that can take a unique value for each instance of the task type. In this case, it's intended to provide each Furnace instance with a unique number. The body looks the same as for a single task.

The task body may contain variable declarations. The variables are allocated on the task's stack. *Permanent task variables* remain as long as the task exists.

Temporary task variables are declared in inner blocks, in subprograms called by the task, and the like. They are no different than temporary variables declared in a sequential program, but it's important to remember that each thread has its own set. If two threads happen to call some procedure at the same time and the procedure declares a variable X, then each thread will have its own copy of X on the thread's stack. X is *not* a shared variable that would need exclusion synchronization.

2.3.1.2 Instantiation of Task Types

Once a task type has been specified, individual tasks can be created by instantiation. A single instance of Furnace with the discriminant Num = 4 is declared as follows. (The discriminant value can also be specified by means of an expression.)

```
Fur : Furnace (4);
```

This declaration of Fur appears in the declaration part of a block and is *static*. Task types can also be instantiated *dynamically*, that is, during execution. This is done by means of *access types*. (They are the same as references in Java and pointers in other languages.[37]) An access type F_Ptr_Type referencing instances of Furnace is declared as follows:

```
type F_Ptr_Type is access Furnace;
```

Once F_Ptr_Type has been declared, we declare variables of the type like this:

```
F_Ptr : F_Ptr_Type;
```

Once an access variable such as F_Ptr has been declared, we can create a task instance by means of an *allocator* consisting of the reserved word **new** followed by the task-type identifier. The following statement creates a new instance of the task type Furnace with the discriminant Num = 5. F_Ptr is a handle to the task instance.

```
F_Ptr := new Furnace (5);
```

Any variable may be assigned an initial value upon declaration, and this goes for an access variable such as F_Ptr. If the variable is of an access type referencing a task type, then a task instance is dynamically created as a side effect of the variable declaration. In the following declaration, an instance of Furnace is created, and F_Ptr receives the reference to the newly created task instance as its initial value:

```
F_Ptr : F_Ptr_Type := new Furnace (6);
```

Dynamic instantiation of task types is useful if the tasks represent domain entities that are short-lived and may start and/or cease to exist at runtime.

2.3.1.3 Task Activation

The program unit where a task is declared or a task type is instantiated is called the *parent unit* of the task or task-type instance. Single tasks and statically declared task-type instances start running concurrently with the parent as soon as the parent reaches **begin** after the declaration. A task created by means of an allocator starts running upon creation. For example, assume that the declarative part of the parent includes the following declarations:

```
task type Furnace (Num : Integer);
type F_Ptr_Type is access Furnace;
```

---

[37]The name "access type" is unfortunate in this book where, otherwise, we are mostly concerned with (exclusive) access to shared resources.

```
F_Ptr : F_Ptr_Type := new Furnace (3);
Fur : Furnace (7);
begin ...
```

Here, Fur starts running when the parent reaches **begin**, while the task referenced by F_Ptr starts at once after the declaration of F_Ptr completes.

2.3.1.4 Task Priorities

Task access to a processor is normally first come–first served, but this can be changed with priorities (Barnes, 2006; Burns and Wellings, 2007). The programmer can assign a priority to each task by means of the **pragma**[38] Priority (X), where X is a static expression of the Integer subtype Priority. The pragma is used as follows:

```
task A is
        pragma Priority (X); ...
end A;
```

2.3.1.5 The delay Statement

Like a Java thread, a task can control its own timing by rescheduling itself for execution after a specified interval or at a specific point in time. A task can suspend itself for a specified amount of time *T* by means of the **delay** statement:

```
delay T;
```

Here, T is of type Duration. It's a fixed-point type that specifies the delay in seconds. In a statement such as "**delay** 3.0;" the delay is specified by a fixed-point constant.

We say that the execution of the task is *resumed* when the delay interval has expired. (Resumption may be delayed if other tasks with the same or higher priority are running at that time.)

A **delay** statement where the parameter is zero or negative causes no delay but may cause a context switch, whereby another, ready task with the same priority gets control.

2.3.1.5.1 The Statement delay until

The built-in package Calendar provides the type Time as well as such time-related subprograms as

```
function Clock return Time;
```

Clock returns the current reading of the system clock in terms of seconds and parts thereof. A value of type Time is the parameter in the statement **delay**

---

[38]A **pragma** is a directive to the compiler.

until, which causes a delay until a certain time. Here's a task that needs to call a procedure Proc every minute on the minute:

```
with Calendar; use Calendar;
declare
    Interval : constant Duration := 60.0;
    Next : Time := Clock;              -- Next start time
    loop
      Proc;
      Next := Next + Interval;
      delay until Next;          -- Delay until next scheduled start time
    end loop;
end;
```

This solution assumes that Interval is much longer than the possible slippage caused by other tasks and also that the execution time of Proc is always less than Interval.

A variable of type *Time* is automatically reset to zero when it reaches its maximum value. *Next* in the excerpt above appears to increase steadily, but the *Numeric_Error* exception that would normally occur when the maximum value is exceeded isn't raised.

2.3.1.6 Exceptions in Tasks

Exceptio probat regulam in casibus non exceptis
The exception proves the rule in cases not excepted.

I never make exceptions. An exception disproves the rule.
Sir Arthur Conan Doyle, The Sign of the Four, 1890

Exception handlers may be included in tasks as in other Ada structures. If an exception is raised in a task and not handled inside the task, the task will execute its final **end**. There is no higher level to which the exception can be propagated. When a task executes its final **end**, it expires. This in turn can cause the software to degrade quite disgracefully. If there is any possibility that an exception is raised in a task, the task should handle it.

2.3.2 Protected Objects

In Ada, safe objects are called *protected*. Thus, a protected object is Ada's counterpart to a synchronized object in Java. Protected objects can have *protected operations* of three kinds: *functions*, *procedures*, and *entries*. These are declared in the specification of the protected type[39] as in the following example:

```
protected type X is
    function F1( ) return Type1;
    procedure P1 ( );
    entry E1 ( );
```

---

[39]As with tasks, Ada also provides for singleton protected objects.

```
private
    - - Attribute variables
    - - Private operations including interrupt handlers
end X;
```

All protected operations have exclusion synchronization built in. Their logic is defined in the protected body, which complements the specification. The differences between protected functions, protected procedures, and entries are as follows:

- **Protected functions** are read only. They cannot change the protected object's data and are subject to a read lock: Multiple function calls on a given object are allowed at any one time, but not during a procedure or entry call on the object.

- **Protected procedures** are allowed to change data values. They are subject to a write lock: Only *one* procedure (or entry) call at a time is allowed on a given object, but not during any function call.

- Like procedures, **entries** are allowed to change attribute-variable values and are subject to the write lock. In addition, an entry can provide condition synchronization by means of a *barrier condition*, which appears in the declaration of the protected body. An entry call proceeds only when the condition holds. For instance, an entry Get, which is allowed to execute only when the number (Num) of items in a buffer is greater than zero, may be declared as follows:

```
entry Get ( ... ) when Num > 0 is ...
```

A task that calls Get when Num ≤ 0 is put on a queue. Each protected object has one queue *per entry*. (This is different from Java, where each *object* has a single wait set. That aside, the barrier provides condition synchronization much as a wait loop placed at the very beginning of a synchronized operation in Java.)

The variables in the barrier condition are supposed to be attribute variables of the protected object, on which the entry operates. The values of those variables can be changed only by calls to protected procedures and entries on that object.

At the end of each procedure call and entry call on a given object, all its barriers are evaluated. If an entry's barrier is found to be true, the most eligible task in the entry's queue is activated and executes the entry body.

The principle of "internal progress first" gives tasks already in a queue precedence over new callers. Besides that, the entries with open barriers are served in arbitrary order. The callers queued for each entry are served according to the queuing policy in force, typically FIFO or FIFO within priorities.

The protected object is a safer construct than Java's synchronized object. *All* operations on a protected object are protected; in Java it's up to the programmer to designate some operations as "synchronized." In Ada, you achieve concurrent execution when multiple tasks call a protected *function* at the same time.

*2.3.2.1 Protected Interfaces

In Ada 2005, a type can implement any number of interfaces in addition to extending a base type. As in Java, an interface is similar to an abstract class without data where all the operations are abstract.[40]

In Ada 2005, protected types can implement *protected interfaces*.[41] Like other interfaces, they allow polymorphism. This addresses to a degree an awkwardness in Ada 95, which introduced both protected types and extensible types but didn't combine the two by allowing protected types to be extended (Wellings et al., 2000).

If a number of protected types implement the same protected interface, *S*, we can reference their instances by means of access variables with a target of type *S'Class*. (Ada makes a distinction between a type such as *S* and the polymorphic, "class-wide" type *S'Class*, which can refer to instances of *S* and its descendants.)

EXAMPLE (Sandén, 2006). Assume that a program deals with devices of various types where each type needs it own driver. We can declare a protected interface with an operation Initialize like this:

```
type Device_Handler is protected interface;
procedure Initialize (D: in out Device_Handler) is abstract;
```

The interface is implemented by device handler types such as *Device_Type1* as follows. Those implementing types inherit the obligation to provide a concrete implementation of *Initialize*.

```
protected type Device_Type1 (Device_Number : Natural) is
     new Device_Handler with
     procedure Initialize;
     ...
end Device_Type1;
```

The body of this protected type contains the logic of the procedure *Initialize* for this type of device. Device_Number is a *discriminant* (Section 2.3.1.1), which allows us to give such unique information as a device number to each instance. We can now declare an array of pointers to device drivers as follows:

```
Driver_List : array ( ... ) of access Device_Handler 'Class;
```

---

[40]Ada interfaces can also have **null** operations, which are concrete but have no effect.
[41]A *synchronized* interface can be implemented by protected types and tasks. A *task interface* can be implemented by task types. I don't discuss interfaces for task types in this book.

A loop such as the following invokes the right initialization procedure for each array element:

```
for D in Driver_List'Range loop
    Driver_List(D).Initialize;
end loop;
```

For each value of D, the call *Driver_List(D).Initialize* binds at runtime to the *Initialize* procedure for the type of the device at *Driver_List(D)*.

2.3.2.2 Requeuing

The Java solution with a wait loop deep inside a synchronized operation (Section 2.2.3.1) has no Ada counterpart. To the same end, Ada uses **requeue**, which lets a task that is executing an entry suspend itself and place itself on the queue of the same or another entry. The syntax is as follows:

```
requeue Get;
```

The requeue statement has no parameters. The target entry (Get, in this case) must have the same parameters as the one where the **requeue** statement appears.

Requeuing can be useful in protected objects that allocate resources to calling tasks. Say that tasks call a memory resource server with a parameter indicating the amount of memory requested. The barrier condition cannot refer to such a parameter. Instead, the protected entry can accept the call and then, if necessary, put the caller back on a queue. When its time comes, the caller again tries to secure the resource.

2.3.2.2.1 Home Heater Example (Requeuing)

A home-heating system (Sections 2.2.3.1.1 and 6.5.2) serves a group of five homes. Due to undersized fuel lines, no more than four homes at a time can be heated, so now and then a home must forgo heating in favor of another. The system ensures that no home is forcibly without heat for more than 10 minutes at a time. When a home has been without heat for 10 minutes, heat is turned off in whichever home has had heat the longest.

Each home has a task of type *Heater* that handles the heating cycle, which takes the home's furnace through the steps needed to turn heating on and off. The protected object *Token_Pool* models a pool of four heating tokens. Before starting its heater, each *Heater* task must obtain a token. It tries to do this by calling *Acquire*. If it cannot obtain a token for 10 minutes, it calls *Token_Pool.* *Insist*, which calls the *Force_Off* operation on the *Switch* object of the task that has had heat the longest and then waits for that task to turn off the heat. It does the waiting by calling **requeue** and putting itself on the queue of the entry *Wait,* as shown below. A *Heater* task releases a token by calling *Release*.

```
protected body Token_Pool is
    procedure Acquire is ...
```

```
      entry Insist when True is
         ...
         Switch (Oldest).Force_Off;
         requeue Wait;       -- Requeue to wait for a token to become available
      end Insist;
      entry Wait when Active < Home_Num - 1 is
                              -- The barrier is true when a token is available
         begin
                              -- Continue here when a token has become available
         end Wait;
      procedure Release is ...
end Token_Pool;
```

2.3.2.3 Conditional and Timed Entry Calls

Normally, a task making an entry call on a protected object is blocked until its turn comes to access the object. If we don't want the caller to be blocked, we can let it make a *conditional* entry call. A conditional entry call to the entry E of a protected object P has the following syntax:

```
select P.E( ... );
   else <sequence of statements>;
   end select;
```

A conditional entry call is effective only if the protected object is available for immediate access; that is, it's not locked. Otherwise, <sequence of statements> executes. The *timed* entry call is a variation of the conditional call, where the caller gives the protected object a certain time to accept the call. It has the following syntax:

```
select
   P.E ( ... );
   <sequence of statements 1>;
or
   delay D;
   <sequence of statements 2>;
end select;
```

If the protected object becomes available for access within D seconds, the call is effective. Then, <sequence of statements 1> executes. If not, <sequence of statements 2> executes.

2.3.2.4 Interrupt Handling

As discussed in Section 2.1.5, an interrupt handler is a segment of code designed to handle one particular kind of interrupt. Each type of interrupt has its own handler. In Ada, an interrupt handler is implemented as a protected procedure.

By means of a **pragma**, the procedure name is tied to the proper kind of interrupt.

The whole-house fan controller (Sections 3.5.1 and 5.2.1.1) has a handler for a single interrupt from a button that controls the fan. The protected object that contains the interrupt handler is roughly as follows:

```
protected Fan_Handler is
private
   procedure Handle_Button;
   pragma Attach_Handler (Handle_Button, ...);
   ...
end;
protected body Fan_Handler is
   procedure Handle_Button is
   begin
      ...
   end Handle_Button;
end Fan_Handler
```

2.3.2.5 Timing Events

Timing events are introduced in Ada 2005 as a means to define code to be executed at a future time. They are similar to *OneShotTimers* in *RTSJ* (Section 2.2.5.3). A timing event can be set to go off at or after a certain time and can be canceled. When the event goes off, it causes a handler to execute. We can get a similar effect in Ada 83 or Ada 95 by means of a task with a **delay** statement (Section 2.3.1.5). Timing events offer a simpler alternative. They are defined in the package Ada.Real_Time.Timing_Events.

Like an interrupt handler, a timing event handler is implemented as a protected procedure. In the window elevator for a car in Section 5.2.1.2, Auto_Time is declared as a variable of type Timing_Event, and Time_Amount is a constant of type Time_Span. The handler is the procedure Time_Out of the protected object Window_Control. The following call ties Auto_Time to Time_Amount and to the handler and starts the countdown:

```
Set_Handler (Auto_Time, Time_Amount, Time_Out'Access);
```

Such a call to Set_Handler also cancels any previous Set_Handler call for Auto_Time. The following call cancels the timing event Auto_Time. (Cancelled is a Boolean **out** parameter.)

```
Cancel_Handler (Auto_Time, Cancelled);
```

A timing event can serve as a *watchdog timer* that goes off when it's determined that some event hasn't happened as it should. For instance, we may want a system to wait a certain time for a response from a device. If the device hasn't responded by then, it's deemed inaccessible.

In the bicycle odometer in Section 5.2.1.3, timing events drive the solution. This is a little more complex than the single event in the window elevator and explains why the Set_Handler needs such an involved parameter list. There is a single timing event, but both the Time_Amount and the handler vary with the state of the odometer, that is, whether it's currently displaying the distance traveled, the speed, or something else. When the biker switches from distance to speed, a single call to Set_Handler cancels the next distance display and, instead, arranges for the speed to be displayed at once.

2.3.2.6 Controlling Access to Shared Domain Resources

As discussed in Sections 2.1.4.2.1 and 2.2.4, we use condition synchronization to control the sharing of such resources in the problem domain as a forklift truck in the automated factory application. The jobs on the factory floor, which need forklift service from time to time, are represented by *Job* threads. Depending on the pattern of simultaneous exclusive access, there are two possible solutions: monitors and semaphore safe objects (Section 2.1.4.2.1).

2.3.2.6.1 Semaphore Solution

With a semaphore solution, access to a single forklift is controlled by a semaphore protected object, *F* of type *Forklift_Semaphore*:

```
protected Forklift_Semaphore is
entry Acquire;
procedure Release;
private
   Busy : Boolean := False;
end Forklift_Semaphore;
protected body Forklift_Semaphore is
entry Acquire when not Busy is
   begin
      Busy := True;
   end Acquire;
procedure Release is
   begin
      Busy := False;
   end Release;
end Forklift_Semaphore;
```

A task, *J*, representing a job that needs the forklift, calls *Forklift_Semaphore. Acquire*. Once *J* gets past the barrier, *Busy* is set to true, which guarantees the job exclusive access to the forklift. Task *J* releases the forklift by calling *Release*, which sets *Busy* to false. Each statement sequence where the forklift is operated is bracketed by calls to *Acquire* and *Release* as follows:

```
Forklift_Semaphore.Acquire
// Critical section where the forklift is used
Forklift_Semaphore.Release
```

While one job has the forklift, other *Job* tasks can call *Forklift_Semaphore. Acquire* and be queued. The variable *Busy* serves as the lock on the physical forklift while the protected object *Forklift_Semaphore* controls the access to the variable *Busy* and the queue.

2.3.2.6.2 Monitor Solution

When possible, it's safer to collect the critical sections in one place. If the forklift management can be encapsulated in a single operation, *Use_Forklift,* say (or a few like operations), the entire semaphore handling is in one place, inside a monitor protected object (Section 2.1.4.2.1). Here's a monitor for a single forklift:

```
package Forklift_Monitor is
   procedure Use_Forklift;
end Forklift_Monitor;
package body Forklift_Monitor is
   protected Forklift_Semaphore is ...     (as in 2.3.2.6.1)
   protected body Forklift_Semaphore is ... (as in 2.3.2.6.1)
   procedure Use_Forklift is
   begin
     Forklift_Semaphore.Acquire;
     ...          -- Critical section: Operate the forklift
     Forklift_Semaphore.Release;
   end Use_Forklift;
end Forklift_Monitor;
```

2.3.3 Asynchronous Transfer of Control

Asynchronous transfer of control lets us abandon an ongoing activity—such as a computation—when an event occurs. (The event is often a time-out.) In Ada, ATC is implemented by means of abortable tasks rather than exceptions as in *RTSJ* (Section 2.2.5.7). This makes for a lighter syntax. A common case is a calculation that improves iteratively an approximate result until it converges to a value with a given precision (Section 2.2.5.7.1). If the calculation fails to converge by a certain time, a real-time system may opt to terminate it and settle for the best approximation available so far. Ada provides an *asynchronous select* statement for this:

```
select delay until Next_Reading;
then abort
     <some computation>
end select;
```

This works as follows: <some computation> starts. If it doesn't end by the time *Next_Reading*, it's aborted. (*Next_Reading* might be when new sensor data are available, making the ongoing computation moot.)

Asynchronous transfer of control has the following general syntax:

```
select trigger
   [optional sequence of statements]
```

```
then abort
  <abortable sequence of statements>
end select;
```

The trigger is either a **delay** statement—or **delay until** as in the example above—or an entry call. The construct works as follows:

- If the trigger is a delay that has already expired by the time the **select** statement executes, then the optional sequence of statements executes, and control passes beyond the **select** statement.

- If the trigger is an entry call or a delay that hasn't expired, the <abortable sequence of statements> begins running.

- If the triggering event occurs before the <abortable sequence of statements> finishes, that sequence aborts. Then the optional sequence of statements executes, and finally control passes beyond the **select** statement.

- If the <abortable sequence of statements> completes first, then the trigger is canceled, and control passes beyond the **select** statement.

In the *concurrent-activities* pattern (Section 5.4.2.2.1), activity tasks normally communicate with a state machine protected object by calling its operations at a pace determined by each task. Sometimes, the state machine protected object (*PO*, say) may need an activity task to react to a state transition at once, in the midst of computation. For this, *PO* has an entry, *E*, say, whose barrier is normally closed. The activity task contains the following:

```
select Po.E;
  [optional sequence of statements]
then abort
  <normal computation>
end select;
```

As soon as *E*'s barrier opens, the task aborts its normal computation, executes the optional sequence of statements, and then continues past the asynchronous select statement.

2.3.3.1 Example: Bumping an FMS Job

From ghoulies and ghosties and long-leggety beasties and things that go bump in the night, Good Lord, deliver us!

THE CORNISH OR WEST COUNTRY LITANY

Asynchronous select statements can capture certain intricate situations in the problem domain. In one solution of the flexible manufacturing system (Section 7.3.2), such a situation arises when a job, *j*, is waiting on a workstation's outstand having requested the next workstation it needs. If *j* hasn't acquired the next workstation and left the outstand by the time the next job needs it, *j* is bumped and sent to storage. The following construct in the body of task type *Job* lets the job wait for the first of those two events (Carter and Sandén, 1998):

```
select
      WS_Mgr.Request (…);        -- Get workstation
then abort
      WS_Ptr.Clear_Out_Stand;    -- Be bumped
      exit Floor;                -- Exit loop if bumped
end select;
```

Here, the trigger and the abortable sequence of statements both start with calls on protected entries. This effectively puts the job task in two task queues: one waiting for a workstation to become available and one waiting for the barrier on *Clear_Out_Stand* to open, indicating that the next job needs the stand. There are two possible outcomes:

- The call to *Request* is accepted, meaning that the job has obtained a workstation. The call to *Clear_Out_Stand* is then aborted, and processing continues beyond **end select**.

- The *Clear_Out_Stand* barrier opens, and the call is accepted. The job task then exits the loop Floor (not shown in the excerpt) that surrounds the asynchronous select statement and goes on to travel to storage. In this case, the call to *WS_Mgr.Request* is cancelled.

*2.3.4 Rendezvous

In Ada 83, task interaction always takes the form of a *rendezvous,* a scheme for synchronization and intertask communication that doesn't rely on protected objects. The rendezvous was made redundant when Ada 95 introduced protected objects, but all Ada versions support it (Barnes, 2006; Burns and Wellings, 2007).

A rendezvous is the synchronization of two tasks that I shall label the *caller* and the *callee*. It can also involve data exchange. Like a protected object, a task can have entries. The callee defines certain entries and accepts calls by means of **accept** statements referring to those entries. A task can be called at any one of its entries. The following is a specification of a task Simple with a single entry Simple_Entry without parameters:

```
task Simple is
   entry Simple_Entry;
end Simple;
```

In the body of the callee, one or more **accept** statements refer to an entry such as Simple_Entry as follows:

```
accept Simple_Entry;
```

When a task reaches an **accept** statement, it waits for an entry call from another task (the caller) unless a call is already outstanding.

The caller makes an *entry call*, exactly as for a protected entry. The following statement appears in the body of a task calling the entry Simple_Entry:

```
Simple.Simple_Entry;
```

When the caller reaches an entry call statement, it waits for the callee to arrive at an **accept** statement for the same entry unless the callee is already waiting there. The rendezvous is when a caller executes an entry call statement, and a callee executes a matching **accept** statement at the same time. (Section 7.5.4 has another small example.)

2.4 PTHREADS

Pthreads (POSIX® threads or Single UNIX® Specification threads) is an interface standard (IEEE POSIX 1003.1c, 1995) for packages that provide threading in such languages as C and C++ where it's not built in (Butenhof, 1997; Hughes and Hughes, 2008; Nichols et al., 1996). The interface lets us define threads and, for each thread, indicate a function where the thread starts executing. (Such a function plays the role of the *run* operation in Java.)

Pthreads also lets us define semaphores, which are called *mutexes*, short for "mutual exclusion." It also provides condition variables for condition synchronization. This brief summary lists a subset of the POSIX routines and illustrates their use. The intent is to show that Pthreads provides the basic threading support discussed in this chapter, albeit at a rudimentary level.

2.4.1 Managing Pthreads

As with any other language, a C program starts with a single *default thread*, which executes the function main. To create an additional thread, **pthread_create** is called as follows:

```
pthread_create (thread, attr, start_routine, arg)
```

The parameters are as follows:

- **thread** is of type **pthread_t** and returns the new thread's identity.
- **attr** defines thread attributes.
- **start_routine** is the C function where the thread starts executing once created.
- **arg** is an argument passed to **start_routine**. It's akin to a discriminant in Ada (Section 2.3.1.1) and lets us supply distinct data to each of the thread-type instances that share a **start_routine**.

A Pthread terminates when it reaches the end of its **start_routine**. A call **p_thread_exit** (status) is also available and can be used to terminate the default thread in such a way that the threads we have created will continue to execute.

2.4.1.1 Example of Pthreads

The excerpt below[42] creates a single thread. It continues executing until the default thread executing **main** sets the variable **thread_run** to false. The statement **pthread_join**(**thread_id, status**) makes the default thread wait in **main** until the newly created thread has terminated. **pthread_join** blocks the thread calling it until the thread **thread_id** terminates. (Java has a similar construct.)

```
#include <pthread.h>
void* thread_function(void*);
BOOL thread_run = TRUE;
pthread_t thread_id;
main(int argc, char* argv[]){
    if (pthread_create (&thread_id, 0, thread_function, NULL)!= 0)
    { ... error: cannot create thread ... }
    thread_run = FALSE;
    pthread_join(thread_id, NULL);
}
void* thread_function(void* args){
    while(thread_run){
    /* Do Something */
    }
    pthread_exit(NULL);
}
```

2.4.2 Mutex Variables and Exclusion Synchronization

Mutex semaphore variables are of type **pthread_mutex_t**. A semaphore is created unlocked. A thread acquires a semaphore called *m* by calling **pthread_mutex_lock** (*m*) and releases it by calling **pthread_mutex_unlock** (*m*). If the semaphore is closed, **pthread_mutex_lock** stalls the calling thread until the semaphore opens. To avoid stalling, we can call **phtread_mutex_trylock**, which instead returns a "busy" error code if the semaphore is closed.

2.4.2.1 Example of Pthreads and Mutexes

This excerpt creates two threads **t_one** and **t_two**, and one mutex semaphore *m*. Each of the threads acquires and releases the semaphore.

```
#include <pthread.h>
#include <stdio.h>
#include <unistd.h>

pthread_mutex_t m; /* Allocate a mutex semaphore*/
void* thread_one( void* arg );
void* thread_two( void* arg );
int main(){
```

[42]The examples in Sections 2.4.1.1 and 2.4.2.1 are courtesy of Danny Maupin (Colorado Technical University, January 2002)..

```
        pthread_t t_one, t_two; /* Allocate thread ids */
        pthread_mutex_init(&m, NULL); /* Initialize mutex */
        printf("starting\n");
        pthread_create(&t_one, NULL, thread_function, NULL);
        pthread_create(&t_two, NULL, thread_function, NULL);
        sleep(2);
        return 0;
  }
  void * thread_function(void *arg){
        pthread_mutex_lock(&m); /* Stall until lock available */
        sleep(1);
        pthread_mutex_unlock(&m);
        return NULL;
  }
```

To study the effect of the program, we could supply the two threads with different arguments and instrument `thread_function` with print statements that reflect each thread's progress.

The example shows that the Pthreads program must include statements dealing with the naked semaphores. In Java, the compiler takes care of this for synchronized operations; an Ada compiler does it for protected objects.

Pthreads programmers do well to stick as much as possible to a programming style that emulates monitors (Section 2.1.1.2.2; also Sections 2.2.4.2 and 2.3.2.6.2). Rather than inserting the mutex operations in the `start_routine` for each thread, we should make our own safe objects. Each semaphore should be local to such an object, and each operation on the object should start with a call to `pthread_mutex_lock` and end with a call to `pthread_mutex_unlock`. The style in the excerpt just above, where the lock and unlock operations appear in `thread_function`, isn't generally recommended.

2.4.3 Condition Variables and Condition Synchronization

Condition variables are of the type `pthread_cond_t`. Like the wait loop in Java, operations on condition variables exist inside a critical section with respect to a certain mutex variable. This variable is a parameter in the `pthread_cond_wait` call. The following calls are similar to Java's *wait, notify,* and *notifyAll*.

- `pthread_cond_wait (condition, mutex)` blocks the calling thread until the specified condition is signaled. The lock on `mutex` is automatically released when the thread blocks. It's reinstated before the thread returns from `pthread_cond_wait`.
- `pthread_cond_signal (condition)` is akin to Java's *notify* and activates a thread that is waiting on `condition`.
- `pthread_cond_broadcast (condition)` is analogous to Java's *notifyAll* and is used if more than one thread may be blocked on `condition`.

`pthread_cond_signal` and `pthread_cond_broadcast` must be followed by a call to `pthread_mutex_unlock` so that the (first) activated thread can reacquire `mutex`, and its call to pthread_cond_wait can complete. In Java and Ada this is done by the compiler.

2.4.4 Pthreads: Conclusion

This short overview shows that Pthreads provides the basic multithreading facilities supported by Java—and often at a similar level of abstraction. The main difference is that exclusion synchronization is built into the Java syntax so that the Java programmer need not deal with naked semaphores. Ada represents yet higher abstraction with condition synchronization built into the protected-entry syntax.

2.5 CONCLUSION

There are no substitutes to a "bottom-up" understanding in any field of human enterprise.

PAGELS, 1989

Ada and Java and, to a degree, Pthreads offer quite elaborate constructs for thread manipulation, resource sharing, and so forth. The chief purpose of this book is to show how such language features can capture such phenomena as concurrency and resource sharing in the problem domain. Beginning with Chapter 4 this kind of modeling is demonstrated.

Once we know how threads work, it becomes clear that we can use them in more or less optimum ways. For instance, context switching is overhead, and we want to leverage it by doing a reasonable amount of computation for each switch. This is no stranger than optimizing an inner loop. But it's not quite as easily done and may require a thread-architecture redesign.

Entity-life modeling lets us design to the strengths of threads and avoid inefficiencies. If you are a thread programmer, the threads as provided by your language or system are your working material. Paraphrasing Glegg (1969): Make your material your ally! Work with it! Don't fight it!

EXERCISES

There can be no question, my dear Watson, of the value of exercise before breakfast.

SIR ARTHUR CONAN DOYLE, THE ADVENTURE OF BLACK PETER, 1904

2-1 Threads versus modules. Write a small program illustrating that a thread (task) is quite separate from the run operation (task body) where it starts executing and that a subprogram isn't a shared resource requiring mutual exclusion. The program contains the following:

■ A static function (procedure) called *infinite-loop* that takes a text string *s* and a time period *t* as parameters. In an infinite loop, it repeatedly displays *s* and delays *t* time units.

■ Two or three threads (tasks), each of which calls *infinite-loop* once with its own specific parameter values.

Once started, these threads (tasks) spend their lives executing the common code of *infinite-loop* each using its own instances of *s* and *t*.

2-2 Wait-loop variants. According to Section 2.2.3, a wait loop in Java is while (*cond*) wait( );. What can happen if we instead use the following statements:

(a) if (*cond*) wait( );
(b) while (*cond*) yield( );   // yield the processor to another thread

2-3 Shared memory in spacecraft software. In software onboard a spacecraft, a safe object *Infobus* is a shared memory area.[43] The high-priority thread *Manager* accesses *Infobus* frequently to move data in and out. A low-priority thread *Gatherer* accesses *Infobus* to publish its data. A medium-priority thread *Comm* runs on the same processor without using *Infobus*. When *Manager* tries to access *Infobus* while *Gatherer* is holding it locked, *Manager* is stalled on the lock. In this situation, if *Comm* becomes active, it preempts *Gatherer*. *Manager* then finds itself waiting not only for *Gatherer* to release the lock but also for *Comm* to finish so that *Gatherer* can get on with its business.

(a) What are some technical ways to avoid this situation?

(b) Could the system be redesigned to make the situation less likely on a uniprocessor?

(c) How would the situation be different with multiprocessors?

2-4 Phase lock. In an avionics system, the fuel flow rate is determined from the angular position, $-80° < \Theta < +80°$, of a certain shaft (Silvasi-Patchin, 1995). Two sensors emit synchronized sine waves whose amplitudes are proportional to $\cos(\Theta - 60°)$ and $\cos(\Theta + 60°)$. The sine wave is 400 Hz, so it peaks every 1.25 msec. The waves are sampled pairwise and the values of the two cosines let us calculate Θ.

The phase lock issue arises because the two signals should be sampled near their peaks so that the amplitude can be measured accurately. To lock the sampling into the sine-wave frequency, the signals are first sampled repeatedly until their magnitudes are $< \varepsilon$. If this happens at time t, further readings are scheduled for $t + 0.625 + N \times 10$ milliseconds to synchronize with peaks. Each time, two sample pairs are taken so that any drift away from the signal peaks can be detected. If drift is detected, the next delay interval is adjusted slightly.

(a) Design a thread (task) that locks into the phase of the sine waves and then periodically samples the fuel rate.

(b) Solve the same problem by means of timing event handling without threads/tasks.

[43]This is loosely based on a description of the Mars Pathfinder at http://research.microsoft.com/en-us/um/people/mbj/Mars_Pathfinder/, accessed November 16, 2009. Ben Herr brought the problem to my attention (Colorado Technical University January 2009).

2-5 Speed-and-distance safe object. Write a protected object (Ada) or a synchronized class (*RTSJ*) that keeps track of a car's speed and distance traveled. The speed is expressed as the *time for 1000 driveshaft revolutions*. The object must do the following:

■ Handle a revolution-complete interrupt.

■ Count drive-shaft revolutions.

■ Calculate the current speed in terms of time per 1000 revolutions.

■ Return the current revolution count in response to the function call *dist*

■ Return the current speed in response to the function call *speed*

Disregard the following two issues: (1) The speed value will be incorrect when the car first starts since there haven't yet been 1000 revolutions. (2) The revolution counter will eventually overflow. How can we solve the overflow problem?

2-6 Circular buffer. Design a synchronized class (protected type) containing a circular buffer (Sommerville, 2007). The buffer connects the acquisition threads and the processing threads in a data acquisition system (Sections 5.4.3.2 and 6.5.1). The buffer is implemented as an array. After the bottom of the array is reached, storing continues at the top. At their own pace, the processing threads read buffer items in the same order. The number of unread items in the buffer is maintained in a counter incremented by acquisition threads and decremented by processing threads. Acquisition threads must block when the buffer is full, and the processing threads when there are no unread items.

2-7 Internode communication. In a distributed system, each connected computer can contain one or more logical nodes. Application programs in each logical node communicate with applications in other logical nodes through a module *Msgcomm*, which in turn uses a module *Network* to send messages between computers. There is one instance of *Msgcomm* and one of *Network* in each computer. *Network* has the operation *send*, which takes a message and a computer address as parameters.

Msgcomm contains one message queue Qi for each logical node i in its computer. Each message queue has two operations: *submit*, which adds a message to the end of the queue, and *receive*, which removes the first message in the queue and returns it to the caller.

Msgcomm as a whole has one operation *submit* that calls *Qi.submit* when called by a thread in *Network* with a message for logical node *i*. It also has the two operations *send* and *receive* called by application threads. *send* first determines whether the receiving logical node is local or remote. If it's remote, *Network.send* is called with the appropriate computer address. If it's local, *Qi.submit* is called for the appropriate logical node, *i*.

At the application level, each logical node, *i*, has its own thread that calls *Msgcomm. receive* with *i* as a parameter. It calls *Qi.receive* from within *Msgcomm.receive*. If there's no message in *Qi*, it blocks until one arrives.

(a) Design the necessary safe objects.

(b) Assume that new logical nodes can be added to a computer at any time, even during message traffic. What additional safe objects does this require?

2-8 Iterator. Design a synchronized class (protected object) *Datafile* with an iterator consisting of the two operations *get-first* and *get-next*, where *get-first* returns the record 1 in *Datafile*, and each successive *get-next* call returns record 2, record 3, ..., and finally an end-of-file indicator. Each *get-first* call locks *Datafile*. The *get-next* that returns end-of-file unlocks *Datafile*.

State modeling **3**

3.1 INTRODUCTION

*The process . . . can be interpreted as a modeling activity that begins with informal
(or conceptual) models and converts them into formal models.*

BLUM, 1992

State diagrams [also known as *state transition diagrams* (Wagner et al., 2006),
state machine diagrams (Fowler, 2004), and *statecharts* (Harel, 1987, 2009;
Samek, 2008)] are among the most helpful formal notations for software specification. They are rigorous yet intuitive and suitable for reactive systems.

A state diagram is a representation of a *finite-state machine (FSM)*, also
called a *finite automaton*. Some state machines cannot easily be represented as
diagrams, so state modeling means describing something as a state machine, not
necessarily as a state diagram. A state machine is a formal, analytical model.
It captures the behavior over time of some entity type in the problem domain
in terms of the *states* in which the entity can exist and of the *events* that may
change the state.

The logic of many a mechanical or electromechanical device from
toasters and up can be modeled that way. Everyday gadgets include automated
garage doors as well as cruise controllers and window elevators for cars. Some
are becoming sophisticated, such as a car lock with "one-button customization," which adjusts seats and mirrors to driver preferences, depending on which
remote unlocks the car. At the other end of the spectrum are large real-time
systems that control satellites or aircraft and have such major modes of operation
as *airborne*.

The *user interaction* with an automated teller machine (ATM), gas pump,
or their ilk can also be represented in a state model (Section 1.6.1.2). A single state
diagram can often cover the main use-case flow as well as various exceptional
flows. Some find such a representation more difficult than an activity diagram
or bulleted list, so state diagrams are chiefly for stakeholders accustomed to
abstraction.

In this book, we use state models to design software that controls such physical devices or makes such user interaction possible. Implementing a state model is usually straightforward: Once we have it, we also have the essence of the program logic. That way, a state model comes close to being an executable specification.

Sections 3.2 and 3.3 discuss "classic" state diagramming. Section 3.4 describes superstates, which were introduced as part of *statecharts* (Harel, 1987; Wieringa, 2003; Jorgensen, 2009). The distinction is no longer important in practice, so I use "state diagramming" and "state diagrams" throughout.

I have relegated some esoteric aspects of state modeling to footnotes. It's best to avoid unusual notation that a reader may not understand. The strength of state modeling is its expressiveness in spite of limited graphical vocabulary.

3.1.1 State Modeling and Object Orientation

State modeling was used long before object orientation became popular. It has been integrated into object-oriented analysis and is part of UML. In UML, we tie each state model to a class.

Each class may have a state model and, if so, normally also has a single **state variable**[44] among its attributes. It's an instance variable whose value indicates the instance's current state. Ideally, it's of an enumerated type with exactly one unique value for each state. The events typically map onto operations defined for the class.

3.2 STATE-MODELING TERMINOLOGY

This section introduces the terminology used in state modeling:

- An **event** is something that happens *to* an entity in an instant. An event is *instantaneous*, that is, *takes no time*. It's an *external* impulse: It comes from outside the entity. To illustrate, a light switch has events such as *turn-on* and *turn-off*. Someone other than the switch turns it on and off.

- Event **occurrence**. A single event can have multiple occurrences.

- **State.** Entities commonly exist in different modes at different times. The light switch, for instance, is either in the state *On* or the state *Off*. At any given point in time, an entity is in exactly one of its states. Each entity has a finite number of states.

- A **state transition** is a change of state. In the kind of state machine I discuss here, it's always caused by an event.

- An **action** is an instantaneous operation performed by an entity *in response to* an event. It's the entity's response to an impulse from the environment. It may itself affect the environment. Unlike an event, it's done *by* the entity, not *to* the entity.

- An **activity** is an operation with extension in time. It's performed by an entity throughout a certain state.[45]

---

[44]With orthogonal composition (Section 3.4.4), we need one or more additional state variables.
[45]Unfortunately, the terminology isn't entirely stable. UML 2.0 refers to what I call activities as *do-actions* (Eriksson et al., 2004) or *do-activities* (Fowler, 2004).

- A **state machine** is a set of events, a set of states, and a set of state transitions defined for a given class.
- A **state diagram** is one representation of a state machine. It shows states as rounded rectangles and state transitions as arrows between states, where each arrow is annotated with the triggering event, any conditions guarding the transition, and any action.

  A state machine can also be represented as a **state table** (Section 3.3.3) and in mathematical notation.

We say that an event makes an entity *go* or *transition* to a state, or *enter* a state. An event *causes* or *triggers* an action and/or a transition. A state machine accepts a series of events and performs the necessary transitions and actions.

*Note In an alternate view a state machine accepts *input symbols* and generates *output symbols*. A compiler reading a source program text could be modeled that way.

3.2.1 States and Events

Novice state modelers sometimes confuse events and states, although the distinction becomes very clear with time. We can often associate state with "status," as in marital status: A person can be married, divorced, widowed, and so forth. Those are states in the life of a human being. A wedding may be an elaborate social or religious event that alters one's marital status. But legally, what changes the status is *instantaneous*: The couple may be pronounced "married" by some official or may sign a contract. If the ceremony is cut short earlier, they legally remain unmarried. Here are some additional examples of events:

- The mouse is clicked.
- Flight 123 leaves Chicago.
- The engine stops (or starts).
- A library book is returned.
- Forty seconds have passed since event *x* occurred.

Here are some examples of states:

- A screen is being displayed (as on an ATM).
- A window is in focus (on a computer screen).
- A web page is being displayed.
- Flight 123 has arrived (as displayed at an airport).
- The engine is off (on).
- A library book is out on loan.

Some of the events and states above are related: A mouse click may bring a new window into focus, where it remains until another mouse click causes another window to be highlighted. The event "the engine stops" may occur in the state "the engine is on" and cause the engine to enter the state "the engine is off," remaining there until some other event occurs.

The event and state names above aren't typical. What entity a certain state model represents should always be clear from the context and usually isn't part of the names. If the entity is an engine, "off" and "on" are sufficient names. If it's a car, the same states might be called "engine off" and "engine on." By and large, we should name states with adjectives as "off" and "on" or adjective phrases; for events, we prefer verbs such as "start" and "stop."[46]

Events typically originate in the external environment and may reach the software as *interrupts*. This is likely the case with "the engine stops" and the mouse click. In the case of the flight or the library book, an operator executing a transaction probably causes the event to occur by pressing a key or clicking a mouse button.

Events are used in a similar manner in web programming. A mouse click is simply known as *click*; *mouse over* is when the user moves the mouse over a link; and *submit* is when the user submits a form (Conallen, 2003). Like the ones mentioned earlier, such an event can cause a state transition and/or an action: It may bring up a new web page. A mouse-over event on the PC desktop may cause an icon to be highlighted.

3.2.1.1 Time Events

"Forty seconds have passed since event *x*" is a *time event*, which is an important category. A **time event**[47] is the event that a certain amount of time has passed since some reference point, such as another event. In a diagram, it might show up as "40 seconds" on a transition from a state, meaning that 40 seconds have passed in that state.

When the state machine has been implemented in software, the stimuli for time events come from an internal clock. A Java programmer can create a time event by calling *sleep* (Section 2.2.1.1) or by supplying a time-out parameter to some operation call such as *wait*. The time event occurs when the given number of milliseconds has passed. In real-time Java, time events can also be created by instances of *timer* classes (Section 2.2.5.3). Likewise, an Ada programmer can use a **delay** or **delay until** statement in a task (Section 2.3.1.5) or a *timing event* (Ada 2005; Section 2.3.2.5). Time events are also discussed in Section 3.3.4.4.

A time event is instantaneous just as any other event. It doesn't include the wait leading up to it. The event is the alarm clock starting to go off, not its steady ticking through the night.

*3.2.1.2 Determinism

All state machines in this book are *deterministic*. This means that if a certain event occurs in a certain state under certain conditions, the next state is well defined. Mathematically, we can also define *nondeterministic* state machines, where we don't know for sure what will happen when a certain event occurs in a given state. Furthermore, a nondeterministic state machine can change its state spontaneously—without any event occurring. Nondeterministic state machines are of little use in practical software development.

---

[46]Some recommend naming events with verbs in the past tense, such as "started" and "stopped," to emphasize the causality: The event happens, and the transition follows (Ambler, 2005). But the present tense is usually shorter and doesn't cause confusion in my experience. Use either form consistently.
[47]Other names are *timing event* and *clock event*. *Temporal event* (Wieringa, 2003) is yet another synonym.

3.3 BASIC STATE MODELING

The first asset in making designs is a good notation to record and discuss alternate possibilities.

SHNEIDERMAN AND PLAISANT, 2005

3.3.1 A Simple Example

Figure 3-1 is a simple example of a state diagram. In addition to states, transitions, and events, it includes notation that's introduced successively in the following sections. The class Book has the attributes *State* and *Due date*. It has the following operations: *buy, classify, discard, checkout, return, renew,* and *check for overdue.*

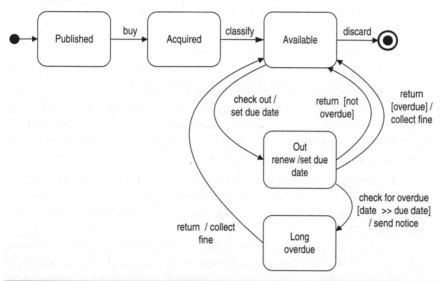

Figure 3-1 State diagram of a library book.

At each point in time, each instance of the class Book exists in exactly one of the following states: *Published, Acquired, Available, Out,* and *Long overdue.* In Figure 3-1, the arrow with a bullet on its tail marks *Published* as the **initial** state. The rest of a book's life transpires as follows:

- The event *buy* occurring in *Published* causes a transition to *Acquired.*

- The event *classify* occurring in *Acquired* causes a transition to *Available.* The event *classify* cannot occur in state *Initial,* or has no effect in that state. Even if the classification takes minutes or more, there is some instant, we shall assume, when the book becomes fully classified. Likely it's when someone hits *enter* at the end of a transaction.

- The event *checkout* occurring in *Available* causes a transition to *Out* and the **action** *Set due date,* which is the entity's reaction to the event *checkout.* In this case, it happens as part of the transaction where a librarian checks out the book. A slash "/" separates the event and the action.

- The event *return* occurring in *Out* causes a transition to *Available*. If the **guard condition** *overdue* holds when *return* occurs, the action *collect fine* is taken. The guard condition *not overdue* is obviously the complement of *overdue*; exactly one of the two must be true. The two arrows from *Out* to *Available* account for the two cases where the book is overdue and where it's not.

- The event *check for overdue* occurring in *Out* causes a transition to *Long overdue* and the action *send notice* if the book is indeed long overdue when checked. If the guard *date >> due date*[48] is false at that time, then there is no state change, and no action is taken. By convention, this case isn't shown in the diagram. (See "Convention" below.)

- The event *renew* occurring in *Out* causes the action *set due date*. There is no transition. The book remains in state *Out*.

- The event *return* occurring in *Long overdue* causes a transition to *Available* and the action *collect fine*.

- The event *discard* occurring in *Available* makes the book transition to the unnamed, *final state* marked with a bull's eye.

A *state–event pair* refers to a specific state and a specific (conditional) event occurring in that state. A *valid* state–event pair is one where the event can physically happen in the state. *Invalid* state–event pairs in Figure 3-1 include the event *buy* occurring in any state but *Published*.

Convention Invalid state–event pairs and valid pairs that cause neither action nor state transition are omitted from the diagrams. Thus the conditional event *check for overdue [date not >> due date]* isn't shown because it leaves the book in state *Out*.

I follow this convention in this book. It simplifies the diagrams but cannot always be used. If a state diagram—or a state table; Section 3.3.3—is the official specification of a critical system, every state–event pair should be accounted for whether or not it causes a state transition and/or an action.

The bullet with an arrow pointing to the initial state *Published* is sometimes referred to as the *initial pseudostate*. Every state diagram should have one initial state. Not all state diagrams have a *final* state. For instance, a window elevator for a car loops through a set of states forever. We don't care that the device will some day be scrapped. So it is with most examples in this book.

3.3.2 Guard Conditions

A **guard condition** (or simply "guard" or "condition") is a Boolean function such as *temperature < 32* or *time > T-time*. It guards a transition in the following sense: If the triggering *event* occurs, the transition is made only if the condition holds.

In the diagram, the guard is enclosed in brackets and immediately follows the event as in *return [overdue]/collect fine*. The interpretation is as follows: *When the event happens*, the condition is evaluated. Only if the condition holds, the transition is made and the action taken. Unlike an event, which takes no time, a guard condition remains true or false during some space of time.

---

[48]By the expression *date >> due date* I mean that *date* is much greater than *due date*. In the library book example it may mean that *date* is two weeks beyond *due date*.

When an event is guarded, the state machine must define what happens whether or not the condition holds. In the diagram in Figure 3-2, when the event *e* occurs in state *S1*, a transition is made to either *S2* or *S3*, depending on the ambient temperature. Clearly, the guards must be mutually exclusive and cover all possible cases.

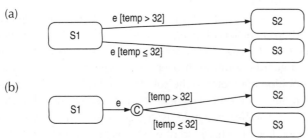

Figure 3-2 Two equivalent notations for conditional transitions.

Figure 3-2 shows two possible notations. The one in Figure 3-2*b* is most helpful if there are many different guard conditions.[49]

The conditions are mutually exclusive, meaning that exactly one is true at a time. Specifying the two guards in Figure 3-2 as *temp ≥ 32* and *temp ≤ 32* would provide two possible behaviors for *temp = 32* and make the state machine nondeterministic (Section 3.2.1.2).

By the convention in Section 3.3.1, we suppress event–condition combinations that cause neither transition nor action. In Figure 3-2, if the event–condition combination *e[temp > 32]* left the entity in state *S1*, then the upper arrows in Figures 3-2*a, b* wouldn't be shown.

*Note 1 All state models in this book are *event driven,* meaning that each transition is caused by the occurrence of a specified event. Other versions of state modeling let the condition *[overdue]* alone on a transition indicate the event that the book *becomes* overdue (Section 8.2.4). This requires some mechanism behind the scenes that polls all the books and finds out which ones have become overdue since the last poll.

Note 2 In Figure 3-1, an arrow with a bullet on its tail points to the initial state. We can attach multiple arrows to the bullet with a guard condition on each to indicate that the initial state depends on which condition is true. Exactly one must be true at a time.

*3.3.2.1 Guard Conditions Based on Modeled-Entity Attributes

A state diagram describes the behavior over time of each instance of some class. We draw it with an arbitrary but fixed instance, *o*, say, in mind. A condition usually refers to the state of some entity other than *o* (or on time, the ambient temperature, or the like; Section 3.3.2.2).

A condition based on one or more of *o*'s own attributes can be a state in disguise. If so, it should be modeled as a state. (Figure 3-4 below shows

---

[49]With the notation in Figure 3-2*b*, you can tie an action to the event (*e,* in this case). The action is taken before the condition is evaluated and can determine which branch is chosen.

an infelicitous state diagram with conditions based entirely on such attributes; Section 3.3.3). There are common exceptions to the rule:

1. A condition can be expressed in terms of entity *o*'s attributes if the state model applies to multiple entity types whose treatment is mostly the same but varies here and there.

   Case in point: If the state diagram describes luggage handling, perhaps oversized luggage is handled differently in specific ways. If the class *Luggage* has a Boolean attribute *oversized*, it could be used as a guard condition. If oversized luggage represents a subclass, the condition may refer to the subclass of the item at hand. Or, the guard condition could be *weight > 30 lb*, based on the attribute *weight*.

   Another example is a car wash, where steps are skipped depending on what kind of wash has been purchased. With the wash type as a guard, we avoid having to represent the various kinds of wash in separate but probably very similar superstates (Section 3.4).

2. A common case is where a set of states essentially represents the values of a counter. For instance, an ATM may confiscate the card after three invalid pass codes. Here, the pure solution would include such states as *one failed attempt* and *two failed attempts*, but most designers probably instead introduce a counter, *attempts*, the action *increment attempts*, and the guard condition *attempts < 3*. (See also Sections 3.3.3 and 3.5.2.)

3.3.2.2 Ambient Guard Conditions

The guard can be some environmental condition such as the current temperature or time. In the library book example, the condition *overdue* compares the current date with the book's due-date attribute. The comparison is made at the time of the *return* event. Likewise, the comparison *date >> due date* is made at the time of the overdue check.

3.3.2.3 Complex Guard Conditions

A practical example of an event with a complex guard is a mouse click on a PC or laptop. When the click occurs, the system determines whether the cursor is at an icon. If so, it starts the corresponding program. We can express such a condition as *Mouse at icon X*.

3.3.2.4 Example: Traffic Light

Figure 3-3 is a simple state diagram with conditional transitions (Blaha and Rumbaugh, 2005; Rumbaugh et al., 1991). It describes a traffic light at the intersection of a north–south road and an east–west road. Each road has separate lanes for left-turning traffic. Each state represents a constellation of green lights indicating one of the following traffic flows:

- Northbound and southbound traffic may go straight through the intersection.
- Northbound and southbound traffic may turn left.
- Eastbound and westbound traffic may go straight through the intersection.
- Eastbound and westbound traffic may turn left.

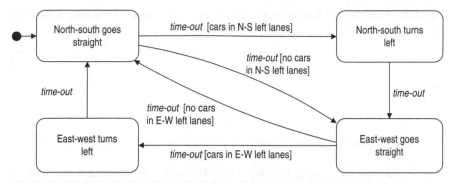

Figure 3-3 State diagram of an intersection (Blaha and Rumbaugh, 2005; Rumbaugh et al., 1991).

In this particular intersection, the north and south through traffic goes first (state: *North–south goes straight*). This continues for *time-out* seconds. Then, if there is left-turning traffic on the north–south road, it gets green lights for *time-out* seconds (state: *North–south turns left*), and then the east–west through traffic gets to go. Absent turning traffic, there is a direct shift from *North–south goes straight* to *East–west goes straight*. The same procedure is followed for the east–west traffic. In this model, all events are time events. The turn-lane sensors are objects apart from the intersection as a whole. Each sensor object has a Boolean operation that returns true when cars are waiting and false otherwise.

Note This state diagram is very simple, even if we were to give each transition its own time-out value. State diagrams can easily describe much more realistic intersections where, for example, the left-turn lights go to red as soon as there's no more traffic. A camera system could determine when no car has appeared for a given time.

*3.3.2.5 State Machines Associated with Aggregate Entities

The traffic light in Section 3.3.2.4 illustrates an important point about state modeling. The entity shown in Figure 3-3 is an aggregate of multiple traffic light fixtures, each of which may have three lights: red, amber, and green.

Each *fixture* is a simple device, usually with the three states *Red*, *Amber*, and *Green* and the three transitions from *Red* to *Green* to *Amber* to *Red*. (To go even further, each light can be represented by a state diagram with the states *On* and *Off*.) We could represent the intersection as a number of diagrams showing individual fixtures, but such diagrams tend to be tightly coupled and awkwardly dependent on each other.

It's much easier to describe the behavior of the entire intersection in a single diagram as in Figure 3-3. The trick is to find the right level of aggregation. (See also Section 3.4.4.2.1.)

3.3.3 State Tables

Some state machines don't lend themselves to diagramming because the number of states is either too large or unspecified. A typical entity with an unspecified number of states is a queue with room for n elements. It's often shown in a state diagram such as in Figure 3-4. The queue has $n + 1$ states, one for each possible number of items, but because *n* is undefined, we cannot show each state by itself.

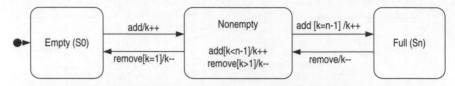

Figure 3-4 State diagram of a queue.

The state diagram in Figure 3-4 is unfortunate. Almost all the information is in the guard conditions, which are expressed in terms of the attributes of the queue object. While we could flaunt the rules and let an ellipsis ". . ." represent additional states, it's much better to realize that the queue actually has n + 1 states and list the transitions for each state–event pair in a table (Wieringa, 2003, Wagner et al., 2006) as follows:

From State	Event	Condition	To State
S0	Add		*S1*
Sk, k = 1, . . ., n − 1	Add		*S(k + 1)*
Sk, k = 1, . . ., n − 1	Remove		*S(k − 1)*
Sn	Remove		*S(n − 1)*

A column for actions can be added but isn't needed in this example. The actions and conditions in Figure 3-4 involving the index *k* have been replaced by state transitions: The state variable keeps track of the number of items queued.

Note This table describes a simple algorithm which can be implemented easily (Section 3.3.2.1). We don't have to glorify it as a state machine at all.

3.3.4 Actions and Activities

3.3.4.1 Actions

An **action** is an entity's instantaneous response to an event (in addition to any state change). If an event is implemented as an operation call, the action defines what the operation does: It can change entity attribute values and/or call other operations on the same or other entities. An *event* happens *to* an entity, and as a response, *the entity takes the action*.

In the label on a state transition arrow, a slash "/" separates event and action. In Figure 3-5, the event *on-hook* occurring in *S1* triggers the action *disconnect* and the transition to *S2*.

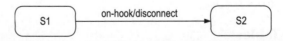

Figure 3-5 Event–action pair.

In Figure 3-1, actions on the library book include *collect fine* and *send notice*. If a single event triggers multiple actions, they are separated by slashes as in the instance *event/action1/action2/action3*.[50] Like the state transition, all the actions are subject to any guard as in *event [cond]/action1/action2, ...* If *event* causes different actions depending on the value of the guard, there must be multiple transition arrows as in Figure 3-2, even if they lead to the same state.

Most actions have some effect upon the domain as *close* and *disconnect* do. Operations on attribute variables such as "i++" are also common (Section 3.3.2.1).

3.3.4.1.1 Internal Actions

An *internal action* is one that is specified inside a state symbol and not on a transition arrow. The event–action pair *renew/set due date* in state *Out* of the library book is an example (Figure 3-1). Figure 3-6 shows a state, *S*, with the following internal actions:

- **entry**/*a1* means that *a1* is taken whenever *S* is entered.

- **exit**/*a2* means that *a2* is taken whenever *S* is exited.

- *e1/a3* means that if the event *e1* occurs in *S*, action *a3* is taken, but the state doesn't change.

- **do**/*actity* means that the *activity* called *actity* continues throughout *S* (Section 3.3.4.2).

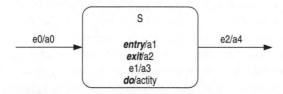

Figure 3-6 State with internal actions and an activity.

We can *guard* internal actions and activities. Thus, *entry [cond]/a1* means that action *a1* is taken upon entry to the state only if *cond* is true. The same state may also specify *entry [not cond]/a2*. The entry action chosen depends on the value of *cond*.

*3.3.4.1.1.1 Order of Actions and Activities

Conceptually, events and actions are instantaneous, so when event *e0* happens, causing a transition to *S* in Figure 3-6, then *a0* and the entry action *a1* are taken at the same time. In practical programming the actions are *nearly* instantaneous. If the actions depend on each other, the order becomes important. A practical convention is that action *a0* is taken first, and then *a1*. Likewise, when event *e2* happens in state *S*, action *a2* is taken before *a4*. (See also Section 3.4.3.)

If a state has multiple entry or exit actions, we can stipulate that they are taken in order from top to bottom. That way, we can also indicate whether a certain entry action should be taken before or after an activity is started and

---

[50] This is an awkward notation introduced by UML. It's clearer to separate the actions with semicolons as in this example: *event/action1;action2;action3*.

whether a certain exit action should be taken before or after an activity ends. With multiple activities, we can stipulate that the first one listed starts first and ends last, and the last one starts last and ends first. This means that the activities are nested, which should be of little consequence because they all start when the state is entered and stop when it's exited.

Note There were originally two kinds of state machines (Sandén, 1994, Wagner et al., 2006). In *Mealy* machines, every action is tied to a *transition* as with *e0/a0* and *e2/a4* in Figure 3-6 (Wieringa, 2003). In a *Moore* machine, all actions are *entry actions* as with *a1* in Figure 3-6. Merging the two has proven quite workable although it affords diagrammers rather too much combinatorial freedom for their own good.

3.3.4.1.2 Self-Transitions

A *self-transition* is shown as an arrow from a state symbol back to itself (Fowler, 2004). It looks like a jug handle and is labeled with an event and any actions. Such an event is similar but not equivalent to an event-internal-action pair such as *e1/a3* as in Section 3.3.4.1.1. The difference is that by convention, a self-transition triggers the state's exit and entry actions. (An internal event does not.) State *S* in Figure 3-6 could have a self-transition marked *e3/a5*. When *e3* occurs, the exit action *a2* is taken and the activity *activity* stopped. Then *a5* is taken. Finally, the entry action *a1* is taken and *activity* is restarted.

Often, an action such as *a5* is periodic and taken every *x* seconds. The self-transition is then marked *x seconds/a5* based on the convention that an implicit timer is restarted every time *S* is "reentered."

The term "self-transition," the graphical notation, and the convention all suggest that the entity somehow leaves a state and goes right back to it. This isn't so. There is no transition at all; *the entity remains in S throughout*. It's even more misleading with superstates (Section 3.4). If *S* is in superstate *U*, you can draw an arrow from *S* back to itself in a way suggesting that not only *S* but also *U* is exited and reentered.

Besides, the difference between a self-transition and an internal event is subtle so the implementer of the state machine may well miss it. It's clearer to use an internal event and reset a timer, *T*, say, explicitly: *T = x seconds/a5/reset T*[51] (Section 3.3.4.4).

3.3.4.2 Activities

The notation *do/activity* in Figure 3-6 indicates that an activity named *activity* is performed throughout state *S*. An **activity** is an operation that takes time, unlike an action, which is instantaneous. It's often a computation. Other possible activities include sounding an alarm (in a security system), sounding a ring tone, and recording a message (in an answering machine). It may be periodic and sample or display some quantity every *n* seconds. An activity such as *activity* is sometimes specified in terms of the two actions called *start activity* and *stop activity* or the like.

Activities are less common than actions. Unlike an action, which is tied to a transition, an activity is tied to a *state*. The activity *activity* in Figure 3-6 is

---

[51] I also sometimes use the informal notation do/take action … every X seconds.

performed when the entity is in state *S*. An activity is a process without internal states that needs no detailed explanation.

*3.3.4.2.1 Software *Activities and* Nominal *Activities*

nom·i·nal ... 3 a: *existing or being something in name or form only.*

MERRIAM-WEBSTER, 1993–1996

I shall call an activity such as *sound alarm* that needs no software involvement other than for starting and stopping it a **nominal activity**. I define **software activity** as any activity that needs software involvement throughout. A lengthy computation is a software activity, as is periodic sampling. A control thread's wait for access to a shared resource is also a software activity since it occupies the thread (Section 5.1.1.1.2).

The difference between nominal and software activities becomes important when we discuss the *concurrent-activities* and *sequential-activities* patterns in Chapter 5. In multithreaded implementations, a software activity often needs its own thread; a nominal activity does not.

3.3.4.3 Actions or Activities?

Like an event, an action conceptually takes no time at all. In practical programming, actions must be *nearly* instantaneous—short enough that we needn't worry about anything happening *during* the action (Section 3.6.4.1). Time stands still. What this means in practice depends on the application. For any kind of real-time processing, it's quite a stringent criterion. An action can be a short computation or possibly a file access. Any lengthy computation must be represented as an activity.

The terms "action" and "activity" are often confused, even in the UML literature. Anyone dealing with any kind of real-time processing in the widest sense must understand the difference. An *activity* needs a state in which the entity exists while the activity is carried out. An *action*, by contrast, takes no time.

3.3.4.4 Actions on Timers

Many state transitions and actions are triggered not by physical impulses but by *time events* (Section 3.2.1.1): After an elevator has spent 30 seconds in the state *Doors opened*, it may start closing the doors and go to *Doors closing*, on the condition that there is no obstacle. This is shown in Figure 3-7.

Figure 3-7 Time event.

If we need more precision, we can define a timer, *T*, say, and use actions such as *start timer T*. The time event can then be *T = 30 seconds*, as in Figure 3-8. Note that it's different from a guard condition such as *[T > 30 seconds]*. The code lock in Section 3.5.2 uses such a timer.

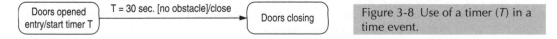

Figure 3-8 Use of a timer (*T*) in a time event.

*3.3.4.5 Actions on Other Attribute Variables

Just as guards can be expressed in terms of the attribute variables of the entity modeled by the state diagram (Section 3.3.2.1), it's sometimes convenient to let some actions modify those (or other) variables even though it may seem that we're introducing additional state variables.

For instance, some automated gas pumps ask, "Do you want a receipt?" early on, before we fill up. A state model of the pump could transition to one state for "Yes" and another one for "No," but we would then have to duplicate the rest of the dialog. The practical solution is, instead, to let a Boolean variable capture the answer and use it in a guard later on.

*3.3.5 Multiple Events with the Same Effect

At times, different events occurring in a certain state trigger the same transition and actions. Here's an example: In some apartment buildings, the door to the basement garage can be opened by running a card through a reader, by pressing an *Open* button, or by driving across a sensor wire embedded in the garage floor. To avoid three transition arrows from a state *Closed* to a state *Opening*, we can define an abstract event *opening-event* and let *read-card*, *press- open*, and *trip-sensor* be specializations thereof. This can be shown in a class diagram (Figure 1-1). The state diagram now has a single arrow marked *opening-event* from *Closed* to *Opening*.

3.3.6 Basic State Modeling: Summary

A state model shows the states in which an entity can exist. The entity remains in each state for some time. A state is the result of the succession of events leading up to it and defines how the entity is going to respond to further events. For this, knowing the state is enough; which particular events led up to it doesn't affect future behavior. The following definition holds:

> The state of an entity o at a given time is all the information necessary to determine all future actions (and activities) taken by o, given the future events that happen to o and given the states of other entities.

An event occurs at a point in time and is *instantaneous*; that is, *it takes no time*. The event is an external impulse to the entity; an *action* is the entity's response to an event. Like events, actions are (at least nearly) instantaneous.

Time passes in states only. Any *activity* is an operation that takes time. It goes on throughout a state. This includes the degenerate activity where the entity waits idly until a given point in time or for a certain amount of time. Waiting requires a state. We cannot treat "delay 5 seconds" as an action; it obviously takes time.

3.4 SUPERSTATES

A **superstate** is a group of states with some common properties (Harel, 1987). The state diagram in Figure 3-9 contains the states *S1*, *S2*, and *S3*. Event *i* triggers a transition from *S1* to *S3* and from *S2* to *S3*. That is, *i* causes a transition to *S3* whether the current state is *S1* or *S2*. So, *S1* and *S2* have the common property that event *i* causes a transition to *S3*.

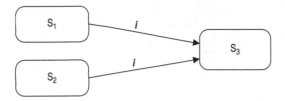

Figure 3-9 Two states with identical transitions.

In this situation, a superstate is a convenient notation. In Figure 3-10, *S1* and *S2* are enclosed in the superstate *U*. The transition on *i* to state *S3* is shown as a single arrow from *U*'s border to *S3*. This abbreviated notation means that a transition to *S3* happens whenever the event *i* occurs in any substate of *U*.

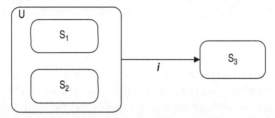

Figure 3-10 *S1* and *S2* enclosed in the superstate *U*.

A superstate isn't an additional state. The entity whose behavior is shown in Figure 3-10 is in superstate *U* exactly when it's in either *substate S1* or *S2*. The notation is visually misleading because the superstate seems to extend beyond the substates.

A superstate can have any number of substates. Superstates can also be nested so a substate can be a superstate with its own substates. If *S1* and *S2* in Figure 3-10 had substates, they in turn had substates, and so on, then the transition to state *S3* upon event *i* would apply to any substate within *U*, no matter how deeply nested.

Just as an arrow from a superstate border has a special meaning, so does an arrow pointing *to* a superstate border. Figure 3-11a shows this. Event *i* occurring in state *S1* causes a transition to the **default entry state** of superstate *V*. This default entry state is *S21*, as indicated by an arrow with a bullet on its tail inside *V*.[52]

A superstate border is porous in the sense that a transition arrow can pass through it on its way from a substate to an outside state, or vice versa. Event *r* in Figure 3-11a causes a transition from substate *S21* to state *S4* outside *V*, and event *k* causes a transition from *S4* to substate *S22*. Clearly, transitions between substates are legal, such as those on events *q* and *p* between *S21* and *S22*. Finally, the event *m* may occur in any substate of *V* and trigger a transition to *S3*, similar to the effect of event *i* in Figure 3-10.

As a way to modularize the diagrams, we can suppress the internals of superstates as shown in Figure 3-11b. The assumption is that those details are shown separately. This is particularly useful if multiple superstates have the same internal structure, which is then shown only once.

---

[52]Like the bullet indicating the initial state, this one can have multiple arrows pointing to different states. If there is more than one such arrow, exactly one of the guard conditions must be true.

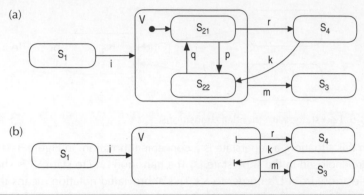

(a)

(b)

Figure 3-11 (a) Example of superstate and transitions. (b) Variation of the diagram in part (a) indicating that V's internals are shown elsewhere.

"*S* seconds" on an arrow from a superstate border is the time event that *S* seconds have passed since *the superstate as a whole* was entered. To measure time from a different starting point, we can define a timer (Section 3.3.4.4).

State diagrams without superstates are called *flat,* and, in a sense, superstates add a dimension to state diagramming. Because a transition can pass through a superstate border, it's usually easy to add a superstate to an existing diagram and take advantage of the conventions for reducing the number of arrows. Except for the arrows thus replaced, the superstate leaves the existing diagram structure as it is.

3.4.1 Exceptional Events

A transition from the border of a superstate often corresponds to some exceptional event that can occur in many states. The diagram fragment in Figure 3-12 describes the behavior of a phone connected to a "plain old telephony" system (POTS) exchange (Davis, 1993).

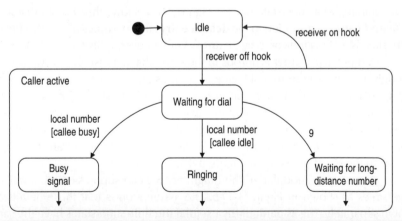

Figure 3-12 Telephony example (Davis, 1993): The event *receiver on hook* causes a transition to *Idle* from any substate of *Caller active*. The informal arrows at the bottom are meant to suggest that *Caller active* has many more substates than shown.

It starts in the *Idle* state. When the receiver is taken off the hook for an outgoing call, a superstate *Caller active* is entered. It has multiple substates: First, *Waiting for dial* is entered, and then, depending on the number dialed and whether the callee is busy, such states as *Busy signal*, *Ringing*, and *Waiting for long-distance number* are entered.

The informal arrows at the bottom of the superstate are meant to suggest that the phone can enter various other states. But no matter where it ends up inside *Caller active*, the event *receiver on hook* always takes it straight back to *Idle*. A single arrow from the superstate *Caller active* to *Idle* can replace any number of arrows from individual substates.

3.4.2 Arrows between Substate and Superstate Border

A transition arrow to the superstate border can come from within the superstate, as with the arrow labeled *x* shown in Figure 3-13. This arrow represents a transition from substate *S3* to *S1*, which is *W*'s default entry state. Figure 3-13 also shows that a transition arrow from the superstate border can lead to a substate. By the general rule in Section 3.4, the event *t* causes a transition to *S2* from any substate of *W*. Events such as *x* and *t* can have associated actions.

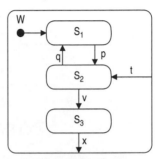

This is consistent with how we interpret arrows between the superstate border and a state *outside* the superstate (Figure 3-11), but much less intuitive: It's easy to believe that *x* somehow triggers an exit from *W* and that *t* is related to a transition from outside *W*.

*Note If event *t* occurs in *S2*, there is no transition at all, and the entity remains in *S2*. *S2*'s entry and exit actions are *not* triggered, and any action associated with *t* is treated as internal in *S2* (Section 3.3.4.1.1).

Figure 3-13 Transition arrows from a substate to the superstate border and from the superstate border to a substate.

3.4.2.1 Superstates for Reducing Clutter

Superstates let us get away with fewer arrows. Not only can this make a diagram clearer, it also reduces the risk of inconsistencies and omissions. In Figure 3-12 a single arrow *from* the superstate border represents transitions from any substate *on one given event*, in this case, *receiver on hook*.

Arrows *to* the superstate border work in a similar way. Each one represents a transition to the default entry state. In Figure 3-13 the arrow marked *x* replaces a longer arrow from *S3* to *S1*. It doesn't reduce the number of arrows, but it avoids an awkward, long one. This can be important in larger superstates. See also Figure 3-19 and Figure 3-20 later in the chapter.

3.4.3 Activities and Internal Actions for Superstates

We can specify internal actions for a superstate by means of the notation **entry**/*action*, **exit**/*action*, and so forth, mentioned in Section 3.3.4.1.1. When deciding whether a transition triggers an entry or exit action, we must always compare the entity's exact state, *S1*, when the transition occurs and its exact state, *S2*, immediately after the transition. By "exact states" I mean that *S1* and *S2* are not superstates. Each can be a substate of any number of superstates. The following rules hold no matter how the transition from *S1* to *S2* is expressed in the diagram:

- An entry action of a superstate, *W*, is taken upon any transition from a state, *S1*, outside *W* to a substate, *S2*, of *W*.
- An exit action of a superstate, *W*, is taken upon a transition from a substate, *S1*, of *W* to a state, *S2*, outside *W*.

In Figure 3-14, when event *e1* occurs in state *S*, action *a1* is first taken. Then *W*'s entry action *a6* is taken and *W*'s activity *c2* starts. Finally, action *a3* is taken and activity *c1* starts. *S* is clearly outside *W*, and *T* is a substate of *W*, so *W*'s entry action is taken and its activity *c2* is started.

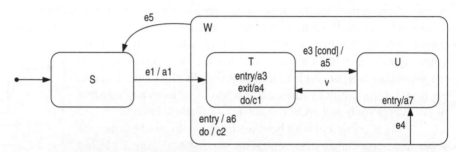

Figure 3-14 Nested states with entry actions, exit actions, and activities.

When *e3* occurs in state *T* and *cond* is true, action *a4* is taken and *c1* stops. After that, action *a5* is taken and then the entry action *a7* of state *U*. The entity remains in *W*.

The arrow marked *e4* defines a transition from any substate of *W* to *U* upon event *e4*. The entity remains in *W* in either case. If the entity is in state *T* and *e4* happens, *U* is entered, action *a4* is taken, activity *c* stops, and action *a7* is taken. If the entity is in *U* when *e4* happens, it remains there.

The activity *c2* is specified for *W*. Such an activity can continue throughout several substates. It starts whenever *T* or *U* is entered from outside *W* and continues until some transition from *T* or *U* to a state outside *W* takes place.

Note Wisely used, the keywords **entry** and **exit** work well but the notation is easily abused. Nested superstates with their own entry and exit actions make it difficult to figure out what actions a given event triggers. The conventions for arrows to/from superstate borders can also lead to confusion. A diagram such as the one given later in Figure 3-25 may be thought provoking but isn't in good style.

3.4.4 Orthogonal Composition

When you make two descriptions of an existing, visible, tangible, APPLICATION DOMAIN, the domain itself embodies the result of composing them. It demonstrates the answer to the question: What do you get if you have something of which both this description is true and that description is true? Check each description separately against the domain, and if they are both true separately then their composition is a true description of the domain you can see.

The complete state of a system at a given point in time is composed of the state of each of its entities. If a system consists of multiple entities and each one has multiple states, the total number of system states can be enormous. For the most part, we separate concerns by breaking the system into classes and giving each class its own state diagram.

Some entities are themselves best described by the orthogonal composition of two or more state diagrams. The **orthogonal composition** of two state machines *B* and *C* is a state machine where each state is the *composition* of a state of *B* and a state of *C*. We can subdivide a state in any number of **regions** such as *B* and *C* by means of dashed lines (Harel, 1987).

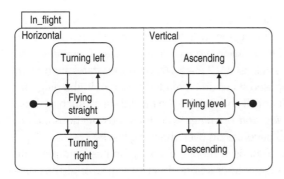

Figure 3-15 The state of an aircraft in flight has two orthogonal components represented by the two regions *Horizontal* and *Vertical* of the state *In-flight*.

Figure 3-15 shows the state of an aircraft. The superstate *In-flight* is the orthogonal composition of the regions *Horizontal* and *Vertical*. When the aircraft is *In-flight,* it can be in any combination of exactly one state from the *Horizontal* region and exactly one state from the *Vertical* region. Thus, the six substates shown in the diagram allow us to describe nine aircraft attitudes such as *Turning left and ascending*.

We use orthogonal composition and not two objects in this case because the horizontal and vertical components of the aircraft attitude aren't different entities. In other cases we can use it for practical convenience. In the state diagram of a workstation in Figure 5-13, this technique lets us combine a major state machine and a much simpler machine in one diagram.

Orthogonal states are called "*and* states" because at any one time the entity is in exactly one state per region. States such as *Flying straight, Turning left*, and *Turning right* are then called "*or* states" because the entity is in no more than one of them.

No arrow can *cross a dashed line.* If the regions must communicate, an action in one region can be an event in the other region. We can also let a guard condition refer to the current state in the other region.

*3.4.4.1 Orthogonal States and Multithreading

orthogonal *[from mathematics] adj. Mutually independent; well separated; sometimes, irrelevant to. Used in a generalization of its mathematical meaning to describe sets of primitives or capabilities that, like a vector basis in geometry, span* *the entire "capability space" of the system and are in some sense nonoverlapping or mutually independent.*

RAYMOND, 1993

Sometimes orthogonal composition is confused with multithreading, but the two concepts are unrelated (Harel, 2009). In Figure 3-15, letting two threads *Vertical* and *Horizontal* describe the aircraft has no merit. All we need are two state variables such as *vertical* and *horizontal*. Each variable can take three values, and together the two variables define nine states. With orthogonal states, we generally use multiple state variables. (This is the exception from the general rule that a single variable should describe an entity's state.) Orthogonal states are sometimes referred to as *concurrent states*, but I avoid this term for fear of confusion with multithreading.

3.4.4.2 Know Your States!

Don't abuse orthogonal composition! We could describe an elevator's state as an orthogonal composition of a *direction* region (with the states *up* and *down*), a *movement* region (with *moving* and *still*), a *door* region (with *open, closed, opening,* and *closing*), and so on.[53] The result is at least $2 \times 2 \times 4 = 16$ *composed states* such as *up **and** still **and** closing*. These composed states aren't readily apparent in the diagram. Still, we must take inventory of them all and remove the invalid states, such as those with *moving **and** open* or *moving **and** opening*. With hundreds or thousands of states, picking out the valid ones becomes an overwhelming task.[54]

In such an orthogonally composed model, each region has a simple state diagram, and the complexity is in their interaction—but that's all wrong! The complexity should be where the expressiveness is the greatest: in the individual state diagrams. The interactions between diagrams should be kept to a minimum.

In the elevator case, we start with a well-defined state such as where the cabin is sitting at a floor. Then we determine what events are valid in that state and what transitions they trigger. (Valid events include correct ones such as a button being pressed or a floor sensor tripped as well as error events such as a power cut.)

We continue in the same vein from each of the new states, making sure we know and understand each state and giving it a meaningful name. This way, we identify all valid states. (In the process, we may reach the same state more than once without realizing it. It's sometimes possible to use names that make such *equivalent* states easier to detect; Section 3.6.2.)

We add superstates as necessary to group all states where the elevator is still, for example. Should we also need to collect all states where it's headed up, we can introduce another, *overlapping* superstate (Section 3.4.5.2).

3.4.4.2.1 Complex State Machines

The complexity is there, and it is a major benefit of a method if it forces you to recognize . . . complexity when it is present in a problem. In software development, a complexity ignored is a disaster waiting to happen.

JACKSON, 1995

---

[53]This is sometimes referred to as *factoring*.
[54]This is like a traditional programming style with flags [also known as history variables (Sandén, 1994)]. Each flag is a Boolean indicating whether the elevator is moving or not, for example. It's a state machine with two states.

Like the elevator, a complex device such as an ATM could be described using orthogonal states (Harel, 1987): One such state could show the inner workings of the printer and another those of the card reader. It's cleaner, however, to decompose the device into different classes, each with a set of operations. We can introduce a class *ATM* representing the entire teller machine, which calls operations on the printer and card reader objects. The state of each class is encapsulated. With this approach, the state machine of the class *ATM* captures the high-level logic. At need we can drill down to the printer or card reader state machine but often we don't have to.

3.4.5 Additional Superstate Concepts

*3.4.5.1 History Marker

In response to some exceptional event, an entity may have to leave a superstate, *U*, visit another state, *T*, and then return to the substate of *U* where it was. To show this, we can use a *history marker*[55] consisting of the letter "H" within a circle as shown in Figure 3-16. The marker is placed inside the superstate *U*.

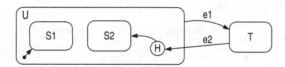

Figure 3-16 History marker. *e2* causes a transition to *S1* or *S2*, whichever substate of *U* was visited last. If no substate has been visited, a transition to *S2* occurs.

Event *e1* triggers a transition from either *S1* or *S2* to *T*. The arrow from *T* to the history symbol signifies a transition to the substate of *U* last visited. So, upon event *e2*, the entity transitions to either *S1* or *S2*. The arrow from the history marker to *S2* is for when *U* is entered via the history marker and no prior substate is defined.

The history marker is one of those esoteric features that are best left out unless we are sure that our readers understand them (Ambler, 2005). Besides, the implementation of the history marker can be complex.

*3.4.5.2 Overlapping Superstates

Overlapping superstates is an advanced state diagram feature. In Figure 3-17, *U* has the substates *S1* and *S2*, and *V* has the substates *S2*, *T1*, and *T2*. Each overlapping superstate can have its own entry and exit actions and activities. This feature can be elegant in the hands of a virtuoso but can get a beginner into trouble.

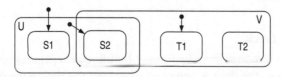

Figure 3-17 Overlapping superstates.

---

[55]It's also referred to as *history symbol, history state,* and *history pseudostate* (Fowler, 1997; Rumbaugh et al., 2005).

In Figure 3-17, *T1* is *V*'s default entry state, and *S2* is *U*'s default entry state, as indicated by the place of the bullet at the end of each tail. In the same vein, the arrow pointing to *S1* with its bullet outside both *U* and *V* indicates that *S1* is the *initial state* of the whole state machine shown in Figure 3-17. With overlapping superstates we can define any group of states as a superstate although some such superstates cannot be shown graphically.

3.5 EXAMPLES

3.5.1 Whole-House Fan

The control system of a *whole-house fan* is connected to a button and to the fan motor. The fan is initially off. Pressing the button once starts the fan going at high speed. Pressing the button once more makes it go at low speed. The third time, the fan is turned off. The button causes an interrupt to the controller. The motor commands are *High*, *Low*, and *Stop*. The state diagram is shown in Figure 3-18. It illustrates that one and the same event can trigger different actions, depending on the state where it occurs.

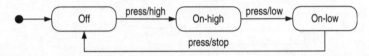

Figure 3-18 State diagram of a fan controller.

Note Figure 3-18 not only shows the domain entity, which could be described without the actions, but also specifies the control program. Even though the states are named *Off*, *On-high*, and *On-low*, the controller must take explicit actions to change the speed. The programmer must insert these motor commands. The states are internal to the controller and merely serve to remember what events have occurred.

Arguably, a diagram of a domain entity shouldn't show those actions; they should be inserted in a separate design step. Often when we attempt to describe the problem domain, we find ourselves describing a software solution instead (Jackson, 2005). In state diagramming this can be unavoidable, and sometimes we must introduce variables in both actions and conditions. For example, an ATM may allow three incorrect attempts at a personal identification number (PIN) code before confiscating the card. A state diagram can show this by means of a counter. Actions increment the counter, and guard conditions are based on its value.

3.5.2 Code Lock

A code lock to the door of an apartment building accepts an infinite sequence of digits as input. The door is *unlocked* whenever the digit sequence *XYZW* has been entered. (At each point in time, *X* through *W* stand for specific digits.) Once the door has been physically opened, it's again locked. It's also locked after *T* seconds even if it hasn't been opened. While the door is unlocked, any succession of digits may be pressed with no effect.

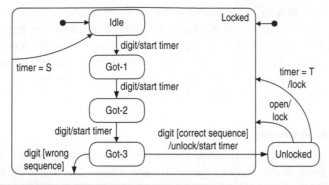

Figure 3-19 Basic code lock solution.

This example reinforces the state concept: With each digit, a new state is entered, and it defines what events are acceptable next. Figure 3-19 shows a practical programming solution. The successive digits are saved in a buffer. After the fourth digit, the entire sequence is compared to the correct sequence, *XYZW*.

Note the arrow from the superstate border to *Idle* marked *timer = S* and the action *start timer* triggered by *digit* events. The timer measures the time spent in each substate, *Got-1*, *Got-2*, and *Got-3*; and the transition to *Idle* is taken after *S* seconds in any one substate. That way, the user is given the same time to enter each digit (Section 3.3.4.4).

The solution in Figure 3-19 is practical but relies on a buffer of digits. Figure 3-20 shows a purer state machine solution relying on states alone.[56] A state name such as *Got-XY* indicates that the correct sequence *XY* has been received while *Got-2* indicates that some other two-digit sequence was received. When the fourth digit is received, it's already known whether the first three were correct or not.

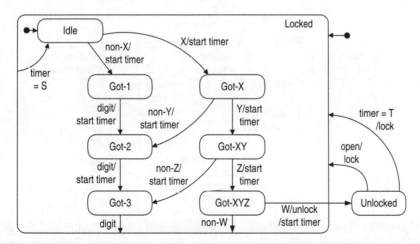

Figure 3-20 State-only solution for the code lock.

[56]This solution was suggested by Thai Tran, Colorado Technical University, summer 2001. The diagrams with *Idle* inside the superstates were suggested by Matthew Deichsel, Colorado Technical University, winter 2006. They are nice and compact but may be too elaborate as working tools. Flat diagrams without superstates may well be easier to understand.

With a state table instead of a diagram, we can generalize the solution to *n* digits (Section 3.3.3). In the table, we can name the states generically so that *GotCorrectDigits*$_i$ is the state where *i* correct digits have been entered, and *GotDigits*$_i$ is the state where *i* digits have been entered that aren't the correct sequence. It's best implemented with a counter of digits entered and a Boolean showing whether an incorrect digit has been entered (Section 3.3.2.1).

3.5.3 Car Window

A power car window is manipulated by means of a little lever that can be held in the positions *up* and *down* and springs back to a neutral position when released (Sandén, 1994). Normally, the window moves down while the lever is held in the *down* position and up when in the *up* position until the window reaches its fully opened or fully closed position. But if the control is held *down* for *S* seconds, the window continues down automatically after the lever is released. In that automatic mode, we can stop the window by pushing the lever *up*. The events *top* and *bottom* occur when the window reaches its top and bottom positions.

A state diagram with *Closed* as its initial state covers the above events. But if we program it, we will have an initialization problem: We don't know in which state the program should start after the ignition is turned on. The physical window can be in any still state, *Open, Closed,* or *Stopped*; and the control software shouldn't be expected to retain its internal state once the car's ignition is turned off. The example shows the practical importance of the initial state: Each time the ignition is turned on, the window control program starts in the initial state, no matter the current position of the window.

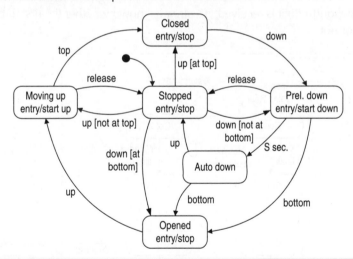

Figure 3-21 First car window solution. *Stopped* means stopped partway.

We could attempt to solve the problem by making *Stopped* the initial state as in Figure 3-21. Sadly, that creates ambiguity: When the window is physically fully open, its state may be either *Open* or *Stopped*. It's better to consolidate those states where the window isn't moving. In Figure 3-22 they have been replaced by a single *Still* state.

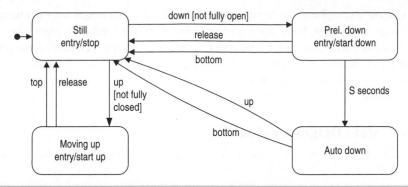

Figure 3-22 Corrected state diagram of the car window.

Note 1 The entry actions can be replaced by nominal activities: *Moving up* could have the activity *raise window*. *Prel. down* and *Auto down* could each have the activity *lower window*, but then it would be stopped and restarted at the transition to *Auto down*. To avoid this, we can instead enclose *Prel. down* and *Auto down* in a superstate with the activity *lower window*.

Note 2 In each of the diagrams in Figures 3-21 and 3-22, we could have replaced *Prel. down* and *Auto down* with a single state, *Moving down*, say, and used the time spent in that state in a guard condition. But states are more expressive than guard conditions, and the network of states is what makes the diagram such an intuitive, visual tool. Involved conditions make it harder to understand. Many of my solutions have evolved from having more guards to having more states.

3.6 STATE MODELING IN PRACTICE

Aesthetic considerations are fundamental to design, whether in art or technology. Simplicity, elegance, and clarity of purpose distinguish products of outstanding quality from mediocre products.

FAIRLEY, 1985

Identifying well-defined states pays off directly. Draw such a state diagram on a whiteboard, and the class will rip it apart arrow by arrow. A team of engineers will keep at it until they get it right.[57] It's an effective tool for a collaborative analysis effort or a design review, and it makes for concrete work at a level abstracted from the actual programming. No tool is better if we want to convince some recalcitrant "real programmer" that co-workers can provide valuable input and that an abstract model can support actual problem solving.

The incomplete, hand-drawn diagram is the real tool according to Blum (1992), and Fowler (2004) talks about diagramming in "sketch mode." A designer does well to tie up loose ends and produce a clean diagram, but others may see a polished diagram as an unassailable work of art. Yet, clean diagrams that document the final solution are important to maintainers. When it comes to

[57]Harel (2009) reports a similar experience.

modifying a state-based program in any nontrivial way, it's much safer to change the state model first. If no up-to-date state diagram is available, a maintainer is well advised to create one by reverse engineering the relevant part of the program. The same may be true for a tester (Beizer, 1990). A state diagram can be part of a requirements specification (Davis, 1993). If it's not, making one forces the designer to scrutinize and question the requirements.

3.6.1 State Diagram Layout

A lot of the communication value in a UML diagram is still due to the layout skill of the modeler.

EVITTS, 2000

Even on a whiteboard, it's sound to let the state diagram layout reflect the symmetries of the problem (Ambler, 2005, Lieberman, 2006). In Figure 3-21, the still states are arranged down the middle with movement states up and down on either side. (I first had *Auto down* lined up vertically with the still states, but it was misleading.) Don't expect your audience to find missing arrows in a "ball-of-yarn" diagram as in Figure 3-23, which can be understood only by laborious path tracing.

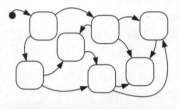

Figure 3-23 Typical "ball-of-yarn" state diagram.

At times, path tracing—also called "walking" the diagram—may be helpful and even necessary. But we may also feel a need to walk a diagram because its states aren't intuitively clear. This could be a simple matter of naming but may also mean that the states are ill conceived.

*3.6.1.1 Conversations with Materials; Backtalk

You say to brick, "What do you want, brick?" And brick says to you, "I like an arch."

KAHN AND TWOMBLY, 2003

Donald Schön has studied designers in various professions at work. His thoughts on designers' *conversations* with their materials and the materials' *backtalk* have made their way into the realm of software design (Pescio, 2006; Winograd, 1996). Good design tools and diagramming styles should give a kind of feedback. Thus Figure 3-21 may feel a bit asymmetric and ask whether a state *Auto up* is missing,[58] while Figure 3-23 likely has little to contribute beyond a half-hearted "Trust me; I'm fine." The graphical layout is important, and for that same reason a diagram may engage us in conversation more readily than a state table (Section 3.3.3).

3.6.2 State Names

In naming there is no place for humor. Life is real, life is earnest; naming is a serious, though not necessarily cheerless affair.

MCQUEEN, 1977

A good state diagram separates concerns so we can study each state by itself. For this, states need meaningful names. "Meaningful names raise expectations"

---

[58]For safety, the car in my example has no automatic window closing.

(Jackson, 1995), however, so we'd better avoid names flavored with irrelevant associations lest people read too much into them. Finding good names isn't always easy. If it proves utterly impossible, something may be wrong with the state model itself.

Pólya sums this up beautifully: "A good notation should be unambiguous, pregnant, easy to remember; it should avoid harmful second meanings, and take advantage of useful second meanings; the order and connection of signs should suggest the order and connection of things" (Pólya, 1957, p. 136).

State names should be short and easy to remember. If a short name doesn't capture the essence of a state, we can add a separate, full state definition such as "the elevator is moving up" or "only north–south through traffic has green lights." Each such definition should hold in exactly one (super)state. A substate name need only be unique within its superstate.

It's usually a bad idea to think of a state only as the place where we end up after some series of events. That amounts to path tracing. Instead, we should be able to look at any state in isolation, understand the situation it represents, and determine what events can happen next.

Some states can be named for the event(s) that the entity is waiting for. *Waiting for dial* in Figure 3-12 is an example. (Clearly, the names must still tell the states apart. The whole-house fan in Section 3.5.1, for instance, is waiting for the event *press* in every state.)

Naming each state for the events awaited can reveal *equivalent* states. Two states are equivalent if every sequence of event occurrences starting from one produces exactly the same sequence of actions and activities when started from the other (Beizer, 1990). Such duplication of states is to be avoided. It's not only imprecise but also error prone.

The production line workstation discussed in Section 5.5.2.1 (Figure 5-13; page 167) has a number of states where it's waiting for one or more of the events *arrival*, *info*, and *picked*. In that particular case, we avoid equivalent states by using names such as *Waiting for arrival* and *Waiting for arrival or info*.

3.6.3 Consistent Point of View

It's important to make clear what entity a state model represents and to be consistent. Say that we need a state diagram of a motorist's interaction with a gas pump for a simulation. The diagram can describe the workings of the pump or it can describe the doings of a motorist. While the person is buying gas, the two points of view coincide: The gas pump and the motorist both participate in events such as *insert credit card*, *choose octane level*, and *unhook nozzle*. If we are describing the pump, the sequence starts and ends with the pump in an idle state. If we're taking the person's point of view, it may start with state *Driving up* and end with *Driving away*. If a diagram starts in *Idle* and ends in *Driving away*, it has suffered a point-of-view change midway.

3.6.4 Time Scale of State Models

The time scale of a state model should be that of the domain, where an entity may spend seconds, minutes, or more in each state. Typical computations, by comparison, are nearly instantaneous and are modeled as actions, not activities.

If an entity spends several seconds in most states, having other states where it spends mere milliseconds is awkward.

*3.6.4.1 Near Instantaneity

As mentioned earlier, an action triggered by an event is *nearly instantaneous* if it's short enough that we need not worry about events happening *during* the action. That is, any event occurs either before or after the action. For our practical purposes, the action takes no time.

More precisely, the whole handling of the event occurrence—including any latency and the entire action—must be nearly instantaneous. In the common case where an event is signaled by an interrupt, we achieve this by making the interrupt handling short (Section 2.1.5). If the interrupt handler needs exclusive access to a safe object, *all* operations on the safe object must then be short to minimize the time the handler may be stalled (Section 2.1.4.1).

*3.6.4.2 State Models of Devices with Embedded Software

A state model of a device with embedded software must capture the system behavior of the hardware and software together. In response to an event, the software may need to perform a lengthy computation before it actuates on the device. If the computing time is noticeable in the world outside the software, we need a state to account for it. That means that there may be states where the device is waiting only for an embedded computation to complete. Events may occur during the computation, and their effect must be defined. The completion of the computation is itself an event and may trigger a state change and/or actions (Section 5.1.1.1.1). (For more about such *software-detected* events, see Section 4.2.1.4.1.)

3.7 STATE MACHINE IMPLEMENTATION

State machines have the important benefit that they can be implemented easily and directly. In fact, once we have represented the behavior of a device as a state machine, we have essentially designed a program that controls the device.[59]

In the simplest implementation of a state machine without activities, the current state of each instance of a class is kept in a state variable, *state*, say, which takes exactly one unique value for each state. When the state changes, *state* is assigned a new value. I refer to this situation where the state is kept in a variable as **explicit** *state representation* (Sandén, 1994). (In some cases it's helpful to complement the state variable with a counter; Section 3.3.2.1.)

In an alternate implementation, the state is instead always defined by the current locus of control.[60] For example, the entity may be in a certain state exactly while a particular loop executes. This kind of implementation needs no state variable. Since the identity of the current state isn't explicit in a variable, I call this **implicit** *state representation* (Sandén, 1994). In the following I first discuss explicit and then implicit state representation.

---

[59]Using many superstates may complicate the implementation.
[60]The **locus of control** is the place in the code of the machine instruction that the thread will execute next. The *program counter* contains the memory address of that instruction.

Both representations are used in multithreaded software (as well as in sequential programming). With explicit state representation and multithreading, the state machine is usually represented by a safe object and any software activities by threads. Implicit state representation, on the other hand, is found in the *run* operation of some thread classes. All this may seem confusing but only serves to show the versatility of state modeling. State machines in multithreaded software are the topic of Chapter 5.

3.7.1 Explicit State Representation

ex·plic·it … 3 : *unambiguous in expression*

MERRIAM-WEBSTER, 1993–1996

Say that a state machine describes the behavior of each instance of a class, *C*. To represent the state explicitly, we can include an attribute variable, *state*, in *C*. Ideally, this variable should be of an enumerated type, *state-type*, say, so that *state* can take on exactly one value for each state.[61] (Otherwise, we must deal with errors where *state* has a value that maps to no state.)

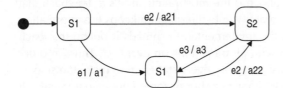

Figure 3-24 Simple state diagram with events and associated actions.

Figure 3-24 shows a simple state diagram for *C*. Let the state variable, *state*, take exactly the values *S1*, *S2*, and *S3*. Its initial value is *S1*. For simplicity, we shall assume that each action *a1*, … is represented by a "void" operation with the same name.

The software can become aware of an event in various ways. We shall assume here that the occurrence of event *e1*, *e2*, or *e3* causes a call to one of *C*'s *event handlers e1*, *e2*, and *e3*. That is, operation *e2* is called after event *e2* has occurred. We can then implement *e2* as follows. (Operations *e1* and *e3* are similar.)

```
void e2 ( ) {
   switch (state)
      case S1: a21 ( );          // Perform action a21
         state = S2;
         break;
      case S2: break;
      case S3: a22 ( );          // Perform action a22
         state = S2;
         break;
   }
}
```

[61]In Java we can create a class, *StateClass*, say, and instantiate it exactly once for each state. A state variable of type *StateClass* can then take on exactly those values that map to states.

With a procedure (without parameters) for each action, the Ada equivalent is as follows:

```
procedure E2 is
begin
   case state is
      when S1 => A21; state := S2;
      when S2 => null;
      when S3 => A22; state := S2;
   end case;
end E2;
```

This straightforward implementation is usually the best. It lets each event handler such as *e2* have its own unique set of parameters. Moreover, subclasses of *C* can override individual event handler operation. If there are superstates, we can flatten the state model and implement it as shown above.

*3.7.1.1 Alternate Implementation: A Single Handler for All Events

While the implementation just above is the most practical, it's a drawback that it effectively inverts the state diagram: While the diagram keeps the information about each state in one place, the implementation spreads it out so that each event handler such as *e2* deals with all transitions on event *e2*. Thus, in order to construct the handler, we must inventory every state to find those transitions. An alternate implementation is less practical but of some conceptual interest. It has a single event handler *event* with a parameter of type *event-type*, which, like *state-type*, should be enumerated. The operation *event* can then be implemented with an outer switch statement over states and, for each state, an inner switch over events. This implementation mirrors the state diagram closely. It's easy to go from one to the other as they are both organized first by state and then by event. One disadvantage is that each event cannot have its own unique parameters. Moreover, if we need to modify the state machine in a subclass, we must override the entire operation *event* and inherit nothing.

3.7.1.2 Other Implementations of Explicit State Representation

The Golden Rule of Style: A program should be as easy for a human being to read and understand as it is for a computer to execute.

COOPER AND CLANCY, 1982

With explicit state representation, the implementations above, where each state is represented by the value of a state variable, are usually the most efficient: A state transition is implemented as an assignment statement. There are, however, other ways to implement the state explicitly:

1. Many freely available tools take some definition of a state machine and generate a program.
2. We can implement a state table (Section 3.3.3) as a data structure and calculate the result of each event by means of table lookup. Rather than hard coding the state table into our program, we could even keep it in a file that's read at initialization.

3. The *State Pattern* (Gamma et al., 1995) represents a state machine as a superclass with one subclass for each state. The superclass has an abstract event operation for each event in the state machine. Each subclass overrides each event operation with its own operation, which defines the effect of state–event pair.

The polymorphism is elegant, and, arguably, the implementation is easily modifiable and extensible. But the programmer may have to worry about the overhead for the dynamic binding of operations to the operation calls. Besides, the pattern may well suggest that state machine implementation is much more involved than it really must be.

3.7.2 Implicit State Representation

im·plic·it ... **1 a**: *capable of being understood from something else though unexpressed.*

MERRIAM-WEBSTER, 1993–1996

A state machine may be implemented without a state variable, especially if its structure is simple. In a program that sequentially reads n different inputs, $i1$, $i2, \ldots$, each input can be thought of as an event that takes the program from one state to the next. From the initial state, $S0$, input $i1$ takes the program to a state $S1$ where it expects input $i2$ and so forth.[62] The plainest implementation merely lists statements such as *read i1*, *read i2*, and so on, after each other in the program text. The states are implicit and no state variable is needed. There's typically no need to actually draw a diagram of such a simple state machine; pseudocode is sufficient.

As the state diagram grows more complex, implementing it with implicit state representation in a structured program does become difficult (Section 9.3). Most state diagrams can be implemented with implicit state if we permit *goto* statements. The program text for each state has essentially this structure (super-states aside):

State *X*

> Take any entry actions.
>
> Wait for the next event (*e*, say) while performing any activity defined for state *X*.
>
> Depending on the type of event *e* and any guard condition, either
>
> ■ perform only actions triggered by *e* or
>
> ■ perform state *X*'s exit actions and any actions triggered by *e*. *Go to* the next state.

The structure resulting from this programming style is no better than with explicit state representation.

Examples of implicit state representation abound. For instance, when an item travels along an assembly line and is worked on by various workstations, its state changes, probably at least once per workstation. Each workstation knows the item's state and there is no need to maintain it explicitly anywhere.

---

[62]Jackson structured programming (Section 9.3) is a design approach based mainly on implicit state representation.

3.8 CONCLUSION

[C]'est par la logique qu'on démontre, c'est par l'intuition qu'on invente.

[I]t's through logic that we prove; it's through intuition that we invent.

POINCARÉ, 1908

Some object-oriented texts let state diagrams merely show the behavior of the software, and many states represent longer or shorter computations. This is legitimate—a program can be said to exist in a certain state during a certain computation—but may suggest that state diagrams are little more than flowcharts. In this chapter, I make a point of letting the state models capture *the workings of things in the problem domain* such as various devices. (Chapter 5 includes additional examples.) On the time scale of those devices, many computations are nearly instantaneous and modeled as actions, while most states represent the wait for some external event. In my experience, this is where state modeling becomes truly profitable.

In much computing, such as compilation, it doesn't matter that a computation takes time. Time during execution is decoupled from time in the world, and we can let it stand still by not allowing any input during the computation. Dealing with reactive systems and with real-world events as they happen adds an element of practical engineering to state modeling. We must exercise our judgment as to whether the computation is short enough to be nearly instantaneous.

Like entity-life modeling, state modeling provides a bridge between the informal problem and a formal solution in a programming language. The greatest strength of these techniques is their appeal to the modeler. State *diagrams* are particularly intuitive and more helpful for capturing the problem than other state machine representations.

ELM uses state diagrams to capture the behavior of entities in the world. Chapter 5 shows how to implement them with threads and safe objects. We use them for entities of some complexity; far from every thread is intricate enough to deserve a state model.

EXERCISES

Most of these exercises call for the construction of a state machine for a given problem. Many other similar problems are possible. A microwave oven, a home security system, and a single-family home garage door are but a few. Because problems can be stated in many different ways, they may work best as projects where the features of a particular system are worked out in tandem with the state modeling.

3-1 Seatbelt. Draw a state diagram of an automatic car seatbelt. The belt is affected by the events that the door *opens* and *closes* and that the ignition is turned *on* or *off*. Initially, the door is closed, the engine is off, and the belt is unfas-

tened. The seatbelt controller takes the actions *fasten* and *unfasten* in response to the following events and situations:

Event	Situation	Action
open	Belt is fastened	*unfasten*
on	Belt is unfastened and door is closed	*fasten*
close	Belt is unfastened and ignition is on	*fasten*

3-2 Whole-house fan variations. Here are two variations on the example in Section 3.5.1, Figure 3-18.

(a) Suppose there are three buttons—*off*, *high*, and *low*—which can be pressed in any order. Use a superstate to show this without arrows from every state to all other states.

(b) Assume that *off*, *high*, and *low* are mechanical buttons that stay pressed even through a power cut. With a new state *Power-off* and with the substates *Off*, *On-high*, and *On-low* in a superstate *Power-on*, show that the controller ends up in the last visited substate upon return to *Power-on*.

3-3 Exit gate. Draw a state diagram of the automatic, software-controlled exit gate of a gated community. Add states and events to those mentioned below, as necessary. Use superstates if you wish.

The gate is normally closed. It can be opened by a *signal* either from a remote control or from an electromagnetic sensor in the roadway. In response to the signal, the software issues the command *start-open* to the machinery. The gate is in an *Opening* state while it swings open. Once the gate is fully opened, a timer is started.

After *t* seconds in the *Opened* state, the software attempts to close the gate:

■ If no object is detected at the roadway sensor, the command *start-close* is issued and state *Closing* is entered. When the gate is fully closed, a state *Closed* is entered.

■ If an object is detected, the timer is restarted and the gate remains open. After *t* seconds, another attempt at closing is made, and so on.

Regardless of state, *power-cut* causes the gate to open fully (on back-up power). For this, the software issues the command *start-bkp-open* in response to the *power-cut* event. The gate remains open until power is restored. When this happens (as indicated by the event *power-up*), the gate automatically closes unless there is an object at the roadway sensor. If an object is detected, another attempt at closing is made after *t* seconds, and so on, in the same manner as if the gate had been opened normally.

3-4 Basement garage. Draw a state diagram of the door of the basement garage in an apartment building (Sandén, 1994). The door is opened from the outside by means of a magnetic card and from the inside by an exiting car tripping a floor sensor. Sensors in the doorframe are tripped when the door reaches the fully opened and fully closed positions. When the door has been either fully opened or stopped for 1 minute, it starts

moving down automatically as soon as there's no obstacle.

There are three buttons: *stop*, which stops the door; *open*, which makes it move up; and *close*, which makes it move down absent any obstacle.

A light source in one doorpost and an optical sensor in the other detect obstacles. Any obstacle breaks the light beam, which stops the door if it's closing.

A warning sign CAR IN RAMP flashes whenever the door isn't fully closed. Refer to the different stimuli as follows:

top	The door reaches the fully opened position.
bottom	The door reaches the fully closed position.
open, close, stop	The *open, close*, or *stop* button is pressed, respectively.
card	A card with a correct code is read.
floor	A car trips the floor sensor.
break	An obstacle breaks the light beam.
unbreak	The obstacle is removed from the light beam.
time-out	The door has been stopped or fully opened for 1 minute.

The actions controlling the warning sign and the door motor are:

on, off	Turn flashing warning sign on and off, respectively.
up, down	Start the motor moving the door up and down, respectively.
halt	Stop the motor.

The following conditions exist for the optical sensor in the doorway:

Beam	The light beam is unbroken.
No beam	The light beam is broken.

3-5 Superstate conventions. Given the state diagram in Figure 3-25, determine what states are visited and what actions are taken successively in response to the following sequence of event occurrences:

#1: e1; #2: e9; #3: e5, #4: e4; #5: e9; #6: e2; #7: e3

The whole sequence is part of one scenario: Event 1 occurs in state *S0* and causes a transition to a certain other state. Event 2 *occurs in that new state*, and so on.

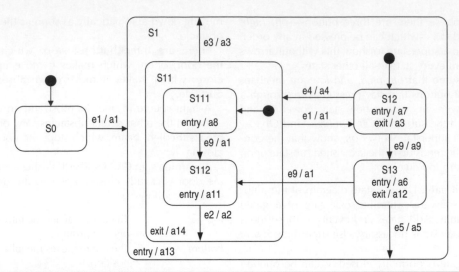

Figure 3-25 A rather overelaborate state diagram.

3-6 Turing machines. A Turing machine (Brookshear, 2009) is an imaginary device consisting of a control unit with a read/write head. A *tape* extends indefinitely to the left and to the right and is divided into cells. Each *cell* contains a *symbol* from a finite *alphabet*. (For this exercise, the alphabet is {0, 1, *}.) At each point in time, the machine is in exactly one of a finite number of *states*. It begins in state *Start* and ends in state *Halt*.

The machine executes a program. At each program step, the control unit reads the symbol in the current cell, writes a symbol into the cell, may move one cell to the right or left, and may change state. The program can be described by a state machine where each event is the symbol read and each action consists of writing a symbol and optionally moving left or right.

(a) Draw a state diagram of a Turing machine that places 0s in all cells to the left of the cell where it starts until it reaches a cell with an asterisk (Brookshear, 2009).

(b) Let a pattern of 0s and 1s on the tape be flanked by an opening asterisk on its right and a closing asterisk on its left (Brookshear, 2009). Draw a state diagram of a Turing machine that starts at the opening asterisk and then rotates the pattern one cell to the left. (At the end of this operation, the value originally to the right of the closing asterisk will be to the left of the opening asterisk.)

3-7 Remote car door opener. Draw a state diagram of a remote control that provides "one-button customization": Depending on which remote unlocks the car, the driver's seat and the mirrors are adjusted to driver preferences. When the car is locked with a clicker, the system saves any seat or mirror settings that have been changed since the car was unlocked and associates them with that clicker.

THE ELM WAY

Entity-Life Modeling

4

And first with nicest skill and art,
Perfect and finished in every part,
A little model the Master wrought,
Which should be to the larger plan
What the child is to the man,
Its counterpart in miniature;
That with a hand more swift and sure
The greater labor might be brought
To answer to his inward thought.

HENRY WADSWORTH LONGFELLOW, THE BUILDING OF THE SHIP, 1849

4.1 INTRODUCTION

Based on the preliminaries in Part I, this chapter introduces *entity-life modeling (ELM)* as a design principle for multithreaded, reactive software (Sandén, 1994, 1997a, 2001, 2003; Sandén and Zalewski, 2006). ELM maps certain problem-domain phenomena onto threads and safe objects.

In object-oriented software development, classes and relationships found in the problem domain are carried seamlessly into design and implementation. ELM extends this idea into the time dimension. With ELM, we identify sequences of event occurrences in the problem space and model the control threads in the software on them. Such sequences are called **event threads**.[63]

Event threads exist in the problem domain. They aren't the same as Java or C# threads, Pthreads, or Ada tasks. Whenever there's risk for confusion, I use the term "control threads" for such threads provided by a language. (Pthreads are also control threads.) The control threads and the safe objects make up a system's *thread*

---

[63] Event threads are akin to *event streams* (Bass et al., 2003), which are also sequences of event occurrences. I define **event thread** more precisely in Section 4.2.2.

architecture.[64] In this chapter in particular, I use "thread" without qualification in situations where one can think of it as either an event thread or a control thread.

The distinction between event threads and control threads is fundamental, as is their relationship: With ELM, each control thread corresponds to an event thread in the problem space. The event thread justifies the control thread. Some event threads need no control thread; instead, all the events are dealt with by event handlers. This is a design decision; the event thread in the problem domain stays the same.

ELM assumes that we are looking for a thread architecture. We are not analysts attempting to describe the problem as a goal in itself or to specify requirements. We are designers, rather, seeking in the problem realm a sound foundation for our software architecture.

*Note 1 The event-thread concept allows us to discuss the problem and the software architecture apart. The two aren't the same. As we saw above, some event threads need no control threads. Once we grasp the idea, the distinction fades in our minds. It's like object orientation where we design software by reasoning about objects in the domain and juggle domain objects and software objects quite freely.

Note 2 I have found it necessary to introduce quite a number of ELM-specific concepts. The Glossary indicates which terms are of that nature. Of course, creating a special little language for ELM is no goal in itself. The purpose is to give us words for what different problems and solutions have in common. While I define each concept, I believe we understand a term such as event thread the best by studying a few, selected examples to find out what they have in common.

4.1.1 Concurrency Structures in the Problem Domain

Certain structures in the problem intuitively suggest concurrent software architectures. This happens when there are event series unfolding more or less independently. Here are some such concurrency structures:

- **Independent Processes** (Douglass, 2009). In many applications, users carry on their work independently of each other. Examples include customers at the ATMs of a bank. In the software, each ATM may have a thread. The processes running on a PC also represent independently unfolding developments. (Each such process has one or more threads.)

- **Asynchrony.** In some problems, multiple activities are going on, each at its own pace. For instance, a jukebox in a diner is connected to panels at the booths where customers can put in money and select songs. Customers pick songs at their pace. The jukebox's CD player plays one song after another. During the playback, customers can pick more songs. That asynchrony between song ordering and playback can be captured by *Panel* threads, which deal with customer inputs, and a *CD-player* thread that deals with the player (Section 4.4.2.2). In the software, the *Panel* control threads are connected to the *CD-player* control thread by a buffer of song requests. An additional illustration of

---

[64]"Thread architecture" is quite similar to the concepts "concurrency architecture" and "concurrency and resource management architecture" (Douglass, 2009).

asynchrony is a data-entry application where one thread captures data blocks from a keyboard in a buffer while another thread writes each block to disk (Section 4.2.2.1).

■ **Resource Contention.** Some control systems deal with resource contention between *resource users* in the domain. In the software, we can give each resource user a control thread and let safe objects represent the resources (Section 4.4; Chapters 6 and 7). One example concerns a flexible manufacturing system (FMS) where jobs contend for workstations and automated vehicles (Section 7.3.2).

■ **State Machines with Concurrent Activities.** As we saw in Chapter 3, many devices can be modeled as state machines. A state machine can be implemented as a safe object and the activities as threads (Section 4.2.5.1; Chapter 5).

We shall return to these cases throughout the chapter. Multiple concurrency structures can coexist and overlap in a given problem. Thus, the *Panel* threads in the jukebox are independent processes because customers in different booths can order songs at the same time. That way, they are like the ATM threads. We can also treat the jukebox as a resource-sharing problem where customer threads contend for access to the one CD player. In the FMS, the jobs are independent to the degree allowed by the resource sharing. The processes running on a PC can also share such resources as a printer.

In this section I've made no distinction between event threads and control threads to emphasize that multithreading affords quite intuitive software solutions. Thread architectures suggest themselves where each control thread has a counterpart in the problem domain.

4.1.2 Thread Architectures

ELM has these objectives for thread architectures:

■ A thread architecture should be easy to understand and give a clear mental picture of the software in problem-domain terms. Each thread should have a problem-domain justification that can be grasped at once, as in these cases:

■ *One thread per ATM* in a bank system

■ *A periodic thread that gathers meteorological data* in a planet rover

■ *One thread per emergency vehicle* in a metropolitan traffic light preemption system[65]

Many an architecture consists of multiple instances of one or a few thread types as with the ATM or the traffic light preemption system.

■ The thread architecture should be efficient. ELM takes a restrictive view of concurrency and aims to eliminate unneeded threads and context switches. It introduces the notion of a *concurrency level*, which

---

[65]The system alters traffic signal timing to give the emergency vehicles green lights along their path. (Bryan Curtis brought this example to my attention; Colorado Technical University, fall 2005.)

indicates the number of threads that is, in a certain sense, optimal for a given problem (Section 4.2.3).

- With symmetric multiprocessors (SMP), the thread architecture should adapt fluidly to the number of processors available.

"Thread architecture" may sound grand, but many are very simple. Simpler is better, to be sure. Some architectures in this book are in fact degenerated and have no threads at all. I still use "thread architecture" to tell a software solution apart from a thread model of the problem domain.

Entity-life modeling takes its name from the idea that each control thread is modeled on an **entity** in the problem domain such as an ATM, a jukebox user, or an FMS job. An *entity*[66] is an object in the domain whose "life"—or life *history*, if you will—is an event thread.

In some problems, event threads stand out, while no entities readily present themselves. We can then avoid the indirection and name the thread itself. The meteorology thread illustrates this. So does a *screen-redraw* thread on a PC, although we could also associate it with a window or screen entity.

In any case, each thread must have meaning in problem-domain terms. ELM doesn't produce internal threads that repeatedly read a message from a queue, perform some computation, and place the result in another queue. In that kind of *data-flow threading*, each input visits a number of threads (Section 8.3). In ELM, each impulse, such as an interrupt or other input, is normally handled to completion by a single thread (or by an interrupt or event handler).

4.1.2.1 Analogical Modeling

A control thread is an *analogical* model of an event thread, just like the artisan's little ship in Longfellow's poem that opens this chapter: Its form corresponds to that of the original in some essential respects (Section 1.4.1.2). The control thread becomes a software *analog* of the event thread—they share the same structure.

Note that "model" and "modeling" are often used in the looser sense of abstract description. I use "event-thread model" for a problem-domain description in terms of event threads and "state model" for a description centered on states and transitions. They are not analogical models.

4.1.2.2 Few But Significant Thread Types

Basing each control thread on an event thread in the problem is a powerful principle. A statement such as "each emergency vehicle has a control thread" is simple enough, yet as a guide to understanding a reactive software system, it's much more pregnant than a module breakdown. The modules are static and don't tell us what makes the system "tick," but the key idea behind the thread architecture can (Section 1.4.2.1).

A key idea can carry much meaning because a thread architecture tends to contain far fewer thread types than there are classes in an OO design. Most threads are critical to the architecture. Little harm is done if a programmer adds a class that no one else knows about. Adding a thread of a new type can prove

---

[66]The term "entity" is used in this sense in simulation (Banks et al., 2001).

much more fateful: Obscure threads that access all manner of safe objects can complicate debugging and maintenance dramatically.

The number of instances of each thread type is also a concern, even though some applications may have thousands (Allman, 2004). Each thread instance, necessary or not, has its own stack and other control data. It also requires context switching.

All this means that the thread architecture is strategic. We shouldn't go about it in a piecemeal manner; it's not like adding classes here and there and later refactor. Adding a thread type is an architectural decision; adding a safe object is perhaps less so, at least as long as it's never held with exclusive access together with other objects.

4.2 MODELING SOFTWARE ON EVENT THREADS

Imagine there is an observer with a notebook who watches the process and writes down the name of each event as it occurs. We can validly ignore the possibility that two events occur simultaneously; for if they did, the observer would still have to record one of them first and then the other, and the order in which he records them would not matter.

HOARE, 1985

In ELM, we model control threads on **event threads**. An event thread is defined as a sequence of event occurrences in the problem domain. A customer's inter-action with an ATM is an event thread, which might start as follows:

1. Insert card.
2. Enter password.
3. Choose "withdraw money".

Important for the moment are not the specific events or their order but that they occur one after the other, with a space of time in between. A sequence of event occurrences separated in time that way can be handled by a single control thread, which can keep up with the events as they occur.

4.2.1 ELM Rationale

While object-oriented software does a reasonably good job of modeling "things," it does not model processes, events, behaviors, and interactions well. This is partly because programmers have not yet shaken off the mindset that incorrectly equates the technical concept of "object" with the intuitive concept of "thing."

DEUTSCH, 1991

In light of the quote from Deutsch just above, this section justifies ELM as a way to extend the ideas of object orientation into the time dimension. This isn't done by letting objects represent processes and behaviors, however. Instead, event threads and control threads are seen as orthogonal to objects and their relationships.

4.2.1.1 Object-Oriented Modeling

Object-oriented software design is analogical modeling when classes and objects in the software build on classes and objects in the problem. The idea emerged first in programming languages such as Simula and Smalltalk and later in design and analysis. If we want to program in terms of classes and objects, we first identify phenomena in a problem that map onto those programming constructs. This is object-oriented analysis. Ideally, the analysis model seamlessly becomes a design model: The relationships between objects in the analysis model also hold for their software counterparts.

Basing the software structure on what exists undisputedly in the real world lends soundness and legitimacy to the design. It's in keeping with the "principle of deferred invention" (Jackson, 1995), which suggests that the design should rest as much as possible on the given properties of the problem. Only when they are exhausted should the designer resort to inventing things.

4.2.1.2 Modeling in the Time Dimension

If we want to base threading on analogical modeling, we need to identify phenomena in the problem domain that map onto control threads (Sandén, 2003). For this we note that threading deals chiefly with time. It's common to visualize control threads by laying out the computation of a multithreaded program along a timeline as shown in Figure 4-1a.

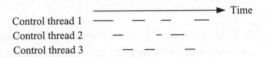

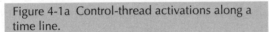
Figure 4-1a Control-thread activations along a time line.

The control threads may be Java or C# threads, Ada tasks, or Pthreads. The diagram shows a series of *activations* of each thread. Each activation is represented by a short, horizontal line which corresponds to a time interval. On a single processor, the activations are interleaved; with multiprocessors, they can overlap.

With this view of threads, how can they capture some aspect of the problem domain? We shall assume that each thread activation is caused by the occurrence in the problem domain of an *event* to which the software must react. An event occurs when a sensor is tripped, a key is struck, a button is pressed, or the like. We assume that a thread spends a finite (nonzero) amount of time processing each event occurrence.

In the diagram in Figure 4-1b, each thread activation shown in Figure 4-1a has been replaced by a dot indicating the event occurrence that caused the activation. An event such as "sensor S is tripped" normally occurs over and over. Each such *occurrence* of the event is shown separately in Figure 4-1b. The informal diagram shows the sequence of all the event occurrences in the problem partitioned into *event threads*.

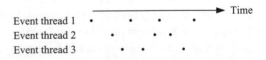

Figure 4-1b The event occurence causing the activations in Figure 4-1a.

If Figure 4-1b depicts the jukebox in Section 4.1.1, thread 1 can be the events at one of the panels, thread 2 can represent another panel, and thread 3 can be the events created by the CD player. In the traffic light preemption system in Section 4.1.2, each thread can be the events happening to a particular emergency vehicle.

To be precise, we look for events that are *shared* by the problem domain and the software. An event is shared if the domain and the software both participate in each of its occurrences (Jackson, 1995).

4.2.1.3 Time Events

Quite often, software must take actions of its own, such as refreshing a display or sampling some quantity in the environment. It must do it at certain, given times—not in response to events such as keystrokes. For this, we must include in the model **time events** defined as "x seconds have passed since event y" (Sections 3.2.1.1 and 3.3.4.4).

In practice, a time event is created by the software itself and specified in the program logic.[67] Yet we can validly think of time events as referring to real time: The computer's clock keeps up with the passage of time in the world as accurately as most other clocks.

Time events are everywhere. All sorts of electronic household devices use timers for one purpose or another. Any periodic thread is driven by time events (Section 4.3.1.2). In human–system interaction, they may trigger warning messages or log out a user for inactivity. ELM is concerned only with time events that are shared by the software and the problem environment (Section 4.2.1.4). We aren't concerned with times that are figments of the design and exist in the software only. Thus, if a thread checks its internal message queue every n milliseconds, this is *not* a time event in the ELM sense and isn't included in an event thread.

Time events are common in simulation software. Take the simulation of a bank system where customers arrive at random times and wait to be served by a teller. The interarrival time and the service time are considered random variables with known probability distributions. (The exponential distribution is typical.) In the simulation, we make the next arrival occur after a certain space of time, which is determined by a properly distributed random *variate*.[68]

*4.2.1.4 Events Shared by Problem and Software Domains

In the simplest kind of control system problem, there is a tangible domain, *external to the* machine, *to be* controlled. *This domain is connected to the machine directly, by* SHARED PHENOMENA.

JACKSON, 1995

Many events in a problem domain are *not* shared by the software. Most elevator systems don't keep track of each individual entering or leaving a cabin, for example. Likewise, the software has many internal events that are *not* shared by the problem domain. A time event prompting a thread to check its internal message queue is a case in point.

If the software is distributed over multiple nodes, it may very well make sense to study each node apart and treat its inputs from other nodes as external

---

[67] A *sleep* statement in Java (Section 2.2.1.1) or a `delay` or `delay until` statement in Ada (Section 2.3.1.5) creates a time event when the specified delay expires. RTSJ has *Timer* classes that produce time events (Section 2.2.5.3). Ada 2005 has timing events (Section 2.3.2.5).
[68] A random-number generator produces a sequence of uniformly distributed integers. From that, we can calculate a sequence of random *variates* with some other distribution.

events. This is illustrated by the production line workstations in Section 5.5.2.1, where each station sends a request for a part to the upstream station and an information message to the downstream station indicating that a part has been sent.

Another case is a database server that receives commands from various other computers. Each such command is an event occurrence. Multiple commands arriving simultaneously justify multiple threads in the server.

If we're putting together a simulation model with the process interaction worldview (Section 1.1.1), the software's problem domain is a *simulated* reality, and events are shared between it and the software. They remain the same even if we change the internal logic of the simulation program.

4.2.1.4.1 Software-Detected Events

To complicate matters, some relevant events in the life of an entity are detected by the software alone. Thus they aren't really shared: The domain only sees any action the software takes in response to the event. Still, the ELM designer must include them in event threads. Examples are:

- The end of a computation (or the end of a set of parallel computations)
- The allocation of a shared resource (which I shall call an **allocation event**)

These events are independent of any particular software design: In many problems a lengthy computation is necessary no matter how the software is structured.

In a way, time events are also software detected, but we can think of them as shared because the software and the problem environment can follow the passage of time independently.

The cruise controller (Section 5.4.3.1.4) has a similar type of event: that a certain speed is reached. The software keeps track of the speed and detects and acts on the event occurrence, but the speed of the vehicle could also be known independently by some device in the problem domain. So, we can consider this event shared.

4.2.2 Event Threads and Event-Thread Models Defined

[N]ew methods of construction demand new forms

...

AYN RAND, *THE FOUNTAINHEAD*, 1943[69]

An **event thread** is a time-ordered sequence of shared-event occurrences that are *separated in time*.[70] Events originating in the problem domain and time events are included.

An **event-thread model**—**thread model** for short—of a given problem is a set of event threads that together include all relevant shared-event occurrences in the problem and where each occurrence belongs to exactly one event thread.

Thus the event threads in a thread model of a problem *partition* the set of event occurrences in the problem. An event-thread model is a description of the problem that concentrates on the events while abstracting away all other aspects.

---

[69]Reprinted by permission of the Ayn Rand Institute.
[70]The separation allows for the processing of each occurrence, but the definition abstracts away from this practicality. An alternative, suggested by Jan Hext (Macquarie University, Sydney, Australia, 1994), would be to associate each event with the processing time explicitly.

Here's a summary of ELM's problem-domain and software-domain concepts:

Problem-Domain Concept	Software-Domain Concept
Event thread	Control thread
Event-thread model	Thread architecture

The concepts don't map perfectly one to one: Not all event threads become control threads, and the thread architecture includes both threads and safe objects.

4.2.2.1 Data-Entry Example

A simple data-entry application repeatedly prompts an operator to input blocks of 100 numeric sales figures into a buffer and then uses the values to update a revenue spreadsheet on a single disk (Asche, 1993; Sandén, 2003). The events in this problem are *keystrokes* on one hand and disk *writes* on the other.[71]

Below is a possible trace of event occurrences in the data-entry system. It shows occurrences along a timeline left to right where k *n* indicates a keystroke into block *n* and w *n* is a write from the same block. In this and the following traces, I have simplified things drastically so that each block requires only three keystrokes and three writes:

```
k1 k1 k1 w1 w1 k2 w1 k2 k2 w2 k3 k3 k3 w2 w2 w3 k4 . . .
```

The keystrokes are separated from each other in time, as are the writes. Because each block is first captured and then written to disk, the keystroke occurrences for a given block are also separated from the write occurrences for that block. This offers two possible event-thread models.

Model 1 One *Operator* thread (*O*) and one *Disk* thread (*D*). *Operator* consists of all the keystrokes. *Disk* consists of all the writes. This yields the following partitioning:

```
O: k1 k1 k1      k2      k2 k2      k3 k3 k3                k4
D:           w1 w1      w1      w2            w2 w2 w3
```

The occurrences in the *O* thread are separated in time, as are those in the *D* thread. On the other hand, occurrences in different threads (such as the bold-faced **k3** and **w2**) can be arbitrarily close and effectively simultaneous. Model 1 captures quite vividly the asynchrony between the data capture and the writing of the data to disk.

Model 2 Two *Block-sequence* threads (*BA* and *BB*). Each *Block-sequence* thread consists of the keystroke occurrences for one block followed by the disk write

---

[71]For the moment we assume that it always takes longer to key in a block than to write it to disk, so there will never be a queue of blocks waiting to be written (Section 4.2.3.3). Also, strictly speaking, a write is not an event but rather an action taken by the software in response to a hardware-created event such as write complete.

occurrences for that block. Then follow the keystroke occurrences for the next block, the write occurrences from that block, and so forth. Here's the resulting partitioning:

```
BA: k1 k1 k1 w1 w1    w1              k3 k3 k3        w3
BB:                k2    k2 k2 w2            w2 w2    k4
```

In Model 1, *Operator* and *Disk* are the entities. Model 2 has two entities, both of the type *Block-sequence*. Both models are reasonably practical. Each implementation has two control threads due to the asynchrony inherent in the problem. In an implementation of Model 1, at most one of the *Operator* and *Disk* control threads at a time has access to a given data buffer.

The implementation of Model 2 uses a synchronization mechanism to ensure that no more than one *Block-sequence* control thread at a time has access to the keyboard and no more than one thread at a time accesses the disk. Each control thread has its own buffer.

*4.2.2.2 Impractical and Counterintuitive Event-Thread Models

Some formally correct event-thread models are impractical or counterintuitive. Consider a multielevator controller for a hotel or office building, where a number of cabins move in parallel shafts, each serving all floors. In a typical solution, each elevator entity, *E1, E2* ..., keeps its own control thread, *t1, t2* ..., which accounts for all events happening to that elevator cabin: *t1* is modeled on an event thread capturing the life of *E1* and so on.

Suppose that *E1* and *E2* are idle at a given point in time. Technically, we can swap control threads at that point so that *t1* handles *E2*, and *t2* handles *E1* from then on. In such a solution, *t1* implements an event thread that contains events happening to *E1* followed by events happening to *E2*. The model is implementable but makes little sense once the relationship between thread and elevator entity is lost. Tying a thread to an entity ensures a consistent point of view (Section 3.6.3).

Note Control-thread-swapping elevators may seem bizarre, but the solution can fit other problems with very many entities, only a few of which are ever active at once. Those entities could share a *pool* of control threads. Each thread would for a time be tied to one entity, and then for a time to another (Section 7.3.2.2.1).

It's best to not look at the pool as a mere implementation device but to make clear in our minds what each control thread represents. In the elevator system, we can identify the entity type *Trips* and let each thread in the pool be its software surrogate. *Trips* consists of one complete trip by one elevator, a trip by another, and so on. Unlike *"Elevator,"* the word *"Trips"* doesn't associate *all* the trips with one elevator.

*4.2.2.3 Exceptional Events in a Thread

Even if most of an entity's life is a well-defined event thread, it may also suffer exceptional events that aren't neatly separated in time from other events. These situations have to be allowed as exceptions to the general definition of event thread. The implementation can often rely on special language features. Thus, an event may cause an exception to be raised in a control thread modeled on the life of the entity.

If an entity waits for the first of two possible event occurrences, asynchronous transfer of control can deal with the situation where the two events occur arbitrarily close in time (Sections 2.2.5.7 and 2.3.3).

4.2.3 Concurrency Levels and Optimal Event-Thread Models

By choosing Models 1 and 2 in the data-entry example in Section 4.2.2.1, we dismissed other event-thread models that comply with the definition at the beginning of Section 4.2.2. Programmers would find those models impractical, but they have conceptual interest. Here they are:

Model 3 Each data block *n* is given its own thread, *Blockn*, which consists of the keystroke occurrences for that block and the corresponding disk writes. Model 3 partitions the trace in Section 4.2.2.1 in the following way. (A period indicates the last occurrence in an event thread.)

```
Block1: k1 k1 k1 w1 w1    w1.
Block2:            k2    k2 k2 w2          w2 w2.
Block3:                    k3 k3 k3        w3
Block4:                                    k4
```

The implementation of this model creates a new control thread whenever a new block must be captured and destroys it once the block has been written. This is busy and wasteful; a single control thread can handle a sequence of blocks just as easily. Thus, in terms of event threads, *Block3*, *Block5*, … can be tacked onto *Block1* while *Block2* can be extended with *Block4, Block6, …* . This leads to Model 2.

Model 4 is less wasteful yet has the same kind of redundancy as Model 3. It consists of the following four event threads:

  OperatorA (OA) containing the keystrokes into buffer A

  DiskA (DA) containing the disk writes from buffer A

  OperatorB (OB) containing the keystrokes into buffer B

  DiskB (DB) containing the disk writes from buffer B

  Model 4 partitions the trace as follows:

```
OA:  k1 k1 k1                  k3 k3 k3
DA:           w1 w1    w1                    w3
OB:              k2    k2 k2                    k4
DB:                       w2          w2 w2
```

This model is redundant because the threads are pairwise synchronized: When one thread in such a pair has events occurring, the other one is always passive. Thus *OperatorA* is synchronized with *DiskA* because a buffer is never being filled and written at the same time. First, *OperatorA* has some event occurrences, then *DiskA* has some, and then *OperatorA* again. At the same time, *OperatorA* and *OperatorB* are synchronized because only one buffer can be filled at a time. So, we can combine threads in one of the following ways:

1. Combine *OperatorA* and *OperatorB* into one thread named *Operator* and combine *DiskA and DiskB* into another thread named *Disk*. This brings back Model 1.

2. Combine *OperatorA* and *DiskA* on the one hand and *OperatorB* and *DiskB* on the other and get two *Block* threads. This brings back Model 2.

From the discussion of Models 1–4, we can conjecture that a solution with two threads is optimal in the data-entry problem. No matter which model we choose, only two event threads are making concurrent progress during any given interval, one thread representing keystrokes and the other writes. We may choose to include more threads, but in a significant sense, this is a two-thread problem.

4.2.3.1 Coincidental Simultaneity

An observer, real or imaginary, can follow the progress of an event thread as its events occur. We want to capture the idea of event threads progressing concurrently. For this, ELM introduces the notion of *coincidental simultaneity*. If multiple threads are making concurrent progress, then their events can *occur at the same time by coincidence*. That is, threads are progressing concurrently if and only if *there can be times when they all happen to have events occurring*. An observer patient enough will ultimately see multiple events occurring at the same time. Conversely, if some constraint prohibits two threads from progressing concurrently, then it imposes some order on their event occurrences such that they cannot be at the same time.

4.2.3.1.1 Coincidental Simultaneity in Data-Entry Example

A keystroke and a disk write can occur at the same time if they involve two different buffers. In Model 1, this means that the *Operator* thread, which consists of keystroke occurrences, will now and then have an event occurring at the same time as *Disk*, which consists of write occurrences.

The same holds in Model 2 with the two *Block-sequence* threads *BA* and *BB*, one of which can be capturing keystrokes while the other one is updating the disk. But if we were to add a third *Block-sequence* thread, *BC*, there's never a time when *BA*, *BB*, and *BC* each have an event occurring. In an implementation, one of the three control threads has exclusive access to the keyboard, a second one has access to the disk, and the third one must be waiting; it needs one of those resources to make progress.

The *Block* threads in Model 3 are the same way. *Blockn* can have an event occurring at the same time as *Blockn-1* or *Blockn+1*, but threads numbered further apart have no events occurring anywhere near each other. (*Blockn-1* and *Blockn+1* have no simultaneous occurrences.)

4.2.3.1.2 Co-occurrence

Events are instantaneous, so strictly speaking, the likelihood that they occur at the same time is zero. Here is a more careful definition directly related to the notion of coincidental simultaneity:

*Two or more threads in a thread model **co-occur** if it's possible to construct an arbitrarily short time interval where each of them may have a different event occurrence.*

In Model 4, *OperatorA* and *DiskA* do *not* co-occur because they need exclusive access to the same buffer. But *OperatorA* and *DiskB* co-occur because one buffer can receive a keystroke at the same time that the other buffer is being written to disk. Likewise, *OperatorB* and *DiskB* do not co-occur, but *OperatorB* and *DiskA* do.

The *Block* threads in Model 3 co-occur pairwise only; there's no arbitrarily short interval where more than two of them have events occurring. Yet, we could argue that a solution such as Model 3 is optimal because it never has more than two threads at any one time.

4.2.3.2 Concurrency Levels and Optimality

Co-occurrence allows us to define the concurrency level of a problem as follows:

*The **concurrency level** of a problem is the maximum number of event occurrences in an arbitrarily short time interval.*

As we have seen, the concurrency level of the data-entry problem is 2: At any given time, at most one keystroke and one write can occur. For more realistic problems, it's not as easy to determine the concurrency level. It may even be impossible, but we can often find at least a reasonable upper limit, which is enough for design purposes.

*An **optimal** event-thread model is one where all the threads co-occur.*

The number of threads in an optimal event-thread model of a problem is equal to the concurrency level of the problem. Co-occurrence and optimality let us evaluate a thread architecture by comparing its number of threads to the concurrency level. That way, optimality can be a safeguard against redundant and counterproductive threads.

4.2.3.3 Nonoptimal Event-Thread Models

Because we cannot always determine the concurrency level, optimality can be no absolute requirement of entity-life modeling. Furthermore, a designer may have reasons to prefer a nonoptimal model. More threads may help to separate some concerns better or accommodate possible future changes.

Model 4 of the data-entry problem (with the *Operator* threads *OA* and *OB* and the *Disk* threads *DA* and *DB*) is nonoptimal, as discussed above. For a slightly less contrived nonoptimal solution, say that we have settled for Model 2 (with two *Block-sequence* threads, *BA* and *BB*). In the implementation, *BA* has buffer *A*, and *BB* has buffer *B*. Somehow, an especially fleet-fingered operator manages to get ahead of the updating and must wait. In the following trace, this occurs after the third block has been entered. (The keystrokes for the third block are shown as k3.)

```
BA: k1 k1 k1 w1 w1    w1           k3 k3 k3          w3
BB:              k2    k2 k2 w2            w2 w2    k4
```

After the three keystrokes **k3** into buffer *A*, buffer *B* is still being written, as shown by the **w2** occurrences that follow in thread *BB*. The operator must wait until *B* is available for keystrokes. This can be avoided by adding a third *Block-sequence* thread *BC*. The result could play out as follows:

```
BA: k1 k1 k1 w1 w1    w1           k3 k3 k3          w3
BB:              k2    k2 k2 w2            w2    w2
BC:                                              k4
```

BC translates into a third control thread in the implementation. After the operator has filled buffer *A*, *BC*'s control thread makes its buffer, *C*, available, and the operator can make keystroke k4 into it while buffer *B* is still being written to disk.

As we saw in Section 4.2.3.1.1, this is a nonoptimal model where one control thread is always waiting. In the example, thread *BC* waits for access to the keyboard until keystroke k4. BA then waits for disk access until w3.

This nonoptimal model works, but Model 1 offers an optimal and more practical solution in the case of the fleet-fingered file clerk. In the implementation of Model 1, the buffers are passive objects without threads, and an extra one can be added with little overhead.

Yet another illustration of a nonoptimal model is a PC application with multiple windows where each open window has a thread even though only one window at a time is in focus, and perhaps a few others are computing in the background. A designer may favor this model for its simplicity. The number of windows that most PC users keep open at a time may be small enough that the extra threads are of little concern.

*4.2.3.4 Multiprocessors

ELM doesn't expressly address the issue of parallelizing a program to take advantage of multiprocessors. Some computations such as image processing can be arranged to let different processors work in parallel on distinct parts of the image. Hence, in addition to the ELM modeling, a designer may have to take parallelization into account and add threads as necessary, typically by means of subprogram libraries. (Ideally, such parallelization is handled by a compiler without direct programmer involvement.)

Threads that execute independently on different processors are very much in the spirit of ELM. While they may not correspond to event threads in the problem domain, they certainly make progress concurrently, thanks to the hardware at hand.

4.2.4 Latitude for the Designer

There are some enterprises in which a careful disorderliness is the true method.

HERMAN MELVILLE, *MOBY-DICK*, 1851

In practice, it's up to the analyst/designer to determine how far apart the occurrences in one event thread must be. This is like state modeling where it can be a judgment call whether an operation can be abstracted as an action or must be thought of as an activity with extension in time (Sections 3.6.4.1 and 3.8).

4.2.4.1 Accidental Constraints

When determining whether two events can occur at the same time, we ignore constraints that are temporary or accidental. In the data-entry problem, the reason that only one block can be written at a time may be that there's a single disk. If there's any chance that the data may be distributed on more disks in the future, that constraint is accidental or temporary and can be ignored. By leaving such constraints aside, we can justify more threads, which may come in handy at a later date when the computing environment may have changed.

The constraint that only one instruction at a time can execute on a uniprocessor is similar. If the program may some day run on multiprocessors, the constraint is accidental and can be ignored.

4.2.4.2 Many Simultaneous Occurrences

The concurrency level is defined as the number of events that can theoretically happen at once. In some systems, this may exceed the feasible number of control threads. What's feasible changes as the hardware capacity increases, but still, the memory available for thread stacks is a finite resource. It's reasonable to bring to bear the laws of probability and note that the likelihood of n simultaneous occurrences decreases as n increases.

At times, the ELM analyst can opt to treat a phenomenon in the problem domain either as an event or as a state or condition with certain duration. In an elevator system, people may press all the *up* and *down* buttons and all the buttons inside the cabin at the same time. For some purposes, we can look at this as multiple, simultaneous occurrences of an event *press*. But closer scrutiny reveals that we aren't dealing with an instantaneous event: A button is held pressed for several milliseconds, which creates a condition that the elevator system can sense at any time during the interval (Section 6.7.1.2).

ELM's mission is to do away with superfluous threads. It doesn't stop a program from having *fewer* control threads than the concurrency level. On a single processor, a sequential program—without threads—may be the best.

4.2.5 Design Based on Event Threads

Before beginning to compose something, gauge the nature and extent of the enterprise and work from a suitable design. ... Design informs even the simplest structure, whether of brick and steel or of prose. You raise a pup tent from one sort of vision, a cathedral from another.

STRUNK AND WHITE, 2000

Every event-thread model for a given problem is potentially the foundation for a software architecture. Control threads are modeled on the event threads. Basing the control threads on an event-thread model ensures that each event occurrence is handled completely by one control thread, and no thread is inundated with simultaneous events. Each simultaneous event occurrence is taken care of by its own thread, and the threads may run on different processors.

A thread architecture based on an optimal model has no redundant threads. Sometimes, more control threads than event threads are needed. One such case is when an event cannot be attributed to a certain thread without further analysis of its associated input data.

4.2.5.1 Design Patterns for Implementing Threads

In ELM, every control thread requires an event thread as its justification. The reverse isn't true, for the occurrences in an event thread may be dealt with by interrupt handlers. In other words, an event thread is a necessary but insufficient justification for a control thread. The rest of this section discusses a couple of possible software designs.

4.2.5.1.1 Single Control Thread Modeled on an Event Thread

A control thread modeled on an event thread can often represent the state implicitly (Section 3.7.2). Implicit state representation means that the state is defined by the current locus of control in the thread, that is, the value of the program counter. Thus a particular state may exist exactly while a certain loop executes.

This book has several examples of this expressive way to capture the life of an entity (Sections 5.3.1, 6.2.2 and 7.3.1.1). A thread representing a participant in the game musical chairs is a toy example[72] (Exercise 6-3). The player's life may unfold as follows:

```
while (true)
    Wait until music stops
    Take a seat
        Break out of the loop if no empty chair is found
    Wait until music starts
    Get up
```

This translates to a program control structure quite easily. As further explained in Section 5.3, such a thread is called a *sequential-activities* thread. The same programming style works for animation and similar software too.

4.2.5.1.2 State Machine Safe Objects

For the case where events are dealt with by a handler, ELM introduces a *state machine safe object* as an implementation of a state machine. Any ELM event thread can be described as a state machine. A state machine safe object is like the class C in Section 3.7.1 adapted to a concurrent environment. If the state machine has no activities, a state machine safe object is all we need to handle interrupts and time events (Section 5.2).

A state machine with software activities (Sections 3.3.4.2 and 5.1.1) can define more than one event thread because the activities may define co-occurring threads. In that case, the implementation will contain *activity threads* in addition to the state machine safe object (Section 5.4). The periodic sampling of some quantity and a lengthy computation are two such activities.

---

[72]Drew McPheeters made this simulation model as a class project (MCI, fall 1999).

4.3 DISCOVERING AND CHOOSING EVENT-THREAD MODELS

The first rule of discovery is to have brains and good luck.

PÓLYA, 1957

As we have seen, we analyze the problem domain for possible event-thread models, where each thread consists of event occurrences separated in time, and each occurrence belongs to one thread. This is the basis of ELM.

Theoretically, we could discover event-thread models by making a trace of all relevant event occurrences and partitioning it into threads. But identifying *all* possible models in a realistic problem is a huge and thankless undertaking. As we saw in the data-entry problem, most models turn out to be impractical. I do some trace partitioning as a pedagogical tool in this chapter only.

In practice, it's better to start with some intuitive entities or event threads. Section 4.3.1 suggests some useful kinds of thread to look for. Section 4.4 discusses problem domains involving resource sharing. In that case, we often have a choice: We can give a thread to either each resource user or each resource. Early identification of resources and resource users is especially important when entities hold multiple shared resources at once (Section 4.4.1; Chapter 7).

Once we have found some candidate entities, we need to make sure that each actually represents an event thread and that our thread model accounts for all event occurrences in the problem. Here's a checklist:

1. Do the entities/event threads account for all event occurrences in the problem? If not, find additional entities and/or threads.

2. Do any simultaneous event occurrences belong to different event threads? If not, partition the candidate entities or threads.

3. Is the solution close to optimum? If not, is each event thread justified or can it be eliminated?

4.3.1 Identifying Individual Entities and Event Threads

This section discusses some useful kinds of event threads and general rules of thumb.

4.3.1.1 Operator Threads

An **operator thread**[73] consists of the events where a human[74] operator or user interacts with a system. The operator or user is the entity. Whenever there's such interaction, one or more operator control threads are often a viable design. They typically implement one or more use cases (Section 1.6.1). The ATM system offers one illustration (Section 4.1.2). Other operator threads mentioned in this chapter are the following:

■ The *Operator* thread in the data-entry application (Section 4.2.2.1) is typical. (The solutions with *Block-sequence* and *Block* threads have no operator threads.)

---

[73]"User thread" might be a better name but clashes with "resource-user thread" (Section 4.4.1).
[74]Animals can be operators, too, just as they can be actors (Section 1.6.1.1).

- Both the *Customer* thread and the *Panel* thread in the jukebox example (Section 4.4.2) qualify as operator threads because they capture a human–system interaction. A new *Customer* thread is created for every new customer, while the *Panel* threads are long-lived.

- The *Teller* threads in the bank office queuing system (Section 4.4.3.2) are operator threads. The *Customer* threads in the bank system (Section 4.4.3.1) barely make the cut because their interaction with the system is minimal.

Operator threads are typically implemented as *sequential-activities* threads (Section 4.2.5.1.1). Implicit state representation is often suitable, especially for lengthy operator–system exchanges.

4.3.1.2 Periodic Threads

A periodic event thread is a series of time events indicating when the software must prompt some action in the problem domain. The periodicity can vary over time. For example, there can be an initialization phase of some kind. There are some different kinds of actions:

1. **Sampling** (also known as **polling**) is when the software reads or gauges some external quantity, such as the temperature or pressure of a physical or chemical process. Other examples: the planet rover samples meteorological data at a certain pace and the software in Exercise 2-4, which first locks phase with a certain sine wave and then samples its amplitude periodically.

2. **Output generation** refers to periodical outputs. For instance, music synthesizer software may contain a control thread *metronome* that gives the beat to connected instruments. The weather buoy in Section 5.4.3.2 includes additional examples of output generator threads.

3. **Regulation** is when the software periodically samples some quantity and creates output or takes action based on the values returned. The common case is feedback control. Thus the *speed control* thread in a cruise controller (Section 5.4.3.1) repeatedly senses the current speed, compares it to a desired speed, and adjusts the throttle as needed.

As always, the sampling, generation, and regulation should involve phenomena that are shared by software and the problem domain. It can be implemented as control threads—samplers, generators, and regulators—or by event handlers in languages supporting time events (Section 4.2.1.3).

Note We may feel that the sampling doesn't really belong in the domain. The physical or chemical process is the domain entity, and the temperature and pressure are continuous functions of time. ELM doesn't reach that far into the problem environment, however. It lives in a discrete world, where such functions have been reduced to so many series of samples.

4.3.1.2.1 Organizing Periodic Threads

At times, we can arrange time events so as to simplify the software. Say that each of a large number, N, of sensors must be polled every second. It's often practical to define a number—much less than N—of control threads, each of which polls a number of sensors, one after the other.

A single sampler control thread can poll multiple, different quantities at the same or harmonic frequencies. This reduces the number of threads, but the software may become more difficult to modify. Along the same lines, we could combine sampling, output generation, and/or regulation, especially if the quantities involved are logically related.

In some situations, the sampling frequency is left to the designer. A novice may program a sampler thread with no timing control at all: After taking one sample, the thread loops right back and takes the next. Such a thread never lets up. On a uniprocessor, it will starve all lower priority threads. Multiprocessors may let us get away with some processor monopolization, but it's still poor style.

4.3.1.3 Long-Lived Threads

Some event threads make only brief appearances in a problem. In Model 3 of the data-entry application (Section 4.2.3), each *Block* thread consists of the events for capturing and writing a single block of data. We can create a control thread for each block and destroy it once the block has been stored on disk.

Sometimes, such short-lived threads represent the most intuitive entities. Thus the job in the FMS problem domain (Section 7.3.2) is a prominent and stable abstraction. While *Job* threads aren't as short-lived as the *Block* threads, many *Job* threads are created and destroyed at runtime. An alternative is to consider an architecture with *long-lived* threads defined thus:

> A **long-lived** thread is one that begins its existence when the system is first started and ends its existence when the system is stopped. It may also start or end its existence when the system is reconfigured.

Long-lived threads are common enough. The *Operator*, *Disk*, and *Block-sequence* threads are all long lived and so are the *CD-player* and *Panel* threads in the jukebox (Section 4.4.2.2). The definition allows us to create a fresh *Panel* thread when a new panel is installed, which is system reconfiguration. It can alter the problem's concurrency level.

Note The cost for creating and destroying threads may be negligible, really. But an experienced programmer knows to avoid things that tend to be error prone. Minimizing thread creation is like using fewer moving parts in mechanical design: It keeps us on the safe side.

4.3.2 Example of Thread Identification: Elevator System

It is surprising how often the initial over-simplified model will convey additional insight, to assist in the solution of the problem as a whole.

HOARE, 1985

A multielevator system for a hotel or office building (Section 4.2.2.2) can illustrate thread identification. A number of elevator cabins move in parallel shafts, each serving all floors. We shall name the elevators E1, E2 . . ., the doors D1, D2 . . ., and the floors F1, F2 . . . . To simplify, we shall deal with the following events only:

Ex arrives Fy	Elevator x arrives at floor y.
Ex leaves Fy	Elevator x leaves floor y.
Dx opens Fy	The door of elevator x opens fully at floor y.
Dx closes Fy	The door of elevator x closes fully at floor y.

We shall also assume for now that the system is well behaved such that the doors open only after the elevator arrives at a floor and close before it departs. Here is a possible trace of event occurrences:

E2 arrives F2

D2 opens F2

E3 leaves F1

D2 closes F2

E1 arrives F1

E2 leaves F2

E3 arrives F2

D1 opens F1

D3 opens F2

D1 closes F1

D3 closes F2

E1 leaves F1

E2 arrives F3

E3 leaves F2

E1 arrives F2

Let's attempt to partition the event trace in various ways until we find a valid event-thread model. Each partitioning attempt involves one or more tentative entity types such as *floor*, *elevator*, and *door*.

    1. Floor Entities. Separating the event occurrences by *floor* yields the following:

	E2 arrives F2
	D2 opens F2
E3 leaves F1	
	D2 closes F2
E1 arrives F1	
	E2 leaves F2
	E3 arrives F2

D1 opens F1

D3 opens F2

D1 closes F1

           D3 closes F2

E1 leaves F1

                  E2 arrives F3

      E3 leaves F2

      E1 arrives F2

This approach clearly partitions the event occurrences, for each affects exactly one floor. But the occurrences at a floor aren't necessarily separated in time. For example, *E2 leaves F2* and *E3 arrives F2* can well happen at once. Consequently, the event occurrences at a floor don't form an event thread, so this is *no* legitimate event-thread model.

2. **Simple Elevator Entities and Door Entities.** Partitioning the occurrences into one set per *elevator* and one set per *door* produces the following:

    E2 arrives F2

           D2 opens F2

       E3 leaves F1

           D2 closes F2

E1 arrives F1

    E2 leaves F2

      E3 arrives F2

        D1 opens F1

            D3 opens F2

        D1 closes F1

            D3 closes F2

E1 leaves F1

    E2 arrives F3

      E3 leaves F2

E1 arrives F2

With the occurrences thus realigned, those in each thread are separated in time. But alas, we detect a new flaw: Because each elevator and its doors are synchronized, the partitioning appears more concurrent than it is. An elevator's doors at a given floor open only while the elevator remains stopped at the floor.

3. **Elevator Entities** To remedy this new flaw, we combine the events occurring to each elevator with those occurring at its door. One

event thread for each elevator including its door yields the following partitioning:

	E2 arrives F2	
	D2 opens F2	
		E3 leaves F1
	D2 closes F2	
E1 arrives F1		
	E2 leaves F2	
		E3 arrives F2
D1 opens F1		
		D3 opens F2
D1 closes F1		
		D3 closes F2
E1 leaves F1		
	E2 arrives F3	
		E3 leaves F2
E1 arrives F2		

This is an optimal model. It's as concurrent as the problem itself, no more, no less. In an implementation we may have one control thread per elevator, which handles the door events too. (We could also let interrupt handlers deal with all the events without any control threads.)

More easily than the first two, the third solution can be captured in a key idea: It's driven by *Elevator* threads and looks at the problem and the software from the point of view of an elevator. Likely there will also be *Floor* and *Door* objects. They're always called by an *Elevator* control thread as when an elevator cabin reaches a floor. ELM's rules let us not only eliminate unneeded threads but also achieve an economical and clear architectural style (Section 1.4.2.1).

4.4 EVENT-THREAD PATTERNS FOR RESOURCE SHARING

[E]ach pattern describes a problem which occurs over and over again in our environment, and then describes the core of the solution to that problem, in such a way that you can use this solution a million times over, without ever doing it the same way twice.

ALEXANDER ET AL., 1975

In some problems, we find not only entities or event threads but also *patterns* of interacting entities. Many problems involve resource sharing; at times, entire thread architectures can be based on resource-sharing patterns. This appears to be quite intuitive: In my experience, design teams easily identify resource contention in a problem and model it in software.

ELM recognizes two resource-sharing patterns. These are *analysis patterns* in the sense that they view the problem differently and generate different event-thread models.

- In the **resource-*user*-thread** pattern, *resource-user* threads, each representing a resource-user entity, contend for shared resources. The corresponding control thread blocks on a safe object while waiting for each resource. It's a *sequential-activities* thread because waiting for a resource is a software activity (Section 4.2.5.1.1).

EXAMPLES In a database system, each thread may represent a human operator, while the shared resources are database records. In the data-entry problem, the *Block-sequence* threads represent resource users that need exclusive access to the keyboard and the disk in an alternating fashion.

- In the **resource-*guard*-thread** pattern, *resource-guard* threads represent resources. Such threads are often arranged in a virtual *assembly line* and connected by queues implemented as safe objects.

EXAMPLE In the data-entry application, *Operator* and *Disk* form a circular assembly line with two stations. A buffer object travels along the assembly line and is queued for each resource along the way.

Each pattern ensures that the operations on each shared resource are completed in a serial fashion, without interfering with each other. The patterns are widely used in practice but not under these names.

Each event occurrence where a resource user operates on a shared resource must be included either in a *resource-user* event thread or a *resource-guard* event thread, not both. The definition of an event-thread model forces us to choose one or the other.

As long as each resource user has exclusive access to no more than one resource at a time, the designer can usually choose between a solution with *resource-guard* threads and one with *resource-user* threads. In this sense, the two patterns are dual. Models 1 and 2 of the data-entry problem illustrate this, as do the examples in Sections 4.4.2 and 4.4.3. Resource-sharing patterns are discussed in greater detail in Chapter 6.

The jukebox (Section 4.4.2) illustrates the patterns. In one solution, a new *Customer* thread is started each time a customer begins to pick songs. It waits until any prior song requests have been served and then gains access to the CD player, a shared resource. Each *Customer* thread is kept until all the customer's requests have been played. In the dual solution, the customer uses a thread only (1) while requesting songs and (2) while each song is played. The rest of the time, each request exists as an entry in a queue.

4.4.1 Simultaneous Exclusive Access to Multiple Resources

The resource-user-thread pattern often applies when resource users need exclusive access to more than one resource at a time (Chapter 7). In the FMS

(Section 7.3.2) (Sandén, 1994, 1997a), jobs being processed in a factory have simultaneous exclusive access to multiple resources. In one solution, each job has a resource-user thread, and safe objects guard the resources. *Job* threads waiting for resource access are held in FIFO queues. When one *Job* thread releases a resource, then a waiting *Job* thread, if there is one, is notified. The FMS is a more involved and realistic ELM application than the other problems discussed in this chapter.

4.4.2 Example: Jukebox

The jukebox mentioned in Section 4.1.1 lets customers request songs at the same time from the panels in their several booths and must arrange for the songs to be played one at a time on the CD player. Events in the problem environment include *song selected*, *song ends*, and so forth.

4.4.2.1 Resource-User-Thread Model: A Thread per Customer

Figure 4-2 shows a *resource-user-thread* design as a UML communication diagram (Section 1.6.2.2) (Booch et al., 2005). Each panel starts out with a *Customer* thread that interacts with the first customer who inserts money and requests songs. This thread has exclusive access to the panel until the customer completes the selection. It then creates another *Customer* thread instance for the next customer and requests exclusive access to the player for the first customer's songs. This occurs in the operation *play-songs* on *CD-player*. Each *Customer* thread instance remains until all of a customer's songs have been played.

Figure 4-2 Communication diagram: *Customer* thread design of the jukebox.

Customer is a class of resource-user threads that may be queued for access to the player. The *Customer* threads are also operator threads (Section 4.3.1.1) and are implemented as *sequential-activities* threads.

4.4.2.2 Resource-*Guard*-Thread Model: A Thread per Panel

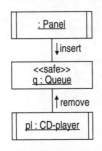

Figure 4-3 Communication diagram: *CD-player* thread design of the jukebox.

Figure 4-3 shows an alternate, *resource-guard-thread* solution. There's a *Panel* thread for each panel resource. It allows customers to enter money and choose songs, which it inserts into the *Queue* object. The thread *CD-player* owns the physical player and successively plays songs from the queue. The resource-guard threads *Panel* and *CD-player* form a little assembly line with two stations (Section 6.3).

4.4.2.3 Comparison of Thread Models and Architectures

At each point in time, the *Customer* thread design has as many threads as there are customers whose songs have been requested but not all played yet plus one per panel. It can theoretically have quite a few threads, but only in the unlikely event of a run on the jukebox with all customers throwing themselves at the panels. *Customer* threads are short lived and are created and destroyed all the time. This is a drawback.

The *Panel* thread design always has as many threads as there are panels plus one for the player. This number is the concurrency level: At any one time, at most one event at each panel and one related to the player can occur. Like *CD-Player*, the *Panel* threads are long lived.

4.4.3 Example: Queuing System for a Bank Office

Many bank offices maintain a single waiting line of customers rather than one per teller position. Each customer gets a numbered ticket from a machine and can sit down or mill about while waiting. Perhaps this is less stressful for tellers than having a row of impatient people bearing right down on them.

A customer entering the office presses a button on the machine, which then issues a ticket with a queue number. Whenever a teller position becomes available, its number is displayed overhead together with the customer number in turn to be served.

The system includes these events: Customer n arrives (cn), teller m gets customer n ($tmcn$), and teller m is done with customer n ($dmcn$). Here is a possible trace of events at the bank office:

Customer 1 arrives	c1
Teller 1 gets customer 1	t1c1
Customer 2 arrives	c2
Teller 2 gets customer 2	t2c2
Customer 3 arrives	c3
Customer 4 arrives	c4
Teller 3 gets customer 3	t3c3
Customer 5 arrives	c5
Customer 6 arrives	c6
Teller 1 done with customer 1	d1c1
Teller 1 gets customer 4	t1c4
Teller 2 done with customer 2	d2c2
Customer 7 arrives	c7
Teller 3 done with customer 3	d3c3

The following event-thread models can be identified:

1. A resource-*user*-thread model with multiple *Customer* threads
2. A resource-*guard*-thread model with *Teller* threads and an *Arrivals* thread that represents all the arriving customers

4.4.3.1 Resource-*User*-Thread Model: A Thread per Customer

Figure 4-4 shows a solution with multiple instances of a resource-user thread *Customer*. From the customers' point of view, the tellers form a resource pool. Multiple *Customer*

Figure 4-4 Communication diagram of the *Customer* thread solution.

threads ($c1$, $c2$, ...) represent the resource users, and the tellers are represented by the singleton safe object *tc* of class *Teller-control*.

The singleton *Teller-control* object is an unencapsulated *semaphore safe object* (Section 2.1.4.2.1.1): It gives each customer exclusive access to a teller but doesn't encapsulate the critical section where the customer and teller interact (Section 6.2.1.2). In this solution, the trace is partitioned as in Figure 4-5.

C1	C2	C3	C4	C5	C6	C7
c1						
t1c1						
	c2					
	t2c2					
		c3				
			c4			
		t3c3				
				c5		
					c6	
d1c1						
			t1c4			
	d2c2					
						c7

Figure 4-5 Bank event occurrences partitioned into *Customer* threads.

4.4.3.2 Resource-*Guard*-Thread Model: A Thread per Teller

Figure 4-6 shows the bank system as a little assembly line with a singleton *Arrivals* thread called *arr* and one thread per teller. Class *Teller* has the instances *t1*, *t2*..., which form a station with multiple servers. The *Arrivals* thread and the *Teller* threads are connected by the *Wait-line* object, which represents the customers waiting to be served. (In an alternate implementation, the *Arrivals* event thread may become a sequence of interrupts, which are handled by *Wait-line*'s operation *get-ticket*.) Figure 4-7 shows the trace of event occurrences partitioned into one event thread *Arrivals* and three *Teller* event threads.

4.4.3.3 Comparison of Thread Models and Designs

It's a drawback that the *Customer* thread solution creates and destroys an endless series of short-lived *Customer* threads. Yet it may be the more flexible solution. Say that we want to simulate the queuing system. We may then be interested in more varied customer behavior, such as when a customer tires of waiting and leaves. For this, a *Customer* thread must be able to take itself out of the queue. This isn't as easily done in the *Teller* thread solution, which doesn't keep track of individual customers. On the other hand, it has a fixed set of long-lived threads.

Many a software architecture has a dominant pattern that defines its *architectural style* (Perry and Wolf, 1992). In a resource-sharing problem, both a resource-guard style and a resource-user style may be possible, as shown by the small illustrations in this section. Quite likely, other event-thread patterns are yet to be discovered that may define thread architectural styles.

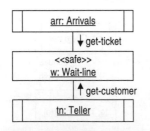

Figure 4-6 Communication diagram of the *Teller* thread solution.

Arrivals	Teller 1	Teller 2	Teller 3
c1			
	t1c1		
c2			
		t2c2	
c3			
c4			
			t3c3
c5			
c6			
	d1c1		
	t1c4		
		d2c2	
c7			
			d3c3

Figure 4-7 Bank event occurrences partitioned into teller threads.

*4.5 PORTRAYING THE WORLD IN SOFTWARE

Unlike arithmetic and school math drill, the computer offers a glimpse into the aesthetic dimension of mathematics and science. And, unlike arithmetic and school math, it provides an expressive medium to which soft masters are drawn.

TURKLE, 1984

Earlier in this chapter, I liken ELM to object orientation: ELM builds thread architectures in the image of concurrency structures in the problem, and object orientation fashions software objects after their counterparts in the domain. Objects and event threads are abstractions that form bridges between the problem world and the software world: An event thread abstracts both a process in the actual world and a control thread in the software.

The object-oriented view oversimplifies many a multifaceted, real-world object—but it's easily implementable. Stronger abstractions exist. For instance, an analyst could allow objects to change their class dynamically and let the programmers implement them as best they could. We don't do this, however, but stick to the conventional, simple model that programming languages support. That's what makes the transition from analysis to design and implementation seamless: All is based on the same categories.

While object orientation invented a new abstraction to capture domain objects, ELM starts with control threads and safe objects as they already exist in various languages and uses them to capture aspects of the problem domain. As with object orientation, the world model is imperfect, but it puts control threads to good use. ELM sides with the software designer who wants an optimum solution given the software tools at hand rather than with the analyst who wants to describe the problem as faithfully and completely as possible without regard to implementation. Event threads have no higher purpose than to help us identify control threads.

Event threads don't map onto control threads one to one, as some event threads can be implemented by event handlers alone. An event thread may also extend beyond a single control thread. In some distributed systems, for instance, it may be implemented as multiple control threads running on different nodes. (For another illustration, see Section 6.4.1.1.)

In object orientation, we don't expect every software class to trace its roots back to a domain class. Frameworks and patterns add their own classes and objects. In fact, classes have proven useful for internal structures as illustrated by the Real-Time Specification for Java (RTSJ; Section 2.2.5) (Bollella and Gosling, 2000; Wellings, 2004). Threads can have similar internal uses, but aren't as versatile and elaborate building blocks as classes. One internal use in the spirit of ELM is the parallelization of algorithms (Section 4.2.3.4).

A usage that generally violates ELM's principles is where threads are subordinated to objects. In some approaches to concurrent object-oriented programming, each object may have a thread that invokes the object's operations for each message (Section 1.3.2.2) (Caromel, 1993). Such a thread may have its benefits but is unrelated to any problem-domain concurrency.

4.6 CONCLUSION

The important thing in science is not so much to obtain new facts as to discover new ways of thinking about them.

Sir William Lawrence Bragg[75]

With reactive systems, the control threads in software can be grounded in concurrent structures found in the problem domain, just as software classes and objects are modeled on domain objects. Entity-life modeling creates control threads in that fashion and at the same time limits the number of thread types and thread interactions. As a result, ELM programs tend to be easy to explain and document. We can usually paint a vivid picture of the software as a whole by describing each thread from beginning to end.[76]

A brief statement that relates control threads to entities in the problem often captures the key idea behind the thread architecture. When I teach ELM, it provides a critical checkpoint: If a student team has developed a viable, central principle of what they want to build, whatever goes wrong later tends to be fixable (Section 1.4.2.1).

ELM is best introduced and explained with small, textbook examples as in this chapter, but it's justified only in larger and more realistic cases. Some are discussed in the next three chapters.

ELM classifies threads and thread patterns in two ways. On the one hand, there are certain kinds of *event* threads; on the other, different sorts of *control* threads. In fact, a single thread may be both an operator thread and a resource-*user* thread and may be implemented as a sequential-activities thread.

Untidy though it may seem to an orderly mind, such is the way of pattern-oriented design—no pigeonholing of threads here. Instead, we want threads to participate in multiple patterns that "dovetail and intertwine to produce a greater whole" (Gamma et al., 1995, p. 358).

---

[75]Quoted in Mackay (1991), which in turn cites Koestler and Smythies (1969), where Holger Hydén is quoted as referring to "Bragg's statement"

[76]This is not the case with any design approach. With data-flow threading, for example, the software is broken into transforms implemented as threads. With such a solution, describing each transform apart is often insufficient; instead, a cross-cutting narrative is added that follows each input on its way from one transform to the next (Section 8.3.2.4.4).

Michael Jackson points out that analysis is rarely a simple matter of breaking a problem into discrete pieces. Teasing the concerns apart is more akin to color separation. With that metaphor, we look at a thread architecture through a concurrent-activities-colored lens and a consistent pattern of activity threads emerges. Likewise, a resource-user-colored lens lets us see patterns of resource-user threads. Without lenses, the patterns may look hopelessly entangled with some threads participating both as activity threads and as resource-user threads.

Strive as I may to explain ELM in pedagogical detail, it's vain to aim for complete sets of rules and exceptions. ELM should be mastered, not pedantically followed. As Pólya (1957, p. 148) writes in *How to Solve It*:

Pedantry and mastery are opposite attitudes toward rules. . . .
To apply a rule with natural ease, with judgment, noticing the cases where it fits, and without ever letting the words of the rule obscure the purpose of the action or the opportunities of the situation, is mastery.

Should the rules conflict or not cover the situation at hand, draw on your own judgment in the spirit of ELM. "Always use your own brains first" (Pólya, 1957, p. 149).

APPENDIX 4A: SUMMARY OF TERMS

A vast new terminology can easily overwhelm the reader. I hope the following summary can help by shedding new light on it. The Glossary is yet another resource.

The main tenet of ELM is that each *control thread* in the software—such as those provided by Ada, Java, and C#—should correspond to an *event thread* in the problem space.

Looking first at the problem, we identify threads of events occurring over time. Reactive systems typically have many such event threads. Together they form an *event-thread model* of the problem.

There are event threads of many kinds. When there's resource sharing in the problem, it's important to identify either *resource-user* event threads or *resource-guard* event threads. The life of a resource-user or resource-guard entity can often be described by a state machine. We shall discuss resource-sharing problems further in Chapter 6.

We can often identify other state machines, too, in the problem domain. In fact, each event thread can be captured as a state machine. The opposite isn't true, because a state machine may define more than one event thread.

Turning now to software implementation, its *thread architecture* consists of *control threads* and safe objects. Only state machines with software activities need control threads; in other cases, event handling by means of a state-machine safe object is sufficient. Chapter 5 explains how a state machine can be implemented. It introduces two important kinds of *control* threads: *activity* threads associated with state-machine safe objects and *sequential-activities* threads. An activity thread implements a software activity in a certain (super)state, while a *sequential-activities* thread represents a series of consecutive software activities throughout the life of an entity.

There's a relationship between certain event threads and event-thread patterns on one hand and the design patterns on the other. So, for example, *resource-user* threads are typically implemented as *sequential-activities* threads, where the wait for a resource is the activity in many a state.

EXERCISES

4-1 Entity and event-thread discovery. Identify useful entities and/or event threads in the following problem sketches. Are they operator entities, resource-user entities, resource-guard entities, periodic threads, or something else? (Each entity/thread can be of more than one kind.) Are different thread models possible? Justify your answers.

(a) In a mail order company, clerks accept orders via phone and enter them into a database. The database also contains such product attributes as style, color, size, availability, and price.

(b) A boy and a girl toss a ball back and forth to each other.

(c) A CD player produces sound by continuously interpreting the data on a compact disk. At the same time, it allows the user to adjust such attributes as the volume and balance by means of various controls.

(d) A server communicates with clusters of terminals. The terminals in each cluster are polled in a given order. Each terminal is given 0.1 second to respond to a poll. (If it doesn't respond in time, it's considered down.) Terminals in different clusters can be polled in any order.

(e) A conveyor belt feeds letters to a mail-sorting device. (Operators along the belt manually put a bar-coded zip code on each letter and place it on the belt.) The device sorts the letters into slots by zip code. The device controls the speed of the conveyor so that it has time to place each letter in its slot before the next one arrives.

4-2 Operator threads. Many examples of systems with operator threads can be found in daily life. Design an appropriate user thread based on your experience with one of the systems described below. Capture the exchange between user and system in either informal structured English or a state diagram and implement it as the control structure of a thread.

(a) An automated gas station. The thread represents an iteration of customers, each going through a series of steps: The customer first uses a credit card reader, which validates the card by calling a clearing center. If the card is accepted, the pump is turned on and the customer selects gasoline quality, uses the nozzle to fill up the car's tank, and hangs up the nozzle. Finally, the charge is communicated to the clearing center and a receipt is printed if the customer so desires.

(b) An ATM. A simplified version of an ATM operator thread is discussed in Sections 4.1.2 and 4.2. Complete the thread by taking into account situations where the transaction is aborted for various reasons.

(c) A vending machine for metro-transit tickets. Some transit systems issue tickets for repeated use. Each ticket holds magnetically registered information that is initialized when the ticket is purchased and updated each time the ticket is used. The vending machine must:
- Accept a used ticket for trade-in
- Accept bills and coins up to a certain maximum amount
- Allow the user to adjust the amount
- Make change, if necessary
- Issue the ticket

Account for various error conditions.

4-3 Bank office simulation. For a simulation of a bank, design a *Customer* thread as discussed in Section 4.4.3.3. After waiting a certain amount of time, the customer may leave with a probability that increases with the wait time.

4-4 Towed-array simulator.[77] Design the thread architecture for an *acoustic simulator* system used for sonar operator training. A towed-array signal-processing system is used to detect and localize submarines. The simulator is used for training purposes when the towing vessel is in port.

A towed array is a long—a significant fraction of a mile—cable with over 100 hydrophones

[77]Adapted from "Towed array acoustic simulator controller (TAASC)" by Denise Chambers, Pete Dietert, Larry Gray, and Howard Morris, George Mason University, 1995.

attached at regular intervals near one end. The other end of the cable is attached to a towing vessel and electrically connected to the towed-array signal processor on board. The system can detect the presence of a submarine as well as additional information about it. (Every submarine emits a slightly different acoustic signature, with energy components at various frequencies corresponding to machinery on board.)

The simulator electrically replaces the towed array and includes five analog signal generators and hundreds of variable delay lines configured so that realistic analog signals for each of the replaced hydrophones can be fed into the towed-array processor.

The simulator is controlled by digital commands that determine the amplitude, frequency, bearing, and other acoustic information for each of the five signals. We're here concerned with the software that controls the acoustic simulator in such a manner that the hydrophone signals that are output from the simulator represent realistic, time-varying, at-sea-like signals.

The software must simulate the movements of the towing vessel and up to five submarines and use resulting range and range-rate information to continuously determine realistic signal amplitudes and Doppler shifts for the acoustic energy emitted by each submarine.

Design patterns based on event threads

5

5.1 INTRODUCTION

My view of software engineering is that it is the discipline of resolving problems with software solutions.

BLUM, 1992

Chapter 4 introduced *event threads* as abstractions for analyzing the problem domains of reactive software systems. Every event thread can be modeled as a state machine, but a state machine can also include multiple, co-occurring event threads defined by *software activities* in individual (super)states. This chapter discusses the design of multithreaded programs based on state machines and introduces design patterns for the following situations:

1. If the state machine has no software activities, it needs no control thread and can be represented by an object. If some of the events are interrupts or time events, it must be a state machine *safe* object (Section 5.2). This is a degenerated case of the *concurrent-activities* pattern.

2. When each software activity is performed in a different state, the state machine together with its activities defines one event thread and can often be implemented as a single control thread. At each point in time, the thread executes the activity defined for the current state. This is the **sequential-activities** pattern (Section 5.3). The control thread can often be implemented with implicit state so that it reads from top to bottom.

3. With co-occurring software activities included in a state diagram, the state machine proper is implemented as a safe object and the activities as multiple activity threads. This is the **concurrent-activities** pattern (Section 5.4). In this case, we use the misalignment between threads and state machines to discover additional threads. Co-occurring activities defined in a state diagram suggest necessary threads that we may not have thought of.

Reactive software must handle each event so quickly that, for practical purposes, it takes no time at all. We say that the event and the actions are *nearly instantaneous*. In other words, we need not deal with events happening during the action (Section 3.6.4.1).

5.1.1 *Software* Activities and *Nominal* Activities

Each (super)state can have one or more activities going on throughout it (Section 3.3.4.2). In some cases, the software merely starts the activity upon state entry and stops it upon exit. In a toaster, for instance, the heating activity may be reduced to turning the heat on when the state is first entered and off when the time expires. Such an activity is *nominal*.

Other activities require software involvement throughout. This is so with computation and may be with periodic activities. Thus a high-end toaster may sense the toast's condition ever so often and recalculate and adjust the heat. Those are *software* activities. We define the two kinds as follows:

> A **nominal activity** is one that requires no software involvement other than for starting and stopping it when the state is entered and exited.

> A **software activity** is one that requires some software involvement throughout the state.

We cannot tell software and nominal activities apart by looking at a state diagram. In the diagram, most activities are indicated by *do/* as in *do/heat*, but action pairs such as *entry/start heating* and *exit/stop heating* are also common (Sections 3.3.4.1.1 and 3.3.4.2). Section 5.1.1.1 discusses how specific software activities are shown in a diagram and implemented.

5.1.1.1 Particular Kinds of Software Activity

A software activity keeps a control thread occupied much of the time. It's plain that a thread is busy when it's computing but it's also occupied when it's waiting for a processor or another resource. In those cases, the thread plays its important role as a queuable resource user. (In ELM, it's often a surrogate for a resource-user entity that needs access to a domain resource; Sections 2.1.4.2.1, 2.2.4, 2.3.2.6, and 6.2). In similar cases, the thread may be waiting for an operation such as a blocking read to complete. Activities of different kinds are further discussed in the following.

5.1.1.1.1 Computation

A computation that's too long to be negligible is an activity and should be tagged by *do/* in a state diagram. Such a computation needs a state that accounts for the time it takes. In the implementation, it needs a control thread that does the computing outside any safe object (Sections 2.1.4.1 and 2.1.4.1.3). With multi-processors, multiple such control threads can run in parallel.

Quite often, the completion of a computation is an event that triggers a state transition and perhaps an action (Section 4.2.1.4.1). To report the event, the activity thread can call an event handler. With multiple threads computing in parallel in a single state, the event that the last one completes may be important.

A simple way to keep track is to let each thread call a certain event handler when it's done and to keep a tally.

5.1.1.1.2 Waiting for Access to Resources and for Blocking Operations

A thread that's waiting for access to a resource sits in a queue or a wait set (in Java; Section 2.2.3). The situation with a blocking read operation or the like is similar: A blocked or queued thread is taken out of commission; it can do nothing. For this reason, such waits are software actitivities even though the thread is actually dormant.

The wait for a resource, *r*, is typically not spelled out as an activity in a state diagram. Instead, an action such as *acquire r* is taken going into a state and the allocation event—*r acquired*—triggers a transition to another state. Access to shared resources is the topic of Chapters 6 and 7. There are two kinds of event-thread models: one with *resource-user* threads and the other with *resource-guard* threads (Section 4.4). A resource-user thread is implemented as a sequential-activities control thread where the activities involve waiting for and using shared resources.

Note The allocation event is detected by the software, which usually goes on to take further action (Section 4.2.1.4.1). This can be handled seamlessly in a sequential-activities thread with implicit state representation (Section 5.3.1). By contrast, assigning a handler to an allocation event may not be as easy.

5.1.1.1.3 Periodic Activities

Many an activity consists of taking some action repeatedly with intervals that are often but not always of constant length. I tend to specify such activities somewhat informally as in *do/display speed every 500 msec.*

Increasingly, languages provide time events and time event handlers similar to interrupt handlers. Thus, RTSJ provides timer classes (Section 2.2.5.3) (Bollella et al., 2000) and Ada 2005 has timing events (Section 2.3.2.5). A state machine safe object can handle time events the same as other events, including interrupts. With built-in time events, an activity such as *display speed every 500 msec* can be replaced in the state diagram by internal actions (Section 3.3.4.1.1) such as

`display-event/display speed; reset display-event`

where **display-event** is the name of the time event.

If a language lacks built-in time events, we can usually create them by means of threads. To create a time event, a thread executes a statement such as *sleep* or **delay** (or **delay until**) and then remains dormant until the event is due. The need for a thread makes the periodic activity a software activity in this case.

When a periodic activity involves computation, it's convenient to let the computing thread do the waiting as well. During the activity *do/maintain speed* in a cruise controller (Section 5.4.3.1), the throttle is actuated periodically, based on a computation of the delta between the current and desired speeds. After the computation, the thread suspends itself until it's time for the throttle adjustment. If necessary, the computation can be cut short so it fits between adjustments (Sections 2.2.5.7.1 and 2.3.3).

Sampling may be the commonest periodic activity (Section 4.3.1.2). It's a standard way to detect event occurrences. Albeit sampling is an activity going on in certain (super)states, it's often not shown in state diagrams. This may be intended to avoid overspecification, as the rest of the diagram often remains the same whether events are detected by sampling or by interrupts.

*5.1.2 A Note on Complexity

The activities patterns build on statecharts. As pointed out in Chapter 3, statecharts go beyond basic state diagramming. They let us create complex state models with activities at different superstate levels and in overlapping superstates. This can be abused, but it's not for me in this book to limit the number of nested states, superstates, and the like. Keeping this under control must be left to the designer (Section 3.4.3 Note; Exercise 3-5).

5.2 STATE MACHINES WITHOUT SOFTWARE ACTIVITIES

An entity whose life is described by a state machine without software activities needs no thread and can be implemented as a *state machine object*. In multithreaded software, such an object can be implemented as a safe class, often—but not always—with a singleton instance. It's a simple version of the **state machine safe object** in Section 5.4.1.

Attributes include a **state variable** (Section 3.7.1), which holds the current state, and **parameter variables,** which can record the results of some actions. For instance, a bicycle odometer state machine object has a variable that holds a reference time (Section 5.2.1.3.1). The state machine safe object can have the following kinds of operations:

1. An **event handler** registers an event occurrence with the state machine object. If the event causes a state transition, the handler updates the state variable and takes any action triggered by the event. Event handlers can deal with interrupts and time events. They can also be called from other state machine safe objects.

   ■ In Ada, a state machine protected object can have protected procedures that are interrupt handlers (Section 2.3.2.4) (Burns and Wellings, 2007) or timing event handlers (Section 2.3.2.5).

   ■ In RTSJ, the operations can be called by asynchronous-event handlers (Section 2.2.5.2) (Bollella et al., 2000).

   Conceptually, the events and actions are instantaneous (Section 3.3.4.3), so the event handling must be *nearly* instantaneous.

2. A **state query** either returns the current state or takes a parameter indicating a (super)state and then returns true exactly when the state machine is in that (super)state.

3. A **parameter query** returns the value of a parameter variable (or some derived value). In the case of the bicycle odometer, it may return the reference time.

Note A state machine object without threads represents an event-driven programming style. This is altogether in the spirit of ELM, which promotes threading in moderation. Other design approaches implement every state machine as a thread serving a queue of event messages from other threads (Section 8.3.2). Such an implementation has no real benefit but typically means that every event occurrence requires two context switches even if it involves no action and no state change.

5.2.1 Examples

The examples below concern the software embedded in simple devices. The entire system consists of a state machine that receives its inputs from interrupts and RTSJ timers (Section 2.2.5.3) or Ada timing events (Section 2.3.2.5).

5.2.1.1 Example: A Simple Fan

A simple fan (Sections 2.3.2.4 and 3.5.1) is controlled by a single button. The fan is initially off. Pressing the button once makes the fan go at high speed. Pressing it once more makes it slow down, and pressing the button yet again stops the fan. Here's an Ada protected object for controlling the fan:

```
protected Fan_Handler is
private
   procedure Handle_Button;
   pragma Attach_Handler (Handle_Button, ...);
   State: State_Type := Off;
end;
protected body Fan_Handler is
   procedure Handle_Button is
   begin
      case State is
         when Off =>
            State := High;
            Motor_Control.High;
         when High =>
            State := Low;
            Motor_Control.Low;
         when Low =>
            State := Off;
            Motor_Control.Stop;
      end case;
   end Handle_Button;
end Fan_Handler;
```

The state machine protected object Fan Handler is nothing more than a handler for the button interrupt, which keeps track of the current state of the fan.

5.2.1.2 Example: Window Elevator for a Car

A car window is manipulated by a lever on the car door (Sandén, 2006). Figure 5-1 is a simplified fragment of the state model in Section 3.5.3 (Figure 3-22).

The window starts in state *Still*. By pushing the lever down, the driver puts the window in state *Prel. down* (short for "preliminary down"). Releasing the lever takes the window back to *Still*.

Auto_Time is the event that the window has spent *Time_Amount* milliseconds in *Prel.down*. It causes the window to enter *Auto down*, where it keeps on opening even after the driver releases the lever.

Figure 5-1 State diagram fragment of the car window.

In an Ada solution, the state machine protected object *Window_Control* controls the window. The handlers for the interrupts *Lever_Down* and *Release* and the timing event handler *Time_Out* are protected procedures. The window's state is kept in the variable *Wstate* of *State_Type*.

The following program fragment includes type and instance declarations and part of the specification and body of *Window_Control*. I have left out the **pragmas** tying the interrupt handlers to the interrupts:

```
type State_Type is (Still, Prel_down, Auto_down, ....);
Auto_Time : Timing_Event;
Time_Amount : constant Time_Span := ....
protected Window_Control is
private
   procedure Lever_Down;                        -- Interrupt handler
   procedure Release;                           -- Interrupt handler
   procedure Time_Out (Event : in out Timing_Event);  -- Timing-event handler
   Wstate : State_Type := Still;                -- State variable with
                                                --    initial value
end Window_Control;
protected body Window_Control is
   procedure Lever_Down is
   begin
   if Wstate = Still then
      Wstate := Prel_down;
      -- Define the timing event Auto_Time, the requisite amount of time
      -- and the handler, Time-Out:
      Set_Handler (Auto_Time, Time_Amount, Time_Out'Access);
      -- Start window motor going down ...
   end if;
end Lever_Down;
procedure Release is
   Cancelled : Boolean;
begin
   if Wstate = Prel_down then
      Wstate := Still;
      Cancel_Handler(Auto_Time, Cancelled);
      -- Stop window motor
```

```
       else ...                   -- For when Release happens in other states
    end if;
end Release;
procedure Time_Out (Event : in out Timing_Event) is
begin
    if Wstate = Prel_down then
        Wstate := Auto_down;
    end if;                        -- Time_Out is ignored in other states
end Time_Out;
end Window_Control;
```

This kind of example shows that Ada 2005's timing events fit right in with interrupt handlers.

5.2.1.3 Example: Bicycle Odometer

A particular bicycle odometer has four states: *Distance*, *Speed*, *Mileage*, and *Time* (Figure 5-2) (Sandén, 2001). In each state, it repeatedly displays one quantity—distance traveled, current speed, total mileage, or elapsed time—with a refresh rate specific to each quantity. (In the program below, the period for the activity in each state is *Distance_Delay*, *Speed_Delay*, and so on.)

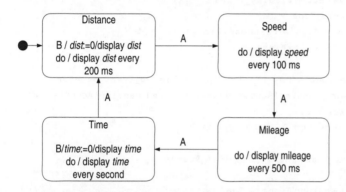

Figure 5-2 Odometer state diagram.

The odometer has two buttons, *A* and *B*. By pressing *A*, the biker switches to the next state cyclically from *Distance* to *Speed* to *Mileage* to *Time* and back to *Distance*. Pressing *B* in *Distance* resets a reference distance. In *Time*, it resets a reference time. *B* has no effect in the other states.

5.2.1.3.1 Bicycle Odometer Solution

In an Ada solution, the protected object *Wheel* (not shown) receives an interrupt every time the bicycle wheel completes a revolution. Its protected functions *Wheel.Dist* and *Wheel.Speed* return the current distance and speed in a type, *Display_Type,* suitable for display. (The procedure *Display* isn't shown.)

The odometer is represented by a protected object *Odometer*. As in the window-elevator solution in Section 5.2.1.2, a timing event (Section 2.3.2.5), here named *Refresh*, triggers display refreshment. Even though each state has its own refresh rate and timing event handler, there's only one timing event. That way, whenever *Set_Handler* is called, the previous *Refresh* timing event is automatically canceled.

A peculiarity with this solution is that the odometer displays nothing until it receives an input from button *A* or *B*. In practice, this can be solved by means of a power-up event or the like.

```
subtype Distance_Type is ...;
type State_Type is (Distance, Speed, Mileage, Time);
subtype Display_Type is ...;
Refresh : Timing_Event;
Cancelled : Boolean;                      -- Return status from Cancel
protected Odometer is
private
   procedure A_Pressed;
   procedure B_Pressed;
   pragma Attach_Handler (A_Pressed, ....);
   pragma Attach_Handler (B_Pressed, ....);
   procedure Distance_Handler (Event : in out Timing_Event);
   procedure Speed_Handler (Event : in out Timing_Event);
   -- and so on
   function Rel_Dist return Display_Type;
   function Rel_Time return Display_Type;
   Ref_Dist  : Distance_Type := 0;
   Ref_Time : Calendar.Time := Calendar.Clock;
   State     : State_Type     := Distance;
end Odometer;
Handler_Array : constant array (State_Type) of Timing_Event_Handler :=
   (Odometer.Distance_Handler'Access, Odometer.Speed_Handler'Access, ...);
protected body Odometer is
   function Rel_Dist return Display_Type is
   begin
      return Display_Type (Wheel.Dist - Ref_Dist);
   end Rel_Dist;
   function Rel_Time return Display_Type is
   begin
      return Display_Type (Calendar. "-" (Calendar.Clock, Ref_Time));
   end Rel_Time;
   procedure A_Pressed is
   begin
      if State = Tyme then State := Distance;
      else State := State_Type'Succ (State);
      end if;
      Set_Handler (Refresh, Time_Span' (Seconds (0)), Handler_Array (State));
      -- Cancel old display. Schedule new display immediately
   end A_Pressed;
   procedure B_Pressed is
   begin
      if State = Distance then Ref_Dist := Wheel.Dist;
      elsif State = Tyme then Ref_Time := Calendar.Clock;
      end if;
   end B_Pressed;
```

```
procedure Distance_Handler (Event : in out Timing_Event) is
begin
    Display (Rel_Dist);
    Set_Handler (Refresh, Delay_Array (Distance), Distance_Handler'access);
    -- Schedule next display
end Distance_Handler;
procedure Speed_Handler (Event : in out Timing_Event) is
begin
    Display (Wheel·Speed);
    Set_Handler (Refresh, Delay_Array (Speed), Speed_Handler'access);
end Speed_Handler;
procedure Mileage_Handler (Event : in out Timing_Event) is ...
procedure Tyme_Handler (Event : in out Timing_Event) is ...
end Odometer;
```

The solution is simple enough, but as any protected specification or body, this one just lists procedures and functions. There's no trace of the state diagram structure. Compare the sequential-activities solution in Section 5.3.3.

5.3 SEQUENTIAL-ACTIVITIES DESIGN PATTERN

If a state machine has at least one software activity but *no co-occurring activities*, we can implement it and its activities together as a **sequential-activities thread**. This thread is the only participant in the *sequential-activities pattern*. At each point in time, the thread executes the activity defined for the current state. (If there's no software activity, the state machine should be implemented as a passive object; Section 5.2).

> A **sequential-activities thread** is a control thread that keeps track of the current state of an entity and performs the software activities defined for the entity sequentially.

Sequential-activities threads are common. Resource-user threads that acquire one resource after the other can often be programmed to that pattern: Waiting for access to a shared resource is a software activity even though the thread actually does nothing (Sections 4.4 and 5.1.1.1.2).

Sequential-activities threads are handy for implementing entity types with multiple instances. They let us get away with a single thread per instance and no safe objects. By contrast, the concurrent-activities pattern gives each instance a state machine safe object as well as activity threads (Section 5.4).

5.3.1 Implicit State in Sequential-Activities Threads

Representation is the essence of programming.

Brooks, 1995

Although a sequential-activities thread could use a state variable to keep track of the state, representing the state implicitly is an attractive option (Sections 3.7.2 and 6.2.2). With implicit representation, the current state of the entity is determined by the current locus of control in the thread's *run* operation or task body. That way, the thread logic, read from top to bottom, can convey much of the structure of the state model.

In some cases, the programmer interface of a language, package, or operating system forces implicit state representation. This is so whenever a call to a system function blocks the calling thread (Section 5.1.1.1.2). That state of blocking exists from the time the program calls the function until it returns, that is, exactly while the program counter is at the call statement.[78] Here are some examples of implicit state representation built into system functions:

1. sleep or **delay**: A Java thread that calls *sleep* or an Ada task that calls **delay** or **delay until** exists in a suspended state from the time the program counter reaches the call until the thread is reactivated and proceeds past the statement.

2. Waiting for access to a shared resource.

3. Blocking I/O.

The sequential-activities implementation of the bicycle odometer in Section 5.3.3 illustrates implicit state representation. Another example is an operator thread (Section 4.3.1.1) that steps through a series of interactions with a human user. Thus an ATM thread may be in a state *S1* when waiting for a card to be inserted, in state *S2* when waiting for a password, in state *S3* when waiting for the user to choose a function, and so on. Identifying and naming all those trivial states is tiresome, unneeded, and sometimes even error prone. We are quite accustomed to such calls appearing one after the other in the program text however.

The *Job* threads in the FMS problem (Section 7.3.2.2) are sequential-activities threads, too. They are chiefly resource-user threads and can spend much of their time waiting for access. Here's a slightly simplified version of the *Job* thread pseudocode:

```
Get information about first job step
   while (not done)
      Acquire workstation instand
      Acquire storage stand
      Acquire forklift
      Travel to storage stand
      Release forklift
      while (True)
         Acquire AGV
         Travel to instand
         Release storage stand or outstand, and AGV
         Wait for job to appear on outstand
         Get information about next job step
         Break from inner loop if job done
         Acquire instand of workstation for next step
      Acquire storage stand        // Continue here when job done
      Acquire AGV
      Travel to storage stand
      Release AGV
      Acquire forklift
      Travel to bin
      Release storage stand and forklift
```

[78]Aside from the time spent executing parts of the function before and after the blocking.

This pseudocode is *structured* in the sense that it consists only of sequential statements, loops, and *if* statements (Section 9.3). An entity that mostly transitions sequentially from one state to a second to a third is a good candidate for implicit state representation. The FMS *Job* does this as it acquires and uses its resources.

Yet another example is the resource-user-thread solution to the home heater (Section 6.5.2.1), where the logic of a heating cycle for a home furnace reads from top to bottom.

5.3.2 Sensing Events That May Change the State

A sequential-activities thread must be able to sense event occurrences that may change the state and/or trigger actions. Allocation events and the completion of a blocking operation are software detected: The thread is alerted when a read operation or a call to a safe object returns control.

The more difficult situation is when the thread is waiting for whichever of multiple events occurs first. Often, one of the events is a time event. In Java, a sleeping thread can be roused by an *InterruptedException* (Section 2.2.1.1). In Ada, the `delay` statement can be part of a timed call (Section 2.3.2.3) on such a protected entry as *Buttons.Pressed* in the body of the *Odometer* task in Section 5.3.3.

Buttons is a safe object acting as a broker: It handles the interrupts and provides operations for the sequential-activities thread to call. Multiple thread instances can often share such a broker object. The need for a broker in addition to the thread takes away from the attraction of the sequential-activities pattern.

Asynchronous transfer of control (Sections 2.2.5.7, 2.3.3 and 5.4.2.2.1) lets a thread break out of a computation when the event occurs. Often it's a time event that prompts a thread to cut short an iterative algorithm and output the best result available.

5.3.3 Example: Odometer as a Sequential-Activities Thread

Common sense and clarity, more than any abstract rule of correct usage, should be the programmer's guide.

COOPER AND CLANCY, 1982

We saw a state machine object solution to the bicycle odometer problem in Section 5.2.1.3. Because each state has a distinct activity, the sequential-activities pattern offers an alternate solution where a thread keeps track of the state (Sandén, 2000). In the Ada solution below, *Odometer* is a sequential-activities task. In the *Distance* state, it displays the distance traveled; in *Speed*, the current speed; and so forth. Each quantity has its own display-refreshing frequency.

The protected broker object *Buttons* handles the interrupts from *A* and *B* and has an entry that *Odometer* uses in a timed call to sense when a button is pressed. A variable of an enumerated type *Button_Type* indicates which button was pressed. *Buttons* is as follows:

```
protected Buttons is                      -- Broker object
   entry Pressed (Button : out Button_Type);
   -- The entry Pressed is called by the Odometer task
```

```
private
   procedure A_Pressed;
   procedure B_Pressed;
   pragma Attach_Handler (A_Pressed, ....);
   pragma Attach_Handler (B_Pressed, ....);
   Occurred : Boolean := False;
   Which_Occurred : Button_Type;
end;
protected body Buttons is
   entry Pressed (Button : out Button_Type)
      when Occurred is
   begin
      Button := Which_Occurred;
      Occurred := False;
   end;
   procedure A_Pressed is                    -- Handler for button A
   begin
      Occurred := True;
      Which_Occurred := A;
   end;
   procedure B_Pressed is                    -- Handler for button B
   begin
      Occurred := True;
      Which_Occurred := B;
   end;
end;
```

The *sequential-activities* task *Odometer* spends most of its time suspended and uses a timed entry call (Sections 2.3.2.3 and 5.4.2.2.1) to sense when the *A* or *B* button is pressed during the suspension.

The state is represented implicitly, so each state corresponds to a portion of the program text. Thus, the odometer is in the state *Distance* exactly while control remains within the loop *D*. State transition corresponds to the **exit** statement transferring control to the construct related to the *Speed* state.

```
task body Odometer is
   Ref_Dist     : Distance_Type := Wheel.Dist;
   Ref_Time, Next : Time := Clock;
   Button          : Button_Type;
begin
   loop
      Next := Clock + Dist_Delay;
      D: loop                               -- Distance state
         select Buttons.Pressed (Button);   -- Timed-entry call
            case Button is
            when A => exit;                  -- Exit to Speed state
            when B => Ref_Dist := Wheel.Dist;  -- Reset the reference distance
            end case;
```

```
        or delay until Next;
            Display (Wheel.Dist - Ref_Dist);
            Next := Next + Dist_Delay;
        end select;
    end loop D;
    Next := Clock + Speed_Delay;
    S: loop                                    -- Speed state
        select Buttons.Pressed (Button);       -- Timed-entry call
            case Button is
            when A => exit;                    -- Exit to Mileage state
            when B => null;                    -- Ignore B button
            end case;
        or delay until Next;
            Display (Wheel.Speed);
            Next := Next + Speed_Delay;
        end select;
    end loop S;
    -- etc., for the Mileage and Time states
    end loop;
end Odometer;
```

With such a simple state machine and absent co-occurring activities, this implicit-state program is attractively straightforward even though it needs a broker object for the interrupt handling.

We could also implement the *Odometer* task with a state variable, *State*, say, of an enumerated type that takes the values *Distance*, *Speed*, and so on. *Odometer* would then contain a loop with a case statement over the different values of *State*. But without implicit state representation, it's more difficult to justify a task, and we may as well revert to the implementation in Section 5.2.1.3.

Solutions with a thread or task representing the odometer have the little advantage that the odometer can begin displaying the distance as soon as the program starts. This takes some extra doing otherwise.

5.4 CONCURRENT-ACTIVITIES DESIGN PATTERN

A state machine that includes co-occurring activities can be accommodated in the concurrent-activities pattern. Its participants are the **state machine safe object** and **activity threads**. They are further described in Sections 5.4.1 and 5.4.2. An automobile cruise controller and other examples are covered in Section 5.4.3.

5.4.1 State Machine Safe Objects Revisited

State machine safe objects were introduced in Section 5.2 for the simple case without software activities. Here is the full treatment.

A state machine safe object's attributes include a **state variable**, which holds the current state, and **parameter variables,** which can record the results of some actions. Thus, in a cruise controller, a parameter variable may contain the desired speed (Section 5.4.3.1.3). The operations are of the following types:

1. An **event handler** registers event occurrences. If an event causes a state transition, the handler updates the state variable and notifies

any threads blocked on that state change. It also takes any action triggered by the event occurrence. One event handler can contain calls to others.

Event handlers can deal with interrupts and other events such as time events:

■ In Ada, a state machine protected object can have protected procedures that are interrupt handlers (Section 2.3.2.4) (Burns and Wellings, 2007) or timing-event handlers (Section 2.3.2.5).

■ In RTSJ, the operations can be called by asynchronous-event handlers (Section 2.2.5.2) (Bollella et al., 2000).

Event handlers can also be invoked by activity threads, such as samplers (Sections 4.3.1.2 and 5.1.1.1.3). Thus the cruise controller may have a thread that samples the driver's controls and reports any newly pressed or newly released button by calling an event handler.

2. A **state query** either returns the current state or takes a parameter indicating a (super)state and then returns true exactly when the state machine is in that (super)state.[79]

3. A **state wait operation** blocks the calling thread until a certain (super) state is entered. (It must be called by a thread, not by an interrupt handler.)

4. A **parameter query** returns the value of a parameter variable (or some derived value). In the case of the cruise controller, it may return the current, desired speed.

5. A **state-dependent operation** is helpful if an activity defined for a superstate has different effects in different substates. It may be that the activity must continue at a given periodicity independent of substate but take effect only in certain substates. For instance, a periodic output may be suspended in an emergency substate (Section 5.4.3.2).

Operations must sometimes be combined. Thus a state query may have to return both the state and a parameter value. This is common with multithreading because a thread must exchange all required information with a safe object in one go while it has the object locked. (If the thread were to make two calls, another thread might intervene and change variable values.)

As we saw in Section 5.1, all the operations on a state machine safe object must be *nearly* instantaneous (Section 3.6.4.1). In any reactive system, the operations on a safe object should always be kept short. A safe object works on the assumption that no thread ever holds it locked for a significant amount of time (Section 2.1.4.1).

An operation that isn't nearly instantaneous is deemed a software activity and implemented in a thread. The state machine must include a state where the entity waits for the operation to complete.

---

[79] With overlapping superstates (Section 3.4.5.2) we can make any set of states a superstate.

5.4.2 Activity Threads

An **activity thread** is a control thread that implements one or more software activities associated with a state machine safe object.

As a rule, each co-occurring software activity needs its own activity thread. Even a single state can define two or more co-occurring activities, each of which may require an activity thread. Computation actitivities that can be performed in parallel may need separate threads for that reason. A superstate-related activity often warrants its own thread, as in the following two situations:

- When one activity is defined for a superstate and another for a substate
- When the activities are defined for overlapping superstates (Section 3.4.5.2)

Activities belonging to different states can sometimes be combined in one control thread. In the cruise controller, the activities *maintain speed* and *increase speed* are defined for different states, so they are mutually exclusive. Because they are also semantically related by operating on the throttle, we can conveniently let them share one control thread called *speed-control*. The change of activities at state transitions is often much easier if activities in the old and the new states are handled by the same thread(s) as is the case with *maintain speed* and *increase speed*. Otherwise, an elaborate and costly *state change protocol* may be needed, which may penalize all threads.

5.4.2.1 Multiple Instances of a State Machine Safe Class

A state machine safe class can have multiple instances—N, say—if the corresponding entity type has N instances. Each activity thread may then also exist in N instances. Sometimes, a single activity thread can implement a certain activity for multiple instances of a state machine safe class and call each instance's event handlers: Thus, one activity thread may well be able to do the sampling for multiple state machines.

*5.4.2.1.1 Resource-Dependent Activities

With N instances of some entity type, an activity may be constrained by shared resources so that no more than n of the instances (with $n < N$) can engage in it at once. If so, n activity threads can each handle one instance at a time while the others await their turn in a different state. The home heater in Section 6.5.2.2 offers an example—if somewhat contrived. Often, $n = 1$ so that only one instance at a time can proceed.

We typically want to keep the waiting instances in a queue organized as FIFO or perhaps FIFO within priorities. This is discussed in connection with the resource-guard-thread pattern in Section 6.3.

5.4.2.2 Communication with State Machine Safe Object

An activity thread normally communicates with the state machine safe object by calling its operations and detects state transitions through state query or state wait operations. In the simplest case, the thread queries the state periodically at a constant pace. This is handy with threads that perform some periodic action anyway. The *speed control* thread in the cruise controller is again an example (Section 5.4.3.1.3).

*5.4.2.2.1 Communication Initiated from State Machine Safe Object

Sometimes, an operation on the state machine safe object must communicate with an activity thread immediately. How this can be done is language dependent. In Java, an *InterruptedException* can be thrown to the activity thread (Section 2.2.3). In RTSJ, there's also the *AsynchronousInterruptedException* (Section 2.2.5.7).

In Ada, we can achieve the same effect by letting an activity task make a timed or conditional call on a state wait entry (Section 2.3.2.3). There are two cases as follows:

1. If a task is suspended until a point in time, *Next*, say, it may need to be awakened prematurely. For this, it can use a timed entry call. The following excerpt assumes that E is a state wait entry in the state machine object SM:

```
select SM.E;
    [optional sequence of statements]
or
    delay until Next;
end select;
```

E's barrier is normally closed, and the task is delayed until *Next*. If E's barrier opens, E executes the optional sequence of statements (if provided) and then continues after **end select**. This arrangement is useful if a thread's period may change. If it's shortened, the thread may have to be awakaned and take its action sooner than planned (Section 6.5.1.1).

2. The activity thread may need to be interrupted during computation. It can then use an asynchronous select statement (Section 2.3.3) such as the following:

```
select SM.E;
    [optional sequence of statements]
then abort
    <abortable sequence of statements>
end select;
```

The computation that may need to be interrupted is placed at <abortable sequence of statements>. When E's barrier opens, the call SM.E is accepted, the abortable sequence of statements aborts, and the optional sequence of statements executes. After the optional sequence, processing continues after **end select**. One case where this may be necessary is when an operator can cancel a command before it completes.

5.4.2.3 Activity-Thread Creation

We don't normally create an activity thread every time the activity's state is entered (and destroy it when the state is exited). It's more practical to create threads when the program starts or when a superstate is entered.

A *long-lived* thread is one that—essentially—exists as long as the whole system does (Section 4.3.1.3). In the examples in Section 5.4.3, allocating long-lived threads once and for all is a reasonable solution. In Ada, such threads are defined statically.

5.4.3 Examples

A great discovery solves a great problem but there is a grain of discovery in the solution of any problem.

Pólya, 1957

5.4.3.1 Cruise Controller

A cruise controller is a well-known device that offers a straightforward illustration of the *concurrent-activities* pattern. It has been a favorite guinea pig for experimentation in reactive-software design since the early 1980s (Atlee and Gannon, 1993; Awad et al., 1996; Birchenough and Cameron, 1989; Bollinger and Duffe, 1988; Caromel, 1993; Carter, 1989; Gomaa, 1993, 1994, 2000; Hatley and Pirbhai, 1987; Jones, 1989, 1990, 1994; Magee and Kramer, 2006; Mellor and Ward, 1986; Sandén, 1994; Sandén and Zalewski, 2006; Shaw, 1995a, b; Wellings, 2004; Yin and Tanik, 1991). See also Section 8.3.4.

The classic cruise controller problem is stylized and reflects the state of automotive engineering in the 1980s. It's a stand-alone system that determines the speed of the car by means of its own sensors. At the current state of the art, electronic subsystems can provide such data. (Automotive technology has moved on to more demanding closed-loop systems for engine control and for stability control—and from there to collision avoidance and autopilots.)

5.4.3.1.1 Cruise Controller Problem Description

The cruise controller regulates the speed of a car with automatic transmission by adjusting the throttle periodically. The driver sets a desired speed in an analog fashion by either pressing or releasing a button when the car reaches that speed. This is the event *cruise*. By holding down a button, the driver can also let the cruise controller accelerate the car. Pressing the button causes the event *accel*.

The driver can override cruise control by pressing the accelerator. The action of the accelerator on the throttle then physically overtakes the action of the cruise controller. (The throttle is controlled by means of a wire.) Automatic cruise control resumes as soon as the driver steps off the accelerator.

The cruise controller receives a signal when the driver brakes; it then suspends cruising. The driver can later *resume* cruising at the earlier defined, desired speed. This arrangement affords sufficient system safety: Should anything go wrong with the automatic control, the driver can always disable it and reach a *safe state* by touching the brake pedal. The driver can also turn cruising off.

The cruise controller gets the speed of the car from some device connected to the driveshaft.[80] The opening of the throttle needn't be proportional

---

[80]In reality, the system should have at least two independent means of determining the speed. In a modern car, the cruise controller may have electronic access to the speed as well as other quantities such as the torque.

to the difference between the actual and desired speeds. The calculation can also take into account speeds recorded over a period of time and thereby allow proportional-integral control.

There are some time-critical aspects to the cruise controller. Thus, if the speed is calculated by counting driveshaft revolution interrupts, each interrupt must be handled before the next one comes. There are, however, no *conflicting* deadlines that would justify elaborate thread scheduling (Section 8.2.2.1) (Klein et al., 1993). Throttle adjustment isn't deadline dependent. Small variations around the average time between adjustments are more acceptable than adjustments that are always made within a predefined period but with considerable jitter (defined in Section 8.2.2.1.2).

This classic cruise controller has no potential complications such as multiple computers or multiprocessors. A simple software structure with a few threads and objects is perfectly suitable.

5.4.3.1.2 Cruise Controller State Model

The behavior of the cruise controller can be captured in a state diagram.[81] Figure 5-3 shows that the controller enters the *Initial* state when the ignition is turned on. When the driver selects *accel*, the controller enters *Accelerating* where it normally remains until the driver selects *cruise*. At that point the controller saves the current speed and enters *Cruising* where it maintains the speed automatically. If the driver selects *accel* while the controller is in *Cruising*, it reenters *Accelerating*. If the driver brakes while the controller is in the superstate *Automated control*, it transitions to *Cruising suspended*. Then, if the driver selects *resume*, the controller reenters *Cruising*, unless the brake is being operated. If the driver selects *off*, the cruise controller returns to *Initial*.

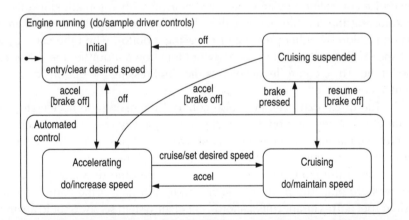

Figure 5-3 Cruise-control state diagram assuming that the driver-control events cause interrupts. [Based on a similar diagram in Sandén and Zalewski (2006).] In an alternate design, a sampling activity would be defined for the superstate as indicated by (do/sample driver controls).

[81]This diagram is close to one used in a data-flow-based solution discussed in Section 8.3.4.

5.4.3.1.3 Cruise Controller Software Design

The ELM recipe for a problem such as the cruise controller is the concurrent-activities pattern. The state diagram is implemented in a safe class *Cruise-control* with a singleton instance. The diagram includes three software activities: *sample driver controls*, *increase speed*, and *maintain speed*. As discussed in Section 5.4.2, *increase speed* and *maintain speed* are combined in the activity thread *speed-control*.

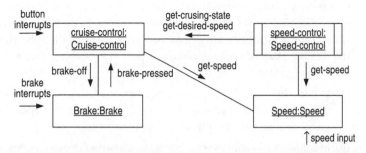

Figure 5-4 Cruise controller communication diagram. [Based on a similar diagram in Sandén and Zalewski (2006).]

The state diagram can lead us to further classes if we identify things that the cruise controller must interface to or maintain data about. The communication diagram in Figure 5-4 shows the interactions between the following objects, all singleton instances of their respective classes:

Safe Class *Cruise-control*; Singleton Instance *cruise-control*

■ The variable *state* has a unique value for each state in Figure 5-3 (except the superstates). The variable *desired-speed* contains the current desired speed.

■ There's a handler for each of the events *accel, resume, cruise, off,* and *brake-pressed*. They can be called either by sampler threads or as a result of interrupts.

■ The state query *get-cruising-state* returns one of the values *Initial, Accelerating, Cruising,* and *Cruising suspended*.

■ The parameter query *get-desired-speed* returns the desired speed.

Safe Class *Brake*; Singleton Instance *brake*

■ *brake* hides the brake–sensor interface and has a state variable that indicates whether the brake is currently applied.

■ The event handler *press* takes the object from state *Unpressed* to state *Pressed* and calls *cruise-control.brake-pressed*. The operation *release* takes the object back to state *Unpressed*. We assume that *brake.press* and *brake.release* are interrupt handlers.

■ The Boolean state query *brake-off* returns true if the brake is currently in the *Unpressed* state and false otherwise. This corresponds to a condition in the diagram in Figure 5-3.

Safe Class *Speed*; Singleton Instance *speed*

- *speed* hides how the current speed is determined and has the operation *get-speed*, which is a safe operation in case speed determination should involve threads not included in this discussion.

Class *Speed-control Extends Thread*; Singleton Instance *speed-control*

- *speed-control* implements the algorithms for maintaining and increasing speed defined in the private operations *maintain-speed* and *increase-speed*. *Speed-control*'s *run* operation defines a periodic thread, which queries the state of cruising once per period by calling *cruise-control. get-cruising-state*.

  (a) When the state is *Cruising*, *speed-control* calls *speed.get-speed* and *cruise-control.get-desired-speed*, computes the speed difference, and adjusts the physical throttle accordingly.

  (b) In state *Accelerating*, *speed-control* maintains constant acceleration.

The software as described here has a single thread and a few objects. If the input required sampling, there would be additional threads.

5.4.3.1.4 State Modeling and Control Laws

The cruise controller illustrates the separation of concerns between a state model and a control algorithm (also called a control *law*), such as the one that computes the pull on the throttle as a function of the speed difference (and possibly other inputs). This issue is common to many control problems.

In Figure 5-3, the cruise controller is in *Cruising* whenever it's attempting to maintain a desired speed automatically. The control algorithm may have internal states, such as where the actual speed is much lower than the desired speed and where it's much higher (as when driving downhill). The algorithm may be different in each state or may adjust continuously. In the spirit of separation of concerns, we let the algorithm *maintain-speed* worry about this.

The state modeler doesn't know and shouldn't care about the workings of the control algorithm. This is the separation of concerns. The state model and the control algorithm are different software modules and should have the simplest interface possible. The control algorithm shouldn't normally have to report its internal states to the state machine module.

5.4.3.2 Example: Weather Buoy

In this example, a number of free-floating buoys broadcast navigation and weather data to air and ship traffic at sea (Booch, 1986; Sandén, 1989a, 1994). Under normal circumstances, each buoy makes a periodic, *regular transmission* of current wind, temperature, and location information every minute on the minute.

In addition, a passing vessel may request a *history transmission* of all data collected over the last 24 hours. This transmission may go on for several minutes and takes precedence over the regular transmission.

Moreover, a sailor in distress who physically reaches the buoy may engage an emergency switch and initiate an *emergency transmission* that continues until it's explicitly reset. The emergency transmission takes precedence over all other transmissions.

This kind of system that collects data from sensors for subsequent processing and analysis is known as a *data acquisition system* (Sommerville, 2007). The weather buoy also falls in the category of *repository* problems discussed in Section 6.7.

5.4.3.2.1 Weather Buoy State Model

The state diagram in Figure 5-5 shows the three transmission states *Regular* and *History* (both in the superstate *Normal*) and *Emergency,* as well as the transitions described above. Each state has an activity, whether regular transmission, history transmission, or emergency transmission.

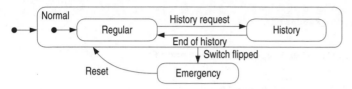

Figure 5-5 Buoy state diagram.

5.4.3.2.2 Weather Buoy Solution[82]

An Ada solution has the following three activity tasks: *Regular*, *History*, and *SOS*, output generators all:

- *Regular* prepares a regular transmission every 60 seconds and then calls the state-dependent operation *Reporter.Regular_Msg*, which sends the message if the buoy is in state *Regular*. (This has the advantage that *Regular* can stay on schedule throughout.)

- *History* blocks on the state wait operation *Reporter.Hold_History* while waiting for a history request and then repeatedly calls *Reporter. History_Msg* with history data messages until the relevant history information has been exhausted. It then again blocks on *Hold_History*.

  History_Msg is a state-dependent operation. It transmits history messages while the buoy is in state *History* and suppresses them in *Emergency*.

- *SOS* repeatedly generates an *SOS* message and calls *Reporter.SOS_Msg*, which is a state wait operation with a barrier that lets calls through in the *Emergency* state alone.

In Ada, the state machine protected object *Reporter* is as follows:

```
type State_Type is (Regular, History, Emergency);
protected Reporter is
    procedure Regular_Msg (....);      -- Regular, periodic msg
    procedure History_Request;         -- Request for history data
    entry History_Msg (....);          -- Send history message
    entry Hold_History;    -- State wait operation for History_Task
    entry SOS_Msg (....);  -- Send SOS if needed (state wait operation)
    procedure Reset;       -- Emergency reset
```

---

[82]This solution was suggested by Alan Brown (George Mason University, Spring quarter 1991). At the time, I had a sequential-activities solution (Sandén, 1994). Alan suggested one with a thread per output type and a protected object serving as a filter that lets the appropriate output through in each state. (See also "key idea," Section 1.4.2.1.)

```
private
   procedure Switch;              -- Emergency switch flipped
   pragma Attach_Handler (Switch, ...);
   State : State_Type := Regular;
end Reporter;

protected body Reporter is
   procedure Regular_Msg (....) is
   begin
      if State = Regular then <send message>[83] end if;
   end;
   procedure History_Request is
   begin
      if State = Regular then State := History; end if;
   end;
   entry History_Msg (....) when True is
   begin
      if <end of messages> then
   if State = History then State := Regular; end if;
   requeue Hold_History;          -- For requeue see 2.3.2.2
      elsif State = History then
         <send message>;
      end if;
   end;
   entry Hold_History (....) when State = History is
   begin
      null;
   end;
   procedure Switch is
   begin
      State := Emergency;
   end;
   entry SOS_Msg (....) when State = Emergency is
   begin
         <send message>
   end;
   procedure Reset is
   begin
      if State = Emergency then State := Regular; end if;
   end;
end Reporter;
```

   The *History* task illustrates the awkwardness of the state change. When
Emergency is entered, *History* continues with its output suppressed until it has
exhausted its data. Making *History* and *SOS* into one task would eliminate the
overlap but seems rather inelegant and unintuitive because the two tasks aren't
closely related semantically.

[83]If <send message> were a blocking operation, *Regular_Msg* would be an entry.

As an alternative, *History* could requeue on *Hold_History* when *Emergency* is entered. When the *History* state is reentered later, the *History* task would resume the interrupted broadcast. This may or may not be desirable because the emergency broadcast may continue for some time.

5.5 COMMUNICATING STATE MACHINES

Some systems can be modeled as networks of state machines. The network may reduce to a chain as in the toy car factory in Section 5.5.1.1, where each workstation along a production line is an entity represented as a state machine and implemented as a safe object. Once a workstation has delivered the toy car in the making to its downstream neighbor, it alerts the state machine representing the upstream workstation by calling one of its event handlers.

The workstations could be represented as orthogonal regions in one state machine (Section 3.4.4), but I find it easier and clearer to treat them as different objects that call each other's operations (Section 3.4.4.2.1). This makes for flexible, loose coupling of the state machine implementations.

By and large, the state machines can be implemented as safe objects (Section 5.4.1) or as sequential-activities threads (Section 5.3). The assumption is that the workstations operate concurrently, each on a different item. In steady state, as many toy cars are under construction as there are workstations. For this reason, activities at one workstation will co-occur with any activities at other workstations.

State machine chains are somewhat similar to the virtual assembly lines of *resource-guard* threads discussed in Section 6.3. The difference is that those assembly lines involve queuing.

5.5.1 Communicating State Machines without Activities

A simple system such as the toy car factory can be controlled by software that handles interrupts and time events and issues commands. There are no activities. Such software can be implemented by a network of state machine safe objects without activity threads (Section 5.2).

The state machine safe objects can communicate by calling each other's event handlers and state and parameter queries. They cannot call state wait operations (Section 5.4.1) because they lack threads that can be queued during the wait.

5.5.1.1 Example: Toy Car Factory

The Division of Automatic Control at Linköping University in Sweden http://www.control.isy.liu.se uses a factory of simple toy cars for student laboratory exercises (Strömberg, 1991). The factory is put together from LEGO® blocks, as are the cars. Figure 5-6 shows the little assembly.

Each station hands over one car in the making at a time to the next station. The hand-over proceeds from the end of the assembly line to the beginning. Stations can operate concurrently on their assemblies but must await the slowest station downstream before handing over the assembly to the next station in line. In other words, a station that has done its processing is blocked until the downstream station is ready.

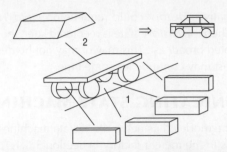

Figure 5-6 Toy car assembly: The chassis blocks (1) are pressed onto the bottom block. The roof (2) is pressed onto the chassis. (From Strömberg, 1991. Used by permission.)

Figures 5-7 and 5-8 show the first half of the little factory. The cars are assembled at a series of stations along a conveyor which moves from right to left in Figures 5-7 and 5-8:

- A pusher pushes bottom blocks from a store onto the conveyor. (The pusher motor E1 is also shown.) An optical sensor (F1) detects when the store is empty.

- Another pusher pushes chassis blocks from a store onto each bottom. Its motor is indicated as E3. An optical sensor (F2) detects when the store is empty.

- A mechanical stop and an optical sensor (F3) control the position of a bottom on the conveyor. The sensor indicates only that a bottom is present while the stop ensures that the bottom is placed in the exact position for chassis blocks to be attached on top of it. Motor E2 moves the stop forward (into position) and back (out of the way).

- The press is powered by motor E5 and secures the chassis blocks to the bottom block. The stop is driven by motor E4. The optical sensor F4 signals that the bottom block is in position.

- The turner flips the toy car over for part 2 of the assembly line. (Part 2 isn't shown.)

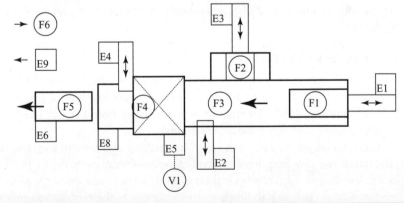

Figure 5-7 Layout of part A of the toy car factory. (From Strömberg, 1991. Used by permission.)

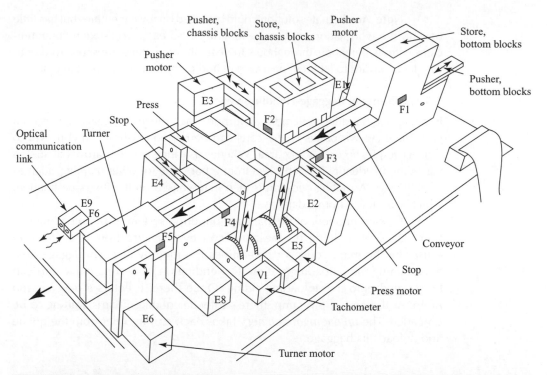

Figure 5-8 Perspective drawing and plan of part A of the toy car factory. (Translated from Strömberg, 1991. Used by permission.)

5.5.1.1.1 Toy Car Factory: Solution

The production line can be modeled as a chain of state machines, each of which can be implemented as a safe object. For instance, the *Bottom-station* state machine handles the following events:

- Main switch on/off
- Bottoms store empty/nonempty
- Chassis station ready (for a bottom to be pushed in place)
- Bottom pusher in forward/back position

The *Bottom-station* safe object sends commands to the bottom-pusher motor. The *Chassis-station* state machine handles the following events:

- Bottom at stop (interrupt from optical sensor F3)
- Chassis store empty/nonempty
- Press ready
- Chassis pusher in forward/back position
- Press station ready (for bottom and chassis to proceed beyond stop)
- Stop in forward/back position

The *Chassis-station* safe object sends commands to the chassis pusher and the stop and calls the *Bottom-station* safe object's handler for the event *Chassis station ready*.

Note An alternate solution could be based on toy car entities but has little benefit. The workstation entities are long lived, so each workstation communicates with its neighbors throughout. Toy cars in the making are short-lived entities. It's awkward to let them be aware of and communicate with each other.

5.5.1.2 Example: Baggage-Handling System

In a baggage-handling system for an airport, each piece of luggage travels on a cart. There are waypoints where carts can be routed off the main conveyor to a baggage pickup or loading area. Whenever a luggage item arrives at such a waypoint, its identity is established from a bar code (or other marking, such as an RFID tag). A routing decision is then made based on the item's destination, which is retrieved from a database.

One component of the baggage-handling system is an unloading station placed at a siding off the main conveyor (Figure 5-9). A *destination sensor* by the main conveyor determines the identity of each luggage item approaching the unloading station. Depending on its destination, a cart can be shunted onto the unloading siding. Once there, it enters a *deceleration ramp*. At the end of the ramp, there's a feeder queue of carts waiting to be unloaded. The *unloading machinery* takes each cart in order from the queue and unloads its baggage.

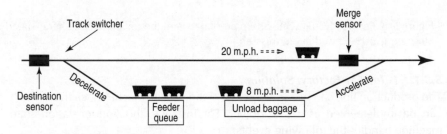

Figure 5-9 Unloading station.

After unloading, the cart is placed in a queue of empties to be merged back onto the main conveyor (Figure 5-10). Each cart needs a lull in traffic for at least *N* seconds in order to merge. For this, a *merge sensor* along the main conveyor creates an interrupt for each cart that passes by it. The distance between this point and the merge point is an exclusion zone that takes *N* seconds to travel. As soon as the exclusion zone is free of traffic, an empty cart can accelerate along an *acceleration ramp* onto the main conveyor.

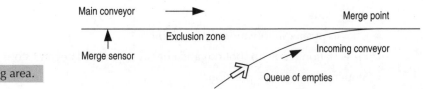

Figure 5-10 Merging area.

The parts of the unloading station form a set of communicating state machines. There's no need for the state machines of different loading and unloading stations to communicate. The stations are only coupled by the stretches of conveyor that connect them.

5.5.1.2.1 Solution Sketch for Baggage-Handling System

The controlling software for the unloading station can consist of objects that perform the following functions:

- A *track-switcher* safe object handles the interrupts from the destination sensor and manages the track switcher. It calls *feeder-queue* to report the arrival of a new cart.

- The safe object *feeder-queue* maintains a count of carts in the feeder queue. (To guard against the queue overflowing, it must also have the means to either stop the main conveyor or turn off the track switcher.)

- Depending on the details of the unloading, the *unloader* may be implemented as a safe object or as a sequential-activities thread that pends on *feeder-queue*. When a cart is available, *unloader* takes it through the unloading steps, then moves it to the merge queue, and finally calls an event handler on *merger* indicating a new cart. This activates the thread *merger* if it's in its *Open* state (Figure 5-11).

- *merger* launches empty carts ("empties") when the exclusion zone is free of traffic. This is discussed in some detail in Section 5.5.1.2.2.

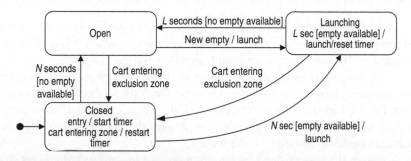

Figure 5-11 State diagram of the merging operation.

5.5.1.2.2 Merging Operation

Figure 5-11 is a state diagram of *merger*. It's in state *Open* if there's no cart in the exclusion zone and no cart is being launched. It's in *Closed* if there may be a cart in the exclusion zone. An empty that arrives while *merger* is in *Open* is launched onto the main conveyor, putting *merger* in *Launching* for the amount of time (L seconds, with $L < N$) necessary to launch the cart. As soon as a cart enters the exclusion zone, *merger* transitions to *Closed*.

If *merger* is still in *Launching* when the cart has been launched and another empty is available, *merger* launches it and remains in *Launching*. If no empty is available, *merger* transitions to *Open*. When a cart enters the exclusion zone, *merger* remains in *Closed* for N seconds. After N seconds have passed, an empty may or may not be waiting. If one is waiting, it's launched, and *merger* transitions to *Launching*. If there's none, it transitions to *Open*.

5.5.2 Communicating state machines with activities

A network or chain of communicating state machines may include state machines with software activities. Each machine can be implemented to either the sequential-activities pattern (Section 5.3) or the concurrent-activities pattern (Section 5.4). An activity thread or sequential-activities thread can call state wait operations on other state machine safe objects in the network.

The example in Section 5.5.2.1 uses the concurrent-activities pattern because of co-occurring activities.

5.5.2.1 Production Line Workstation

In an environment like the distributed factory automation system in Gomaa (1993), a number of workstations are arranged along a production line with a conveyor as shown in Figure 5-12. Except for the first and last ones, each workstation, *W1*, sits between an upstream workstation, *W0*, and a downstream workstation, *W2*. I'll refer to *W1* as a prototypical workstation.

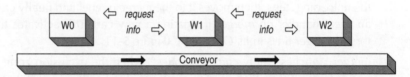

Figure 5-12 Production line showing the workstation communication.

Each workstation has a microprocessor, a pick-and-place robot, and an assembly robot. An item on the conveyor trips a sensor when it gets close to a workstation. This generates an interrupt, signaling the event *arrived*.

The microprocessor program can make the robot arm *pick* an item off the conveyor and *place* an item on the conveyor. The interrupts *picked* and *placed* signal the completion of those robot operations. Once an item has been picked off the conveyor, the assembly robot can perform the operation *assemble*. The interrupt *assembled* signals its completion.

When *W1* is ready for a new item, it sends a *request* to *W0* and receives an *info* message in return. Thus, *info* can arrive only after *W1* has sent a *request*. On the other hand, *W1* can expect a *request* from *W2* at any time.

To send a message, the microprocessor program performs the non-blocking operation *send-message*. To receive a message, it performs the blocking operation *receive-message*.

The state diagram in Figure 5-13 shows that a typical workstation *W1* functions as follows:

1. As it enters superstate *Winfo* and its substate *Waiting for arrived or info*, *W1* sends a request to *W0*. It then awaits one of the events *info* and *arrived*, whichever occurs first.

2. *W1* passes through different state sequences, depending on the order of events. Each state is named for those events that the station is waiting for.
   - In response to *arrived*, it takes the action *pick*. The signal *picked* from the robot indicates that it's done.

3. Once the *info* message has been received and the robot has picked the part, *W1* takes the action *assemble* and enters the state *Waiting for assembled*.

4. When the assembly is done (indicated by the event *assembled*), *W1*'s actions depend on whether a request has been received from *W2*.
   - If none has been received, *W1* enters the state *Waiting for request*.

5. Once the request arrives, *W1* takes the actions *send-info* (to *W2*) and *place* and then enters state *Waiting for placed*.

6. In *Waiting for placed*, the event *placed* causes a transition to *Waiting for arrived or info*. As mentioned earlier, this event also causes *W1* to send a *request* to *W0* and start waiting for an *info* message.

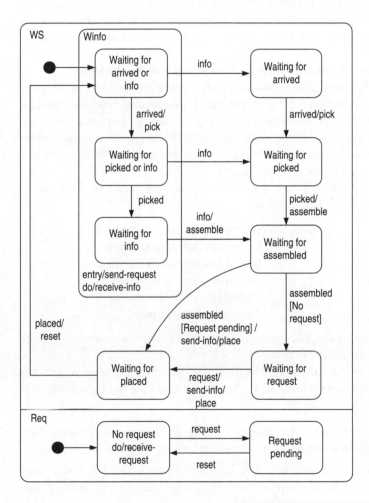

Figure 5-13 State diagram of the workstation with orthogonal states.

Because *receive-message* is a blocking operation, there are two activities, *receive-info* and *receive-request*. They block on *receive-message* in order to wait for an *info* message or a *request* message.

An *info* message can arrive only in state *Winfo*, so Figure 5-13 shows *receive-info* as an activity in that state. *W1* acts on the *info* message at once by making a state transition.

While a *request* can come from *W2* at any time, the workstation doesn't act on it until it's done assembling. For this reason, I introduce the orthogonal region *Req* with the substates *No request* and *Request pending* (Section 3.4.4).

The other orthogonal region, *WS*, uses the current substate of *Req* in the two guards tied to the event *assembled*. Furthermore, whenever the workstation returns to *Waiting for arrived or info*, it takes the action *reset*, which is an event that causes a transition from *Request pending* to *No request* in the orthogonal region *Req*.

Note 1 The request handling is an unfortunate case where state modeling complicates a rather simple reality. In real-life software development, I would have left *Req* out of the state diagram. All we need is a Boolean variable that keeps track of whether the request has arrived. I opted for a more complete solution for this book. If nothing else, it illustrates how orthogonal regions communicate: *WS* uses the state of *Req* as guards, and *reset* is an action in *WS* that turns up as an event in *Req*. Both action and event effectively go away in the implementation.

5.5.2.1.1 Software Solution Sketch for Production Line Workstation

Because they block on *receive-message*, both *receive-info* and *receive-request* are software activities (Section 5.1.1.1.2) and may have blocking reads outstanding at the same time. They co-occur because a *request* message from *W2* can come at the same time as the *info* message from *W0*. This suggests the *concurrent-activities pattern* with a state machine safe object and two activity threads, one for *receive-info* and one for *receive-request*.

The state machine safe object has the following handlers, each corresponding to an event in Figure 5-13:

arrived	Called because of an interrupt
picked	Called because of an interrupt
placed	Called because of an interrupt
assembled	Called because of an interrupt
info	Called by activity thread
request	Called by activity thread

It also has the state wait operation *wait-for-Winfo*, where the *receive-info* activity thread awaits a transition to *Winfo*.

Because of the orthogonal regions, the state machine safe object has two state variables, where the one for *Req* is reduced to a Boolean (Note 1 in Section 5.5.2.1):

1. The event *reset* in *Req* happens as a result of *placed* occurring in WS. We let the event handler *placed* change *Req*'s state to *No request*.

2. The activity thread *receive-request* should really pend on a state wait operation on *No request* but can just as well use the existing state wait operation *wait-for-Winfo*.

(As an alternative, each activity thread could call *receive-message* right after reporting a message arrival. In that solution, no state wait operation is needed.)

Note 2 In safety-critical systems, it's important to account for all *valid*—that is, physically possible—state–event pairs, including erroneous ones. For example, a spurious *info* event could occur in the state *Waiting for request*. The event handler *info* can test the current state and do nothing in states where *info* has no meaning. Other similar situations may call for some kind of error handling.

Note 3 I have assumed that the state machine safe object itself calls the nonblocking *send-message* to send its *info* and *request* messages. If this is impractical, the *receive-info* thread can send the *request* just before calling *receive-message*, and the *receive request* thread can send the *info*. This is consistent semantically: We can associate *receive-request* with the downstream workstation (*W2*) and *receive-info* with the upstream workstation (*W0*).

*5.5.3 Broader Use of Activity Threads

In state diagramming, an activity may be dismissed with a short description such as *sample X every Y seconds* (Section 3.3.4.2). Activities specified in a state diagram should be that simple and have minimal logic of their own.

We can, however, use a state machine safe object to activate and deactivate much more complex threads that are needed only in certain states, such as threads that are active only while a vehicle is airborne. It may be convenient to let them block on a state wait operation until the right (super)state is entered. When active, they can also query the current state periodically and discontinue their operation if necessary.

5.6 CONCLUSION

Discovery consists of seeing what everybody has seen and thinking what nobody has thought.

ALBERT SZENT-GYÖRGYI, QUOTED IN BERNAL, 1962

This chapter introduces patterns for designing and implementing thread architectures. They deal with programming mechanics that can live in the shadow of grander design aspects. Thus a cruise controller is chiefly a feedback problem, and the whole state machine business can be thought of as little more than a glorified on/off switch.

The cruise controller implementation follows the concurrent-activities pattern, which is useful for state machines with complicated transitions whether there are activities or not. It offers some built-in flexibility as in a software product line that may range from very simple systems without threads to others with multiple activity threads.

A concurrent-activities design without activities becomes pure event handling. An *event-driven* programming style has become popular because of the nature of graphical user interfaces and web applications. There are drawbacks to using such a style excessively, however. When a program with an event loop needs to get some input (Gustafsson, 2005, p 44):

> [It] can't simply stop and wait for the data. Instead, it needs to set up an I/O request and then return to the event loop. When the data is available, the event loop will invoke an I/O completion callback function to process it. This forces the programmer to ruin a perfectly fine program by chopping it up into a series of short callback functions.

This captures precisely the advantage of sequential activities over concurrent activities in cases where the state machine has a simple structure. If the program includes a series of blocking reads, for example (Section 5.3.1), the completion of each read is an event, and for each read there's a wait. A sequential-activities thread with implicit state lines up the read calls one after the other in the program text and abstracts away the states and events.

The sequential-activities pattern is an ELM showpiece of sorts. With state represented implicitly, it lays out an entity's life history plainly in the control structure of a thread. The *Job* thread logic in Section 5.3.1, read from top to bottom, tells us how a job goes about its business.

EXERCISES

5-1 Code lock implementation. Implement the control software for the code lock in Section 3.5.2. Use a state table and generalize the solution to *n* digits (Section 3.3.3). Maintain a counter of digits entered and a Boolean showing whether an incorrect digit has been entered (Section 3.3.2.1). Call the operations *lock* and *unlock* to operate the electric lock.

5-2 Brass lamp with touch control. Design the control software for a lamp that lets a person change the light intensity by touching the metal casing. The controller for the lamp connects to:

- A sensor that causes an interrupt as soon as the lamp is touched

- A switch that causes an interrupt when it's turned on or turned off

- A digital potentiometer that can be set anywhere between 0 and 120 volts

The switch is initially off. Turning it on activates the touch control, but the intensity is still none. Touching the brass successively turns the intensity to low, medium, high, and back to none.

5-3 Toaster. Design the control software for a motel-style toaster that functions as follows: A piece of bread is inserted into the toaster on a metal bar. When the bar has been lowered into the toaster, the software turns on the heating elements. The user selects the degree of toasting by means of a knob. The software calculates the toasting time based on the knob setting. When the time is up, it turns off the heat and releases the bar, which then ejects the bread. Also, the user can manually release the bar and stop the toasting.

There are three interrupts:

- *bar-lowered* indicates that the bar has been lowered into the toaster.

- *bar-released* indicates that the bar has been manually released.

- *overheating* indicates that the temperature exceeds a certain value.

The software can use the following operations:
- *heat-on* and *heat-off* turn the heat on and off.

- *compute-time* returns the toasting time in seconds.

- *eject* releases the bar.

In response to the interrupt *overheating*, the heating must be turned off, and the toaster mustn't turn it back on until *cool-down* seconds have passed even if the bar is lowered.

5-4 Modified cruise controller. Modify the cruise controller solution by adding a calibration feature that works as follows: The driver turns calibration on at the beginning of a measured mile and turns it off at the end. The cruise controller counts the number of driveshaft revolutions and measures the time to drive the mile. When calibration is turned off, the software calculates a conversion factor between driveshaft revolutions and speed, and, if it's reasonable, stores it for future reference.

5-5 Tank control. Design a software system that controls the filling and emptying of a tank. It does this by monitoring the liquid level and by opening and closing an inlet and an outlet valve (Sandén, 1994; Ward, 1989). The inlet valve has two positions: *opened* and *closed*. It's always controlled by the system. The outlet valve has the two positions *opened* and *closed* and also the modes *automatic* and *manual*. It's controlled by the system only when in automatic. Otherwise, it's manually controlled.

Two software modules, *Input-valve* and *Output-valve*, are provided. They both have operations described as follows:

- *closed* returns true if the valve is closed and false if it's open.

- *close* closes the valve unless it's in manual.

- *open* opens the valve unless it's in manual.

Output-valve has the following additional operation:
- *automatic* returns true if the output valve is in automatic and false if it's in manual.

A module *Tank* is also provided, with this operation:
- *level* returns the current liquid level of liquid in the tank.

The program must:
- Display the maximum fill level for the tank on request.
- Accept and store a desired liquid level.
- Accept commands to fill the tank to the desired level and to empty the tank.
- Report errors if a desired level is entered that's greater than the maximum or if a valve fails to respond to a command. After a *close* (*open*) command, the valve should be completely closed (opened) after *N* seconds.

Hint: Use a transition diagram to show the states of the tank: *filling, emptying,* and *idle.* The state is changed by the events *full* and *empty* and the commands to *fill* or *empty* the tank. In the software design, consider a regulator thread and an operator thread.

5-6 Bottling plant. Make a thread model of a bottling plant in Figure 5-14, which has a number of

bottle lines fed by a single vat (Deutsch, 1988). Each line is independently run by a line operator. Each line fills bottles at its own pace. An area supervisor oversees the operation of several lines connected to one vat.

A software system must:
- Control the level and the pH of the liquid in the vat.
- Manage the movement and the filling of the bottles on the various bottling lines.
- Provide an interface to the line operators and the area supervisor.

The liquid level in the vat is maintained by means of a level sensor and an input control valve. The pH of the liquid in the vat is maintained by means of a pH sensor and a pH control valve. Whenever the pH goes above a given limit, the pH control valve must open to allow a neutralizing liquid into the vat. If the pH in the vat cannot be kept within limits by means of the pH control valve, the area is automatically disabled.

Bottles move in each line as Figure 5-14 shows. One bottle at a time is released onto the chute through the bottle release gate. When the bottle contact shows that a bottle is on the scale, the bottle-filling valve is opened. It's closed when the bottle has reached its full weight as indicated by

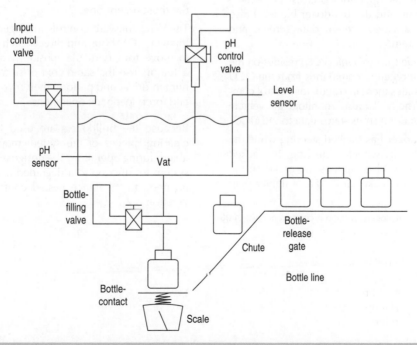

Figure 5-14 Schematic of one bottling line (Deutsch, 1988).

the scale. The system then seals, labels, and finally removes the bottle and releases a new bottle onto the chute.

The area supervisor can disable and enable the entire area at any time. The supervisor's terminal displays the current pH level, the pH limits in effect, the liquid level, the area status (*enabled* or *disabled*), and the status and bottle size of each individual line.

Each line operator's terminal continuously displays the line status (*on* or *off*) and the current bottle size. Each line operator can start and stop an individual line. When the line is stopped, the operator can change the bottle size. The line can be started only when the area is enabled, there's no bottle on the scale, and the bottle-filling valve is closed. (Any bottle remaining on the scale when the line is stopped must be removed manually.)

5-7 Remotely controlled robot vehicle. (May require research.) Make an event-thread model and software architecture for a remotely controlled robot–vehicle system with the following description:[84]

A bulldozer for mine-clearing operations is controlled remotely from an *Operator Control Unit (OCU)*. The same system, with changes in configuration files alone, controls a HMMWV. The *OCU* has a joystick by which the operator controls the vehicle movements and the bulldozer blade. It also contains a video screen, data screen, and audio system.

The *Vehicle Control Unit (VCU)* resides on the vehicle. It receives commands from the OCU and translates them into actuator-control commands. The VCU also monitors all vehicle sensors and transmits status data to the OCU.

The bulldozer has tracked steering while the HMMWV has wheeled steering. In tracked steering, the driver applies the brake on the inner track ("brake turn"). For a tighter "slip

turn," the inner track is instead reversed. Tracked steering involves multiple actuators and more states than wheeled steering.

The joystick automatically centers itself when released. It issues messages indicating a relative offset from its center position. The messages eventually control throttle, steering, braking, and transmission. Each message is a floating-point number between 0.0 and 1.0. The throttle responds to the joystick vertical offset and has maxima at 0 and 1.0, and a minimum at 0.5. The brake is a discrete device and is applied only when the joystick is at 0.5 +/– a preset delta.

The steering responds only to the joystick's horizontal offset. Values less than 0.5 indicate a left turn; values greater than 0.5, a right turn. For tracked steering, the ranges for slip turns are 0.0–0.2 and 0.8–1.0.

The VCU maintains its own set of states, distinct from those of the joystick. This is because the operator can make drastic joystick movements that the vehicle cannot handle right away. The OCU sends a control command whenever a control surface changes its value. It then repeats the same command four times per second until there's another change. For this reason, the VCU doesn't buffer messages but always acts on the most recent one.

The VCU software controls intelligent actuators via a CAN bus and directs each actuator to move to a particular position value. The actuators use the same control surfaces as a human driver and perform their own position and force-feedback operations.

Because the bulldozers are used for mine clearing, pieces of the system may be disabled during operation. The design allows the system to function in a degraded mode with no need to rebalance nested control loops [Section 8.2].

[84]Courtesy of Jim Rogers. (Personal correspondence 2006-2007.)

Event-thread patterns for resource sharing

6.1 INTRODUCTION

Sesquipedalian ... **A.** adj. **1.** *Of words and expressions (after Horace's* sesquipedalia verba *"words a foot and a half long" ...): Of many syllables.*

SIMPSON AND WEINER, 1989

This chapter centers on problem domains where entities need exclusive access to shared resources such as the track segments of a railroad or subway or, for that matter, a model train set or a computer game or animation on a railroad theme. The resources are shared by *resource-user entities*, such as trains.

A resource is *shared* if more than one entity may want to access it exclusively at once, and the software must ensure that each one in turn gets exclusive access.[85] In this chapter, each entity needs only one shared resource at a time. Chapter 7 covers the important situation where an entity needs simultaneous exclusive access to more than one shared resource. This poses the risk of *deadlock* as when one entity holds resource *B* and waits for resource *C* while another entity holds *C* while waiting for *B*.

ELM has two event-thread patterns for resource sharing: the resource-user-thread pattern and the resource-guard-thread pattern.

1. In the resource-user-thread pattern, a **resource-*user* thread** is the life history of a resource-user entity in the domain, such as a train. Each event thread includes the occurrences where that entity acquires, uses, and releases shared resources.

   ■ As we saw in Section 5.1.1.1.2 and 5.3, a resource-user event thread is often implemented as a sequential-activities control thread. Resources are protected by semaphore safe objects (Section 2.1.4.2.1.1). When a real train is waiting for access to a shared track segment, its corresponding control thread is waiting on such a software semaphore.

---

[85]In the toy car factory (Section 5.5.1.1), where each car assembly is processed by one thread in turn, the mechanics force the assemblies into lockstep and enforce the exclusive access.

2. In the resource-guard-thread pattern, each **resource-*guard* thread** is the software surrogate of one shared domain resource. Each thread consists of events where different resource users acquire, use, and release this resource. Resource-guard threads often form a virtual *assembly line* reflecting the order in which the resources are used.

   ■ The corresponding control thread has a queue of items to serve. An item is the software surrogate for a resource user in the problem domain, such as a train. The threads/stations along an assembly line are connected by item queues implemented as safe objects, which the guard threads access under exclusion synchronization.

Resource-user and resource-guard threads are common in multithread programming—if not under those sesquipedalian names. When the context is clear, I shall sometimes write **user threads** and **guard threads** for short.

6.1.1 Duality of the Patterns

We say that the user-thread and guard-thread patterns are *dual* as we can often choose either one for a given problem. When that is so, we shall talk about dual solutions and dual event-thread models. Given a guard-thread solution, we shall call the user-thread solution its dual, and vice versa. We shall never endow both the resource users *and* the resources with threads. That leads to nonoptimal solutions and tends to complicate the implementation.

The jukebox (Section 4.4.2) and bank-queuing systems (Section 4.4.3) are simple problems with dual solutions. In the jukebox case, we build a user-thread model by giving a thread to each customer. Those threads contend for exclusive access to the shared CD player.

If we instead give a thread to each panel (where customers enter requests), the result is a guard-thread solution with a little assembly line where the panel threads form a *multiserver station* and feed a single queue of song requests, served by a *CD-player* thread. In the same spirit, we can construct a user-thread solution for the bank system by giving each customer a thread and letting those threads contend for tellers. One safe object represents all the tellers. Its *acquire* operation returns a teller number (Section 6.2.1.1.1).

For a guard-thread solution, we identify an *Arrivals* thread of all customer arrival events. The *Arrivals* control thread calls the *Wait-Line* object, which represents the queue of waiting customers. The queue is served by a number of teller threads, which together form a multiserver station.

In the following, I first discuss the two resource-sharing patterns apart in more detail and then compare them.

6.2 RESOURCE-USER-THREAD PATTERN

It's striking that the word "user" is associated mainly with computers and drugs.

TURKLE, 1995

A resource-user event thread captures the life of a resource-user entity in the problem domain. Typically, such an entity obtains exclusive access to a shared resource, then operates on it, and finally releases it. This sequence can be repeated for the same or different resources. When such sequences are nested or overlap, there is simultaneous exclusive access to multiple resources (Chapter 7).

Very often, we can implement a resource-user event thread as a sequential-activities control thread. The control thread becomes the entity's software surrogate and acquires and releases shared resources on the entity's behalf. Implicit state representation (Section 5.3) usually works well because allocation events tend to be software detected (Section 4.2.1.4.1): The thread calls a safe object, and when control returns, access has been granted.

Because this is such a common implementation, the distinction between resource-user event thread and the corresponding control thread is blurred. We may have practical reasons, however, to implement a single resource-user *event* thread as a series of resource-user *control* threads, only one of which is in play at any one time (Section 6.4.1.1).

6.2.1 Exclusive Access to Domain Objects

With the resource-user-thread pattern, domain resources are always protected by semaphore safe objects (Section 2.1.4.2.1.1). Whenever possible, the semaphore and the critical sections where a resource is used should be encapsulated in a *monitor* (Section 2.1.4.2.1.2).

It may be helpful to relate semaphores and monitors to how threads access data structures under exclusion synchronization. This is familiar to students of multithreading. I'll use the Java syntax to illustrate the point:

1. The common implementation of exclusion synchronization in Java is a synchronized object. In Java, any operation designated as "synchronized" automatically enforces mutual exclusion (Section 2.2.2). Only the call to the synchronized object appears in a thread's *run* operation. This is essentially a monitor solution.

2. As shown in Section 2.2.2.1, Java also allows *blocks* to be synchronized with respect to some object, *o*, as follows:

```
synchronized ( o )
{
    // block (critical section) where o is used under exclusive access
}
```

This is the semaphore solution: The critical section is part of the *run* operation of the resource-user thread.

In Sections 6.2.1.1 and 6.2.1.2, we return to controlling the access to domain objects. Because the monitor solution relies on a semaphore, I discuss the implementation of semaphores first and then that of monitors.

6.2.1.1 Implementation of *Semaphores* for Domain Objects

A semaphore safe object *s* of class *Sema*, say, has a Boolean variable, *busy*, and the operations *acquire* and *release*. Sections 2.2.4.1 and 2.3.2.6.1 discuss semaphore safe objects in Java and Ada. Each critical section is bracketed by calls to *acquire* and *release* on *s* as follows:

```
s.acquire
// critical section where s is used under exclusive access
s.release
```

s.acquire corresponds approximately to the part "synchronized (o) {"of the synchronized block in Section 6.2.1 and *s.release* matches the final "}". The programmer must create and instantiate the class *Sema* and include the calls *s.acquire* and *s.release* in the program. Two levels of locking are involved: *s*'s hidden lock variable controls the access to the variable *busy*, and *busy* controls the access to the resource.

6.2.1.1.1 Multiple Equivalent Resources
A semaphore safe object can easily control multiple equivalent resources. In that case, *acquire* typically returns a reference to the resource, *b*, say, that the calling resource-user thread actually acquired. The same reference is sent to *release* as follows:

```
b=s.acquire
// sequence where resource b is used under exclusive access
s.release(b)
```

In the customer-thread solution for the bank (Sections 4.4.3.1 and 6.1.1), for instance, *Customer* threads call *acquire* on the singleton instance of *Teller-control* and return with a reference to an available teller.

In the resource-user-thread solution for the home heater in Section 6.5.2.1, a semaphore safe object doles out heating tokens to the resource users (homes). In other cases, each resource user gets a share of a resource such as memory space. Thus in Exercise 6-4, each of various engines onboard a submarine gets a portion of the total electric power available.

6.2.1.1.2 Simultaneous Access to Multiple Resources
Although we prefer to encapsulate semaphores in monitors, unencapsulated semaphores are necessary when a resource needs simultaneous exclusive access to multiple resources and the critical sections overlap (Sections 6.4.2 and 7.3.1). In a train control system, for instance, trains may need to acquire and release track segments in the following fashion:

```
acquire segment n              // Critical section n starts
// The train is on segment n
acquire segment n+1            // Critical section n+1 starts
leave segment n
release segment n              // Critical section n ends
// The train is on segment n+1
leave segment n+1
release segment n+1            // Critical section n+1 ends
```

6.2.1.2 Implementation of Monitors for Domain Objects

A monitor controlling the access to a domain resource is a module that encapsulates a semaphore safe object, *s*, as well as operations on the shared resource. Each of these operations calls *s.acquire* and *s.release*; it's often the first and the last thing the operation does. Sections 2.2.4.2 and 2.3.2.6.2 show monitor implementations in Java and Ada, respectively.

The remote temperature sensor in Section 6.5.1.1 has a resource-user-thread solution with two monitors corresponding to an A/D converter and to a communications line. In the resource-user-thread solution of the jukebox problem, a monitor protects the shared CD player (Section 4.4.2.1).

6.2.2 Programming Style

Good programming is good writing.

SHORE, 1985

The resource-user-thread pattern is reassuringly like a familiar style of sequential programming. Thus, each *train* thread's *run* operation is similar to a main program that calls operations on objects representing tracks. In high-level languages, each control thread has a stack with a frame for each operation call that hasn't returned. The stack also houses temporary variables declared in the operations. If an operation raises an exception,[86] the language's exception-handling mechanism can propagate it up the call hierarchy toward the *run* operation's frame. Moreover, during development and testing, we can start with a simplified system with a single resource-user thread before introducing concurrency.

Implicit state representation is often useful in resource-user threads just as in other sequential-activities threads (Sections 3.7.2 and 5.3.1). Because allocation events are software detected, the state where a thread is waiting on a shared resource is already implicit in the program text (Sections 4.2.1.4.1 and 5.1.1.1.2): The thread enters the state when it attempts to acquire a semaphore that's closed and exits it once access has been granted. The home heater solution in Section 6.5.2.1, for example, has resource-user threads that represent state implicitly. The style is also illustrated by the switchyard and the FMS in Section 7.3.

6.3 THE RESOURCE-GUARD-THREAD PATTERN

The guard-thread pattern offers an alternative to resource-user threads. A *resource-guard* control thread has permanent, exclusive access to a problem-domain resource and works from an input queue of items. As the software surrogate for a resource user, each item may contain state information.

In the guard-thread solution for the jukebox, *CD-player* works from a queue of requests from panels. In Model 1 of the data-entry problem, buffers travel along an assembly line with a *Keyboard* and a *Disk* station: One station fills buffers with data, and the other commits the data to disk. Similar examples

---

[86]Depending on your programming language, you **raise** (Ada) or *throw* (C++, Java) an exception.

abound. Each station on an assembly line can feed more than one downstream station and can be fed by more than one upstream station.

A station may have more than one server, allowing multiple resource users to be served in parallel. Thus the resource-guard solution for the jukebox has multiple *Panel* threads.

6.3.1 Queuing

The queues allow the assembly line stations' processing times to vary around a common average. Queues are also helpful if a station should be temporarily incapacitated. This is so in the remote temperature sensor (RTS) (Section 6.5.1) where an output thread may stop sending packets due to transmission failure. If the failure is of short duration, the packets can accumulate in the queue and be processed later.

As designers we must guard against queue overflow. The RTS copes by overwriting obsolete temperature readings, but such a solution isn't always acceptable. Instead, a thread attempting to put an item in a full queue may have to raise an exception. It'd better not put an error message in another queue, though; queues may be filling up all across the system.

6.3.2 Resource-Independent Processing

An assembly line of resource-guard threads works best if each station represents a shared resource. Processing that needs no shared resource complicates things. There are two ways to accommodate it:

- Add the extra processing to a guard thread. This has the downside that a resource remains busy longer than necessary.
- Add an extra station/thread somewhere along the assembly line. This new station has no matching resource but still serializes processing.

A resource-independent station can have multiple threads if necessary, but if an assembly line has more than one such station, the user-thread pattern offers a cleaner solution: The resource-user threads proceed concurrently whenever they aren't dependent on the same resource; no special arrangements are required. The two home heater solutions in Section 6.5.2 illustrate this.

*6.3.3 Guard Threads Implemented as Concurrent Activities

As items travel along the assembly line, their corresponding problem-domain entities undergo state changes: They wait for a shared resource, use it, release it, and then wait for another resource. A jukebox request, for example, may start in a wait state and then enters a "playing" state. A bank customer may also spend time in a wait state before being served. Their interaction with a resource can be viewed as an activity in a state. This view is helpful when the resource user is stationary as in the home heater (Section 6.5.2.2) where the assembly line metaphor is counterintuitive.

6.4 CHOOSING AND COMBINING PATTERNS

The queuing makes the difference between resource-guard and resource-user threads:

- Resource-user threads themselves queue up while waiting for a resource. Languages that support threading often support such thread queues as well. Ada (Section 2.3.2) and the *RTSJ* (Section 2.2.5) have FIFO thread queues.

- With resource-guard threads, the queues hold items or requests, which are passive objects. Such queues are usually part of the application program.

It's usually redundant to give a thread to each resource user and also to some or all resources. Such a solution is nonoptimal in the ELM sense (Section 4.2.3.3), for each user thread is idle while its entity is using the resource. In the implementation, the resource-user control thread must be parked at some safe object, which can be awkward. Still, user threads and guard threads can coexist in other ways, as illustrated in Section 6.4.1.

6.4.1 Resource-Guard Threads Doubling as Resource Users

Besides its permanent hold on one or more resources, a guard thread can act as a user thread, too, at the same time. That is, it can gain and release exclusive access to additional resources. In one solution to the FMS problem (Section 7.3.2.3), threads that represent workstation resources also gain and release exclusive access to automated vehicles, which carry parts to the workstations.

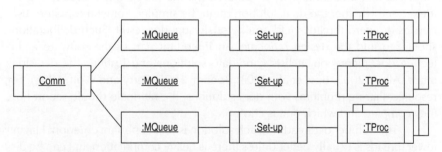

Figure 6-1 Transaction control system: Assembly line where the *TProc* threads are also resource-user threads.

A simple transaction control system (TCS; Figure 6-1) offers another example. One *Comm* thread receives all messages from users and sorts them by size into three instances of *MQueue*. Each such message queue is served by a *Set-up* thread, which creates a *transaction processing* (*TProc*) thread instance for each message. *TProc* completes the transaction and generates output to the user's screen.

Comm, *Set-up*, and *TProc* form an assembly line per message size where *TProc* represents a multiserver station on each line. The assembly line's sole purpose is to prepare for the application processing, all of which takes place in the

TProc instances. Those are resource-user threads operating on database records under exclusive access; the user at the screen is the resource-user entity.

*6.4.1.1 One Resource-User Event Thread—A Series of Control Threads

In a variation on TCS, each transaction consists of a sequence of *interactions* with the user. Each interaction starts with a message from the user and ends with a reply back to the user's screen. In this variant, a fresh *TProc* instance is started for each such interaction. The transaction's record locks and other status information are saved and retrieved by each *TProc* instance.

After a system crash, a restart program restores the database. To make this possible, a transaction that updates a record first stores on disk an image—called a "before look"—of the record before the update. The restart program identifies those transactions that were in progress when the crash struck and thus must be recovered. It creates a resource-user control thread, *RProc*, for each, which effectively inherits the transaction's record locks. It then applies the interaction's before looks, thereby undoing each update made before the crash. After the restart, the interaction can start over.

This kind of solution is hazardous if one transaction can have either two *TProcs* or a *TProc* and an *RProc* running at the same time. If so, two control threads will have access to the same records and may undertake conflicting updates. In TCS, this cannot happen: A new *TProc* thread starts only when the user has received a message and replied, and when an *RProc* thread is created, all *TProc* threads have just perished in a crash.

6.4.2 Choosing Resource-User or Resource-Guard Threads

Once we find one solution to a resource-sharing problem, it's usually a good idea to see whether the dual solution might be simpler. Sometimes, either user threads or guard threads yield an obviously superior result. Such deliberations should go into the design *rationale*, an important part of the software architecture documentation. It lists candidate solutions and justifies the decisions made (Albin, 2003; Bass et al., 2003; Boehm, 1995; Perry and Wolf, 1992). For resource-sharing problems with dual solutions, the rationale should report how they compare and which one is chosen.

The number of threads in each solution is one important criterion: Having fewer threads is usually better unless there is heavy computation that can be distributed over multiple processors. Here are some additional guidelines:

1. *Resource-**guard** threads* are often the best if there are more resource users than resources and almost all processing is dependent on some shared resource. In these problems, the alternate, user-thread solutions tend to be wasteful. The remote temperature sensor in Section 6.5.1 is an example.

2. *Resource-**user** threads* are often the best if much of the computing is resource independent or there are enough resources for almost all resource users. The home heater in Section 6.5.2 is an illustration.

    User threads provide the only reasonable solution if there are very many resources and only a few of them are held exclusively at any one time. For example, a database may have a multitude of individually lockable records. The *TProc* threads in Section 6.4.1 are examples.

3. With *simultaneous exclusive access* to multiple resources, *resource-user threads* tend to make for a simpler solution, as in the train controller in Section 6.2.1.1.2, where the critical sections overlap.

The FMS, too, involves simultaneous exclusive access. Thus an FMS job can have exclusive access to a stand and a forklift at the same time. A guard-thread solution is discussed briefly in Section 6.4.1. A dual solution with *Job* threads (Section 7.3.2.2) is quite intuitive, which is important. On the other hand, it does include many idle threads because each job keeps its thread while in storage waiting for its next workstation.

6.5 EXAMPLES WITH DUAL SOLUTIONS

Few things are harder to put up with than the annoyance of a good example.

MARK TWAIN, *THE TRAGEDY OF PUDD'NHEAD WILSON*, 1894

In the following examples, dual solutions are at least conceivable, but either the resource-guard-thread or the resource-user-thread solution is often a clearly better choice.

6.5.1 Remote Temperature Sensor

The RTS (Figure 6-2) monitors the temperatures of a set of furnaces by means of a thermocouple connected to each furnace and a multiplexed analog/digital (A/D) converter (Sandén, 1989c). First suggested[87] by Young (1982), it has been widely used (Carter, 1988; Cherry, 1986; Howes, 1990; Mills, 1995; Nielsen and Shumate, 1987; Shumate and Keller, 1992; Smith and Williams, 1993).

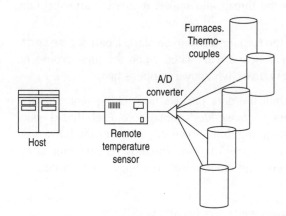

Figure 6-2 Remote temperature sensor system.

The RTS is located near the group of furnaces and sends each temperature reading as a *data packet* to a host computer residing elsewhere. Each furnace is monitored at its own frequency, which can be changed at any time by means of a *control packet* from the host.

---

[87]To my knowledge.

6.5.1.1 RTS: Resource-*User*-Thread Solution

In a resource-user-thread solution, each furnace *n* has an instance *fn* of the thread class *Furnace*. Each instance samples the temperature of one furnace periodically and sends each reading in a data packet to the host.

The A/D converter and the transmitter are shared resources and are represented in the software by the singleton monitors *converter* and *transmitter*. A *Furnace* thread can have exclusive access to one of them at a time. The converter is exclusively held from when the thread issues a sampling command until an interrupt signals that the temperature reading is available in digital form. The transmitter is held until the data packet has been sent and acknowledged. After sending a data packet, each *Furnace* thread suspends itself until its next reading time by means of a *sleep* or **delay** call. The UML communication diagram in Figure 6-3 shows this solution.

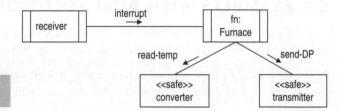

Figure 6-3 Resource-user-thread solution to the RTS.

The singleton thread *receiver* handles all arriving control packets and forwards each to the appropriate *Furnace* thread. *Furnace* threads must be ready to accept new control packets at all times. If the thread is asleep when the packet arrives, it's awakened in case readings must now be more frequent. Here's how this can be done:

- In Java, *receiver* can throw an *InterruptedException* in the *Furnace* thread. This activates the thread and makes it execute an exception handler.

- In Ada, the **delay** of the *Furnace* task can be made a part of a **select** statement such that *Furnace* is reactivated when the time expires or when a control packet arrives, whichever happens first.[88]

If transmission difficulties prevent the data packets from being sent, *Furnace* threads accumulate in the queue of *transmitter*'s semaphore. Each thread waits only up to its next scheduled sampling time, however. At that point, it discards its existing reading and makes a new one. That way, the most recent temperature readings for each furnace are kept, and older, unsent readings are discarded.

---

[88]My solution used the following construct in the *Furnace* task type (Sandén, 1997b):

```
select
    accept Interrupt;
or delay until Next;
end select;
```

Here, *Interrupt* is a task entry called by the *Receiver* task (Section 2.3.4). We can also use an intermediate protected object whose entries the *Furnace* tasks call conditionally. *Receiver* opens the barrier for the appropriate *Furnace* task when its control packet arrives (Section 2.3.2.3).

6.5.1.2 RTS: Resource-*Guard*-Thread Solution

In a guard-thread solution, a singleton thread named *sampler* schedules all the temperature readings and receives the control packages (Sandén, 1997b). It's a guard thread for the A/D converter and forms an assembly line with another singleton guard thread *transmitter* (Figure 6-4). The *sampler* and *transmitter* threads are connected by a queue. Normally, the RTS transmits a data packet as soon as each temperature is read. To protect against transmission difficulties, the queue is implemented as a circular buffer,[89] and the *sampler* overwrites the oldest entry when necessary.

Figure 6-4 Resource-guard-thread solutions to the RTS.

6.5.1.3 RTS: Comparison of the Solutions[90]

The guard-thread solution is simpler and has only two threads, while the resource-user-thread solution has one thread per furnace plus the *receiver* thread. This illustrates guideline 1 in Section 6.4.2. The guard-thread solution is optimal because at most one furnace can be sampled and one data packet sent at once.

One drawback of the guard-thread solution is that the application program itself schedules the temperature readings, while the user-thread solution relies on a built-in thread scheduler. The scheduling is quite straightforward though.

In normal operation, the queue contains no packets as they're sent right away. The sampler and transmitter threads could easily be combined except for when packets back up because they cannot be sent. It's not uncommon for a reactive-system architecture to be determined by an exceptional case in that fashion (Selic and Ward, 1996).

6.5.2 Home-Heating System

A particular home-heating system serves a group of five homes (Hatley and Pirbhai, 1987; Sandén, 1996).[91] The system aims to keep the actual temperature in each home within two degrees of a preset reference temperature for the home. The heating cycle involves starting a fan, letting it rev up before combustion starts, and so forth.

The problem description (Hatley and Pirbhai, 1987) features rather a contrived case of resource contention: The five homes share a fuel tank, but no more than four homes can be heated at a time due to undersized fuel lines. As a consequence, a home must give up heating from time to time in favor of another home. The system makes sure that no home is forcibly without heat for more

---

[89]Compare Exercise 2-6.

[90]The RTS example taught me the importance of considering dual solutions. I first published a user-thread solution (Sandén, 1989c) in response to an earlier, rather involved data-flow solution (Nielsen and Shumate, 1987). When I finally considered the guard-thread solution in detail, it turned out to be much simpler (Sandén, 1997b).

[91]Jan Hext made me aware of this problem at a Workshop on Design Methodologies for Real-Time Systems at Macquarie University, Sydney, Australia, June 1994. According to Hatley and Pirbhai (1987), it was first introduced at a panel session at COMPSAC 86, Chicago, IL, October 1986.

than 10 minutes at a time. It does this by turning off the heat for the home that has had it the longest.

6.5.2.1 Home Heater: Resource-*User*-Thread Solution

In a resource-user-thread solution (Figure 6-5), each home has a control thread, *hn*, of class *Heater*, which handles the heating cycle. The cycle consists of several successive steps largely driven by time events (Sections 3.2.1.1 and 4.2.1.3). In the start-up sequence, for instance, the thread starts the motor, then spends 7 seconds in a wait state, then turns the ignition on and opens the fuel valve, and finally waits 3 seconds.

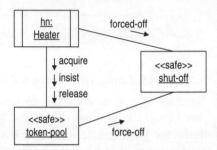

Figure 6-5 Resource-user-thread solution to the home-heating Problwm.

Below is an outline of the thread logic. It's a good illustration of implicit state representation (Sections 3.7.2 and 6.2.2) and also of the sequential-activities pattern (Section 5.3). The heating cycle logic reads from top to bottom. Changes related to precise points in the cycle are easily made. We could start with the logic for a single home and then make some surgical changes (shown in bold) to handle the constraint:

```
Wait for master switch to be On
While system is on:
    While room needs no heating:
        Turn off system when master switch is turned Off
    Acquire a token
    Start-up procedure:
        Start motor; wait 7 seconds
        Ignition on
        Open fuel valve; wait 3 seconds
    While room needs heating:
        Initiate turn-off within 5 seconds of either:
            1. Master switch turned Off
            2. Motor status changes to Off
            3. Fuel flow status changes to Off
            4. Combustion status changes to Off
            5. Another home needs heating
        Indicate abnormal status for 2-4. Furnace restarted only by master
        switch.
    Shut down procedure:
        Close fuel valve; wait 5 seconds
        Deactivate motor and ignition; wait 3 seconds
    Release token. Allow for cool-down.
```

A pool of four heating tokens models the shared resource. It's implemented in the singleton object *token-pool*. Before starting the heater, each *Heater* thread must obtain a token by calling *token-pool.acquire*.

The *token-pool* object is a semaphore safe object but is not limited to the simple *acquire*-and-*release* protocol we have seen so far: There is no wait loop in *token-pool.acquire*, which instead returns to *hn* a status indicating whether a token was obtained. If not, *hn* repeatedly calls *acquire* for up to 10 minutes. It then demands a token by calling *token-pool.insist* and gets one, even at the price of shutting off the heat in another home. From within the *insist* operation it does this by calling the *force-off* operation of the other home's *shut-off* object.

(An alternative would be to place *hn* in *tokenPool*'s wait set with a time-out after 10 minutes. But with the chosen solution *hn* can keep monitoring the main switch while waiting.)

During heating, each *hn* thread senses the room temperature periodically. It also polls the status of a main switch in case heating is turned off and finds out by calling *shut-off.forced-off* whether it must give up its own heat for the benefit of another home.

Note A monitor solution is also possible: The part of the heating cycle logic that requires a token can be placed in a *heat-home* operation in a monitor. But that's the *Heater*'s entire logic from where a token is acquired to where it's released, so breaking it out has little benefit and adds some indirection. Besides, the home is operating its own heater and not some shared resource that the monitor would represent.

*6.5.2.2 Home Heater: Dual Solution

A resource-guard-thread solution is conceivable in the home-heating problem, but the picture of homes traveling on an assembly line of resource-guard threads offends our intuition. It's easier to think of such a stationary entity as a home in terms of state machine with activities. Thus a home has the states *Unheated*, *Waiting for heating*, and *Heated* (Figure 6-6). *Unheated* has the activity *check temperature* and *Heated* the activity *heat*.

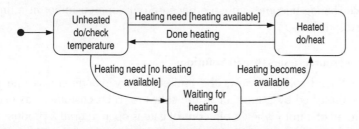

Figure 6-6 State diagram sketch for the home-heating problem.

We can then apply the concurrent-activities pattern (Section 5.4) and give each home a state machine safe object. It also has its own instance of the activity thread *check temperature*. By contrast, there are only four instances of the activity thread *heat* (Section 5.4.2.1.1). The thread *check temperature* polls the home's temperature and determines when heating is needed. At that point, it tries to hand the home safe object over to a *heat* thread. Unless a *heat* thread is immediately available, *check temperature* retries for up to 10 minutes and then forces another home to give up heating. Each *heat* thread takes a home through its heating cycle much as the resource-user thread in Section 6.5.2.1.

With nine threads, this solution is nonoptimal in the ELM sense. Besides, the resource-user-thread solution in Section 6.5.2.1 is more straightforward. But in other cases a concurrent-activities solution may be less far-fetched. Once we have a user-thread solution to a problem with stationary resource users, considering the dual solution based on a state model of the resource user may well be worthwhile.

6.5.3 Automated Store

An automated catalog store sells boxed products: personal video and audio equipment, PDAs, telephones, GPS devices, and whatnot. At any one time, *N* customers can browse an electronic catalog and order merchandise. Figure 6-7 shows six customer stations, each with a *terminal*, *credit-card reader*, *receipt printer*, and *delivery chute*. Each customer follows a step-by-step, menu-guided procedure.

The products of each type are in a vertical *bin* shown from above in the main drawing and from the side in the inset to the right in Figure 6-7. Each item is uniquely identified by a bar code, RFID tag, or the like. When an item has been bought, a *control gate* at the bottom of the bin opens, allowing one box to exit onto a slope leading to a *conveyor belt*. This is shown in the top inset. Each item's identity is read at the gate and associated with the buyer.

Items can back up first on the slopes for access to the conveyor and then on the conveyor. The conveyor ends at an *output dispatcher*, which can target one customer chute at a time. The output scanner reads the item's identity, and the dispatcher delivers it to the right customer. A receipt is printed after the customer receives all her items.

Analyzing the store problem, we easily identify one *Customer* thread for each customer position. (They're long-lived operator threads; Section 4.3.1.1.) Resource sharing becomes an issue because only one customer at a time can use the dispatcher.

6.5.3.1 Resource-*User*-Thread Solution

The user-thread solution views the entire delivery machinery as one shared resource protected by a monitor in the software. Each customer has exclusive access to all of it from when a bin control gate is opened until a product arrives at the chute. If the customer is waiting—rather than browsing the catalog or ordering items—during the delivery, the *Customer* thread can serve as a resource-user thread and call the monitor to request delivery of a product, remain queued until it gains access to the machinery, and then execute the logic that brings about the delivery.

This solution may underutilize the delivery machinery by transporting only one customer's items at a time even though there's room for many more on the slopes and the conveyor. It's acceptable as long as transportation isn't a bottleneck.

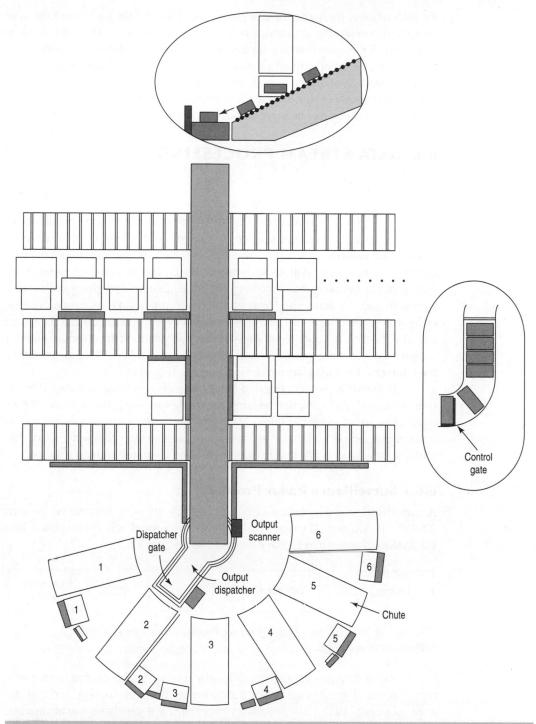

Figure 6-7 Automated store layout. (Ink drawing courtesy of Choa-Chong Lee and Chi-I Hsu.)

6.5.3.2 Resource-*Guard*-Thread Solution

The guard-thread solution is a virtual assembly line with two stations. The first one works off of requests made by *Customer* threads and opens the proper control gate for each request. There may be one guard thread named *Bin* for all the bins, one for each group of bins, or perhaps one per bin for optimum use of the delivery machinery. If there are multiple *Bin* threads, they form a multiserver station.

A guard thread named *Dispatcher* reacts to each product arriving at the output scanner, locates the customer, directs the dispatcher to the correct chute, and updates the customer's delivery status. With this solution, the customer can continue browsing the catalog and ordering products throughout the delivery process.

6.6 DATA STREAM PROCESSING

Never trust any data.

KERNIGHAN AND PLAUGER, 1978

An ELM event thread is a sequence of occurrences with sufficient interarrival time to let a single control thread keep up with it. In some systems, the time between input items or occurrences doesn't allow this, however, because each data item requires extensive computation. With enough processing power, we can then increase the throughput by breaking the processing into multiple steps and giving each step a control thread. All items visit the control threads in the same sequence, so their order is preserved. The result resembles an assembly line of resource-guard threads, just as in Section 6.3, where we stressed that each station/thread should guard a shared resource. In the case of the data streams, we can think of the processor(s) as the resources. The surveillance radar (Section 6.6.1) is an example.

In the MIDI problem (Section 6.6.2), all messages must be handled in the order of arrival, and each one requires minimal processing. The solution comes quite close to an assembly line, except that the outgoing messages are sometimes reordered on purpose. Also, a single input message can be forwarded to multiple destinations. For that reason, there is no clean user-thread solution.

6.6.1 Surveillance Radar Problem

A surveillance radar system was constructed by Ericsson Microwave Systems (EMW)[92] in Sweden (Peterson et al., 2003). The system was decomposed into subsystems, as shown in Figure 6-8. (See also Section 8.3.2.)

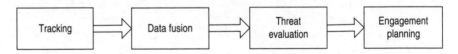

Figure 6-8 Informal data-flow diagram of the surveillance radar software (Peterson et al., 2003).

Radar data processing is traditionally structured along these lines with a typical series of steps: target tracking, data fusion, threat evaluation, and engagement planning. With multiprocessors especially, we can have a real pipeline with each node working on its own input at each point in time. That way, the system can keep up even if the data interarrival time is less than the processing time for each data item.

[92]Now SAAB Microwave Systems.

6.6.2 MIDI Problem

MIDI (Musical Instrument Digital Interface) is a protocol for communication between musical instrument controllers and other units such as synthesizers. A device responds to commands received on its MIDI-IN port and sends commands to other devices through its MIDI-OUT port.

The MIDI protocol calls for asynchronous, byte-by-byte data transfer. Each message consists of a status byte followed by 0–2 data bytes. A status byte that is identical to the previous one may be omitted from the data stream; only the data bytes of the MIDI message are then transmitted. This is referred to as *running status*.

System-real-time messages are one byte long and can appear anywhere in a MIDI data stream, even in the middle of other MIDI messages. They provide the synchronization within a MIDI system. For instance, a *Timing-clock-real-time* message is always issued six times per beat. *System-real-time* messages take priority over all other messages.

6.6.2.1 Programmable Patch Bay

A programmable patch bay has a number of MIDI ports, each of which can be configured for input or output.[93] In addition to forwarding messages to any or all ports configured for output, each input port can also be programmed to translate messages by replacing their status bytes. Moreover, it can drop messages with certain status bytes.

In the Ada solution in Figure 6-9, the protected object *Port_Input* hides a queue of input bytes. It handles the input interrupts and has an entry where the task *Port* retrieves the next byte.

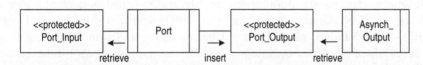

Figure 6-9 Ada solution for the programmable patch bay.

The task *Port* pends for a byte on the *Port_Input* object and performs any necessary translation and transposition. Unless the message is to be dropped, *Port* calls the appropriate *Port_Output* protected object to insert the message into the queue.

The protected object *Port_Output* hides a queue of output bytes. It has the following protected operations:

- Insert a byte at the end of the queue. (Running status adjustments are made as needed.)
- Insert a *System-real-time* message at the head of the queue.
- Retrieve the byte at the head of the queue.

[93]This example was suggested by Paul Sheets, George Mason University, Fall 1992. It can also be looked at as an assembly line where a station can clone an incoming item and send identical copies to multiple other stations.

The task *Asynch_Output* pends on *Port_Output* until a byte needs to be transmitted and then performs the transmission.

6.7 REPOSITORY PROBLEMS

A good problem is one whose solution, rather than merely tidying up a dead end, opens up entirely new vistas.

STEWART, 1987

The resource-user-thread and resource-guard-thread patterns both assume that each item or request needs individual attention throughout an entire transaction, such as when a temperature reading is first sampled and then transmitted in the RTS (Section 6.5.1). (As in the RTS and the MIDI patch bay, this includes the case where an item is deliberately dropped.)

In a *repository system*, by contrast, items don't get individual service. Instead, they're processed according to some other policy and often more than one at a time.[94] The repository resource is shared by the threads that do the collection and those that process the repository data (Bass et al., 2003).

The *weather buoy* in Section 5.4.3.2 is a repository system. It collects environmental data of various kinds, such as air and water temperature and wind speed. Commonly, each kind has its own sampling frequency. Data are stored in a repository. Periodically, all the latest data in the repository are retrieved and broadcast via radio. The *asynchrony* between data capture and data processing is typical for repository systems. Additional examples follow.

6.7.1 Multielevator System

Elevator problems are popular in the literature (Armstrong et al., 1996; Douglass, 1998; Gomaa, 1993; Jackson, 1983; Knuth, 1968; Meyer, 1993; Mills, 1995; Sandén, 1994).[95] As in Chapter 4, we focus on the case where a set of elevator cabins traveling in parallel shafts next to each other serve all the floors in a hotel, department store, or office building. To summon an elevator, a passenger to be presses a button, and a cabin shows up with more or less commendable promptitude. Passengers don't care which particular one it is.

Let's first glance at a distributed solution with one central node and one node per elevator. In this solution, common in textbooks, each elevator has a microprocessor controlling its movements. A dispatcher thread at the central node registers all new requests from *up* and *down* buttons by sampling the button contacts. For each new request, the dispatcher picks one of the elevators based on its current position and direction of travel. Each elevator node maintains a list of requests to serve, including those from its own internal buttons.

---

[94]The term "repository model" is also used for a system where subsystems are arranged around a common database (Sommerville, 2007). Although the systems discussed in this section typically keep data in memory rather than in a database, the principle is similar.

[95]Like the cruise controller (Sections 5.4.3.1, 8.2 and 8.3.4), the elevator example is a "groaner." A single-elevator controller may deserve no better, but a multielevator control is nontrivial.

The drawback is that this solution sometimes sends an elevator to serve requests that another one either has already served or is on its way to serve. Suppose elevator *E* is chosen to serve a *down* request from floor *f*. Before *E* gets to floor *f*, someone presses the *f* button inside a descending elevator cabin, *D*. *D* may stop at *f* before *E* and pick up the passenger. Elevator *E* will then travel to *f* in vain.

Such redundant travel is avoided by replacing the individual lists of requests with a common repository of outstanding requests, as described in Section 6.7.1.1 (Jackson, 1983; Sandén, 1989b, 1994).

6.7.1.1 Solution Sketch

The solution in (Sandén, 1994) has one control thread per elevator. This is typical for the elevator architectures in the literature. The threads can time things, such as how long the doors have been open.[96]

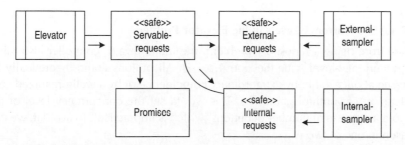

Figure 6-10 Simplified communication diagram of the elevator system.

One or more sampler threads detect pressed buttons and register new requests. One repository, *External-requests*, holds requests from floor buttons (Figure 6-10). This can be an array with two elements (*up* and *down*) for each floor. The repository *Internal-requests* has one instance per elevator, which holds requests from inside that cabin. It needs as many elements as there are floors. Each repository is a safe object. *External-requests* is shared by the elevator threads and the external sampler while each *Internal-requests* instance is shared by one elevator thread and one internal sampler.

The additional, singleton safe object *Servable-requests* is shared by the elevator threads. It has a singleton object *Promises* where an elevator registers its commitment to visit certain floors either going up or down (Jackson, 1983). This prevents elevators from setting out to serve requests that others have already committed to handle.

Each elevator cabin follows an itinerary that is predictable to its users.[97] Repeatedly, it moves as far up as needed, then as far down as needed (Jackson, 1983). When it arrives at a floor, the control thread calls *Servable-requests.stop*. Inside *stop*, it calls the safe operations of *Internal-requests* and, if necessary,

---

[96]A thread per elevator is necessary in the distributed solution, but if the system runs on a single computer, a state machine safe object per elevator suffices (Section 5.2). It can use RTSJ's timers (Section 2.2.5.3) or Ada 2005's timing events (Section 2.3.2.5).
[97]While passengers are moving up to their floor of choice, for example, the cabin shouldn't suddenly go down a couple of floors to pick up another passenger.

External-requests to find out whether the cabin must stop. If it stops, the thread marks the appropriate requests as served, and if it had promised to serve the request, it marks that promise as fulfilled.

When the cabin has visited a floor, the thread calls either operation *continue-up* or *continue-down* on *Servable-requests*. Inside those operations, calls are made to *Internal-requests* and, if necessary, *External-requests* to find any outstanding calls for floors above or below.

The elevator thread finally updates *Promises* with any new commitments. It must serve any internal requests in its current direction. It also commits to serve any external requests in its current direction that no other elevator has already promised to serve. This calculation is done in *Servable-requests* with short calls to *Internal-requests* and *External-requests*. *Servable-requests* is locked for other elevator threads, whereas *Internal-requests* and *External-requests* remain available to the samplers most of the time.

6.7.1.2 Concurrency Levels in the Elevator Problem

Aside from being a repository problem, the multielevator controller also raises a concurrency-level issue (Section 4.2.4.2): All buttons could theoretically be pressed at once either by extraordinary coincidence or by a well-organized confederation of youthful pranksters. This would set the concurrency level of the problem at the total number of buttons, which is impractical. To avoid it, we can reason in one of two ways:

- The probability of many simultaneous presses is so low that we can ignore it. This means that we relax the rule that there should be a thread for each simultaneous occurrence: We need only so many threads that the likelihood of more simultaneous event occurrences is negligible. Missing a few requests in such a rare situation is considered acceptable in this problem.

- Each button stays pressed for a short time, and we only need to sample it during that period.

6.7.2 Traffic Light System

A traffic light system at a road intersection goes through a sequence of phases where each phase allows a set of compatible traffic flows. (See also Section 3.3.2.4.) The length of a phase can depend on the number of vehicles traveling in those directions. A phase can be skipped altogether if there are no such vehicles when its turn comes. A car entering a turn lane or a pedestrian pressing a button doesn't change the lights right away. Only at the proper phase in its cycle, the system checks to see if there is a need to turn on a green arrow or a walk signal.

6.7.3 Repository Problem Solutions

Behind the desire to solve this or that problem that confers no material advantage, there may be a deeper curiosity, a desire to understand the ways and means, the motives and procedures, of solution.

PÓLYA, 1957

The repository problems lend themselves to solutions where one or more threads enter repository data and one or more threads read repository data and act on it. Those sets of threads are connected by the repository rather than by queues.

These problems typically have no reasonable resource-user-thread solutions. An elevator system cannot keep track of a traveler's path from floor to floor; it merely acts on requests to stop. When it opens its doors, it's unaware of whether any passengers exit or enter. Similarly, a traffic light doesn't serve any car or pedestrian in particular but periodically checks whether anyone is waiting.

6.8 CONCLUSION

There is no way to find the best design except to try out as many designs as possible and discard the failures.

DYSON, 1992

For the common situation where resource users in the domain need exclusive access to shared domain resources, ELM offers dual event-thread patterns with resource-guard threads and resource-user threads, respectively. Once you have designed one thread architecture, it's worthwhile to see if its dual might be simpler. Even if it's not, it never hurts to twist and turn the architecture a little and understand it better.

By and large, it's best to consider resource-sharing patterns early, for they tend to dominate the architecture. If we choose to model a resource user in the domain as a thread, we stand to benefit from built-in synchronization and queuing mechanisms (Chapter 2). The choice between the guard-thread pattern and the user-thread pattern tends to determine the major architectural style of the software. The examples suggest that, often, one or the other pattern is clearly the best.

With the user-thread pattern, we need semaphores to protect shared domain resources from conflicting accesses. This presents us with the following additional, more localized choices:

1. We encapsulate the semaphore together with the entire operations on the shared resource—the critical sections—in a *monitor*. This is usually the cleanest separation of concerns.

2. We place unencapsulated semaphores directly in the logic of the user threads. This more primitive solution is often necessary if a resource user needs simultaneous access to multiple, shared resources and if the critical sections aren't neatly nested.

In repository problems, some threads collect data in a repository while others act on the data in due course. The collecting and acting threads form something like an assembly line, but the items don't usually travel intact from one station to the next. For instance, once the system has registered a request from a certain button, identical requests are ignored until the visit has taken place. Also, the requests aren't always served in the order they were made.

EXERCISES

6-1 Event-thread pattern discovery. Identify useful entities (or event threads) in the following problem sketches. What are the resource users and resources? Are dual resource-user-thread and resource-guard-thread solutions possible? Are there any repository problems?

(a) An automated metro rail system controls the movements of trains and ensures that only one train at a time travels on each rail segment.

(b) In a pneumatic mail system, a user at one station may send a packet through a network of tubes and switches to any other station. For each packet, an unbroken path is set up from its origin station to the target station.

(c) In another automatic mail system, each packet has the address of the target station encoded on it. The packet first travels from its origin station to a regional hub. From there, each local packet is sent to its target station while other packets are routed to another hub. Each hub has the capacity to buffer a certain number of packets.

(d) A chat session involves a number of "chatters," each of whom has a window that displays all posts and a text box where the chatter can type a post. A chat server maintains a number of chat sessions, each with a number of chatters. For each session, it receives incoming posts from each chatter by means of a blocking read. It sends each post to each chatter's window.

(e) A device functions as (i) a copier and (ii) an office print server, to which many users can submit print jobs from their personal computers. The printer is shared by the copying jobs, which are done manually, and the print jobs. The device must be programmed to a policy that ensures that jobs aren't interleaved in the single output hopper. What are some possible policies?

6-2 Emergency traffic light preemption. Design a system that alters traffic signal timing to give the emergency vehicles green lights along their path.

6-3 Musical chairs. Design a simulation of the game of musical chairs. The players start out sitting on chairs. When the music begins, they get up and walk around the set of chairs. In the meantime, one chair disappears. When the music stops, each player attempts to find a chair, and one player is out of the game. This is repeated as long as there are players left. The players can be modeled as resource-user entities. Is a dual solution with resource-guard threads possible, however far-fetched?

6-4 Submarine power control. The engines onboard a submarine use an electric source with *max* watts of total power. This means that all the engines together can use no more than *max* watts at any point in time. For simplicity, assume that each engine requires *startup* watts initially and then *steady* watts with *steady* < *startup*. In an onboard control system, each engine has a thread (task) that calls the safe object *Powerguard*. Each engine thread calls *on* to ask for power and is blocked until *startup* watts are available. It calls *on-steady* when start-up is over and *off* when it has shut down.

(a) Design the synchronized class (protected object) *Powerguard*.

(b) Design a thread (task) *Engine* representing an electric engine. *Engine* uses *Powerguard* as described above and a synchronized class (protected object) *OnOff* to wait for start and stop commands from an operator. *Engine* calls the operation *started* to block until a start command is given and *stopped* to block pending a stop command.

Once it receives a start command, an engine thread (task) requests start-up power from *Powerguard*, delays *transtime* seconds, releases the excess power, waits for the stop command, delays for *spin-down* seconds, releases its power to *Powerguard*, and loops back to wait for another start command.

(c) It may be necessary to stop an engine while it's in the start-up phase. How can an engine thread be on the lookout for a stop command while blocked waiting for *transtime* to expire? (Chapter 2.)

(d) How can the onboard power control system allow each engine to request amounts of start-up and steady-state power that are specific to that engine?

6-5 Elevator control (Sandén, 1994). Complete the design of the elevator system described in Section 6.7.1. Here are some additional options:

(a) After the doors have been shut, let the cabin linger for *N* seconds while new passengers press buttons. After that, the elevator thread decides how to proceed.

(b) An idle elevator can either return to the ground floor immediately or remain at the floor of the last request for a while.

(c) Let the software detect unplanned stops between floors.

(d) Give each cabin a *Stop* button. When the button is pressed, the elevator immediately stops at its present position until one of the floor buttons in the cabin is pressed. It then proceeds directly to the indicated floor.

(e) Implement a *Reserve* switch for each cabin. It's useful in certain situations, as when an elevator is used to move furniture. The switch is operated by means of a special key. The elevator is reserved and obeys its own internal buttons only. The automatic door closing is also disabled, and the doors are operated by means of the *Open* and *Close* buttons in the cabin. The reserved status remains until the special key is removed.

(f) Design scaffolding software simulating the behavior of the physical elevator cabins.

Simultaneous exclusive access to multiple resources

7

It's great fun to present lectures and seminars on communicating sequential processes, since the examples give scope for exercise of the histrionic skills of the lecturer. Each example presents a little drama which can be acted with due emphasis on the feelings of the human participants. An audience usually finds something particularly farcical about deadlock.

HOARE, 1985

7.1 INTRODUCTION

This chapter is about problems where each entity needs exclusive access to more than one shared resource[98] at once. In that situation, it's essential to identify those resource-user entities in the problem domain. In the resulting architecture, sequential-activities control threads are surrogates for those entities. With implicit state representation, the entities' life histories as they go about acquiring and releasing resources can be laid out very clearly in the program text of those control threads.

Simultaneous exclusive access poses the danger of *deadlock*. The simplest case is when one entity holds a resource, *B*, while waiting indefinitely for resource *C* and another entity holds *C* while waiting indefinitely for *B*. ELM lets the designer prevent deadlock as part of the analysis and the software design. This is a constructive approach, unlike analytical methods that can detect deadlock in a program but don't indicate how it can be prevented.

Deadlock prevention means that we put our software together in such a way that deadlock cannot arise. This works when we have control over the resource users and their behavior as in the flexible manufacturing system and an automated switchyard. In that situation it's up to the designer to prevent

---

[98]A resource is *shared* if it's needed by more than one entity.

Design of Multithreaded Software, by Bo I. Sandén
Copyright 2011 by the IEEE Computer Society

deadlock. The key is to *identify the resource users and the resources* and impose some convention that prevents deadlock.

In some user-directed systems, the designer has little or no control over how and when entities acquire resources, which makes deadlock prevention impossible (Singhal and Shivaratri, 1994; Stallings, 2008; Tanenbaum and Woodhull, 2006). A typical example is an interactive database where individual users can decide what records their transactions will affect. Deadlock is usually deemed rare enough in such systems that we can pay the price for dealing with it when it happens. Database systems can *detect* existing deadlock by analyzing the resources held and awaited by each transaction at a given point in runtime. If deadlock exists, the database system *resolves* it by rolling back one of the transactions involved.

Transaction rollback means that the database is restored to a state where none of the transaction's updates have been made. Database management systems use rollback in their support for *atomic* transactions. (A transaction is said to be atomic if, when it ends, either all or none of its updates have been carried out.)

7.2 THE DEADLOCK PROBLEM

Deadlock, also known as *circular wait*, exists when entities wait indefinitely for each other to release resources.[99] To hold a resource means to have an exclusive lock on it. To *acquire* a resource means to lock it. For example, one entity of type *X* may hold resource *R1* and want resource *R2*, while another *X* instance holds *R2* and wants *R3*, and a *Y* instance holds *R3* and wants *R1*. This deadlock can be illustrated in a *wait-chain* diagram as follows:

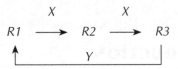

Each arrow is marked with the name of an entity type such as *X* and points from a resource held by *X* to a resource that *X* is waiting for. The circularity is plain to see in the diagram.

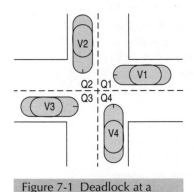

Figure 7-1 Deadlock at a road intersection.

Figure 7-1 shows a deadlock situation. The informal diagram shows four vehicles, *V1–V4*, at an intersection divided into quadrants, *Q1–Q4*. Here, vehicle *V1* is waiting for *V2* to move, which is waiting for *V3*, which is waiting for *V4*, which is waiting for *V1*. The vehicles form a circular wait chain. The quadrants *Q1–Q4* are the resources. *V1* holds *Q1* and is waiting for *Q2*. *V2* holds *Q2* and is waiting for *Q3* and so forth.

Deadlock causes a system (or part of it) to stall but stalemate can arise in other ways. If a Java programmer should forget to put in calls to *notify* or *notifyAll* at all the right places, threads may be stuck in a wait set forever (Section 2.2.3.2). This is no deadlock and cannot be prevented by means of the techniques in this chapter.

---

[99]Deadlock is originally a wrestling term. Another synonym is *hold and wait*. The colorful expression *deadly embrace* usually implies that exactly two entities are involved.

7.2.1 Determining That a System is Deadlock Free

Are you sure that your system cannot deadlock—that is, are you sure that it never reaches a state in which no further action is possible?

Simple wait-chain diagrams can be used to detect a circular wait in a design. In the diagram, each resource is a node, and each entity or thread is represented as an arrow. If an entity of type *X* can hold a resource *R1* while waiting for a resource *R2*, an arrow from *R1* to *R2* is placed in the diagram and marked with the name of the entity type, *X*:

$$X$$
$$R1 \longrightarrow R2$$

If entities of type *X* later release *R1* and go on to acquiring a third resource, *R3*, while still holding *R2*, the following diagram results:

$$X \qquad\qquad X$$
$$R1 \longrightarrow R2 \longrightarrow R3$$

This diagram shows that one instance of type *X* may be holding *R1* and waiting for *R2* while another holds *R2* and waits for *R3*.

If an entity of type *X* attempts to acquire *R3* while still holding both *R1* and *R2*, then *R1* and *R2* and the arrow between them are enclosed in a box:

The box with the arrow to *R3* indicates that an entity of type *X* holds both *R1* and *R2* while waiting for *R3*. The reason for the special notation is that only a single entity of type *X* is involved, first in a situation where it holds *R1* and waits for *R2* and then in one where it's waiting for *R3* while holding both *R1* and *R2*.

If there is circularity in the wait-chain diagram, a potential for deadlock exists. There is circularity if we can start at some resource node *R1*, follow an arrow to another node, then a third, and ultimately get back to *R1* while moving in the direction of the arrows.

Deadlock can exist only if there are enough entities to *populate* the wait chain, however. We can find out how many entities are needed by counting the arrows. In the diagram below, it takes two arrows marked *X* and one arrow marked *Y* to get from node *R1* back to *R1*. That means that it takes two entities of type *X* and one of type *Y* to cause deadlock. If an arrow from a box is included in the count, then the arrows inside the box aren't counted.

Here is a wait-chain diagram for the intersection example:

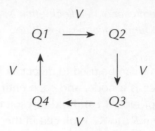

It's obvious from the diagram that four entities of type *V* can deadlock. There are no boxes because no vehicle holds more than a single quadrant of the intersection at once.

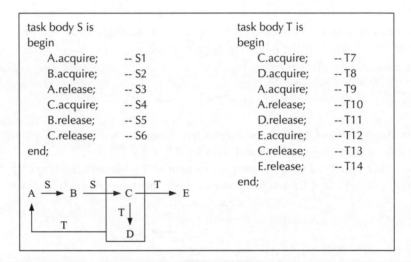

```
task body S is                          task body T is
begin                                   begin
      A.acquire;    -- S1                     C.acquire;    -- T7
      B.acquire;    -- S2                     D.acquire;    -- T8
      A.release;    -- S3                     A.acquire;    -- T9
      C.acquire;    -- S4                     A.release;    -- T10
      B.release;    -- S5                     D.release;    -- T11
      C.release;    -- S6                     E.acquire;    -- T12
end;                                          C.release;    -- T13
                                              E.release;    -- T14
                                        end;
```

Figure 7-2 Deadlock analysis of a schematic Ada program.

Figure 7-2 shows a wait-chain diagram of a schematic program with two task types, *S* and *T*. Each acquires resources *A*, *B*,. . . by means of calls such as *A.acquire* and *B.acquire*. That is, by making the call *A.acquire*, the task attempts to acquire *A*. This may involve a wait. While waiting, the task holds onto whatever resources it has already acquired and not yet released. Upon return from the call *A.acquire*, the task has exclusive access to *A*, which it releases by calling *A.release*.

The diagram shows that a task of type *T* may be holding resource *C* while waiting for access to *D*. This happens when the task has progressed to statement T8, *D.acquire*, and hasn't yet returned from it. Once the task returns, it attempts to acquire *A* (in statement T9) while still holding onto *C* and *D*. This is shown by the box around *C* and *D* and the *T*-marked arrow from the box to *A*.

In statement T12, a task of type *T* attempts to gain exclusive access to the resource *E* while holding *C*. (*A* and *D* have been released in statements T10 and T11.) This accounts for the arrow from *C* to *E*, which crosses the box border. The box isn't involved here.

Given the diagram, we can answer such questions as the following:

1. Can deadlock arise if *enough instances* of S and T run concurrently in one system?

The answer is yes. There is circularity in the diagram. Starting from A, we can follow the arrow marked S to B, then the arrow marked S to C, then the arrow marked T to D, and finally the arrow marked T from the box back to A. It's easy to verify that this deadlock is possible. As the diagram indicates, the following tasks are involved:

- One instance of S holds A and waits for B. It has progressed to statement S2.
- One instance of S holds B and waits for C. It has progressed to statement S4.
- One instance of T holds both C and D and waits for A. It has progressed to statement T9.

2. Can exactly *one instance* of S and *one instance* of T deadlock?

The answer is no. The only circularity in the diagram is the one described above that contains two arrows marked S and one marked T. (The one in the box doesn't count. The same instance of T that once held C and was waiting for D is the one now holding C and D while waiting for A.) This means that it takes at least *two* instances of S and one instance of T to cause deadlock.

7.2.2 Deadlock Prevention

A safety property asserts that the program never enters a bad state. . . . Absence of deadlock is [another] example of a safety property.

ANDREWS, 1991

Now we turn our attention to ways of designing our software deadlock free. All the following criteria must be met for deadlock to exist:

1. Entities must hold and try to acquire resources in such a manner that a *circular* wait chain can form given a sufficient number of entities.
2. There must be enough entities to *populate* the circular wait chain.
3. Each entity must wait *indefinitely* for a resource while keeping any resources it already has.

When we have control over the resource users and their behavior, as in the FMS and the switchyard, we can make sure that at least one of the criteria is unmet by doing one of the following:

1. Manage the resource acquisition so that no circularity can exist. This can be done by a convention governing the *order* in which each entity may acquire shared resources.
2. Limit the number of entities so that the wait chain cannot be populated.
3. Eliminate the indefinite wait for resources.

With resource-user threads, we can usually build such conventions right into their *run* operations. The following subsections elaborate on each alternative.

7.2.2.1 Resource Ordering

A *static locking order* is a rule that dictates the order entities may attempt to gain simultaneous exclusive access to multiple resources (Goetz, 2006). Thus, the rule may allow an entity to hold resource *B* and wait for resource *C*, but not to hold *C* and wait for *B*. Such a rule can prevent the entities from forming a circular wait chain. This is a design or programming *convention,* which is also referred to as an *order rule* (Sandén, 1994). To see why an order rule eliminates deadlock, consider the following circular wait chain:

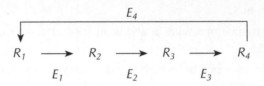

Here, entity *E1* holds resource *R1* and waits for *R2*, *E2* holds *R2* and waits for *R3*, *E3* holds *R3* and waits for *R4*, and *E4* holds *R4* and waits for *R1*. The arrow marked *E4* closes the circle. To prevent circularity we can order resources from *lesser* to *greater* in some fashion and require that each arrow go from a lesser to a greater resource. For example, we can impose the order *R1 < R2 < R3 < R4*. This rule clears *E1*, *E2*, and *E3*—each holding a lesser resource and waiting for a greater one—but not *E4*, which holds *R4* while waiting for the lesser resource, *R1*. (Other orders, such as *R2 < R3 < R4 < R1*, also work, each outlawing a different entity.)

        An **order rule** is *partial order,*[100] "*<,* "such that either *R < S* or *S < R* for any two resources *R* and *S* that are ever held with exclusive access at once by any one entity and with the provision that *an entity (or thread) that holds R may wait indefinitely for exclusive access to S if and only if R < S.*

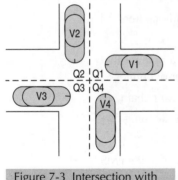

        We can also think of *R < S* as "*R* before *S*" in the sense that an entity in need of both resources at once must acquire *R* before *S*. In the intersection example, an order such as *Q1 < Q2 < Q3 < Q4* breaks the fatal circular symmetry of the problem. This means that *V1* can legally hold *Q1* while waiting for *Q2*, *V2* can hold *Q2* while waiting for *Q3*, and *V3* can hold *Q3* while waiting for *Q4*. But *V4* cannot hold *Q4* while waiting for *Q1*, which means that *V4* cannot enter *Q4*. With *Q4* free, *V3* can move on, liberating *Q3* and eliminating any deadlock (Figure 7-3).

Figure 7-3 Intersection with the resources ordered.

7.2.2.2 Limiting the Number of Entities

Traffic lights and stop signs control the number of vehicles in an intersection. Drivers are expected to respect the conventions and enter the intersection only

---

[100]A partial order such as < is a relation that satisfies the following conditions: (1) If *x < y*, then *y < x* is false and *x* and *y* are not the same. (2) If *x < y* and *y < z*, then *x < z* (transitivity) (James and James, 1976).

when they're supposed to. In the following example we limit the number of entities so that they cannot populate the wait chain.

EXAMPLE In a warehouse system, automated guided forklift trucks travel along wires in the floor (Section 7.3.3). Figure 7-4 shows a portion of the track network. Each forklift must turn around and point its prongs toward the ramp before loading (Magnusson, 1994).

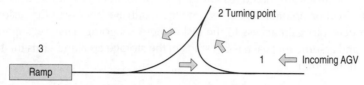

Figure 7-4 AGVs in a warehouse.

A forklift arrives at this portion of the track network via position *P1*, continues to position *P2*, where it's turned around, and then to position *P3* at the ramp. After loading or unloading, it leaves via position *P1*.

If *A1* is an incoming forklift at position *P1*, *A2* is at position *P2*, and *A3* at position *P3*, then there is deadlock (assuming that *A1* cannot back out): *A1* holds position *P1* and is waiting for position *P2*, *A2* holds position *P2* and waits for position *P3*, and *A3* holds position *P3* and waits for position *P1*. It's also clear that if *any one* position is unoccupied, there is no deadlock. The solution in this case is to limit the number of forklifts that can be in this portion of the network at any one time.

Note Another solution exists in this particular example: Once there is a forklift at each of the positions *P1*, *P2*, and *P3*, they can all be started at the same time.

7.2.2.3 Avoiding Indefinite Waiting

Deadlock requires that an entity, *X*, holds onto a resource, *B*, *forever* while waiting for another resource, *C*. The indefinite wait can be avoided in two ways:

1. We empower *X* to force *C*'s release. In the FMS example (Section 7.3.2), a job in a workstation tool can "bump" another job off a stand.

2. We let *X* release *B*. This is what happens in the automated robot-stocking example below. If robot *X* is holding aisle *B* in the front of the store while waiting for aisle *C* in the back, it can release *B* and move to a robot staging area (a robot *corral*) with room for all the robots.

   The storage system in the FMS problem (Section 7.3.2) is a contention-free staging area with room for all jobs in progress.

The approach used in transaction systems (Section 7.1) also eliminates the indefinite waiting. If two or more transactions are found to form a circular wait chain, one of the transactions is aborted (to be restarted later).

EXAMPLE Figure 7-5 shows the layout of an automated supermarket that employs robot vehicles to restock its aisles. The front of the store is organized in aisles, $A1$, $A2, \ldots$, with shelves where customers pick their wares. The back is organized the same way into storage aisles, $S1, S2, \ldots$, which contain crates of cereal boxes and other goods. A fleet of robotic vehicles carry merchandise from the storage aisles to the front aisles. The robots travel on tracks counterclockwise around the store. From the counterclockwise track, a robot can enter any aisle.

The aisles are shared resources: Each robot needs exclusive access to an aisle to load or unload. While keeping the exclusive access to the aisle it's in, it also needs to gain access to the aisle where it's going. First, let's ignore the corral and assume that each robot starts in the storage area and visits the storage aisles in the order

$$S_1 \quad S_2 \quad S_3 \quad \cdots \quad S_m$$

A robot visits only a few aisles on one normal trip—but must do so in that order. It then visits (or passes by) the front aisles in the order

$$A_1 \quad A_2 \quad A_3 \quad \cdots \quad A_n$$

Then it stops. The following order rule is possible:

$$S_1 < S_2 < \cdots < S_m < A_1 < \cdots < A_n$$

So far, so good, but ultimately, a robot in aisle A_k must head to the back of the store. For that, it needs access to aisle S_j while keeping A_k. This violates the order rule.

A robot corral placed somewhere along the track around the store solves the problem. It can be at the point where the robots reenter the storage area as in Figure 7-5. Each robot has a designated space in the corral. Once there, it can release A_k and wait for S_j. It's then no longer holding a resource while waiting for another one, and there can be no deadlock.

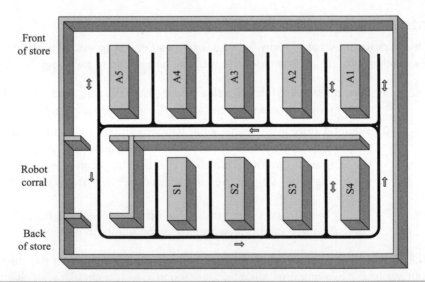

Figure 7-5 Automated-supermarket layout.

7.2.3 Dining Philosophers' Problem

In the end it would be apparent to the inquisitive philosopher that he was waiting for himself—which is the condition for deadlock.

AGHA, 1986

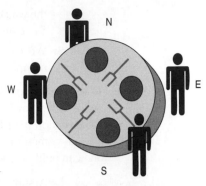

The dining philosophers' problem is a classic example of concurrency and deadlock (Agha, 1986; Bacon, 1997; Dijkstra, 1983; Goetz, 2006; Magee and Kramer, 2006). Figure 7-6 shows four philosophers, *East* (*E*), *South* (*S*), *West* (*W*), and *North* (*N*). Each philosopher has a bowl of spaghetti in front of him. Between each pair of philosophers next to each other, there is a fork. In order to eat, a philosopher must have exclusive access to *both* forks flanking his bowl.[101] We shall also assume that once a philosopher has his forks, he uses them for a finite time. If some philosophers hold onto their forks forever, the others won't eat even though there's no deadlock.[102] Once a philosopher has eaten, he doesn't again contend for forks. The remaining philosophers cannot populate a circular wait chain, so deadlock is impossible.

Figure 7-6 Schematic showing four philosophers around a table.

Figure 7-7 is the wait-chain diagram for the dining philosophers. The forks are marked *F1,. . . F4*. Each philosopher has two arrows representing the situations where he (1) has his left fork while waiting for his right fork and (2) has his right fork while waiting for his left fork. He can populate only one of his arrows at a time. Philosopher *N*, for instance, can either hold fork *F1* and wait for fork *F4* or hold *F4* and wait for *F1*. This means that circularities such as *F1–F4–F1* can never be populated.

Figure 7-7 Wait-chain diagrams for the dining philosophers.

The circularity *F1–F2–F3–F4–F1* can be populated if there are indeed four philosophers who all grab their right-hand forks first. The circularity *F1–F4–F3–F2–F1* can be populated if those philosophers instead grab their left-hand forks first. Either way, deadlock results: One fork in a white-knuckled grip, each philosopher holds out for the other until grim death.

7.2.3.1 Deadlock Prevention in the Philosophers' Problem

Any one of the three ways to prevent deadlock can be applied to the dining philosophers' example:

1. We can eliminate the indefinite wait by assuming that a philosopher—now in a more congenial frame of mind—puts down his fork once he has waited a while for the second fork.

2. We can limit the number of philosophers at the table to one less than the number of forks. That way, there aren't enough philosophers to populate

---

[101]Those of us who have never heard of spaghetti eating with two forks often replace them in this tale with chopsticks even though no one places chopsticks on either side of a plate (Goetz, 2006). At a local Italian restaurant, I saw the light in a yellowed picture of an unkempt cleric—perhaps a philosopher—deftly rolling up spaghetti with a two-fork technique.
[102]In computing, *starvation* is when one or more threads monopolize the available processors so that other threads cannot run sufficiently or at all.

the wait chain. One way is to let the philosophers take turns: First, N and S eat, and when they lay down their forks, E and W get their turn.

3. We can impose an order rule if we number the forks *F1–F4* in any manner.

To explore option 3, we order the forks *F1 < F2 < F3 < F4* and stipulate that no philosopher may hold onto a fork while waiting for a lesser one. This is, of course, a convention, which works only as long as all philosophers can be instilled with enough community spirit and altruism to cooperate.[103] Under the convention, no one can hold onto fork *F4* alone. Here's proof that such a rule prevents deadlock:

> Assume *N* has fork *F1*. He can then legally pick up *F4* and eat unless *W* has *F4*. In that case *W* must have *F3* also and can eat.
>
> If *N* doesn't have *F1*, *E* has it. Either *E* has *F2* also and can eat or *S* has *F2*.
>
> If *S* has *F2*, he may also be able to pick up *F3* and eat.
>
> If *S* cannot get *F3*, *W* has it. But then *W* can eat, since *F4* is available.

It's usually easy to implement the order rule. A simulation of the philosophers might include threads of class *Philosopher*, each of which gains exclusive access to one philosopher's forks in the prescribed locking order. That way, thread *N* and thread *E* both attempt to access *F1* first, and exactly one can proceed.

7.3 CASE STUDIES

Of the following three case studies, the ones about the automated train switchyard and the flexible manufacturing system deal with real-world resource contention problems that can be implemented by means of threads and safe objects. The approaches to deadlock prevention discussed above are used singly and in combination. Section 7.3.3 discusses a simulation done during the design of a storage facility with automated guided vehicles.

7.3.1 Automated Train Switchyard[104]

Look long on an engine. It is sweet to the eyes.

MacKnight Black, *Machinery*, 1929

An automated switchyard is laid out as in Figure 7-8. We shall refer to the layout as a tree of track segments with its root at the bottom of the diagram. This imaginary switchyard is located in Alexandria, Virginia, and trains headed for such places as Richmond and Harrisonburg are being put together on *destination sidings*, each marked with a station name. Incoming freight trains back onto the locomotive siding. An automated uncoupler traveling on the parallel siding identifies cars by bar codes, RFID tags, or the like and partitions the train into groups of contiguous cars with the same next destination. Each such group is taken by a switch engine to the right destination siding.

---

[103]My editor Jessica tried this at home on her own "milk-mustached dining philosophers," but they didn't take well to the altruistic part.
[104]The problem was suggested by Carl Dahlke and Thanh Luu.

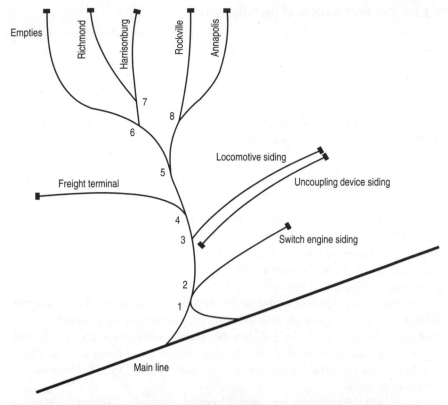

Figure 7-8 Schematic layout of an imaginary automated switchyard at Alexandria, VA, courtesy of Carl Dahlke and Thanh Luu (Sandén, 1994). The root of the tree of tracks is at the bottom of the figure.

The main resources of contention in the switchyard are track segments. The switch engines are their users. In keeping with the resource-user-thread pattern, we endow each engine with a thread. Once a switch engine has hooked onto a Richmond-bound car, say, it must secure exclusive access first to the Richmond siding and then to each track segment (such as 4–5 and 5–6) along the way (Sandén, 1994).

A singleton safe object of class *Segments* represents the shared track segments. It's a semaphore safe object (Sections 2.1.4.2.1.1 and 2.2.4.1). Here's a possible outline in Java-like pseudocode:

```
public class Segments {
    boolean[] busy = {false, false, false, ...};    // Array of track segments
    public synchronized void lockSegment(int s) {
        while (busy[s]) wait();                      // Condition synchronization
        busy[s] = true;
    }
    public synchronized void unlockSegment(int s) {
        busy[s] = false;
        notifyAll();
    }
}
```

7.3.1.1 Deadlock Analysis of the Switchyard

When two trains meet on a track, neither train shall move until the other one has passed.

OLD RHODE ISLAND LAW[105]

The deadlock potential in the switchyard is plain to see: For one thing, a switch engine en route to the Richmond siding may occupy the segment 4–5 while another one, bound for the switch engine siding, sits on segment 5–6. This results in the following wait chain, populated with one engine per arrow:

Such deadlocks can be prevented with an order rule: Order the track segments either up or down the tree. An engine moving across increasingly ordered track segments can acquire them as it goes, but an engine going in the opposite direction must secure its entire path ahead of time by acquiring the segments in the order opposite its direction of travel.

The track segments aren't totally ordered. Specifically, the destination sidings need not be mutually ordered. Further, if segments are ordered from the root up, 4–5 < 5–6 and 4–5 < 5–8, but the relative order of 5–6 and 5–8 is irrelevant as they are never held at once by one engine. An engine on its way from 5–6 to 5–8 must first move from 5–6 to 4–5, then from 4–5 to 5–8. Once on 4–5 it can release 5–6.

Even if the segments are ordered from the root up, the destination sidings are less than other segments. That way, a switch engine on a destination siding can acquire its return path without violating the order rule. Some sidings such as the switch engine siding aren't exclusively held. Instead, multiple engines can be managed there on a last in–first out basis. That siding is a contention-free staging area (Section 7.2.2.3).

We can check compliance with the order rule by inspecting the *run* operation of the class *SwitchEngine*. It includes the following logic for the case where the track segments are ordered from the root up:

```
// Heading toward destination siding
Acquire destination siding
Acquire first track segment
Move onto first track segment
while (not next to destination siding)
    Acquire next track segment
    Move onto next segment
    Release previous segment
Move onto destination siding
Release previous segment
// Switch engine on destination siding
Acquire all segments going from the root up
// Full path acquired
```

[105]According to legend (Cooper and Clancy, 1982).

```
Move onto first segment;
Release destination siding
while (on an acquired segment)
   Move onto next segment
   Release previous segment
```

Note This logic is a typical example of implicit state representation (Sections 3.7.2 and 6.2.2). The switch engine goes through a series of states as it progresses through the *run* operation. This programming style makes the program read from top to bottom (Kernighan and Plauger, 1978) and lets us assert the physical whereabouts of a switch engine at specific points in the program text, as the comments indicate. With *acquire* and *release* calls in line, the text also tells us what segments are held at each step. It's thus clear that the destination siding is acquired first and kept until the engine has turned back toward the root of the track segment tree.

7.3.1.2 Optimization

We follow two rules in the matter of optimization:
Rule 1. Don't do it.
Rule 2 (for experts only). Don't do it yet — that is, not until you have a perfectly clear and unoptimized solution.

JACKSON, 1975

We should forget about small efficiencies, say about 97% of the time: premature optimization is the root of all evil.

KNUTH, 1974B

The return of switch engines can be optimized: Two or more engines can gather on a track segment such as 5–6 or 5–8 in Figure 7-8 and travel down the tree together. That way, the path need be allocated only once for the entire group instead of once per engine.

To bring this about, one engine locks the assembly segment. Each remaining engine enters the segment, ignoring the lock, and releases its destination segment (and any segment in between) after leaving it. As the engines travel down the tree, the first engine acquires each new segment and releases it once all the engines have left it.

*7.3.1.3 Realism

Like many examples in this book, the switchyard case study is idealized to make a point: It centers on the resource-sharing problem. In reality, the software for an automated switchyard or even a model railroad cannot necessarily do with switch engine or train threads alone. The problem domain may well have other events that justify their own threads. Many events in reality are pesky little things going wrong—in the lofty world of textbooks, they are swiftly abstracted away.

John McCormick has used a model railroad control project in his real-time embedded-system courses for years (McCormick, 1992, 2005). Students make their own designs, and typically each train has an Ada task that gains access to the next track segment, powers up each segment before the train enters it, and the like.

One hazard in model railroading—not least in a neighborhood where "devious professors" have been known to lurk—is switch malfunctioning. A train task can issue a command to reposition a switch that the train is approaching. The repositioning is supposed to complete within a certain space of time. A switch task can control the switch adjustment under a timeout and report an error if it isn't completed in due time.

A switch that is always repositioned on behalf of a train waiting nearby could be operated by the train task. But having the train concern itself with the switch mechanics may seem unintuitive. As always, the designer is free to choose a nonoptimal event-thread model with switch threads as well as train threads provided that each event occurrence belongs to exactly one thread.

Similar issues arise in the FMS problem (Section 7.3.2), where automated guided vehicles (AGVs) and forklifts must deal with any obstacles in their paths. These dealings may not belong in the job thread and could instead be handled by software in the vehicles.

7.3.1.4 Hump Yards

A *hump yard* is a kind of switchyard where each car is brought to the top of a little hill and rolls from there to its destination siding under the force of gravity. Each car must always acquire the entire path and have the switches set right ahead of time. If the path segments are ordered from the top of the tree down toward the hump, an engine moving cars from a destination siding to the main line can acquire segments as it goes, stopping from time to time to let a car roll clattering by on its way to its destination siding.

7.3.2 Flexible Manufacturing System

The booms were tearing at the blocks, the rudder was banging to and fro, and the whole ship was creaking, groaning, and jumping like a manufactory.

ROBERT LOUIS STEVENSON, *TREASURE ISLAND*, 1883

The FMS controls the jobs in an automated factory (Carter and Sandén, 1998; Gomaa, 1989; Sandén, 1994, 1997a). A job involves the treatment of one part, which starts as a blank and is then milled, lathed, and drilled (and perhaps ground, cut, formed, or heat treated) in a series of steps at different workstations. The series of such job steps is defined in a *process plan* of each job.

Figure 7-9 shows the layout of a simple FMS. Parts are moved between workstations by AGVs, which travel on a shared system of one-way wires (Section 7.3.3). There is an automated storage and retrieval system (ASRS) for blanks and finished parts, which also serves for contention-free staging of parts taken off the factory floor between job steps. Each job keeps an ASRS bin until done. One or more forklift trucks carry parts between their bins and the storage stands, where the AGVs can pick them up.

There are multiple workstations of each type such as mill, lathe, and drill. Each has an instand, tool, outstand, and robot; the robot moves each part from instand to tool to outstand. I shall refer to the components of workstation n as *instandn*, *outstandn*, and so forth.

Once a blank, p, is present in its bin, the FMS supervisor creates a job by tying the bin to a process plan and queues the job on the right workstation type for its first step. The part remains in its bin until the instand of a suitable workstation, *instand1*, say, becomes available. Having acquired *instand1*, the job acquires a storage stand and then a forklift. The forklift moves the part from bin to storage stand, and an AGV takes it from storage stand to *instand1*.

Part *p* remains on *instand1* until *tool1* becomes available. Then the robot moves it into the tool. When the tool has finished, the robot moves the part onto *outstand1*, and the job is queued on the proper workstation type for its next job step.

Part *p* stays on *outstand1* until the instand of a suitable workstation (*instand2*) becomes available or else when another job needs *outstand1*. If *instand2* becomes available when the part is still on *outstand1*, the part is transported to *instand2* by an AGV. But if part *p* is still on *outstand1* when another part is finished in *tool1*, *p* is *bumped* off the stand and staged in the ASRS. For this, it's removed from the workstation-type queue and then taken by an AGV to a storage stand and by a forklift to its bin.

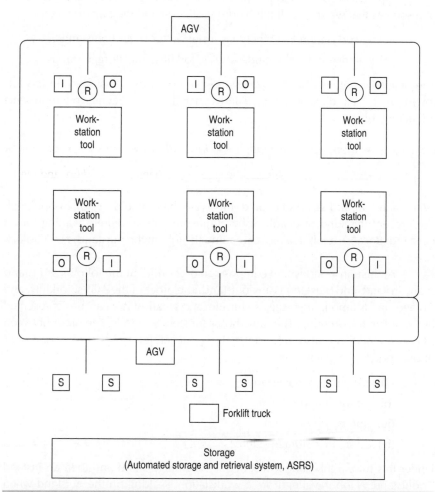

Figure 7-9 Layout of flexible manufacturing system. I: instand; O: outstand; S: storage stand; AGV: automated guided vehicle.

This process continues until the job has completed its process plan. At that point, the part is placed in its bin to be removed by some mechanism outside the scope of this discussion.

7.3.2.1 Deadlock Prevention in the FMS

If there are W workstations, S storage stands, F forklifts, and N AGVs, the resources could be totally ordered as follows:

instand1 < tool1 < outstand1 < instand2 < . . . < toolW < outstandW < storage-stand1 < . . . < storage-standS < AGV1 < . . . < AGVN < forklift1 < . . . < forkliftF

Under this order rule, a job can hold an instand and wait for the tool or hold a tool and wait for the outstand. But a job on an outstand can wait only for the instand of a greater workstation. This would remove much of the flexibility since a job must be staged in the ASRS whenever it's headed from a greater workstation to a lesser one.

A practical solution to this problem is to distinguish between two levels of resources that we shall call the *workstation level* and the *transport level*:

- ■ The workstation level includes instands, tools, and outstands.
- ■ The transport level includes AGVs, forklifts, and storage stands.

The deadlock potential at the workstation level can be illustrated by the following wait-chain diagram for any j and k such that $j \neq k$. Each arrow represents a different job:

instandj ⟶ *toolj* ⟶ *outstandj* ⟶ *instandk* ⟶ *toolk* ⟶ *outstandk*

With each tool and stand occupied, this wait chain would be fully populated. We prevent this kind of deadlock by eliminating the indefinite waiting for an outstand: Because a job in a tool can bump the job on the outstand, no deadlock can arise.

At the transport level, we impose an order rule. In the following, *instand* is any instand, and *outstand* is any outstand. The order of the AGVs, forklifts, and storage stands among themselves is irrelevant, so all AGVs can be represented by "*AGV*" in the ordering. The same holds for storage stands. The order between AGVs and forklifts is also irrelevant as long as each job holds at most one AGV or one forklift at a given time:

- **(i)** *instand < storage-stand*
- **(ii)** *storage-stand < forklift*
- **(iii)** *storage-stand < AGV*
- **(iv)** *outstand < storage-stand*

Under this rule, a job cannot first acquire a storage stand and then an instand or outstand. A job traveling from a workstation is sitting on the outstand when acquiring other resources. A job traveling from storage acquires its destination instand before other resources.

The partial order is transitive so it follows that *instand* < *AGV* and *outstand* < *AGV*. This rule applies to jobs on their way from an outstand straight to their next workstation's instand. Such a job is sitting on an outstand. It must also have an instand to go to before acquiring an AGV.

The order rule is needed even with the bumping. Let's assume there is a single AGV and a single storage stand, that is, $N = S = 1$. Absent the order rule, one job could hold the AGV while waiting for the storage stand, and another could hold the storage stand while waiting for the AGV.

7.3.2.2 Job-Thread Solution for the FMS

We can address the resource contention head-on by identifying job entities.[106] The jobs are the users of all the resources. An architecture with a resource-user control thread for each job can be implemented with implicit state laying out the order in which a job acquires and releases resources. The shared resources are represented by safe objects with operations such as *acquire* and *release*. Here's the job-thread logic:

```
Get information about first job step
while (not done)
      Acquire workstation instand
      Acquire storage stand
      Acquire forklift
      Travel to storage stand
      Release forklift
      while (True)
         Acquire AGV
         Travel to instand
         Release AGV and storage stand or outstand
         Inform workstation about job
         // Process continues at workstation microprocessor
         Wait for job to appear on outstand
         Get information about next job step
         Break from inner loop if job done
         Attempt to acquire instand of workstation for next step
         Wait for either:
            Instand acquired
            or Bumping signal (then break from inner loop)
      Acquire storage stand        // Continue here after break from inner loop
      Acquire AGV
      Travel to storage stand
      Release AGV
      Acquire forklift
      Travel to bin
      Release storage stand and forklift
```

As in the switchyard example, the programming style with implicit state representation lets us easily verify the order in which resources are acquired. An

[106]Jeff Carter worked out the details of this resource-user-thread solution in Ada 95 (Carter and Sandén, 1998).

encapsulated portion such as "Travel to storage stand" can have pre- and post-conditions indicating resources held by a job just before the call and just after the return.

The step "Wait for either: Instand acquired or Bumping signal" is nontrivial and requires asynchronous transfer of control (ATC), which is available in RTSJ (Section 2.2.5.7) and Ada (Section 2.3.3). The Ada implementation of this part of the job task is discussed in Section 2.3.3.1.

The job-thread solution has the drawback that control threads are created and destroyed as parts enter and leave the manufacturing system. One way to avoid this is to tie each thread to a bin rather than a job. Such a *bin* thread would represent the sequence of jobs that occupy a certain bin. We have seen similar solutions such as a thread per ATM representing the sequence of ATM customers (Section 4.1.2). The bin-thread solution would be wasteful if there are many empty bins or if done jobs tend to spend a long time in the bin waiting to be removed.

*7.3.2.2.1 A Job-Thread Pool

A more general way to avoid the repeated allocation/deallocation of memory for newly created/done jobs is to have a pool of job threads. It's implemented as an object, *pool*, which has an operation with condition synchronization. When a job is completed, its thread pends on *pool*, which also keeps track of the number of idle threads available. When a new job is created and the pool is nonempty, one of the threads is activated and takes on the new job. (If the pool is empty, a new thread is created.)

Note It would be more important to use such a pool if the jobs were much shorter so that the time to allocate and start new threads wouldn't be negligible. Also, if each bin often holds a job yet to be done, the pool would have as many threads as there are bins. In that case, the bin-thread solution would be more straightforward and efficient.

*7.3.2.2.2 Variations on the Job-Thread Solution

The job-thread solution is intuitive but nonoptimal because jobs staged in the ASRS keep their control threads. Only a limited number of jobs are ever outside the ASRS at once, which limits the concurrency level of the problem. If the total number of jobs is much greater, it may be tempting to change the software so that a job releases its thread when it enters the ASRS. Unfortunately, this breaks the tidy one-to-one relationship between jobs and control threads.

To justify such a solution, we can identify *floor visits* in the problem domain. Unlike a job entity that represents a job from beginning to end, a *floor-visits* entity represents a portion of a job's life: Each visit starts with a part in storage. The events then take the part to one or more workstations, one after the other, and finally back to storage when the part is either staged between job steps or finished.

Such an event thread can be implemented as a control thread of type *floorvisits*. The software can keep a pool of instances ready to take a part on a visit to the floor. Once a *floorvisits* control thread has left one part in storage, it's free to pick up another. Its life is one long string of visits to the factory floor.

Sadly, the *floorvisits* thread solution contains an ugly asymmetry. In the job-thread solution, a job control thread calls an *acquire* operation on a safe object representing a workstation type and blocks until a workstation becomes available. A *floorvisits* control thread can perform the same service for a job on an outstand. But those jobs in storage that are waiting for workstations lack associated control threads in this solution. Yet, when a workstation becomes available, they too must be taken into account.

So, while *floorvisits* is a valid entity, it's wanting as a resource-user entity. It's at our peril that we settle for such a lopsided architecture. The awkwardness goes away in the workstation-thread solution in Section 7.3.2.3. It, too, has fewer threads than the job-thread solution in most cases.

7.3.2.3 Workstation-Thread Solution for the FMS

*An **elegant** solution is one you wish you'd thought of yourself.*

COOPER AND CLANCY, 1982

As we saw in Chapter 6, an architecture where each resource-user thread holds a single shared resource at a time often has a valid dual solution based on resource-guard threads. This doesn't apply to the FMS as a whole, because jobs hold multiple resources at once. But it works at the workstation level, where the workstations are the only shared resources (Section 7.3.2.1). In a dual resource-guard-thread solution at that level, the workstations have threads, and the jobs are represented by passive software objects that sit in queues and are passed between workstations (Sandén, 1997a). Each station has the following three threads, to which I shall refer collectively as *workstation threads*:[107]

1. An *instand thread*, which finds an eligible job and moves the part to the workstation and into the tool
2. A *tool thread*, which waits for the part to be done and moves it onto the outstand
3. An *outstand thread*, which stages the part in the ASRS if necessary

This is a valid event-thread model because each event occurrence is tied to a workstation—except for the event when a job is first created. It's optimal because, at any one time, one part can be on its way to a given workstation, a second one can be done in the tool, and a third one can be on its way from that workstation to storage. So, a situation—albeit unlikely—exists where all the threads have an event occurring at once.

The workstation-thread solution has the advantage that jobs in storage have no threads. If there are many more jobs than workstations, the workstation-thread solution has fewer threads than the job-thread solution. Furthermore, the workstation threads live as long as the system is running.

7.3.2.3.1 Workstation Threads as Resource-User Threads
In the workstation-thread solution as in the job-thread solution, the deadlock potential at the workstation level is taken care of by means of bumping. We must

---

[107]This solution was suggested by Rob Scott (Section 1.4.2.1).

still prevent deadlock over transport-level resources. The workstation threads are implemented with implicit state. The logic of the *instand* thread, for example, is like this:

```
while ( True )
    Find eligible job
    if job in storage then
        Acquire storage stand
        Acquire forklift
        Travel to storage stand
    Release forklift
    Acquire AGV
    Travel to instand
    Release AGV and outstand or storage stand
    Inform workstation about job
```

As this example suggests, the three threads partition the job logic shown in Section 7.3.2.2 in the sense that each workstation thread takes the job through a part of the logic. (In addition, a supervisor thread queues the job for its first workstation type.)

The workstation threads are resource-user threads for the transport-level resources. The workstation-thread solution leaves those resources essentially as they are handled in the job-thread solution. They are still represented by safe objects, but the calls now come not from job threads but from workstation threads on behalf of jobs.

The order rule in Section 7.3.2.1 holds for both solutions. Thus, when an *instand* thread attempts to acquire a storage stand, a job has already been assigned to it, so rule *i*, *instand* < *storage-stand*, holds for that job. Similarly, when an *outstand* thread attempts to acquire a storage stand, it's on behalf of the job on that outstand. We can verify compliance with the order rule by inspecting the threads' *run* operations.

Note It's convenient that one workstation thread such as an *instand* thread acquires and releases an AGV (and acquires and releases a forklift, if one is needed). Conceivably, a job could keep some shared resource while being handled by more than one workstation thread. For example, the resource might be acquired by the *instand* thread and released by the *outstand* thread. If so, a resource identity would have to be passed between the threads. This would be a strike against the workstation-thread solution but not against the job-thread solution, where only one thread would be involved.

*7.3.2.3.2 Variation on the Workstation-Thread Solution

On the other hand, we cannot ignore efficiency.

Jon Bentley

Although the workstation-thread solution is technically optimal, it's quite unlikely that there will be a time when all the threads have an event occurrence. The *outstand* threads in particular are rarely used. As an optimization, the workstations could share a pool of *outstand* threads. (Compare Sections 7.3.2.2.1 and 7.3.2.2.2.)

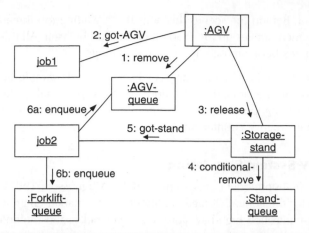

Figure 7.10 Communication diagram of an FMS solution with intuitively active entities (Sandén, 1997a). The operation calls are numbered sequentially.

7.3.2.4 Other FMS Solutions

Besides the job-thread and workstation-thread solutions, other thread models of the FMS problem domain are possible. In one model, AGV, forklift, and workstation entities are chosen because they are physically active (Sandén, 1997a). (There is also a supervisor entity.) The job itself isn't physical and is reduced to a passive object as in the workstation-thread solution.

As long as all entities can be engaged at once, the model is optimal, but it obscures the resource contention. The AGV and the forklift aren't the proper resource users; instead, a resource stays with the job as it's handed from one to the other. This means that the responsibilities aren't as neatly divided as with the job threads in Section 7.3.2.2 or workstation threads in Section 7.3.2.3.

To illustrate the concern, Figure 7-10 shows a scenario with an *AGV* control thread whose AGV has become available. The control thread accesses the *AGV-queue* object to find the job most eligible for service (call 1 in the diagram). If it finds a job, *job1*, say, it must update the job object's state by calling an operation such as *got-AGV* on it (call 2).

Once the AGV has loaded the part from a storage stand, it must release the stand (call 3). In this solution, that's quite an undertaking where the *AGV* control thread must first access the *Stand-queue* object to find any job waiting for the stand (call 4). If it finds such a job, say *job2*, it must then update *job2's* state by calling *got-stand* (call 5). A job such as *job2* on its way to or from storage needs either an AGV or a forklift next. Depending on *job2's* state, the *AGV* thread must put *job2* in either the *AGV-queue* object (call 6a) or the *Forklift-queue* object (call 6b).

All these operations can be encapsulated so that, for example, call 6b is made from within *Storage-stand's release* operation and not directly from the AGV's *run* operation. Still, it's far from obvious why *Forklift-queue's enqueue* operation is called by an *AGV* thread that has just loaded a different job onto the vehicle.

For comparison, the job-thread solution uses a well-understood abstraction, which a maintainer can treat wholesale: A thread simply releases the storage stand. Behind the scenes this activates a waiting job thread (if there is one), which then queues up for a forklift or AGV all by itself. All this is part of a well-known, textbook protocol for resource sharing.

Note The switch engine entities in the switchyard example (Section 7.3.1) and the AGVs in the simulation (Section 7.3.3) are physically active, concrete entities that also happen to be the resource users. This is common, but the FMS provides an instructive counterexample.

7.3.3 AGV System Simulation

This is a simulation model of a system of AGVs (Magnusson, 1994). The system is intended for the central storage facility of a supermarket chain and includes a computer-controlled high-bay store, conveyor belts, and multiple ramps for loading and unloading.

The vehicles travel along a wire buried in the floor. At *places* along this wire are communication devices where the vehicles can receive instructions. Between the places, a vehicle simply follows the wire. This means that the vehicle is sent from place *A* to place *B*, where it can be sent further along, stopped, or delayed until the next place is free. Besides, the vehicles have sensors and automatically stop when they bump into each other or some foreign object.

At places called *interaction points*, the vehicles take part in more complex operations such as loading or unloading. At other interaction points, they can be assigned a new job or sent to a rest area. (Each rest area is an interaction point with room for one vehicle.)

An AGV wiring layout can be viewed at two levels of abstraction. The lower level—the *place graph*—is a network of interconnected places. This is a physical layout where each place is shown exactly once as is each wire connecting two places. The traffic direction on each connection is also shown.

The higher level—the interaction graph—shows the interaction points and the logical flows of traffic connecting them. There may be more than one interaction point per physical place, such as an unloading point, *C1*, and a decision point, *C2*, say. The interaction graph may then show a traffic flow from *C1* to *C2* even though they are at the same place.

Different traffic flows in the *interaction graph* may use the same physical connections. For example, the place graph may show wires from place *P3* to *P4* to *P5* to *P6* to *P7*. The interaction graph may include two flows: One flow may go from a load point at place *P3* to an unload point at place *P5* to another unload point at place *P7*. A second flow may go from the load point at place *P3* straight to the unload point at place *P7*. Physically, a vehicle traveling from the interaction point at *P3* to the interaction point at *P7* must pass through place *P5*, but this is irrelevant at the interaction level and not shown in the interaction graph.

7.3.3.1 Solution Sketch for the AGV System

The structure of the software—in this case, a simulation model—is fashioned after the layered model of the layout:

- The *transport layer* is concerned with moving the vehicles between places while guarding against collisions. Each place is a shared resource that can be occupied by one vehicle at a time. The transport layer also finds a route between two places.

- The *job layer* is concerned with the actions and decisions at the inter-action points and with the distribution of jobs to the vehicles.

In a solution in Simula 67 (Birthwistle et al., 1979; Dahl and Nygaard, 1966), this is represented by a base class *Transport-Layer* and a subclass *Job-Layer*:

- *Transport-Layer* includes the class *Place* and the abstract process class *Vehicle*. (A process in Simula is essentially a thread.[108]) *Vehicle.Move* takes the two parameters *Origin* and *Destination*, which are places that may or may not be connected directly. *Move* finds a route from *Origin* to *Destination* and simulates the physical move.
- *Job-Layer* includes the class *Interaction-Point* and the process class *AGV*, which is a subclass of *Vehicle*.

With this arrangement, *AGV* is a refinement of the abstract class *Vehicle*. Class *AGV* is instantiated; class *Vehicle* is not. *AGV* has its own process body that deals with movements between interaction points and processing at the interaction points, including the assignment of jobs to the AGV. To bring about a physical move between two interaction points, the procedure *Vehicle.Move* is called from the body of *AGV*. This separates the concerns of the two layers.

Interaction-Point is an abstract class with the operation *Action*. The actions taken at each interaction point are defined in several subclasses of *Interaction-Point* such as *Unload-Point*, *Load-Point*, and *Flip-Flop*, which sends vehicles to alternating interaction points. At interaction points of the subclass *Job-Distribution-Point*, each idle AGV is given a job from a job queue and is sent to a suitable load point.

Note In this solution, an (abstract) class, *Vehicle*, represents a basic behavior. A concrete subclass, *AGV*, represents more advanced behavior and calls inherited operations for the basics. This is a way to map levels of abstraction onto the layers of a class hierarchy, which has certain elegance to it.

These days, OO experts recommend a more down-to-earth style where *Vehicle* and *AGV* both are concrete classes, and each physical AGV is repre-sented by one instance of *AGV* and one of *Vehicle*. With this style, *AGV* and *Vehicle* have no superclass–subclass relationship. Instead, *AGV* **delegates** the lower level vehicle operations to its *Vehicle* instance.

7.3.3.2 Complications

In a more complex variation of the problem, wires between places may inter-sect. In that case, semaphores—traffic lights—must be installed to avoid colli-sions. Other complications include deadlock prevention. One such deadlock issue is discussed in Section 7.2.2.2 and involves a subgraph forming a loop with three places. If all three are taken, no AGV can access the place where it needs to go. This deadlock can be broken by starting all three vehicles at the same time. A more general solution is to limit the number of vehicles in the subgraph.

---

[108]Simula's processes are actually implemented as coroutines.

7.4 HEURISTICS

Yes, the solution seems to work, it appears to be correct; but how is it possible to invent such a solution?

PÓLYA, 1957

The "aim of heuristics is to study the methods and rules of discovery and invention" (Pólya, 1957). ELM is chiefly a heuristic approach meant to help the designer discover structures in the problem that can be used as foundations for the software architecture.

The discovery of resource-user entities is key to analyzing resource contention problems and those with simultaneous exclusive access to multiple resources in particular. In the FMS, switchyard, and AGV problems, all resource users are of a single type, be it a job, a switch engine, or an AGV. As we have seen, other entities—no matter how intuitively pleasing—don't qualify as resource users.

7.4.1 Entities Driving the Process

Methinks I see my father—
Where, my lord?
In my mind's eye, Horatio.

HAMLET, ACT I, SCENE 2

One discovery technique is to look for entities in the problem that seem to drive the process. Many entities are mobile or active in some other respect. Focusing on them can let us view the thread architecture in our mind's eye as a mechanism with interacting—perhaps moving—parts. The FMS illustrates this. We looked at the FMS domain in two ways:

1. In the job-thread model in Section 7.3.2.2, each job pursues its own completion by working through its process plan. Intuitively, job entities *drive* the model. In the software, this translates into control: Each job control thread is like a main program that progresses while calling operations on objects (Section 6.2.2).

2. In the workstation-thread model in Section 7.3.2.3, the jobs are passive and the workstations are the drivers. They move the process along by trying to stay busy. This translates into workstation control threads.

We saw in Section 1.4.2.1 that a simple *key* idea can capture the gist of an architecture and allow us to do concrete reasoning at a high degree of abstraction. The key decision to give each job a thread determines how we look at the problem and the software architecture. Most calls on passive objects originate with a job. In that sense as well, the job drives the solution. Such a design decision is also important in what it excludes. With ELM, each event occurrence can be part of no more than one thread, so once we choose job threads, we cannot also have, say, workstation threads.

Other architectures, too, have entities that drive the process, as for instance the AGVs and forklifts in the FMS model in Section 7.3.2.4. (The drawback is that they aren't viable resource-user entities.) Resource-guard threads arranged in a virtual assembly line can also be seen as moving the process forward (Section 6.3).

Such driver entities appear to pursue goals—as with the job entities—or enforce some policy that keeps the system going—as do the workstation entities by striving to stay busy. Looking for such drivers is more productive in some problems than in others.

7.4.1.1 Anthropomorphism?

Mr. Personification is not your friend.

NEWSGROUP POST CIRCA 1993

All this isn't undue anthropomorphism. I'm not suggesting that we think of the jobs as protagonists in a little drama. It's not "Mr. Job talks to Mr. Workstation." The job appears to pursue a goal, not by its own volition but because it has been so programmed, which we could repeat, pedantically, every time. But such shorthand phrases as "the job pursues this goal" and "object so-and-so is responsible for that" are handy and have long been used in engineering (Shore, 1985). They support consistent mental models of what's going on.

7.5 MORE ON DEADLOCK AND ITS PREVENTION

This section broadens the discussion of deadlock prevention and how it informs ELM architectures. The resource-user-thread pattern makes a clear distinction between resource users and the resources they share. The interfaces between resource-user threads are at the safe objects, which each thread acquires and releases. This is the basis of a deadlock prevention strategy. Once we find a convention that prevents deadlock, we can build it into the software design. This approach contrasts starkly with the complex interfaces between the intuitively active entities in Section 7.3.2.4, where an AGV thread becomes involved in the nitty-gritty of enqueuing a job with which it has nothing to do.

7.5.1 Deadlock with and without Threads

Deadlock can exist without threads. Imagine first that we implement FMS as a sequential program. Absent some prevention strategy, such a single-control-thread solution can deadlock. It can put itself in a position where, for example, one job has been assigned the last stand and is waiting for the single forklift and another job has the forklift and is waiting for the stand.

Second, say that we implement FMS with control threads but without aligning them with the resource users. This is so in the solution with AGV and forklift threads in Section 7.3.2.4 and could also be the case in a data-flow-threading architecture (Section 8.3.2). In such a solution, it's clear that jobs can still deadlock, even though the control threads may not. On the other hand, the control threads could engage in their very own deadlocks over internal, shared resources such as job queues. The result could be deadlocks of two kinds. (Section 7.5.2 has an example of deadlock involving internal, shared resources.)

The third case is the job-thread solution to the FMS (Section 7.3.2.2). By definition, the control threads are the users of any internal resources. When we make them the surrogates for problem-domain resource users, they become the sole users of *all* shared resources. A deadlock prevention convention implemented in those control threads can address all combinations of simultaneously accessed resources whether internal or external.

7.5.2 Deadlock Involving Internal Software Resources

A benign case of multiple, *internal* shared objects held simultaneously can be found in the elevator example in Section 6.7.1.1. An elevator thread first calls an operation on the safe object *Servable-requests*. From within that operation, it calls operations on the safe objects *External-requests* and *Internal-requests* (Figure 6-10). (*External-requests* holds the outstanding requests from floor buttons, and *Internal-requests* contains the requests from buttons within cabins.) This requires the order rule

Servable-requests < *External-requests* and *Servable-requests* < *Internal-requests*

Sampler threads detect new requests for service. With this order rule, they can call operations on *External-requests* and *Internal-requests* but cannot call operations on *Servable-requests* from within *External-requests* or *Internal-requests*.

The following example of deadlock over internal software resources arises in an implementation of the observer pattern (Gamma et al., 1995): A safe object of class *Value-holder* updates a number of listener safe objects by calling each listener's *value-changed* operation (Lee, 2006).

Value-holder has the safe operation *add-listener*, which adds an object to the *Value-holder* instance's list of listeners, and the safe operation *set-value*, whereby the instance is given a change that it must propagate to all its listeners by calling the safe operation *value-changed* on each object on its list.

Let *valueholder* be an instance of *Value-holder* and *listener* an object on *valueholder*'s list. If this *listener* has the safe operation *x* in addition to *value-changed*, deadlock exists in the following scenario:

- One thread, *t1*, is executing *valueholder.set-value* and has *valueholder* locked. From within *set-value* it calls *listener.value-changed* and tries to lock *listener*.

- Another thread, *t2*, is executing *listener.x* and has *listener* locked. From within *x* it calls *valueholder.add-listener* and tries to lock *valueholder*.

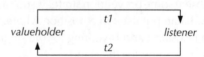

This deadlock can be prevented by means of the order rule *listener* < *valueholder* (where *listener* and *valueholder* stand for any object of each kind). If this problem arises in an ELM architecture, *t1* and *t2* may already be resource-user threads, and the rule would be added to any rules already in place.

7.5.3 Expanding an ELM Architecture

Adhere to the style of the original.

Vermeulen et al., 2000

It happens that we must add entities to an existing architecture such as the job-thread solution for the FMS. If those entities need simultaneous exclusive access to multiple resources that are also used by the jobs, it's clear that they must obey the order rule in Section 7.3.2.1. Intuitively speaking, we make the new entities behave like jobs. The FMS may also need new workstation types—manual inspection and washing stations, for instance. Again, we style them after the existing workstations.

The simple transaction control system in Section 6.4.1 offers another illustration: It has a *TProc* thread that handles each transaction, accesses a common database, and so forth. A *Restart* subsystem runs after a system crash has disrupted the transaction processing. Using information saved on disk for this purpose, *Restart* identifies what transactions were in progress at the crash. Each such transaction is recovered by means of *before looks*, which are record images saved to disk. This happens before normal transaction processing is resumed; no *TProc* threads are running during the restart.

To speed up the recovery by means of some concurrency, *Restart* creates a *TRecy* thread for each disrupted transaction. Each *TRecy* is, in some ways, a *TProc* instance's double and takes over its data and locks. *TProc* and *TRecy* represent the same entity, and *TRecy* must abide by the same conventions as *TProc*. Besides, the transaction control system also uses *utility TProcs*, which performs housekeeping chores and conforms to conventions for *TProcs*.

7.5.4 Problems without Apparent Resources

Some deadlock problems appear to involve no resources—but can usually be converted to a standard form with resources and resource users. The two Ada tasks *X* and *Y* in the example below are deadlocked.

The tasks attempt to engage in a rendezvous, which is a form of synchronous communication (Section 2.3.4). To execute the rendezvous, *X* calls *Y*'s *entry Y1*. *Y* performs an *accept statement* to indicate that it's ready to receive a call to that entry. Either task waits until the other task is ready. That is, either *X* waits in the entry call statement until *Y* executes its accept statement or *Y* waits in the accept statement until *X* issues its call.

In the following example, *X* tries to call *Y.Y1*, and simultaneously, *Y* tries to call *X.X1*. Both tasks wait in vain for the other to execute its **accept** statement.

```
Task X                      Task Y
   begin                       begin
      Y.Y1;                        X.X1;
      accept X1;                   accept Y1;
   end;                        end;
```

Although no resources are visible, deadlock clearly exists. It's easy to restate the problem in terms of resource contention by noting that each connection between the tasks has two ends, one at each task. In order to complete a rendezvous, a task first needs exclusive access to its own end. While holding onto it—and prohibiting incoming calls—it must also gain exclusive access to the other end.[109]

---

[109]The same reasoning holds for a data-flow-threading architecture (Section 8.3.2) where two threads may be waiting on return messages from each other.

With the problem thus rephrased, an order rule such as *End-X < End-Y* allows *X* alone to make a rendezvous call. As an alternative, we could use *timed* entry calls (Section 2.3.2.3) and let at least one of the tasks give up after a period of waiting.

7.5.5 Acquiring All Resources Ahead of Time

We can sometimes let an entity or thread collect *all* the resources it needs before starting to use any of them. There may have to be multiple attempts: If the entity finds that a resource it needs isn't available right away, it doesn't wait long but instead releases those resources it has and starts over. That way, no entity holds a resource indefinitely while waiting for another, and deadlock is avoided. Such a method may be viable in an operating system, when it may be known that a given job needs certain disk drives and printers. The banker's algorithm is sometimes used to allocate resources to jobs (Stallings, 2008; Tanenbaum and Woodhull, 2006).

In Section 7.3.1.1, we saw an example where a switch engine traveling against the locking order must acquire *all* the track segments in the order opposite to its travel. Still, acquiring all resources at once is no solution that can be used across the board because (1) we may not know initially what resources an entity will need and (2) the result may be unacceptably low resource utilization. In the switchyard example in Section 7.3.1.1, a switch engine, no matter which direction it's going, would acquire all the track segments along its route. In the FMS, a job moving to a workstation first on a forklift and then on an AGV would keep the AGV while using the forklift.

7.6 CONCLUSION

The process of preparing programs for a digital computer is especially attractive, not only because it can be economically and scientifically rewarding, but also because it can be an aesthetic experience much like composing poetry or music.

KNUTH, 1968

The various ways to prevent deadlock discussed in Section 7.2.2 are well-understood textbook techniques. ELM's contribution is to put the problem and the software in a form that lets us use the techniques easily and transparently. For this, we identify the resources and the resource-user entities in the problem and feature them prominently in the software. Resource-user control threads serve as the software surrogates for those entities and acquire and release resources on their behalf.

With implicit state representation, we can program those threads in such a way that the program text, read from top to bottom, plainly shows how resources are acquired and freed. By inspecting the program text, we can also verify that any convention put in place to prevent deadlock is observed.

Deadlock, also called circular wait, exists when entities or threads wait for resources held by each other. All deadlocks can be expressed in these terms as long as we identify the resources and the resource-using entities correctly. In addition to circularity, deadlock requires both of the following:

- Each entity waits *indefinitely* for one resource while holding another.
- There are enough entities to populate the wait chain.

It's sometimes possible to falsify one of these conditions and thereby prevent deadlock:

- The entity may be able to release the resource it has, as in the robot-stocking problem in Section 7.2.2.3.
- It may be possible to limit the number of entities in a part of the problem, as in the AGV example in Section 7.2.2.2.

A *locking order*, also known as an *order rule*, offers a third option. If resources are always acquired in a certain partial order, there can be no circularity and no deadlock.

These approaches work when the resource users acquire resources in a pattern defined by a thread's *run* operation. Then the designer can construct a deadlock-free system. They don't work in situations where a human user can cause resources to be acquired in any order.

This chapter assumes that the resources are given. This isn't always so; the designer may well have the option to combine "tiny" resources that are often used together, thereby making it impossible for threads to acquire them in conflicting order. At the same time, the overhead for acquiring multiple locks is avoided. But taken to extremes, such an approach can reduce resource utilization unacceptably, just as acquiring all resources ahead of time can (Section 7.5.5).

EXERCISES

7-1 Variation on the dining philosophers. Show the following situation in a wait-chain diagram: Four philosophers, E, S, W, and N, are seated around a table as in Figure 7-6. There are four forks, and each philosopher needs the two forks next to him in order to eat. The philosophers live by the convention that E and W must pick up the fork on their left before the one on their right. S and N must start with their right fork and may then pick up their left one.

(a) Is there a potential for deadlock? Show evidence one way or the other!

(b) In this example, every other philosopher starts with his left fork. To prevent deadlock, how many philosophers must start with a different fork than the rest?

(c) How must the left-fork first and right-fork-first philosophers be seated? Must every other one be left-fork first?

7-2 Wait-chain diagram 1. There are four resources, A, B, C, and D, and a single thread type with the following logic:

A.acquire;
B.acquire;
A.release;
C.acquire;
B.release;
D.acquire;
C.release;
A.acquire;
D.release;
A.release;

How many instances does it take to create deadlock? In the deadlock situation, what resources does each instance hold (that is, how far has it progressed in the logic)?

7-3 Wait-chain diagram 2. There are five resources, A, B, F, G, I, and O, and two thread types, S and T, with the following logic:

S: I.acquire;   T: O.acquire;
        A.acquire;   G.acquire;
        F.acquire;   A.acquire;
        F.release;   O.release;
        G.acquire;   G.release;
        A.release;   F.acquire;
        G.release;   A.release;
        B.acquire;   F.release;
        I.release;
        B.release;

(a) There are only instances of S. How many does it take to create deadlock?

(b) There are only instances of T. How many does it take to create deadlock?

(c) There are some instances of S and some of T. How many of each does it take to create the circular wait? What resources does each instance hold?

7-4 Entity/event-thread discovery. Identify useful entities and/or event threads in the following problem sketches. Identify resource-user and resource-guard threads. Are there any dual thread models? Is there potential for deadlock, and if so, how can we prevent it? Justify your answers.

(a) A batch data-processing system has one printer and two CD drives. Multiple batch jobs run concurrently. Jobs may need simultaneous access to one or two CD drives and/or the printer. Some jobs need a CD drive and then the printer. Other jobs need a CD and the printer at the same time. Jobs of a third kind need both CD drives at once and the printer separately.

(b) In an automated garage, customers drop off their cars in an area with room for six cars. There are several mobile units. A mobile unit picks up a car in the drop-off area and takes it to an empty parking slot. The garage is made up of aisles of parking slots. The aisles are connected by one-way lanes, where several mobile units can travel at once, behind each other. Each mobile unit needs exclusive access to an aisle so that it can move about freely when parking a car (or when fetching a parked car).

(c) The management system for an aircraft carrier has to account for the movement of aircraft between the hangar deck and the flight deck. Each aircraft has its own parking area on the hangar deck. It's moved to a parking area on the flight deck via a single elevator with room for one aircraft. The number of parking areas on the flight deck is limited. One aircraft at a time is moved from the parking area on the flight deck to the runway, which is also on the flight deck.

Simulation Projects

It's instructive to write programs that simulate problems such as the philosophers, the FMS, or the switchyard. For the latter two, where multiple threads can be waiting for the same resource, you need a language that keeps waiting threads in FIFO queues (or FIFO within priorities). Ada (Section 2.3) does this, as well as RTSJ (Section 2.2.5).

In addition to the thread architecture, the simulation model must include scaffolding threads that simulate the domain entities themselves and their interaction with the simulated software system. Thus a domain entity can be represented by two control threads: One is the entity's software surrogate, and the other is a mock-up of its behavior. To the extent possible, we should keep the two kinds of threads apart.

7-5 Switchyard problem. I simulated the switchyard with the layout in Figure 7-11 in a simple program. Because the destination sidings—rightmost in the diagram—must be acquired first and released last, I ordered all track segments from right to left in the figure. That is, a switch engine traveling from the locomotive siding to a destination siding must acquire the entire path before setting out, while an engine on its way back can acquire segments as it goes.

This seemed like a good idea, as a switch engine that must acquire multiple track segments will start with segments that are relatively little used and only toward the end try to acquire a contested segment near the root. It would be interesting to compare the results from another ordering strategy, most readily the one where the segments are ordered from left to right in Figure 7-11.

By assigning proportionally realistic travel times, we can collect data about the behavior of the switchyard with varying numbers of switch engines. If the engines are too many, they spend a long time trying to acquire the path to a siding, so for given parameters, there is an optimum number of engines.

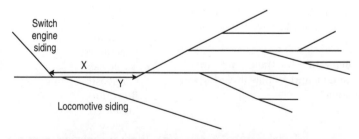

Switch engine siding

X

Y

Locomotive siding

Figure 7-11 Track layout for switchyard simulation.

To avoid a bottleneck, I put in a bypass segment, X, for travel past the locomotive siding in the direction of the arrow. Segment Y is for travel in the other direction. One switch engine at a time can enter the locomotive siding and get cars. With my order rule, it then waits on track segment Y for exclusive access to its destination siding and the path there. The next switch engine can line up behind it but cannot start acquiring track segments until the first one has all its segments.

7-6 FMS problem. Here are some possible extensions to the FMS design that can be tested in a discrete-event simulation:

(a) Error detection: The FMS software may detect the breakdown of a device either when an explicit error signal is received from the device or when an operation times out. When an error is detected, the FMS notifies the supervisor who decides on further action.

(b) Supervisor interface: The supervisor must be allowed to take down a device such as a workstation, an AGV, or a forklift. By taking down a device, the supervisor takes it out of production so it won't be scheduled to a job by the software. The supervisor may take down a malfunctioning device or one in need of preventive maintenance.

(c) Recovery action: The supervisor must be able to decide proper recovery action in error situations. Various actions are possible. For example, if an AGV breaks down with a part on it, there are at least three options:

- If the repair is minor, the part may be left on the AGV.
- If the AGV must be taken down for a long time, the job may be manually moved to its current destination, where normal processing continues.
- The AGV may seriously break down while on its way to pick up a part. In that case, a failure status may be returned to the job control thread, which may then acquire another AGV.

A workstation breakdown may affect jobs occupying the instand as well as the tool proper. (A part on the outstand is unaffected.)

If a workstation breaks down, a decision must be made to scrap the part in the tool or continue processing after repair.

If a part is on the instand of a workstation that breaks down, the simple option is to leave it there and resume processing after repair. But if the job is high priority, it may have to be requeued and the part moved to another workstation.

If all forklifts should break down, the FMS can continue operating for a while in degraded mode with those parts already on the factory floor. Jobs in the ASRS that have workstations, storage stands, and/or AGVs reserved should release them.

(d) Handling of raw material and finished jobs: The solution given in this chapter assumes that a blank is available in the ASRS when the job is defined. Assume instead that the life of a job starts at a port with an outstand, much like a workstation, and that the part must travel by AGV from the port to the ASRS.

Also consider the case where finished and scrapped parts must be carried to a port to be removed from the system. Treat such a port as a station with one instand.

The scaffolding should allow the user to simulate the breakdown of various devices. This may be done with specific commands that are propagated to the scaffolding simulating the devices. These commands are part of the scaffolding and must be clearly distinguished from those supervisor commands that would exist in a real system.

An interesting simulation of a system like the FMS can be found in Chapter 13 of Law (2006). Its purpose is to determine the optimal number of workstations, forklifts, and other resources. It shows how the number of jobs in various queues varies with the number of resources of the different kinds.

BACKGROUND AND DISCUSSION

Real-time software architectures and data-flow design approaches

8

There are two ways of constructing a software design. One way is to make it so simple that there are obviously no deficiencies. The other way is to make it so complicated that there are no obvious deficiencies.

HOARE, 1981

8.1 INTRODUCTION

This chapter covers two different yet related topics. It begins with an overview of architectural styles for real-time software systems ranging from sequential cyclic executives to multithreaded solutions. It then discusses data-flow-oriented design of multithreaded software and contrasts it with entity-life modeling.

Section 8.2 covers the spectrum of real-time software from hard real-time systems that must meet hard deadlines[110] to the kind of soft real-time software with dynamically scheduled threads that ELM produces. With increasing processor capacity, the number of hard real-time systems is probably a shrinking share of the number of all embedded-software devices, which is growing. Many systems may still need to handle interrupts or other inputs by hard deadlines, but as long as there are no deadline *conflicts*, this can be done by assigning priorities judiciously within a soft real-time environment.

In cases where processing capacity is severely limited—such as to a single processor—and there are conflicting, hard deadlines, special thread-scheduling algorithms such as rate-monotonic scheduling can ensure that all deadlines are met. Threads scheduled that way can coexist with dynamically scheduled, lower priority threads.

---

[110]Hard deadlines are defined in Section 8.2.2.1.

8.2 REAL-TIME ARCHITECTURES

If a project has not achieved a system architecture, including its rationale, the project should not proceed to full-scale system development. Specifying the architecture as a deliverable enables its use throughout the development and maintenance process.

BOEHM, 1995

This section reviews the major, standard architecture styles for real-time software. I discuss how each applies to the cruise controller, which was introduced in detail in Section 5.4.3.1 together with an ELM solution. Finally, I show how some established architectural styles can influence the requirements analysis. This happens when a requirements specification makes premature assumptions about the software architecture and thereby ties the architect's hands.

The cruise controller (Section 5.4.3.1) has become something of a model problem for embedded-systems architecture (Shaw, 1995b). Rooted in 1980s engineering, it's now technically passé (Hakim, 2004; Mössinger, 2010). Practitioners see it as a "very trite"[111] textbook example with plain software solutions that needs little analysis. That said, it's also small enough to let us compare different architectures. Here's a summary of the problem statement in Section 5.4.3.1.1: The cruise controller regulates the speed of a car by adjusting the throttle periodically. The driver sets a desired speed by pressing a button. The driver can override cruise control temporarily by pressing the accelerator. Automatic cruise control resumes as soon as the driver steps off the accelerator. The cruise controller receives a signal when the driver brakes, and it then suspends cruising. The driver can later resume cruising at the earlier selected speed.

There are three established architectural styles for embedded real-time systems such as the cruise controller (Laplante, 2004):

- A cyclic executive
- A set of periodic threads
- A set of event-driven threads

Of these, the cyclic executive and the periodic threads are both *time-driven* solutions: They get their input by polling sensors and the like at predetermined times. External events cannot influence the execution directly by means of interrupts or otherwise. In a system of event-driven threads, by contrast, most events are signaled by means of interrupts. I discuss each architecture in the following.

8.2.1 Cyclic Executive

To a hacker, an "exec" is always a program, never a person.

RAYMOND, 1993

A cyclic executive is a sequential program with an infinite loop. Typically, in each loop cycle, it first polls for inputs, then does its calculations, and finally

---

[111]Susan Harbour, comp.software-eng, November 14, 1994.

operates on actuators. This *major cycle* often contains *minor cycles* that execute the same kind of logic more frequently.

A cyclic executive architecture is predictable and also quite simple in principle. It has no threads—and hence requires no real-time kernel to control them. The programmer has full control and may know, for instance, that a given sensor is always polled on the 17th millisecond of each 100-msec interval. Conflicts over shared variables are avoided since no two activities ever execute simultaneously.

On the downside, cyclic executives have a reputation for being hard to maintain. Partly, this is due to a no-frills programming style intended to minimize execution time and memory footprint. Such a style can also make it easier to calculate the exact execution time by summing the instruction times from a CPU manual.

A traditional cyclic executive is a block of Fortran text. The source may be a sequence of **INCLUDE** statements, each representing a set of source statements called a *frame*. The frames usually communicate via global variables. This makes for a potentially fragile structure where frames have assumptions about each other built in. For example, one frame may assume that the preceding frame stored a certain value in a common variable. Such hard coding is heresy to present-day software engineers. We favor loosely coupled modules[112] with restricted, well-defined interfaces. Inscrutable, all-uppercase Fortran identifiers such as **HWSLBUT** and **HGMSTRA** make things even worse.

If the designers hadn't thought the overhead frivolous, they could easily apply information hiding and encapsulate semantically linked variables in modules with well-defined interfaces. Thus modernized, a cyclic executive is no unreasonable architecture for our simple cruise controller: It repeatedly senses the hardware to detect any driver commands and to count driveshaft revolutions. This may be the minor cycle, while the major cycle periodically actuates on the throttle.

8.2.1.1 Cyclic Executive Implementations with Threads

What is essentially a cyclic executive can be implemented as a "main" periodic thread (task). Lower priority threads can then use the CPU after the periodic computations are finished and until the next cycle begins (Vaughan, 1998).

Another option is to allow interrupts during the cycle. To retain the predictability of the executive, the direct interrupt handling is kept to a minimum: The interrupt handler just sets a flag indicating the type of interrupt and stores any associated data. In the proper phase of its cycle, the main thread senses the flag and performs whatever additional processing is called for.

The cruise controller inputs may well be interrupts, making this kind of solution suitable. When an interrupt occurs, a handler updates the state of cruising and, if needed, captures the current speed as the desired cruising speed.

---

[112]The fewer assumptions modules make about each other, the looser their coupling. For example, two modules are loosely coupled if one calls the other's operations and supplies any data as parameters and the other returns the result as a parameter or a return value. They are *tightly* coupled if, for example, they communicate via a global variable.

The main thread's only remaining job is to regulate the throttle. In each cycle, it determines the current state and, if cruising is on, exerts a pull on the throttle wire as needed. This design is quite like the ELM solution in Section 5.4.3.1.3.

8.2.2 Periodic Threads

We can make the software more modifiable by replacing the executive with a set of periodic threads. With proper scheduling and on certain conditions, such a system can be as predictable as an executive. This section discusses *rate-monotonic* scheduling, which lets us calculate ahead of time whether multiple computations will all meet their hard deadlines.

8.2.2.1 Rate-Monotonic Scheduling

Rate-monotonic scheduling (RMS) is a widely known scheduling policy. Each thread is periodic and its priority is a function of the period—the shorter the period, the higher the priority (Klein et al., 1993; Sha et al., 1991). Scheduling is preemptive: As soon as a thread becomes ready to run, it takes over the processor from any lower priority thread (Section 1.3.1).

RMS is concerned only with systems of threads with *conflicting*, *hard* deadlines. A computation has a hard deadline if it must be completed by a given time to avoid dire consequences. Deadlines *conflict* if there are times when more than one deadline-bound computation is ongoing or pending on the same processor. In that situation, it's helpful to give the computations rate-monotonic priorities and find out ahead of time whether all the deadlines can be met.

8.2.2.1.1 Basic RMS

In basic rate-monotonic theory, each thread t has a periodic deadline, say every $T(t)$ seconds. Those $T(t)$ seconds also define the thread's *period*. Each thread has a computation that must be performed once each period. It's known how much time each computation takes. A set of threads is said to be *schedulable* if they all meet their deadlines; that is, each thread gets its computation done during each period.

It's easy to see that assigning priorities by periodicity is an advantage if threads have to meet hard deadlines. Let $t1$ and $t2$ be two threads ready to run. Where $t1$ is activated every 10 msec and uses the CPU for 4 msec each time, while $t2$ is activated every 4 msec and needs 2 msec of CPU time. If $t1$ should run before $t2$, $t2$ will have missed its first deadline before it even starts. But if $t2$ starts before $t1$, it can meet its deadlines at 4, 8, and 12 msec and still let $t1$ complete on time.

RMS is especially attractive if the total CPU utilization is less than about 69% (for a uniprocessor). In that case it can be shown that a set of rate monotonically scheduled threads will all meet their deadlines (Klein et al., 1993; Sha et al., 1991). Total processor use can often be estimated rather easily. With higher total utilization, on the other hand, the proof involves *each thread's* CPU utilization, which may be harder to determine accurately.

8.2.2.1.2 RMS Complications
Simplicity is prerequisite for reliability.

DIJKSTRA, 1971–1979

Certain issues complicate the use of RMS:

- **Processor Utilization.** Determining each thread's processor utilization can be difficult, especially when it performs some iterative algorithm[113]. Such an algorithm is said to *converge*, essentially, if each iteration yields a more precise result. The number of iterations necessary to reach a certain precision sometimes depends on the input data.

  A common solution to this problem is to cap the computation time at M milliseconds, say: If the algorithm hasn't produced a result with sufficient precision after M milliseconds, we settle for the result computed so far. Such a cap can be enforced by means of asynchronous transfer of control (Sections 2.2.5.7 and 2.3.3).

- **Deadlines.** In basic RMS, the deadline is at the end of each period. Each thread is guaranteed to complete its processing *at some point* during the period. This means that the thread may execute up to the very end of one period and be scheduled to restart at the beginning of the next. Such deviation from a regular pace is called *jitter*. To control it, some forms of RMS allow an execution *window* to be specified that is smaller than the full period.

- **Aperiodic Events.** RMS has trouble with *aperiodic* events. (Events are aperiodic if they occur at random times. They may be signaled by interrupts.) RMS deals with such events by means of high-priority, periodic server threads, which are scheduled rate monotonically together with the other threads. (This works for **sporadic** events, which are separated by some minimum time. Other events are called "fully aperiodic.")

- **Resource Sharing.** Resource sharing complicates preemption. If one thread, *t1*, attempts to preempt another thread, *t2*, but needs exclusive access to a resource held locked by *t2*, then *t1* must let *t2* proceed until it frees the resource. Such a situation where a lower priority thread is running while a higher priority thread is stalled is called *priority inversion* (Section 2.1.4.1.1.1).

8.2.2.1.3 RMS Drawbacks
Like any other software design based on formal proofs, RMS calls for special preparation of the maintainers. A person who changes a computation or adds a thread may well have to recalculate the schedulability.

RMS helps only if both the processor is the bottleneck and the competition for processor access is the main concern. In this day and age, processor capacity may be the least of our worries. Instead, the bus may be the bottleneck and the processors mostly idle. If so, RMS is of no help, and there is little reason to build a thread architecture around proving that all threads are schedulable.

---

[113]For example, the Newton–Raphson iterative algorithm is used for solving an equation. Iterative algorithms can also solve systems of equations.

Another drawback is that RMS-based design centers on the technicality of processor optimization rather than on the nature of the problem. Many unwieldy legacy systems were designed to meet the hardware restrictions of their day (Adolph, 1996). There were systems with 80-character record limits long after the last card punch was hauled to a museum. The "Millennium Bug" was the subject of epic hunts because programmers and database designers in the 1970s and 1980s stored the year as two digits only. Back then, storage space was at a premium, and who knew that the system would survive the millennium?

8.2.2.1.4 Deadlines versus Guidelines

The real-time community is much aware that rate-monotonic and other policies let us program to hard deadlines. It makes no sense, however, to invent deadlines just so we can program to them. This would lead to *fictitious deadlines*,[114] by which I mean timing goals that are given deadline status although they aren't *real* deadlines. The need to guarantee multiple deadlines can constrain the design severely, thereby making a system slower and harder to understand and maintain—a steep price if, in fact, the deadlines are just guidelines.

Take, for example, a building monitoring system where a large number of motion detectors and other devices must be sampled every second (Sommerville, 2007). Based on that, 1-second deadlines are imposed, and missed deadlines are counted. But in all likelihood they are mere guidelines as there are *no dire consequences* if a detector goes unsampled for 1.1 or even 2 seconds once in a while. In such systems, a missed-deadline count isn't the best performance metric: The mean and standard deviation of the sampling period are more appropriate and can be remeasured as we add sensors, in case the processing capacity is no longer sufficient.

Other systems, such as the cruise controller, are also elastic that way: It must actuate on the throttle at a roughly consistent pace to ensure a smooth ride, but without hard deadlines. To avoid missed inputs, the interrupt handling (or the periodic scanning of various controls) may need higher priority than the throttle actions.

8.2.3 Dynamically Scheduled Threads

A set of periodic threads that *provably* meets a schedule may be warranted in systems with conflicting, hard deadlines. But software is at its best when it can schedule activities dynamically. As long as processing capacity is plentiful, this makes for modifiable systems: A thread can be expanded or a new one added, and the rest of the system adapts without the intricate reprogramming of a cyclic executive or the schedulability recalculation for RMS.

Much multithreaded software has no conflicting, hard deadlines. Even for many—possibly most—*real-time* systems, only a few computations tend to have hard deadlines. Those computations have periodic threads which coexist with other, dynamically scheduled threads.

That a lengthy high-priority computation may starve more urgent computations is foremost an issue with uniprocessors. As the number of processors

---

[114]It's sometimes called an *artifact* deadline.

grows, a thread is more likely to find one available. This makes scheduling for multiprocessors much easier than for a uniprocessor (Stallings, 2008). To be safer, we can dedicate a processor to a critical thread or set of threads.

With dynamically scheduled threads (Section 1.3.2.1), a designer can choose a thread architecture that separates problem-domain concerns. This is the kind of solution that ELM produces. Such a system may also include some threads that do things on a periodic basis and some rate monotonically scheduled ones. Among the many examples throughout the previous chapters, the switchyard and FMS examples in Chapter 7 show how such dynamically scheduled threads can model problem-domain entities.

8.2.4 Requirements Representations versus Architectures

Principle 46: Avoid design in requirements.

DAVIS, 1995

[T]he separation of the requirements from the design is an abstract goal and not a human reality.

BLUM, 1992

Requirements are supposed to specify only *what* a system must do and stay neutral as to the *how*. Yet, a requirements specification can describe the problem in a manner that constrains the architecture in unfortunate ways. The elevator control problem (Sections 4.3.2 and 6.7.1) may serve as an example. There are at least three ways to specify elevator behavior:

1. **Decision Table or Decision Tree.** Davis (1993) uses nested *if* statements to describe the behavior of an elevator door along the following lines:

   ```
   if door blocked
   then if door not wide open
      then open door
    else if open-door button pressed
      then...
   ```

   This specifies a periodically executed program such as a cyclic executive or a periodic thread. Each time around, the nested *if* statements test the status of several parts of the elevator environment. It's not altogether easy to turn this specification into an event-driven architecture, where the software responds to interrupts. In fact, the designer must reverse engineer the specification and restate it in terms of events.

   *Note The specification captures the state of the elevator as a composition of orthogonal regions (Section 3.4.4), each with two states such as *door blocked* and *door not blocked*. This can produce myriad composed states, many of which are invalid because of the elevator system mechanics.

   The designer of the decision table deals with those states by asking questions such as, "If the door is blocked, which other aspects of the elevator status are important?" Each relevant aspect gives rise to a nested *if* statement. This does seem better than holding up each and every composed state and asking ourselves whether it's valid. Still, the process suggested in Section 3.4.4.2 is even simpler: Start in an intuitively clear state, determine which events can happen, include any new states to which they lead, and continue in that vein from each new state.

2. **Condition-Driven State Machines.** Chapter 3 focuses on *event-driven* state machines, whose transitions are triggered by events. In a *condition-driven* state machine, by contrast, transitions can also be triggered by conditions. This assumes that some mechanism periodically evaluates conditions such as *elevator is stopped*. For example, the state machine for the elevator door can transition from *Closed* to *Opening* on the condition *elevator is stopped and there is a need to visit this floor*.

   Like the decision table specification, a condition-driven state machine can be implemented as a cyclic executive. A frame concerned with elevator movement executes first and sets a flag indicating that the cabin has stopped. The frame concerned with the door executes later and consults the flag.

3. **Event-Driven State Machines.** This is the most common way to represent a state machine; it's covered at length in Chapter 3. Each transition is triggered by an event possibly guarded by a condition. The assumption is that the program is informed of each event occurrence; in the elevator, it's by means of either interrupts or sampling. This representation maps directly onto an event-driven solution, as described in Chapter 5.

8.3 DATA-FLOW DESIGN APPROACHES

Flow gently, sweet Afton, among thy green braes,
Flow gently, I'll sing thee a song in thy praise.

ROBERT BURNS, *AFTON WATER*, 1792

This section deals with designs based on an abstraction where data are viewed as flowing through multiple computational transforms. Such designs were common before object orientation. Data-flow design is of interest in this book because the transforms are sometimes implemented with threads. That is, threading is used as an engineering device to endow a data-flow design with a control structure. This differs conceptually from ELM, where threads reflect concurrency in the problem domain.

8.3.1 Structured Analysis

Structured analysis (SA) is a general-purpose, pre-OO software development method (Blum, 1992; Wieringa, 2003). SA looks at the inputs to a software system and how they are successively *transformed* into outputs. Inputs come from *terminators*, and outputs go to other terminators. A *data-flow diagram* uses essentially three kinds of symbols:

- A *transform* or *transformation*, shown as a circle ("*bubble*")
- A *terminator*, shown as a rectangle

- A *data store*, shown as two parallel, horizontal lines
- A *data flow*, shown as a directed arc from terminator to transform, between transforms, between transform and terminator, or between transform and data store

With structured analysis, a system is usually shown as a hierarchy of data-flow diagrams. The root diagram is called the *context diagram* or *level-0* diagram (Wieringa, 2003). It shows the whole system as a single bubble along with its terminators. This diagram makes a simplified statement about the problem as a whole, which can have "an almost comical obviousness to it" (Blum, 1992).[115] It's the highest abstraction.

The next diagram, *level-1*, shows a first breakdown into transforms numbered 1, 2, ... One of the *level-2* diagrams shows the further breakdown of bubble 1 into bubbles numbered 1.1, 1.2 ...; another shows the breakdown of bubble 2 into bubbles 2.1, 2.2 ...; and so on for each level-1 bubble. Each tier in the hierarchy shows the decompositions of the bubbles one level up.

As a complement to the data-flow diagrams, the logic of each transformation is commonly shown as pseudocode in what is known as a *minispec* (also referred to as a *process description* or *process specification*).

8.3.1.1 Strengths and Weaknesses of Structured Analysis

Hierarchical structure is the sand on which top-down methods are built.

JACKSON, 1995

Structured analysis was never meant to be sophisticated. In the 1970s the SA evangelists consciously sought to make it as simple as possible—even simplistic (Yourdon, 2000). SA's apparent strength is its universality: Most anything can be broken into coherent pieces. To simplify things further, practitioners were told to ignore at first any special cases and exceptions. In administrative systems, deferring special cases that way may be quite possible though not usually in real-time systems where they may determine the whole architecture (Selic and Ward, 1996).

It's difficult, if not impossible, to meaningfully decompose an unfamiliar problem from the top. This seems to belie *stepwise refinement*, a classic but often misunderstood idea (Wirth, 1971). Stepwise refinement works if we "understand all aspects of the situation very thoroughly" (Bell et al., 1997) as when implementing some known algorithm. This is indeed what Wirth does.

When we're working with an unfamiliar problem, SA's top-down nature encourages us to push any difficulties to a deeper level detailed enough to deal with them. Michael Jackson, a staunch critic of top-down approaches, puts it thus: "Top-down became a philosophy of procrastination, of forever deferring the burden of exactness to the next level" (Jackson, 1995, p. 198).

---

[115]A diagram that captures a simple thought may seem harmless. But as design proceeds, many potentially conflicting thoughts must be reconciled, and this is easier while they are in our minds only. The more they are formalized graphically or otherwise, "the more their rigidity resists further modification" (Alexander, 1964, p. 123).

As a result, detecting and resolving the difficulties often fall to the implementers. Bergland uses an administrative program as a simple yet vivid example illustrating how the difficulties can cut across different programmers' domains (Bergland, 1981). What's more, system wide problems can easily go undetected until testing or production. This goes to show that decomposition just isn't enough; we must also think through how it's all going to work.

Ironically, all this may well suit designers and programmers alike: "Unfortunately, it is very tempting to defer problems. This gives an illusion of rapid progress, maintains cash flow, keeps morale high for a while, and keeps the customer happy" (Ford, 1991).[116] Designers get to remain at a grand, strategic level where all difficulties look like implementation issues; and programmers, who never thought much of analysis and design in the first place, get to sweep process aside, roll up their sleeves, and hack away at the software until it works.

8.3.1.2 Design and Implementation Based on Data Flow

As one who has taught students to draw DFDs, however, I also have seen how syntactically correct organizations of bubbles and arcs can convey absolutely no meaning.

BLUM, 1992

Like structured analysis, *structured design (SD)* aims to foster good programming in such languages as Fortran and Cobol, whose primary or only modules are subroutines. Yourdon and Constantine (1979 pp. 10 and 15) lament a state of affairs where "good programming is what appears to be tricky or non-obvious to another programmer" and present SD as "an organized methodology—a 'cookbook'—that will help us develop 'good' designs and discard 'bad' designs as easily as possible."

A *structure chart* shows the subroutines as a hierarchy of boxes with the main program at the top. Lines fanning out from under a box represent subroutine calls. The data flowing to and from the subroutines is indicated by *data tadpoles* placed along the lines connecting a subroutine with its callers. A data tadpole is an arrow (in the direction of the flow) with a bullet on its tail. Control information such as "end of file" is indicated by a tadpole with the ring replaced by a bullet.

8.3.1.2.1 Transition from Analysis to Design

To turn a data-flow description into a running program, we must provide a control structure. In simple cases, the data-flow diagrams can be translated into a structure chart. (Structured analysis combined with structured design is commonly abbreviated *SA/SD*.) In really simple examples, we can hold up the data-flow diagram by its "highest abstraction" transform and let the other transforms hang off of each side. Typically, a set of transforms representing the input processing hangs to the left. This is named the *afferent* branch. Similarly, an *efferent* branch of transforms representing output formatting and the like hangs to the right.

---

[116]This is from an authorless document belonging to a course videotaped by Robert Firth, then with the Software Engineering Institute (SEI). Google finds the quote in an SEI report (Ford, 1991).

The highest abstraction transform becomes the main program. In the structure chart, the afferent branch forms one hierarchy of subroutines under the main program, and the efferent branch forms another.

In more complex problems, translating a data flow into a structure chart isn't so easy. In fact, designing a control structure such that control passes through each transform becomes an engineering project in itself. Pre-OO analysts and designers were well aware of this difficulty and receptive to OO proponents' claim that object orientation affords a seamless transition from analysis to design.

8.3.1.2.2 Hypermodularity

One of the popular fads of the 1970s was blind modularization. Rules such as "No subroutine shall contain more than a hundred statements" were used in the hope of reducing bug frequency.

BEIZER, 1990

SA/SD became identified with the "hypermodularity" trend (Beizer, 1990) of the 1970s when many in the Cobol world first discovered subroutines. In a frenzy, monolithic programs were cut into as many subroutines as reasonably possible. Freshly minted company standards would limit the size of each module to n lines of source program text.

The authors on structured analysis and design realized that a program with too many modules could be confusing and also incur excessive overhead for all the subroutine calls. They tried to limit the excesses by suggesting that some modules in a structure chart could be subsumed into their calling modules. SD views a module as a set of contiguous program statements. If the module is called from one place only, those statements can often be inlined (Blum, 1992). But the motto "if subroutines are good, more subroutines are better" took hold of the popular mind. A related phenomenon was *tramp data* (Aggarwal and Singh, 2006). Because most modules were stateless,[117] the same call parameters tended to travel down the hierarchy from one subprogram to the next.

8.3.1.3 Real-Time Structured Analysis

Structured analysis was originally meant for administrative, punch-cards-in, pajama-striped-listing-out batch programs but was later extended to real-time systems (Blum, 1992; Gomaa, 1993; Hatley and Pirbhai, 1987; Nielsen and Shumate, 1987; Ward and Mellor, 1986). In *real-time structured analysis*, many inputs are typically event occurrences, and the outputs may be actions on actuators.

In real-time structured analysis, the data transforms and the data flow are complemented with *control transforms* and *control flow*. A control transform implements a state machine. The control flow from a terminator to the control transform represents a signal of some kind, such as an interrupt. The control flow from a control transform to a data transform can consist of commands to *enable* or *disable* a computation.

---

[117]Transforms *with state* have local data and are like simple, singleton objects. For example, a formatting module may need to keep track of the number of lines already printed on a page.

8.3.2 Data-Flow Threading

Batch systems seldom use multithreading, but threads have long been associated with real-time software. Threads let us equip a data-flow model with a control structure in a way that seems simple and elegant: In principle, each transform becomes a thread, and each data flow becomes a message queue (Nielsen and Shumate, 1987). This avoids the problematic translation of a data-flow diagram into a sequential program. To reduce the number of threads, we typically first consolidate transforms in some manner.

Some designers use threads to provide an existing object model with a control structure. Much of the discussion in this section applies to such approaches as well as to those where the threading is added to a data-flow model. (In an object-oriented language, transforms become objects.) I use COMET as an example of data-flow design implemented with objects and threads (Section 8.3.3).

8.3.2.1 Mascot

Data-flow threading is perhaps best illustrated by the *Mascot* notation (Bate, 1986; Budgen, 1994). It's quite elaborate and shows not only the direction of the data flow but also the direction of each call from caller to callee. Some Mascot diagrams look like wiring diagrams where the hardware components are replaced by threads and safe objects.

Mascot has two kinds of predefined safe objects: the *channel* and the *pool*, defined as follows:

- A *channel* is a FIFO buffer with a destructive read operation and a nondestructive write operation: A thread that reads a queued message also removes the message from the queue. A thread that enqueues a message leaves the existing messages in the queue intact.

- A *pool* contains values that are updated by one or more threads and are read by one or more threads. It has a destructive write and a nondestructive read operation.

Figure 8-1 shows a fragment composed from Figures 13.18 and 13.19 in Budgen (1994), which illustrate a cruise controller. This fragment is concerned with computing the current speed. (I have simplified the notation somewhat so

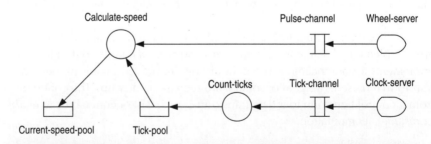

Figure 8-1 Fragment of a Mascot diagram showing the speed calculation in a cruise controller. The arrows show the direction of the data flow.

that Figure 8-1 shows only the direction of the data flow, not the direction of each call.)

- *Wheel-server* and *Clock-server* are interrupt handlers. *Wheel-server* receives a pulse (an interrupt) for each driveshaft revolution, and *Clock-server* receives clock interrupts.

- Each handler inserts data items representing successive interrupts in a channel.

- The thread *Count-ticks* removes each tick item from *Tick-channel* and increments the counter *Tick-pool*. This pool object has a single variable. *Count-ticks* updates the tick count in *Tick-pool*, overwriting any older value.

- The thread *Calculate speed* reads successive pulses from *Pulse-channel*. By accessing the current time in *Tick-pool* for each pulse (or each *n* pulses), it calculates the speed of the car, which it stores in *Current-speed-pool*.

8.3.2.2 Data Flow and Object Orientation

In the OO paradigm, data flow is implicit in the flow of messages between objects and is usually not emphasized. One of UML's precursors, OMT (Rumbaugh et al., 1991), originally included data-flow diagrams but didn't integrate them well with the other OO models. UML doesn't include them.

Some OO approaches use threads in a way similar to data-flow threading. Certain objects are given threads, which essentially execute a *live* routine that accepts messages and calls the object's operations. One benefit is that such a thread can evaluate guards and accept, delay, or reject messages depending on the object's state. The concurrent OO language Eiffel//, for instance, has very elaborate features for selecting the next message to handle from an object's message queues (Caromel, 1993).

Other approaches follow the *implicit-concurrency* style (Eriksson, 2004), where the system is initially described in terms of communicating objects. At that point, the objects are all considered potentially "active," each with its own thread. In a second step, objects are clustered and each cluster is given a thread. This reduction of the initial set of threads is purely pragmatic; no attempt is made to relate the concurrency of the software to the problem.

COMET (Section 8.3.3) (Gomaa, 2000) is a somewhat special case where the objects are transforms. Essentially, each class has an operation that accepts data and then sends the transformed data along to some other object for further transformation.

8.3.2.3 Advantages of Data-Flow Threading

Implementing modules as threads communicating via messages has its benefits. Because of its universality, message passing is often used for communication across some obstacle. For instance, processes with distinct address spaces can communicate by means of messages channeled via the operating system. In distributed systems, messages can pass between threads or processes on different nodes. In RTSJ, no-heap real-time threads can communicate with non-real-time threads via wait-free message queues (Section 2.2.5.6).

Further, loosely coupled modules implemented as threads connected by message queues can afford runtime configurability whether on a uniprocessor or multiprocessors. We can reconfigure such a system at runtime by directing the threads to read messages from other input queues (Section 8.3.2.3.1) (Stewart et al., 1997). The potential downside is performance loss, particularly in reactive systems.

Another motive for using data-flow threading is to obtain a provably schedulable set of threads. A set of periodic, rate monotonically scheduled threads can be proven to all meet given deadlines (Section 8.2.2.1).

8.3.2.4 Drawbacks of Data-Flow Threading

Multiple threads within one program usually face no obstacles that would justify message communication. A message queue simply becomes another safe object. Like structured analysis itself, data-flow threading has a one-size-fits-all character: We can almost always make it work, but it's rarely elegant. This section addresses the issues with data-flow threading.

8.3.2.4.1 Threads as Modules

Each module in a design should represent a single coherent abstraction.

LISKOV AND GUTTAG, 1986

Make sure every module hides something.

KERNIGHAN AND PLAUGER, 1978

Mascot's hardware metaphor may be appealing, but the implementation is unfortunate: Any cohesive part, no matter how minute, can end up with its own thread. The thread *Count-ticks*, which only increments a counter, is an extreme example where the context switching takes longer than the computation.

Unhappily, the hypermodularity associated with SA/SD (Section 8.3.1.2.2) becomes more problematic when the transforms are implemented as threads. With data-flow threading, each thread may represent not a clear abstraction but just a solution fragment that must be understood in relation to other fragments (Section 8.3.2.4.4).

Data-flow threading tends to produce many threads that run to completion one after the other (Sandén, 1989c). That is, one thread does its part of the job and hands control over to the next one. In other words, an input being processed visits one thread after the other. It can be difficult to determine the system's end-to-end response time to a stimulus since its reaction isn't spelled out in one place but consists of a cascade of thread activations (Howes, 1990).

A particular difficulty can arise when threads are scheduled periodically under some policy such as RMS (Section 8.2.2.1). Say that an event requires processing *B* followed by processing *C*. *B* is done by thread *tb*, and *C* by thread *tc*. Both have the same periodicity. If the threads are scheduled independently, it could happen that *tc* always runs before *tb*. This means that processing *C* will always be delayed by one period.

To avoid such a delay, designers may coerce the scheduling so *tc* always runs right after *tb*. This is awkward. The best way to ensure that *B* is always followed by *C* is to line them up one after the other in the same thread. Why first put them in separate threads and then synchronize the threads by forced scheduling?

If *C* is a lengthy computation and always performed by *tc*, only one execution of *C* can be in progress at any given time. That way, *C* becomes a shared resource that users must queue up for. With multiprocessors it's much better to make *C* a subprogram, which multiple threads can execute in parallel.

8.3.2.4.2 *Programming by Context Switching*

Data-flow threading relies heavily on context switching since each input activates a cascade of threads, one after the other. In a real-time system, the overhead for all the context switches may be unacceptable. If the computation by each thread is limited, the switching may take up most of the total execution time.

The Mascot design in Figure 8-1, for instance, may work nicely if every transform has its own processor. Otherwise, it tends to become "programming by context switching": *Clock-server* inserts a tick in *Tick-channel*. This is followed by a context switch to *Count-ticks*, which performs an addition. As soon as *Wheel-server* has stored a pulse in *Pulse-channel*, there is a context switch to *Calculate-speed*, which either increments a counter or performs a division when *n* pulses have been counted. In this example, the context switching between the handlers and threads easily eclipses the trivial operations that each handler or thread performs.

Activating a thread just to increment a counter or perform a single division is offensive to experienced thread programmers. *Clock-sever* could easily maintain a count of ticks in *Tick-pool*. Similarly, *Wheel-server* could keep track of the elapsed time per *n* interrupts, which defines the speed.

A classic example of data-flow threading that appalls many a programmer's sensibilities is where each layer in a communication protocol stack has its own thread. In such a solution, each communication message causes a little cascade of unneeded context switches. Everything changes, though, if each thread does enough computing to dwarf the context-switching time (Section 6.6.2).

8.3.2.4.3 *Message Queues and Data Pushing*

Except for Mascot's pool objects, data flow is usually implemented by means of message queues. Arguably, this captures the concept of data flowing between transforms the best: One thread "pushes" data to the other by adding a message at the end of a queue. The receiving thread either polls the message queue on a periodic basis or blocks until a message arrives.

In some circumstances, messages can accumulate in a queue. The programmer must allow for this and make sure that the queue won't overflow. Also, to prevent memory leakage, every message object must ultimately be deallocated. For these reasons, programmers of safety-critical systems avoid dynamic data structures such as message queues. Some dynamic structures can be eliminated quite easily. Assume, for example, that a thread implementing a control transform sends *enable* and *disable* messages to another thread via a message queue. Such a queue can be replaced by a Boolean variable *enabled* that indicates whether a particular activity should be going on.

8.3.2.4.4 Levels of Abstraction

In the development of the understanding of complex phenomena, the most powerful tool available to the human intellect is abstraction. Abstraction arises from a recognition of similarities between certain objects, situations, or processes in the real world, and the decision to concentrate on these similarities, and to ignore for the time being the differences.

C. A. R. Hoare in Dahl et al., 1972

In a data-flow hierarchy (Section 8.3.1), each higher level transform is made up of a set of interconnected transforms at the next level down. This is an attempt at abstraction: Each transform should convey the essence of what those lower level transforms do. But in practice, many transforms don't quite deliver as abstractions. Far from capturing key concepts, transforms above the lowest level tend to be too vague to allow much concrete reasoning (Jackson, 1995). Essentials, not just details, are lost.

To make up for this deficiency, some data flows come with a narrative—a tour guide of sorts—that cuts across the transform decomposition. It makes no attempt at separating planes of abstraction but proceeds at a detailed level, taking the processor's view as it worms its way through the code. Blum (1992, p. 24) has such a narrative.

With reactive systems in particular, we like to find out how they work. What happens, for example, when an elevator cabin reaches a floor? Below is a short excerpt from a lengthy narrative (Gomaa, 1993). It refers to a state diagram (Figure 24.3 in Gomaa, 1993), a data/control-flow diagram (Figure 24.4 in Gomaa, 1993), and a lower level, data/control-flow diagram (Figure 24.5 in Gomaa, 1993). I don't reproduce the figures but keep the references to show how the narrative cuts across multiple design artifacts (Gomaa, 1993, p. 364):

> When the elevator approaches a floor, Floor Arrival Sensor receives an input from the floor arrival sensor, and sends the floor number to the Check This Floor asynchronous function (Fig. 24.5). Check This Floor reads the Elevator Status and Plan data store, and if it determines that the elevator is due to stop at this floor, it sends the Approaching Requested Floor event flow. The elevator transitions to Elevator Stopping state (Fig. 24.3) and sends the Stop output event flow to the Motor object (Fig. 24.4).

This adds some drama to the dry data flow, yet long software sagas easily overwhelm the reader. We dig for information in a mass of prose, which describes not only essentials but also such implementation minutiae as the internal flow of data and events back and forth.

Lengthy narratives have given all documentation a bad name among programmers. (The attentive reader has probably found one or two in this very book.) Literary preferences vary, but I for one find such prose dull whether in textbooks or in software documentation. The form simply doesn't fit the material.

8.3.2.4.4.1 Recasting the Narrative

[T]he purpose of abstraction is not to be vague, but to create a new semantic level in which one can be absolutely precise.[118]

Dijkstra, 1972

We can use some tricks of the software-engineering trade to lighten up the narrative. First, a formalized style such as pseudocode or even a program language may help. Second, we can put abstraction to good use and separate levels of detail. Here's part of a description in Ada[119] of an elevator system:

```
accept Arrived;                         -- Wait for arrival at floor
while Requests.Continue_Up ( ... ) loop
   if Requests.Visit ( ... , Up) then
      Motor.Stop ( ... ); Door.Open ( ... );
      accept Closed;                    -- Wait for door to close
      Motor.Start ( ... );
      Requests.Visited ( ... , Up);
   else Requests.Passed ( ... , Up);
   end if;
   Floor := Floor + 1;
   accept Arrived;                      -- Wait for arrival at floor
end loop;
Motor.Stop ( ... );
if Requests.Visit ( ... , Down) then Door.Open; ... end if;
Motor.Set_Down ( ... ); Motor.Start ( ... ); Floor := Floor - 1;
```

This excerpt is at some abstraction and includes calls on various objects, shared or not. *Requests* is a shared repository of outstanding requests for elevator service (Section 6.7.1), while each elevator has a *Door* and a *Motor* object. As long as the object interfaces are well defined, we can reason meaningfully about such an excerpt without drilling down for details.[120] While a program text and a narrative alike should read from top to bottom, the program affords the reader better random access.

8.3.2.4.4.2 Integrating Description and Software

Choosing the right medium revolutionized everything. Style is vital. To portray a rainbow you should paint it in water colours rather than model it in clay.

Glegg, 1969

Thus recast, a piece of the narrative has become executable and no longer exists apart from the software itself. Documentation is at its best when it supports the

---

[118]Ideally, levels of abstraction can be "causally decoupled" so we can solve a problem at one level without consulting the lower levels (Pagels, 1989).
[119]I'm using a simplified Ada 83 solution only to make a point.
[120]If we want to describe what happens in less detail than program text but find the narratives tiresome, *use-case maps* provide an alternate graphic notation (Buhr, 1998). The maps' "wiggly lines" can show a control thread's interaction with modules.

program text directly. Meyer's "self-documentation principle" states that "[t]he designer of a module should strive to make all information about the module part of the module itself" (Meyer, 1997, p. 54).

The narrative describes a scenario of internal software events that take place in response to an external event. Such a sequence can often be implemented as a control thread. The Ada description is, of course, an excerpt from a task body. Added comments make it self-documenting. What happens when an elevator arrives at a floor is described at the "one right place" in the program text (Plauger, 1993).

Besides, the task can go on to serve other external events. In fact, it can be a sequential-activities task. This brings us back to ELM. It starts by studying the sequential scenarios—event threads—independently and represents them in software. No separate narrative is needed.

8.3.3 Example Approach: COMET[121]

This section is a fairly detailed description of COMET—*Concurrent Object Modeling and Architectural Design Method* (Gomaa, 2000; Sandén and Zalewski, 2006). It uses UML to describe the design and provides structuring criteria for objects, subsystems, and threads. It builds on the older data-flow-oriented methods DARTS and ADARTS (Gomaa, 1993), which in turn are akin to Mascot (Section 8.3.2.1). COMET retains the data-flow style while implementing the transforms as objects.

We may expect methods to evolve toward greater simplicity over time, but this isn't so with COMET. The process and the resulting software are both much more involved than with DARTS and ADARTS. This is the price paid for grafting a data-flow philosophy onto an OO process.

Requirements analysis in COMET consists of identifying actors, use cases, and their relationships. Typically for OO approaches, the analysis phase includes a static model with class diagrams and a dynamic model with sequence diagrams and statecharts. The COMET analysis phase also produces a *system context model*, which shows how external classes interface to the system being developed. It's like the SA context diagram (Section 8.3.1). I address only COMET's design phase, which consists of the following major steps:

1. Design the high-level architecture.
2. Structure the subsystems.
3. Develop a distributed architecture, if applicable.
4. Design threads.
5. Analyze performance of the design.
6. Design classes for each subsystem.
7. Develop detailed design.
8. Conduct detailed performance analysis.

I discuss each except step 3, which is specific to distributed architectures, and the performance-related steps 5 and 8.

---

[121]Janusz Zalewski provided most of the analysis of COMET (Sandén and Zalewski, 2006).

8.3.3.1 Steps 1 and 2: Designing High-Level Architecture; Structuring Subsystems

A subsystem in COMET is a set of objects. COMET defines the following subsystem types for typical real-time functionality:[122]

- A **control subsystem** receives inputs from an external process and generated outputs to that or some other external process, usually without human intervention. In a cruise controller, the control subsystem receives inputs from the driver's controls, the brake, and the engine and actuates on the throttle.

- A **coordinator subsystem** coordinates activities of more than one control subsystem and may schedule work items to be executed by specific control subsystems.

- A **data collection subsystem** acquires external data such as from sensors. It may also reformat and store the data and perform such elementary analysis as range checking.

- A **data analysis subsystem** may be combined with data collection subsystems. It analyzes the acquired data. Additional functions may include data visualization, report generation, and notification of exceedances.

- A **server subsystem** responds to requests from other subsystems. Server subsystems may provide access to data repositories and I/O devices.

- A **user interface subsystem** functions as an operator interface to other subsystems. It formats and displays data and handles such input functions as parameter changes and starting and stopping processes. Logon and security functions are also handled by this kind of subsystem.

Once the subsystems have been identified, their individual design follows. In step 2, we design classes of passive objects and prepare collaboration diagrams for each subsystem and for the system as a whole.

8.3.3.2 Step 4: Structuring the Threads

Given the classes, we identify threads by applying the following structuring criteria:

- **I/O criteria** identify threads performing I/O operations by mapping device interfaces to I/O threads.

- **Internal criteria** identify threads performing computations. Other internal threads are *control threads* and *user interface threads*. A control thread executes a state machine. (This is in contrast to the concurrent-activities pattern in ELM where the state machine is a passive object; Sections 5.2 and 5.4.1).

- **Priority criteria** distinguish between time-critical and non-time-critical threads.

- **Clustering criteria** consolidate two or more threads into one.

- **Inversion criteria** further reduce the number of threads by merging some of them.

---

[122]There are also I/O and system functions subsystems, which I don't discuss here.

Next, three kinds of thread interfaces are defined: message communication, event synchronization, and access to shared objects. An essential deliverable is the *thread behavior specification*, which includes a thread's interface, structure, timing characteristics, priority, event sequencing, and exceptions.

8.3.3.3 Step 6: Designing Classes

[D]esign is something that is best done slowly and carefully.

KAY, 2004

In this step, we refine the classes identified in the analysis. We determine operations for the classes by analyzing the object interactions as shown in sequence diagrams. Operations are also gleaned from state and class diagrams.

8.3.3.4 Step 7: Detailed Design

Choose a suitable design and hold to it.

STRUNK AND WHITE, 2000

In this step, threads and classes are combined. Major issues include the following:

- Relationship and division of responsibilities between threads and classes
- Synchronization of access to classes
- Interthread communication

Threads are activated by internal and external events. Once activated, a thread calls operations on passive objects. Interthread communication relies on message passing and is done through *connector objects*. COMET distinguishes the following three types of such message communication:

- Loosely coupled (asynchronous) message communication
- Tightly coupled[123] (synchronous) communication without reply
- Tightly coupled communication with reply

This brief summary does poor justice to COMET's over 30 steps and many types of diagrams. With its emphasis on message communication, COMET relies on the simplest aspects of multithreading only. This could be an advantage, for programmers versed in multithreading are in short supply, but it's curious that the architecture is fundamentally the same as one based on data-flow diagrams and implemented with processes. An OO layer has been added, yet object orientation hasn't informed the solution: The objects merely implement transforms.

8.3.4 COMET Solution for the Cruise Controller

This section uses the cruise control example to illustrate COMET (Sandén and Zalewski, 2006). The presentation follows Gomaa (2000) as far as the cruise control is concerned (except that I exclude the monitoring system). I discuss only the most important steps of the COMET design process: subsystem structuring (step 2), designing threads and their interfaces (step 4), and some of the detailed class design (steps 6 and 7).

---

[123] *Tightly coupled* here means that the sender blocks.

The requirements phase identifies a number of use cases. The analysis phase results in a class diagram and a state diagram, which is shown in Figure 8-2.[124]

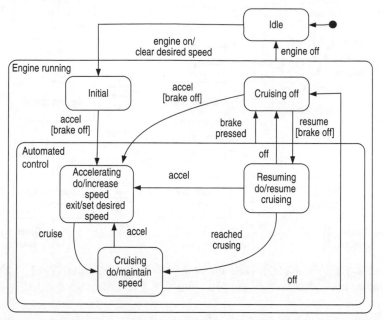

Figure 8-2 State diagram for the cruise controller. (Based on Figure 10-19 in Gomaa, 2000.)

8.3.4.1 Cruise Controller Software Architecture

The subsystem-structuring design phase results in the communication diagram in Figure 8-3. It contains five objects interfacing to external devices:

- Driver Interface, supplying one of the values Accel, Cruise, Resume, and Off
- Brake Interface, supplying one of the values Pressed and Released
- Engine Interface, supplying one of the values On and Off
- Speed Sensor Interface, supplying the current speed
- Throttle Interface, delivering the current position value to the throttle

In addition, Figure 8-3 shows three internal objects:

- *CruiseControl*, which encapsulates the state machine
- Algorithms for acceleration and constant speed
- *DesiredSpeed*, which stores the desired speed

The object interactions are shown in terms of the operation calls one object makes to another.

---

[124]Figure 5-3 is a simplified version of Figure 8-2. I removed the state *Resuming* and the event *reached cruising*, which signals that the actual speed has come within some tolerance of the desired speed. In Figure 8-2, *Resuming* is entered only when the driver presses "resume." Its activity *resume cruising* regains the desired speed and may differ from *maintain speed*. But the speeds can diverge in *Cruising* too, and yet there is no transition from *Cruising* to *Resuming*.

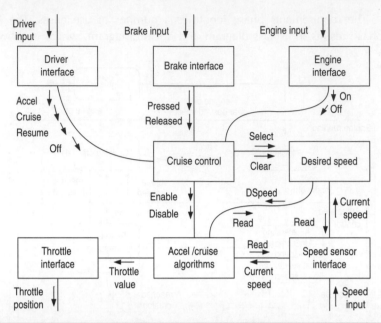

Figure 8-3 Communication diagram for the cruise controller in COMET. (Adapted from Sandén and Zalewski, 2006.)

8.3.4.2 Thread Structuring

Next, the system as shown in Figure 8-3 is structured into threads. Because the sensing of the engine and the sensing of the brake are alike, they are mapped onto a "clustered-periodic-input thread" named *BrakeEngnInterface*. All other devices are handled by their matching threads (shown as boxes with double sides in Figure 8-4) as follows:

- The "asynchronous-device-interface thread" *DriverInterface* handles the interrupts from the driver's controls.

- *SpeedSensorInterface* thread reads the speed-measuring device periodically.

- The "periodic-output-device-interface thread" *ThrottleInterface* actuates the throttle.

In addition, two data-processing threads are introduced:

- *CruiseControl* for state-dependent control; it implements the state machine (Figure 8-2) and receives event messages from other threads.

- *SpeedAdjust* for executing the speed-maintaining algorithm.

8.3.4.3 Thread Interfaces

No matter how beautiful, no matter how cool your interface, it would be better if there were less of it.

Cooper, 1995

Thread interfaces are designed next. Each interface is message based, so the choices are loose or tight coupling and with or without replies. The *CruiseControl*

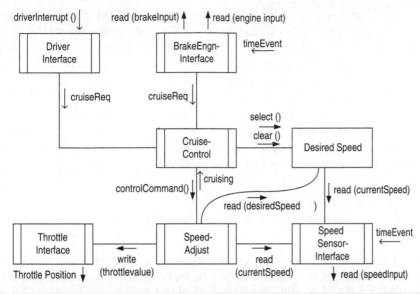

Figure 8-4 Communication diagram of the cruise controller thread architecture in COMET. (Adapted from Sandén and Zalewski, 2006.)

thread is given a FIFO queue for event messages arriving from the threads *DriverInterface*, *BrakeEngnInterface*, and *SpeedAdjust*. All other interfaces are tightly coupled. The communication diagram in Figure 8-4 is the final thread architecture. (Connector objects are not shown.)

The interfaces to classes of shared objects are designed in step 6. There is only one such class, *Desired Speed*. Its operations include *select* and *clear* for setting the desired speed and *read* to read it. Operations on threads are also designed. For device interface threads, they are normally limited to *initialize*, *read*, *write*, and *control*.

8.3.4.4 Comparison with ELM

Simplify, don't complicate—especially processes, procedures and policies.

MORAN, 1993

COMET targets a different audience than ELM, which assumes that the designer is reasonably familiar with concurrency. If ELM is for the aspiring chef who wants to create a dish, COMET gives a cook a recipe to follow. It leads to a solution step by step while requiring little understanding of threading.

8.3.4.4.1 Comparison of Approaches

Lacking any objective measure, we often judge how difficult a program is by how hard a programmer works on it.

WEINBERG, 1971

In COMET, state diagramming follows class diagramming. This order is conventional but usually not ideal for reactive systems of any complexity. A class diagram, once in place, constrains the state model, which is more critical.

A "high-ceremony," detailed process such as COMET gives the inexperienced a sense of security but doesn't guarantee a satisfactory result. The long-windedness and complexity are themselves risk factors: We may lose our way in the many steps and diagrams and confuse different notations. By the time we arrive at threads, their relationship to the problem may be lost.

ELM goes straight to the heart of a problem (Section 5.4.3.1.2). Unlike COMET, it gives the designer an early idea of the possible thread architectures. The state diagram in Figure 5-3 captures all the use-case flows. It's a more fundamental problem description than the class breakdown, which is after all a figment of the analysis and design (Jackson, 1995).

8.3.4.4.2 *Comparison of Software Solutions*
Inside every large program is a small program struggling to get out.

C. A. R. HOARE (QUOTED IN PIERCE, 2002)

The COMET solution rests on a set of thread-equipped modules that communicate via messages. The *DriverInterface* or *BrakeEngnInterface* thread places a message in the queue of the thread *CruiseControl*. (The queue is implemented as a connector object.) After a context switch, *CruiseControl* finds the message, performs any state transition and actions, and may enqueue a message for the thread *SpeedAdjust*, which in turn may enqueue a message for the *ThrottleInterface* thread.

All the thread communication in COMET leads to "programming by context switching" (Section 8.3.2.4.2). Tight coupling with reply, not least, creates situations where one thread sends a message to another and waits for the reply, hence causing two context switches without allowing any concurrent processing.

From an ELM viewpoint, the cruise controller is straightforward. We can easily solve it with thread identification (Section 4.3):

- One thread of events consists of the periodic throttle adjustments while cruising is on. This gives rise to the thread *speed-control* in the software (Figure 5-4).
- The other events have to do with the driver's inputs and occur more rarely. They may be interrupts or we can have additional sampler threads.

That's all the concurrency in the problem. True, the cruise controller is manageable whether we have one or six threads. But in a much larger system the difference could be hundreds or thousands of threads.

ELM lets control threads communicate asynchronously via a variety of shared objects. This way, ELM avoids message queues (Section 8.3.2.4.3). In particular, there should never be a need to queue up a message for a state machine (Chapter 5). By its very nature, it must be able to keep up with events as they occur. Thus, the state machine safe object *cruise-control* replaces the thread *CruiseControl* and two message queues in the COMET solution. The interrupt signaling an event occurrence is handled by an operation that changes the state variable value as necessary. The activity thread *speed-control* queries the state periodically and makes necessary adjustments.

8.4 CONCLUSION

He that will not apply new remedies must expect new evils; for time is the greatest innovator.

FRANCIS BACON, OF INNOVATIONS, 1625

A real-time programmer can easily implement a simple cruise controller without objects and threads. Do-it-yourself designs appear on the Web from time to time. A cyclic executive with global variables is a workable solution in this simple case even though as a rule cyclic executives are hard to maintain. The concurrent-activities pattern, we have seen, uses threads and objects in a simple solution that highlights the dynamic of cruise control.

Normally, we should design to the abstractions of our current languages and systems. ELM does this, so familiarity with ELM reinforces a general understanding of threading. At times, languages have lagged behind our understanding of computing. When structured programming (Section 9.3.1) first came along, we had to implement it with *goto* statements in Fortran until language development caught up. This has been referred to as programming *into* a language rather than *in* it (Gries, 1981).

On the other hand, we may choose to design to a subset of current capabilities to make our program formally provable or give it other known properties. (Ada has such "safe subsets," for example.)

As James Rawson pointed out, the transition from data-flow threading to ELM isn't subtle. ELM takes a discovery approach while Mascot and COMET are traditional, functional methods. Students without much background in traditional real-time programming often take naturally to ELM while some who are steeped in the olden ways struggle with the new paradigm.

The Origins of Entity-Life Modeling

9

Those who are old enough remember the time when things were different as a kind of golden age, an age when a programmer was a skilled artisan who was given a problem and asked to conceive of and craft a solution. For those who are young, the memory of such times remains alive in the collective mythology of the shop.

TURKLE, 1984

9.1 INTRODUCTION

The possibility of writing beautiful programs, even in assembly language, is what got me hooked on programming in the first place.

KNUTH, 1974A

This chapter traces the roots of entity-life modeling and acknowledges significant influences. ELM is based on my practical experience with threading in operating systems, communication systems, and centralized and distributed transaction control systems. Many became aware of multithreading recently, perhaps in Java, and won't believe that it's actually older than they are. My hands-on experience goes back to the summer of 1971. Those were the days when programs consisted of punch cards by the boxful. You could know entire systems—they were smaller then and simpler. A few years later, I was introduced to Jackson structured programming and long-running processes, which map nicely onto threads.

Later, Ada brought built-in tasking even though the original rendezvous concept (Section 2.3.4) was awkward: There were no safe objects; everything was a task. To explain ELM, I had to introduce "subject" and "object" tasks, where the latter were the guardians of shared resources (Sandén, 1994). All this went away when Ada 95 introduced protected objects. The Real-Time Specification for Java (Bollella et al., 2000; Bollella and Gosling, 2000; Wellings, 2004) has similar mechanisms.

Advances in our general understanding of computing and programming have made ELM easier to explain. When object orientation popularized the idea of modeling the software on structures found in the problem environment, designing software by reasoning about the problem became the thing to do.

The software pattern movement starting in the 1990s had a strong impact on ELM. Where I had focused on individual entities and event threads, two widely used patterns of interacting entities and a few software design patterns emerged and took center stage. The following sections expand upon some of these themes.

9.2 EARLY EXPERIENCES WITH SOFTWARE DEVELOPMENT

He who hasn't hacked assembly language as a youth has no heart. He who does as an adult has no brain.

JOHN MOORE (ATTRIBUTED)

My programming education started at the Lund Institute of Technology in the broad yet demanding and math-heavy engineering physics program intended to prepare students to evaluate new technologies as they appeared. The Department of Numerical Analysis housed a relic from computational antiquity: the homebuilt, first-generation computer SMIL.[125] It had a renowned Algol compiler written by Torgil Ekman of Lund University. Wisely, Algol was taught as the first language and headed us students toward computing's block-structured future (Perlis, 1967).

Once a Univac 1108 had been installed at Lund, I had the opportunity to practice Univac's Fortran IV and learn Lisp and Univac-1100 assembly language. I also had a chance to study real software in detail. Besides the operating systems Exec II, I dove into a Lisp interpreter (Norman and LeFaivre, 1975) and the assembler "Sleuth." Univac assembly language technology was taken to dizzying heights in the Meta-Assembler, which appeared a few years later (Sperry, 1977).

It's as important for a software designer to study existing software as it is for an aspiring writer to read.[126] Less engaging than fiction, software is best studied with some purpose, so I made little modifications such as adding a new, built-in Lisp function.

My dissertation work at the Royal Institute of Technology in Stockholm included a discrete-event simulation of a transaction control system that crashes and is restarted. It was done in the object-oriented, Algol-based language Simula 67 with its process interaction worldview (Birthwistle et al., 1979; Dahl and Nygaard, 1966; Sandén, 1976). Simula's *Process Class* was the first high-level-language representation of threads that I came across. (It's beside the point that Simula uses coroutines in the implementation.) The simulation model was an early attempt at combining object orientation with the sequential nature of threads.

---

[125]Swedish acronym for Siffermaskinen i Lund, literally the "Digital Machine at Lund," installed in 1956.
[126]Gates voices a similar opinion (Lammers, 1986).

With ELM, a program that *controls* a real-world entity can be structured the same as one that *simulates* the entity. The idea that a simulation language could work as a real-time language seemed preposterous when Jacob Palme first put it forward (1975), but its symmetry is appealing: Why should a simulation program and a control program for the same phenomenon be *structurally* different? They deal with the same states and events.

9.2.1 Systems Programming

A really advanced hacker comes to understand the true inner workings of the machine—he sees through the language he's working in and glimpses the secret functioning of the binary code—becomes a Ba'al Shem of sorts.

NEAL STEPHENSON, *SNOW CRASH*, 1992[127]

My first industry job involved a Univac-494 computer. Our task was to adapt a transaction control system (TCS) designed for airline reservation to the needs of hospital patient administration.

"Analysts/programmers" all, we implemented our own designs in assembly language, which gave deep insights into the workings of computers and the costs in memory and processor time. This was truly *coding*, and I'm loath to use that term for higher level programming. It has a mechanical ring, which may be appropriate for assembly programming from a good flowchart but not at all for higher level work.

Treated as skilled artisans (Turkle, 1984), we crafted the software by emulating others and visualized their software architectures as we pored over their code. That's how we acquired the tacit knowledge of the trade (Hoare, 1984). One redeeming trait was that almost every assembly instruction was commented. Seeing how reluctant "real programmers" are to document anything, this was a remarkable concession to understandability.

In some ways it was an advantage to be unconstrained by a high-level language. Fortran and Algol were designed for numerical computation and geared to functional decomposition. We worked instead with modules consisting of data and operations, similar to singleton objects. The assembler and linker provided encapsulation: Only those address labels flagged by the programmer became visible to other modules.

Because assembly programming was laborious, systems remained small. We added things one instruction at a time and didn't throw in extra features on a whim. Philips Terminal Systems (PTS), where I worked later, produced teller terminals for banks. Their software had the wonderful property of being correct; once installed, it performed without a glitch. Such were some dedicated systems of old. This one ran a single teller terminal application—albeit with multiple tellers—under the custom operating system TOSS.

9.2.2 Multithreading

Some Algol variants provided for parallelism, but it was largely geared to speeding up algorithms: You could specify that certain blocks could execute in

---

[127]By permission of Penguin Books Ltd.

parallel. Like other aspects of high-level language syntax at the time, this was inadequate for systems programming.

The Univac-494 operating system, Omega, offered multithreading and synchronization somewhat like Pthreads (Section 2.4). It had preemptively scheduled, kernel-level control threads—named "activities"—and a threaded, preemptable kernel, which we studied in detail during debugging efforts. We could follow a thread from the application via Omega's "spigots" into the kernel.

Threads and synchronization were as much at our fingertips as anything else, so we were never tempted to look at threading as some engineering device apart. The transaction control system TCS had an ELM-style thread architecture: A single, high-priority thread received all incoming transactions and sorted them by size into several queues. Each queue was served by a thread, which ultimately spawned a thread for every new transaction (Section 6.4.1). One dedicated, periodic thread invoked the function *pop-all*, which activated all threads blocked on conditions in case the equivalent of a *notify* call should be missing. Once activated, such a thread retested the condition and requeued if necessary as in a Java wait loop (Section 2.2.3).

The TOSS operating system used by PTS provided nonpreemptive threading for the applications. These were written in Credit, a homemade dialect somewhere between assembly and a high-level language. I was involved in the development of DIDAS, a distributed transaction control system also written in Credit.

Assembly programming taught us to do some upfront design, as no one wants to refactor an assembly program. Flowcharting was the basic tool. I found it helpful to overlay the module structure on flowcharts of threads as Figure 9-1 illustrates. These diagrams could capture quite complex logic. In the ELM spirit, they showed threads interacting with safe objects such as *Queue*.

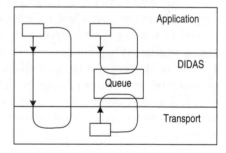

Figure 9-1 Much simplified diagram showing application threads entering DIDAS to send and receive messages and a lower layer thread entering DIDAS to enqueue an incoming message.

9.3 THE JACKSON METHODS

We speculate that professional programmers first create a design using their own personal method. They then legitimise it by casting it into the shape of one of the approved methods.

BELL ET AL., 1997

The first design approach I came in contact with beyond generic divide-and-conquer methods was *Jackson structured programming* (JSP). I took a JSP course from Leif Ingevaldsson in Sweden and later instructor training from Michael Jackson in London. Although the Jackson methods are now rarely used, the central concepts are still relevant for reactive software and threading. In essential ways, ELM builds on Jackson's ideas (Sandén, 2009). For this reason, Section 9.3.1 discusses the JSP process in some detail. Sections 9.3.2 and on discuss how aspects of the Jackson methods relate to ELM.

9.3.1 Jackson Structured Programming

[T]he notion that programming is a set of skills that's separate from any particular computer language is a fairly recent idea. In the early days, people generally wrote programs as they saw fit. Programs were judged by whether or not they ran—not by how well they were written.

COOPER AND CLANCY, 1982

JSP[128] (Jackson, 1975; Marciniak, 1994; Sandén, 1985a, b, 1994) is a technique for designing certain kinds of programs. Like object orientation and ELM, it's based on analogical modeling and creates program control structures in the image of structures found in the problem domain. Excellent accounts are given by Blum (1992), Cameron (1986, 1989), and Ingevaldsson (1979).

JSP appeared in the heyday of structured programming.[129] Corrado Böhm and Giuseppe Jacopini (1966) had found that every computable function can be expressed as an algorithm with three kinds of construct only: *sequence*, *iteration*, and *selection*. Famously, Dijkstra (1968) declared *goto* statements harmful. This inspired such a programming language as Pascal that favors *if-then-else* statements and *while* loops without breaks.

A program consisting of nested sequences, iterations, and selections is structurally equivalent to a regular expression. If we view the structure of our *data* as a regular expression, Jackson observed, the program's structure can be the same.[130] That's the basis of JSP.

9.3.1.1 Structure of Data

Let the data structure the program.

KERNIGHAN AND PLAUGER, 1978

It's convenient to introduce JSP with the help of a simple file-handling program, a typical application of its day. Let *F* be a sequential data file described as follows:

■ First comes one record of type X.

■ Then follow zero or more records, each one of either type Y or type Z.

---

[128]Dick Nelson suggested the name "JSP" (Jackson, 2000) long before the other, unrelated JSP, "Java ServerPages," was invented.

[129]Structured programming is unrelated to structured analysis and design. It's sometimes understood to include stepwise refinement (Floyd, 1979; Wirth, 1971).

[130]In addition to the pure structure represented by sequences, iterations, and selections, JSP allows for exceptions and breaks out of loops.

- Then follow zero or more records of type W.
- An end-of-file marker is implied.

A regular expression for this is X (Y | Z)* W*. JSP shows it as a *tree diagram*[131] (Jackson, 1995) (Figure 9-2). True, the diagram is bulkier than the regular expression but a much handier tool, not the least for group work. Like well-laid-out state diagrams, it tends to bring out flaws (Section 3.6.1.1).

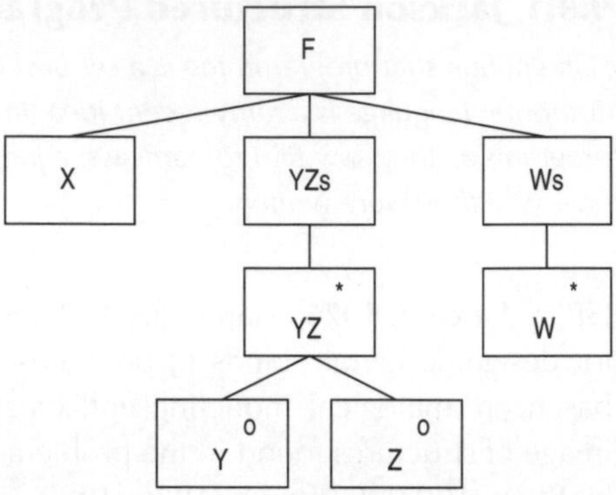

Figure 9-2 JSP tree diagram showing the structure of a file, *F*. An asterisk indicates that an element is iterated, a ring that it's one of two or more alternatives.

Read from left to right, the diagram shows the *order* of the records. The box F represents a sequence: X first, then YZs, and then Ws. YZs is an iteration of the element YZ as shown by the asterisk in the YZ box. In turn, YZ is a selection of Y and Z, each box with a ring. The boxes named X, Y, Z, and W represent individual records and are called *leaves*.

We capture this structure because we intend to work the file sequentially. The structure of a program processing the data can then mimic the structure of the data itself. If *F* is accessed randomly, on the other hand, this tree diagram is of little help.

Sequential file processing has lost much of its importance as random-access storage has become abundant. By contrast, most reactive systems must still handle events one by one as they occur. X, Y, Z, and W could be event occurrences. That is why the Jackson methods are relevant to this book.

Any data tree diagram can be translated into a state diagram. If the tree diagram represents a sequential file, the states will represent various stages of processing (Exercise 9-2).

9.3.1.2 Program Control Structure

The important point, and the one vital to constructing bug-free programs, is that one wants to think about the control structures of a system as control structures, not as individual branch statements. This way of thinking is a major step forward.

BROOKS, 1995

Let *P* be a program that must process file *F* sequentially from beginning to end. The data tree diagram in Figure 9-2 translates to a control structure for

---

[131]The diagrams are called (*data* or *program*) *structure diagrams* in the earlier JSP literature and *sequence diagrams* in (Sandén, 1994; Zave, 1985).

P that starts by processing record X, continues with a loop with an *if* statement that processes Y and Z records, and ends with a second loop handling W records.

The *program tree diagram* is basically the same as Figure 9-2. Each leaf box with a data item is replaced by the program's operations on the item. Under a *read-ahead* rule, a box with a *read* statement is added leftmost in the top sequence, and *read* statements are inserted wherever a record has been processed. That way, a condition such as "Y or Z" can refer to the next record to be processed. The diagram translates to the following pseudocode:

```
read                      Read first record
process X; read
loop while Y or Z         First loop
    if Y then process Y
    else process Z
    end if
    read
end loop
loop while W              Second loop
    process W; read
end loop
```

The program keeps track of its state implicitly (Sections 3.7.2, 5.3.1 and 9.3.2): While processing Y and Z records, it stays in the first loop. When the first W record (or the end of file) is read, it goes on to the second loop. If there's in fact a W record, the program remains in the second loop until the file ends. Read from top to bottom, the little program shows the sequential structure of its data faithfully.

In the prevailing practice, by contrast, programs often keep track of their state by means of state variables or Boolean flags. Thus a program that processes the file *F* sequentially would contain a single loop with a switch statement over the record types X, Y, Z, and W. Repeatedly it would read the next record, determine the current state, and take action.

JSP comes to its fore in more complex applications such as state-dependent, real-time software. The VDU problem is a small yet real example (Sandén, 1985b, 1994). A VDU is a visual display unit—a "dumb" terminal—that shows text only, no graphics. The VDU control program interprets a stream of input characters, which contains text to be displayed on the screen as well as command strings such as "clear screen" (Exercise 9-7).

9.3.1.3 Programs Based on Combined Data Tree Diagrams

The best programmers write only easy programs.

MICHAEL A. JACKSON

In many simple problems, a program's input and output can be shown as two different but easily mergeable regular expressions. Assume that the program *P* prints the following in response to its input:

- Line XO for each X record
- Line YO for each Y record

- Line ZO for each Z record
- Line TO that includes the total number of Y and Z records
- Line WO that includes the number of W records

The regular expression for this output is XO (YO | ZO)* TO WO. We can show this in a data tree diagram, compare it with Figure 9-2, and construct a third tree diagram that combines the two trees (Exercise 9-1). Here's the resulting pseudocode:

```
read
process X
print XO
read
loop while Y or Z                    First loop
   if Y then process Y; print YO
   else process Z; print ZO
   end if
   read
end loop
print TO
loop while W                         Second loop
   process W
   read
end loop
print WO
```

9.3.1.4 Structure Clashes

If a program deals with two or more regular expressions that do *not* combine easily, we have a *structure clash* on our hands. A common case, called a *boundary clash*, is when data elements are grouped in conflicting ways. JSP makes spotting structure clashes quite easy.

The VDU problem features a boundary clash: On the one hand, the input characters form words separated by spaces; on the other, they form fixed-size blocks. The boundaries between character blocks are independent of word boundaries; for example, a block boundary can be anywhere in a command string. The program must detect and handle both the end of each command string and the end of each block.

Such boundary clashes can be tricky and generate many programming errors. (I found out about the VDU problem because Mats Sönnfors, then a programmer with Philips, was struggling with it.) The only clean solution separates the logic of each clashing structure. For this, we put the block reading in a module (or object) *Character-block* with operations such as *get-first-char* and *get-next-char*. Together, they form an *iterator* (Freeman et al., 2004; Gamma et al., 1995). *Character-block* with its iterator lets the main program ignore the blocking altogether.

9.3.1.5 Real-Life JSP Example

I was once involved in a project to convert a compiler for the language Algol-Genius[132] (Asker, 2005; Langefors, 1964), which allowed elaborate output formatting. For one thing, you could embed strings anywhere within a number. An earlier implementation used one loop and multiple flags. Before printing a digit, the program consulted one flag after the other in case it was time for an embedded string or a decimal point.[133] This was computing intensive, making output a bottleneck.

My redesign of the output-formatting routine showed how implicit state representation could improve performance. JSP brought out an intermediate structure: a little iteration of digits. Such iterations were separated by either an embedded string or the decimal point. In the program, each iteration became an efficient, tight loop over digits only. This made for a huge improvement as most output lacked embedded strings. Ordinary programs no longer had to pay a price for the elaborate formatting they didn't use.

9.3.1.5.1 Program Modification

One benefit of JSP, once mastered, is that we can make certain, common program modifications with great ease. This never fails to impress accidental onlookers. Suppose we need to modify a program to allow one or more leading blanks before a command. Such a change is localized in the data tree diagram, and it's very easy to find its exact spot in the program text. (Exercise 9-1d is another little example.)

I had the opportunity to demonstrate this in the output-formatting routine. Not only numbers, it was decided, but also the Boolean values True and False should allow embedded strings. Because of the structural difference between the formatted printout and the number to be printed, I had already factored out the digit generation for integers and floating-point values to separate modules, each with an iterator. The formatting operation invoked *get-next-digit* whenever it needed a digit to print. It was easy to program a similar module where each *get-next-digit* call returned the next letter in "True" or "False," and—Presto!—the same formatting operation worked for Booleans too.

9.3.1.6 The Difficult and the Simplistic

The complexity of software is an essential property, not an accidental one. Hence, descriptions of a software entity that abstract away its complexity often abstract away its essence.

Brooks, 1987

JSP is now dated and decidedly out of fashion. Even at its prime it was widely misunderstood and often trivialized. Program tree diagrams were sometimes taken for structure charts (Section 8.3.1.2). Even some JSP textbooks contained major, conceptual errors.

---

[132]Algol-Genius was a version of Algol designed by DataSaab. "Genius" is the Swedish acronym for "generalized input/output system."
[133]Each flag represents a component of the state, so the approach amounts to composing many very simple state machines (Section 3.4.4.2).

Some viewed JSP simply as a programming notation and didn't bother to identify structures in the data or the domain. Dick Nelson (Saab-Univac), who taught JSP all over Scandinavia, found that many used the diagrams as a kind of structured flowcharts. "But they're happy," he would say about his corporate customers; they were seeking no deeper insights into software design.

Many programmers had trouble using JSP correctly. When it first came out, the conventional wisdom was that programs should be structured so as to be provable formally. Such programming was never easy, and JSP offered one way to do it. For the most part, software developers have come to favor a simple program that is obviously right over a complex one that they can prove things about. Although I had success with JSP as a designer and programmer, I stopped teaching it in connection with ELM long ago. Students saw it as an unneeded complication. Luckily, ELM is much easier than JSP once you understand threading.

JSP and structured analysis/structured design (SA/SD) are at opposite ends of the spectrum of design methods. SA/SD is easy to start but also very general and so delivers on generic goals such as cohesion and loose coupling only; it leaves us to detect and resolve many difficulties on our own (Section 8.3.1.1) (Bergland, 1981). JSP, on the other hand, targets a particular kind of problem. It's more demanding early on because it confronts us with essential difficulties specific to such problems.

Jackson proposes something of a manifesto for design methodologists (1995). It's a good rule of thumb, he suggests, "that the value of a method is inversely proportional to its generality." Further and in the spirit of the Brooks quote above, the *principle of beneficent difficulty* warns against methods that claim to make software development easy (Jackson, 1995): If a method doesn't bring out the difficulties, they will surface later on. Structure clashes (Section 9.3.1.4), which JSP highlights, are such beneficent difficulties, and so is the deadlock hazard, which ELM emphasizes (Chapter 7).

9.3.2 Implicit State Representation

The *run* operation of the *Job* class in the FMS problem (Sections 5.3.1 and 7.3.2.2) is in the JSP style. It's based on a state diagram that easily translates into a structured program: Each state is followed by one next state except for the two cases where transitions lead back to earlier states. The corresponding regular expression is equally simple. Our little program *P*'s states correspond to different parts of the logic, and so it is with the job's *run* operation, too. During execution, the program counter keeps track of the state of the real job on the factory floor.

With or without JSP, this is an intuitive and direct programming style that makes the logic read from top to bottom. Adding steps here and there to the FMS job is simple. Other examples include many operator threads, the switch engine thread in Section 7.3.1, and the home-heating thread, which undergoes targeted editorial surgery in Section 6.5.2.1.

Language *parsers* also represent state implicitly. Often part of a compiler, a parser is usually based on a context-free grammar in Backus-Naur form (BNF) or Extended BNF (EBNF) (Sebesta, 2009). Each production rule in the grammar is implemented as a procedure. When the parser receives a token, the grammatical context is defined by the program counter and the stack of outstanding procedure calls: The counter defines a point in the current syntactic construct, and the call stack represents those constructs in which the current one is nested. Unlike a JSP program, which follows a regular grammar, such language syntax is usually defined recursively.

9.3.3 Explicit State Representation

JSP uses explicit state representation as well as implicit. It arrives at it via a transformation known as *inversion* (Ingevaldsson, 1979; Jackson, 1975, Sandén, 1985a,b). Inversion converts a main program into a module with a single operation and a callback variable, which effectively remembers the current state. The operation is invoked by some other program, which I shall here call the driver. Program *P* in Section 9.3.1.3 can be inverted with respect to either its input or its output. Here's how inversion works in each case:

P inverted with respect to its *input* becomes the operation *put-next-record*, which takes a record as its in-parameter. The driver program reads file *F* sequentially and invokes *put-next-record* for each record. At each place where *P* has a *read* statement, *put-next-record* instead saves a unique callback value and returns control to the driver. When the driver calls next, the callback value directs execution to continue right after the previous return.

P inverted with respect to its *output* becomes the operation *get-next-line* with a line as its out-parameter. The driver repeatedly calls *get-next-line* and prints the line. Wherever *P* has a *print* statement, *get-next-line* instead saves a callback value and returns control. When it's called next, execution continues right after the return.

The callback mechanism works well in assembly and other low-level languages. In higher level languages, it's difficult to transfer control into the middle of loops and *if-then-else* constructs. To make inversion possible, we must dismantle those constructs and substitute *goto* statements.

I have left out some details, but clearly we can invert a main program with respect to any one of its input and output files in a mechanical transformation that leaves the program's logic untouched. The inversion can be automated so that we never see the result, much as we rarely look at the code produced by a compiler. We could use inversion to design *Character-block* in Section 9.3.1.4, but it's easier to construct a *get-next char* operation directly. Another example is *get-next-digit* in Section 9.3.1.5.1.

*9.3.3.1 Inversion with Respect to Event Threads

If the input is an ELM event thread, inversion results in a kind of state machine object. The easiest way to construct such an object, however, is to start from a state model of an entity's life (Sections 5.2 and 5.4). The resulting object typically has a number of event handlers. In contrast, the object we would get by inverting a sequential-activities thread with implicit state—such as the FMS *job*—would have a single event handler and a callback variable representing the state. The solutions fundamentally work the same, and inversion would be justified only under rare circumstances.

Note A single state can actually correspond to multiple callback points produced by inversion. Say that Figure 9-2 shows an event thread with events X, Y, and Z. A programmer converting it into a program tree diagram may place one *read* statement in the Y box at the point where a Y occurrence has been handled and another in the Z box. When the program is inverted, two callback points result. As an alternative, the programmer can just as well make the YZ box into a sequence consisting of the selection followed by a new box with a *read* statement. This is the solution shown in the pseudocode in Section 9.3.1.2 and 9.3.1.3. The two solutions are equal precisely because the *read* statements in the X and the Y boxes correspond to the same state.

9.3.4 JSD, Threading, and ELM

The central activity of software development is description.

JACKSON, 1995

Jackson system development (JSD) extends beyond individual programs (Cameron, 1986, 1989; Ingevaldsson, 1990; Jackson, 1983). Like ELM, it identifies problem-domain entities and captures their life histories as software *model processes*.[134] What is intuitively a single entity can give rise to multiple model processes, each representing an aspect of the entity's life. Thus one process may show only that an elevator cabin leaves a floor, reaches the next floor up or down (without necessarily stopping), then leaves, and so on.

Such assertions of how *any* elevator *must* go about its business are in the *indicative* mood, while statements about how we *want* our particular system to operate are in the *optative* mood. The elevator-scheduling policy is an example of an optative property. Because indicative properties are immutable while optative requirements may change, a requirements specification should separate statements in one mood from those in the other (Jackson, 1995).

JSD goes a step further and carries this *principle of uniform mood* into the software design and implementation. It keeps the model processes and adds separate *function processes* for behaviors in the optative mood. Function processes are introduced at a later step than model processes (Jackson, 1983; Sandén, 1989b).

Ultimately, each model and function process is inverted, and a driver program is added that feeds the system's input to the appropriate inverted programs. They can be very many, but that's acceptable since they incur little overhead. If we change the scheduling policy, the model processes and their corresponding inverted programs stay the same by definition.

ELM's perspective is different. It's that of a thread architect analyzing the problem domain for a foundation on which to erect the architecture. To this end we look for entities whose lives form event threads. We want the entities to be stable in this respect. For example, we know that events related to the elevator cabin movements form a thread. This is an indicative property: The cabin arrives

---

[134]The FMS job thread is an example. Tony Bolt, Richard Rosenthal, and Dan Zuckerman, then master's students, invented the job-thread solution based on my lectures on JSP and JSD at the Wang Institute (Sandén, 2009).

at a floor, stops, opens its doors, and so forth, with some time in-between, no matter how the elevators are scheduled.

We can base a thread model on such entities without knowing more about them. That way, ELM builds certain fundamental, indicative properties right into the thread architecture. The internal logic of a control thread can come later and is easier to change. Because we have technical reasons to limit the number of control-thread types, a single control thread becomes each elevator cabin's software surrogate. Its logic must capture indicative properties as well as optative behaviors such as those imposed by the scheduling (Sandén, 1989b, 2009).

A JSD solution is symmetric with all its inverted programs, some of which are set aside to capture immutable, indicative behaviors. ELM brings control threads with their capacity to run on different processors. We cannot use control threads as freely as inverted programs, but in return, the more restrictive design style brings out the individual character of each architecture to the point where a brief key statement can capture how it differs from other possible solutions (Sections 1.4.2.1 and 4.3.2).

9.3.5 Reconciling the Object and Process Models

As our case is new, so we must think anew, and act anew.

ABRAHAM LINCOLN, *ANNUAL MESSAGE TO CONGRESS*, 1862

Soon after learning about JSP, I came across the "object model" as an established concept (Flynn et al., 1978). Given my experience, I viewed the Jackson principles on one hand and the object model on the other as sound and complementary. The challenge was to reconcile them, especially in concurrent software, without giving preference to either one.

The proponents of each model tended to ignore the other. In JSP and JSD, *everything* is a sequential structure.[135] At the other extreme, object orientation gives the control structure short shrift and focuses on breaking the logic into small operations. Such single-mindedness carried almost ad absurdum is dear to a true programmer's heart, but combined models can be more practical.

ELM views the domain in terms of two kinds of interacting parts: (1) passive objects and (2) event threads, which wind their way through the domain while touching multiple objects. Threads and objects together model the domain; neither is subordinate to the other.

This combined model appears to have another benefit. Treating everything in the software as an object, which is the surrogate of a problem-domain object, blurs the distinction between the world and the software: We may forget whether we are talking about a real object or its surrogate; they are, after all, not the same. In ELM, an event thread doesn't always become a control thread; it may be implemented as a state machine safe object instead. This practical consideration forces us to keep reality and the software model apart.

---

[135]The same is true for Statecharts (Harel, 1987) and CSP (Section 9.4.1).

*9.4 FORMAL MODELS AND METHODS

*Grau, teurer Freund, ist alle Theorie
und grün des Lebens goldner Baum.*[136]

JOHANN WOLFGANG VON GOETHE, *FAUST I*, 1808

Many formal models and methods have furthered practical computing in fundamental ways: Recursive-descent parsers are structured on formal grammars, modern database organization rests on relational algebra, and numerical algorithms are subject to mathematical analysis.

An appropriate formal model—if it can be found—is sure footing for a software design. It's sound to use state machine models as the basis for reactive software and partial-order relations in deadlock prevention (Section 7.2.2.1). Yet, many attempts notwithstanding, formal models have proven of little avail in practical multithreading. (The exception is programming with periodic threads where it can be proved formally that all deadlines are met; Section 8.2.2.1.) The rest of this section discusses why this is so.

9.4.1 Process Algebra

Process algebra is a branch of mathematics that addresses concurrency (Bolognesi and Brinksma, 1987; Hoare, 1985; Milner, 1989; van Eijk et al., 1989). A process is viewed as an algebraic expression that defines sequences of event occurrences. Hoare's *communicating sequential processes* (CSP) (Hoare, 1978) is a good example and the book (Hoare, 1985) a pleasant, compact read. CSP is, however, geared to an architecture consisting of many small processors each with limited local memory and communicating via messages. Multiple threads on a single processor or on symmetric multiprocessors share memory and can inspect and modify the shared state directly (under exclusion synchronization) (Shustek, 2009).

Process algebra produces analytical results but is far removed from the practical construction of reactive software. The algebra lets us define a new process as the concatenation or interleaving of existing ones. Real control threads don't behave that nicely. They aren't just sequences of events but also software objects that must be managed individually at runtime, as well as schedulable units that must be given control of a processor. It proves difficult to abstract away this practical side of threads, mundane though it may seem. Ada 83's rendezvous concept was based on CSP (Sections 2.1.2.2.1 and 2.3.4) and was superseded by the more practical model with threads and protected objects, which ELM uses.

9.4.2 Other Formalism

The implemented product (e.g., the program) is always a formal model, and it is the formality of that model that provides confidence in predicting its behavior.

BLUM, 1992

I understand that Olderog's work on concurrency (Apt and Olderog, 1991) could be a basis for formalizing ELM but haven't pursued it. It seems that this would be

---

[136]Dear friend, all theory is grey, and green the golden tree of life (Goethe, 1967).

justified only if there were significant theorems to prove. ELM is a constructive, heuristic approach that helps us synthesize software solutions. In contrast, the formal methods tend to be better suited for analysis.

So it is with *Petri nets*, a different take on concurrency analysis (Peterson, 1982, Jorgensen, 2009). A Petri net is essentially a resource model: A transition, *t*, is *enabled* when the necessary resources are available in the form of tokens at *t*'s *input places*. In the transition, new resources may become available as tokens at *t*'s *output places* and may, in turn, enable other transitions. Concurrency is defined in terms of transitions that can *fire* simultaneously. There is no concept of a thread of transitions. For this reason, a Petri net doesn't translate directly into a multithreaded program.

9.4.3 The Need for Formalism

[P]rovability is a weaker notion than truth, no matter what axiomatic system is involved.

HOFSTADTER, 1979

In the early days it was felt that formal specifications and proofs were critical to the quality of *all* software. In current practice, they're used only when the correctness requirements are extraordinary, and yet software survives and thrives. Some conclude that those "who suggested that the only way to improve software quality was by using formal methods were clearly wrong" (Sommerville, 2007, p. 218). With ever-increasing computing capacity, others argue, formal proving will be automated and much more widely used, but the cost of producing error-free specifications may be prohibitive (Hoare, 2009).

Declaring a program "correct" if it meets a formal specification may be all right when we implement a known algorithm. Things are murkier in general programming, where much of the difficulty lies in interpreting informal requirements and expectations and in debugging the specification itself (Brooks, 1987). At the same time, some formal elements as assertions and invariants can be fitted into programs neatly and helpfully (Hoare, 2009).

Programming languages are formal, but programmers find them easier to work with than pure mathematical or logical notations. True, preparing a formal specification forces us to look closely at the requirements, but so does any thorough upfront design effort. The programming step in particular forces us to confront ambiguous requirements; its rigor exposes holes in our thinking (Weisenbaum, 1976). Like other authors on reactive systems, I rely on ordinary language for the most part and attempt to write with economy and precision (Wieringa, 2003).

9.4.4 Concurrency in Other Languages

According to some, current design approaches (such as ELM) rely on a "wildly nondeterministic interaction mechanism" and merely attempt to "prune away undesired nondeterminism." As an alternative, they propose graphical or textual *coordination languages* that restrict the set of interaction primitives available to the programmer radically (Lee, 2006).

In a like spirit, some languages hide threads and synchronization from programmers. *CEiffel* (Löhr, 1993) is a concurrent object-oriented language where the programmer defines the thread architecture indirectly by assigning concurrency attributes to individual operations.

The concurrent functional language *Erlang* (Armstrong et al., 1996; Armstrong, 2007, 2010; Cesarini and Thompson, 2009; Larson, 2009) is much in vogue as a tool for harnessing multiprocessors in the service of parallel computation. It seems to allow a more liberal policy for thread creation and context switching than ELM. Yet ELM's chief goal to produce understandable software isn't necessarily furthered by more threads and thread types, no matter how low the overhead may be. This is another area for further study.

9.5 SOFTWARE PATTERNS

A pattern is a small group of interrelated objects and classes that is likely to be useful again and again but not in exactly the same form.

GAMMA ET AL., 1995

The building architect Christopher Alexander's work kindled an interest in software-design patterns, which first became widely known through the classic Gang of Four book. It was something of an overnight success at OOPSLA 1994 (Gamma et al., 1995). Unlike methods imposed from on high, the idea resonated with programmers. Patterns were welcomed as artisans' tools about as concrete as language constructs. A grass-roots pattern movement was soon afoot.

With his patterns for building architecture, Alexander strives toward a "quality without a name," which he explains as "a situation where somehow the essence of life is present".[137] Virtual worlds and games might soar to such levels, but most everyday software patterns—including those in ELM—aim lower. Fittingly, programmers prefer the prosaic acronym QWAN.

Like the Alexandrian patterns, a software design pattern describes a family of solutions to a recurring problem. It's a small constellation of cooperating objects that is likely to be useful over and over. The Gang of Four book catalogs 23 patterns, which are "descriptions of communicating objects and classes that are customized to solve a general design problem in a particular context" (Gamma et al., 1995, p. 3).

A pattern has four essential elements: *name*, *problem*, *solution*, and *consequences*. The name is vital to making patterns "consciously accessible" (Jackson, 2001) and allows programmers to talk about them rather than learn them by copying others. *Intent* is usually also stated, although some argue that the recorder of a pattern ought not to restrict its future uses (Gil and Lorenz, 1998).

The known universe of patterns is reaching grand proportions. It grows as recurring patterns are identified in software designs, "made explicit, codified and applied appropriately to similar problems" (Monroe et al., 1997, p. 49). To show that real trade knowledge is captured, the recorder of a new pattern must cite three uses of it in real systems. Besides design patterns, various other software-related patterns exist. In the sequel, I discuss the evolution of patterns in ELM.

[137]Studio360, http://www.studio360.org, August 15, 2008.

9.5.1 ELM Patterns

It is an inherent property of intelligence that it can jump out of the task which it is performing, and survey what it has done; it is always looking for, and often finding, patterns.

HOFSTADTER, 1979

Before I became aware of patterns, ELM had focused on thread identification, where we look for individual entities and event threads in the problem domain (Section 4.3). When I reexamined various examples with patterns in mind, interesting regularities emerged both in the domain analysis and in the software architecture: In the problem domain, resource sharing could be described in two ways (Sections 4.4 and 6.1), and software based on state machines could also be programmed to a few different patterns (Chapter 5). As a result, ELM patterns exist at two levels:

- *Event-thread* patterns are found in the problem domain. I include two such patterns, which represent ways to look at resource-sharing problems (Section 9.5.1.1). Other event-thread and entity patterns likely remain to be discovered.

- ELM *design* patterns have to do with implementation and focus on state machines (Section 9.5.1.2).

While I don't use the canonical style favored in pattern circles, ELM patterns are in the same general spirit. They limit arbitrary variation as when individual architects or programmers do things differently for no good reason. Patterns introduce a common set of building blocks—a universal "mechanical alphabet"[138] of sorts—which helps developers and maintainers understand each other's software mechanisms.

9.5.1.1 Event-Thread Patterns for Resource Sharing

The *resource-**user**-thread* and *resource-**guard**-thread* patterns (Chapter 6) apply when resource users, one at a time, access a shared resource. Many events in such problems involve a resource user and a resource. We can often choose to thread the events either by resource user or by resource and end up with different event-thread models.

The patterns have undergone some evolution. There was originally an assembly line pattern (Sandén, 1997b), but it seemed better to focus instead on the individual resource-guard thread that represents a station along the line. I use the term "assembly line" to avoid a clash with the established architectural term "pipes and filters" (Garlan and Shaw, 1996). The concepts are alike, but the pipes-and-filters pattern is often formally defined with precise properties, which an assembly line of resource-guard threads doesn't necessarily have.

Resource-guard threads used to be called *resource threads*, but the new name matches resource-user threads better. I'd prefer wieldier names but hesitate to coin such soulless acronyms as *RGT* and *RUT*.

---

[138]Christopher Polhem (1661–1751) was a Swedish inventor, "mechanicus," and industrialist. A set of models of elemental mechanical movements is called Polhem's *mechanical alphabet* (Ferguson, 1994).

9.5.1.2 State Machine–Related Design Patterns

The activities patterns (Chapter 5) are needed because a state machine may specify multiple event threads. There are two ways of designing the corresponding software:

- The *concurrent-activities* pattern maps the state machine onto a safe object with a set of event handlers. Control threads based on the software activities in the several states are called *activity threads*. The first name was *state machine* pattern, but it conflicts with the Gang of Four's *State Pattern* (Gamma et al., 1995), which focuses on the internal representation of a state machine (Section 3.7.1.2).

- The *sequential-activities* pattern came about as a companion piece to concurrent activities. If each software activity belongs to a separate state, the activities and the state machine together can be incorporated in a single sequential-activities control thread. The pattern is often used to implement resource-user threads.

The activities patterns are sufficient for implementing state machine–based reactive systems in software.

*9.5.1.3 Distinction between Event-Thread and Design Patterns

The event-thread patterns for resource sharing came first. The activities patterns followed for what may be called the "cruise control class" of problems without resource contention. I viewed all the patterns as being on the same level. It turned out, however, that *resource-user* event threads were often implemented as sequential-activities control threads. In fact, the activities patterns apply to all reactive software based on state models. This led to the distinction between event-thread patterns and design patterns in ELM.

9.6 CONCLUSION

For any idea that does not appear bizarre at first, there is no hope.

Niels Bohr, according to Ferguson (1985)

This book introduces a principle for the intuitive design of multithreaded software for reactive systems. It isn't all unheard of; many thread programmers have found their way to similar designs. After all, giving each train or each user a thread isn't far-fetched, but it's not the conventional wisdom.

ELM proposes the *event thread* as an abstraction of the problem domain. With any new abstraction that comes along, some believe that it's just the "same old stuff" under a new name. Analysts and designers may have found a new toy, they say, but the resulting software is the same. Not so. Abstractions evolve as computers become more powerful and programming languages more expressive—and as our understanding of software deepens. New abstractions encourage designers to look at things in new ways that can make the software more understandable, easier to change, and less error prone.

A new abstraction doesn't just refine or extend old ones. Thus when object orientation introduces the class, it isn't simply a collection of subprograms with some common data; it's a new abstraction that arches between the problem domain and the realities and constraints of software implementation. It's a workable way to capture domain properties and is also neatly implementable.

It's reasonable and efficient to teach software engineers those abstractions that represent the current state of the art. We once encouraged programmers to embrace data flow and transformations—the productivity tools of the day—and later asked them to transfer their affections to objects.

Adopting a new abstraction may be a paradigm shift, however. If a single paradigm is our entire frame of reference, we are often stuck when a new one comes along. Our brains resist learning new abstractions and prefer to rationalize them as minor variations of the old ones. One way to cope with a new tool or language is to obey its letter but reject its spirit. New languages and tools tend to allow this by being successively more encompassing. Thus we can write Fortran programs in Ada disguise while ignoring the programming style Ada tries to promote and make threads emulate processes and communicate via messages alone.

Methodologists, too, can be stuck in older paradigms and resort to such coping strategies. They can regard new, productive abstractions as mere difficulties that they surmount by complicating their method and adding yet another veneer to their solutions. For example, when most languages are object oriented, some methodologists steeped in structured analysis may comply by implementing transforms as objects. With time, their simple core method is covered by layers of such adaptations, which add little but complexity. An ability to recognize and embrace a superior, new idea—however unconventional—is a welcome trait in architects and methodologists alike.

While the young are usually the first to embrace a new paradigm because they have no baggage, others may appreciate a new software-design concept because they understand what implementation issues are abstracted away. Ironically, those who started when there were no methods and few abstractions have this advantage (Tsichritzis, 1997). They had to grapple with machine instructions, interrupts, and naked semaphores—such stuff as even the fanciest abstraction is made on. Not everyone may want or need such hands-on experience, but it does foster practical software engineering judgment.

In the spirit of all the above, this book attempts to introduce ELM starting from the ground by recapping thread basics and state diagramming. With this foundation, Part II sheds light on ELM itself from various angles, and Part III compares it with other approaches to thread design.

EXERCISES

9-1 Variations on program P

(a) Draw a data tree diagram of P's output as defined in Section 9.3.1.3 by the regular expression XU (YU | ZU)* TO WO.

(b) Combine the output data tree diagram from (a) with the input data tree diagram in Figure 9-2. When a box in one diagram corresponds to a box in the other, collapse them into a single box. If such a collapsed box represents a sequence, it must contain the next-level boxes from each diagram. Some of those may be pairwise collapsible; others not.

(c) Convert the combined data tree diagram from (b) into a program tree diagram by inserting the operations to read and count the Y, Z, and W records and print the various totals according to Section 9.3.1.3. Also, specify the conditions governing the iterations.

(d) Modify the program tree diagram from (c) so that the iteration YZs continues until a W record or end-of-file is read. Include an X record as an alternative in the selection YZ. Modify the combined tree diagram from (b) accordingly and change the program tree diagram from (c) to print an error message when such an X record is detected. After printing the error message, the program continues with the next record.

9-2 State diagrams and JSP tree diagrams. Translate the data tree diagram in Figure 9-2 into a state diagram. Note that the various records play the same role as input characters or events in Chapter 3.

9-3 JSP tree diagrams. Draw a data tree diagram for each of the following examples (Sandén, 1994):

(a) A *semaphore* is repeatedly acquired and released (Section 2.1.1.2.1).

(b) A *circus parade* is led by a *drum major* followed by a *band*. Then follow *animals*: *camels*, *elephants*, and *horses* in any order. The parade ends with either one or two *clowns*.

(c) Change the circus parade so that the animals are grouped. First there is a group of camels, then a group of elephants, and last a group of horses.

(d) A *freight train* consists of an *engine* followed by *cars*. Each *car* is either *refrigerated* or *non-refrigerated*. After the cars comes a *caboose*. Finally there may or may not be a second engine. (An empty part of a selection is shown as a box with only a dash "–".)

(e) The life of a *laser* is as follows: First it's *installed*. Then it enters its *active life*, which consists of *cycles*. Each *cycle* starts with *laser on*. Then follow a number of *releases*. Each release has two steps: *open shutter* and *close shutter*. Each cycle ends with *shutdown*.

9-4 Data and program tree diagrams. Draw a data tree diagram and a program tree diagram for the control system of a *whole-house fan* (Section 3.5.1). The fan is connected to a button and to the fan motor and is initially off. Pressing the button once starts the fan going at high speed. Pressing the button once more makes it go at low speed. The third time, the fan is turned off, and so on. The *data* tree diagram shows a cycle of three inputs called *press*. The *program* calls a blocking *read* operation to wait for the next *press* and issues the motor commands *High*, *Low*, and *Stop*.

9-5 Roman numeral. A program *Roman* reads a string of characters terminated by one blank and determines whether the string is a correct Roman numeral between 1 and 9. If the numeral is correct, the program determines its value. The numerals are as follows: 1: I, 2: II, 3: III, 4: IV, 5: V, 6: VI, 7: VII, 8: VIII, 9: IX (Sandén, 1994).

(a) Describe a correct Roman numeral between 1 and 9 in a data tree diagram such that the characters can be processed in order left to right. (Typically, each character restricts what legal character sequences can follow it.)

(b) Transform the data tree diagram into a program tree diagram or pseudocode. Insert the program logic to determine the value of the numeral. The data tree diagram may include one or more iterations of the character I, and the correctness of the numeral will depend on the number of I's. This constraint must appear in the program tree diagram and the pseudocode.

(c) Include error characters in the data tree diagram from (a). Assume that there is at least one character before the terminating blank.

(d) Transform the data tree diagram from (c) into a program tree diagram or pseudocode.

Hint: Starting with the leftmost character and moving sequentially one character at a time, the program should interpret as many characters as possible as a Roman numeral. If the numeral is correct, the next character is the terminating blank; if not, there is at least one character left over. In that case, the program prints an error message.

9-6 Traffic light. Show a traffic light's phases in a tree diagram (Sandén, 1994). The light serves an intersection of a major east–west road and a minor north–south road. The major road has separate left-turn lanes; the minor road does not. The traffic light has five different, mutually exclusive phases:

NS:	green for north–south traffic only
EW:	green for the through lanes east and west only
LL:	green for both left-turn lanes on the major road only
WL:	green for westbound through traffic and for the left-turn lane off the westbound lane in the major road only
EL:	green for eastbound through traffic and for the left-turn lane off the eastbound lane only

The traffic light steps through phases in a cyclic pattern. A phase may be skipped if there's no appropriate traffic. Make a separate data tree diagram to describe each of the following patterns:

(a) In each cycle, the north–south through traffic first gets a green light, if necessary. Then, if any left-turning traffic is present on the major road, either the two left-turn lanes get green lights or one of the left-turn lanes gets a green light together with the through traffic east or west. Finally, the east–west through traffic gets green lights.

b) In each cycle, the north–south through traffic first gets green lights, if necessary. Then, if there is traffic in both left-turn lanes on the major road, both lanes get green lights. Then, if there is traffic in one of the left-turn lanes, it gets a green light together with through traffic in the proper direction. Finally, the east–west through traffic gets green lights.

Hint: The data tree diagrams indicate only the order of the phases, not the conditions governing the choice of one phase over another or the duration of each phase. Each nonempty leaf in each diagram should contain one of the abbreviations EW, NS, LL, and so on, given above. (An empty box has only a dash "–".)

9-7 VDU control program (Sandén, 1994). A video display unit is equipped with a microprocessor that executes a control program (Section 9.3.1.2). The processor receives a stream of characters from a host via a communication line. The stream consists of three kinds of strings:

■ A *text string* is a series of displayable characters.

■ A *command*, such as "position cursor," is represented by a character sequence bracketed by the characters *ctrl-x* and *ctrl-y*. A correct command has at most *max* characters. After *max* command characters, the next character is regarded as an error character unless it's *ctrl-y*.

■ Any undisplayable character except *ctrl-x* and *ctrl-y* is defined as an *error character*.

(a) Draw a data tree diagram describing the input.

(b) Draw a program tree diagram that uses the following operations:

get	Input one character
put	Display one character on the screen
execute	Execute a stored command
signal	Signal an error character to the host

The program displays text characters, buffers and counts command characters, and calls *signal* when an error character is read. After receiving the signal, the host is expected to continue with a correct character replacing the error character.

(c) Write the pseudocode based on the program tree diagram.

Glossary

activity thread: control thread that implements one or more software activities associated with a state-machine safe object (Section 5.4.2). [ELM term.]

(virtual) assembly line: resource-guard threads connected by queues (Sections 6.1 and 6.3). [ELM concept.]

broker object: safe object that handles interrupts or other events and has operations for control threads to call (Section 5.3.2–3).

composed state: the state of an entity expressed as the state of each of a number of orthogonal regions such as "*up* and *still* and *closing*" (Section 3.4.4.2). [ELM term.]

concurrency level: the maximum number of event occurrences in an arbitrarily short time interval in a given problem (Section 4.2.3). [ELM concept.]

concurrent-activities pattern: design pattern consisting of a state-machine safe object and activity threads (Section 5.4). [ELM concept.]

condition synchronization: ensuring that a control thread can enter a critical section only when a certain condition is met (Section 2.1.4).

control thread: any software thread as in Java or C#, or an Ada task (Chapter 2).

co-occurrence: situation where two or more threads in an event-thread model each can have

an event occurring within an arbitrarily short interval (Section 4.2.3.1.2). [ELM concept.]

critical section: code sequence that is to be executed by no more than one control thread at a time. (Section 2.1.1.2.1)

entity: problem-domain object whose life is an event thread (Section 4.1.2).

event occurrence: a manifestation of a certain event at a particular time and place (Section 1.6.2.1, 3.2).

event thread: time-ordered sequence of shared-event occurrences that are separated in time (Section 4.2.2). [ELM concept.]

event-thread model: set of event threads that together include all event occurrences in a given problem and where each occurrence belongs to exactly one event thread (Section 4.2.2). [ELM concept.]

exclusion synchronization: ensuring that only one control thread at a time operates on a given safe object (Sections 1.3 and 2.1.1.2). Also called mutual exclusion.

explicit state representation: programming technique where the current state of an entity is represented by the value of a state variable (Section 3.7). [ELM concept.]

guard (condition): a condition that must be met for an event to trigger a state transition and/or an action (Section 3.3.2).

guard thread: short for resource-guard thread. [ELM concept.]

implicit state representation: programming technique where the current state of the object is defined by the locus of control of the executing thread (Section 3.7). [ELM concept.]

locking order: see order rule.

locus of control : the place in the code of the instruction about to be executed by a thread.

monitor: a safe object encapsulating a semaphore and a set of operations on a shared resource (Sections 2.1.1.2.2, 2.1.4.2.1.2, and 6.8).

mutual exclusion: see exclusion synchronization.

near instantaneity: something is of short enough duration that for practical purposes it takes no time (Section 3.6.4.1). [ELM term.]

nominal activity : activity that requires no software involvement other than for starting and stopping it when the state where it's defined is entered and exited (Sections 3.3.4.2.1 and 5.1.1). [ELM term.]

nonoptimal thread model: event-thread model where some event threads do not co-occur (Section 4.2.3.3). [ELM concept.]

optimal event-thread model: event-thread model where all the threads co-occur (Section 4.2.3.2). [ELM concept.]

order rule: a partial order ("<") such that either S < R or R < S for any two shared resources R and S that are ever held by an entity at the same time (Section 7.2.2.1). [ELM term.]

protected object/operation/type: safe object/ operation/type in Ada (Section 2.3.2).

resource-guard thread: event thread representing the life of one shared domain resource (Section 6.1). [ELM term.]

resource-guard-thread pattern: event-thread pattern consisting of resource-guard event threads (Section 6.1). [ELM term.]

resource-user entity: problem-domain resource user (Section 6.1). [ELM concept.]

resource-user thread: event thread representing the life of a resource-user entity (Section 6.1). [ELM term.]

resource-user-thread pattern: event-thread pattern consisting of resource-user event threads (Section 6.1). [ELM concept.]

safe object/class: object (class) that enforces mutual exclusion among calling threads. [ELM term.]

safe operation: operation on a safe object. [ELM term.]

semaphore safe object: safe object used for enforcing mutual exclusion on entities accessing a shared domain resource (Section 2.1.4.2.1.1). [ELM term.]

sequential-activities pattern: design pattern consisting of a sequential-activities control thread (Section 5.3). [ELM concept.]

sequential-activities (control) thread: control thread that keeps track of the current state of an entity and performs the software activities defined for the entity sequentially (Section 5.3). [ELM concept.]

shared event: an event such that the domain and the software both participate in each of its occurrences (Section 4.2.1.2)

shared resource: resource that is needed by more than one entity and is to be used by at most one entity at a time (Chapter 7).

simultaneous exclusive access: the situation where an entity or a thread has exclusive access to multiple shared resources at the same time (Chapter 7).

software activity: activity that requires some software involvement throughout the state where it's defined (Sections 3.3.4.2.1 and 5.1.1). [ELM term.]

software-detected event: event that originates inside the software and is part of the life of an entity (Section 4.2.1.4.1). [ELM term.]

state-event pair: a specific state and a specific event occurring in that state (Section 3.3.1).

state-machine safe object: safe object implementing a state machine (Section 5.4.1). [ELM term.]

synchronized object/class/operation: safe object/class/operation in Java (Section 2.2.2).

task: Ada control thread (Section 2.3.1).

thread architecture: the control threads and major safe objects of a software system (Section 1.4.1.1). [ELM term.]

thread model: short for event-thread model. [ELM concept.]

time event: the event that a certain amount of time has passed since some other event (Section 3.2.1.1).

user thread: short for resource-user thread. [ELM term.]

References

A.-R. Adl-Tabatabai, C. Kozyrakis, and B. Saha, "Unlocking concurrency," *ACM Queue*, vol. 4, no. 10, pp. 24–33, Dec./Jan. 2006/2007.

W. S. Adolph, "Cash cow in the tar pit: Reengineering a legacy system," *IEEE Software*, vol. 13, no. 3, pp. 41–47, May 1996.

K. K. Aggarwal, and Y. Singh, *Software Engineering*, 2nd ed., New Age Publications, India, 2006.

G. Agha, *ACTORS: A Model of Concurrent Computation in Distributed Systems*, MIT Press, Cambrige, MA, 1986.

S. T. Albin, *The Art of Software Architecture*, Wiley, Hoboken, NJ, 2003.

C. Alexander, *Notes on the Synthesis of Form*, Harvard University Press, Cambrige, MA, 1964.

C. Alexander, S. Ishikawa, and M. Silverstein, *A Pattern Language: Towns, Buildings, Construction*, Oxford University Press, New York, 1975.

E. Allen, D. Chase, J. Hallett, V. Luchangco, J.-W. Maessen, S. Ryu, G. L. Steele, and S. Tobin-Hochstadt, *The Fortress Language Specification*, Sun Microsystems, available: http://research.sun.com/projects/plrg/fortress.pdf, Mar. 31, 2008.

E. Allman, "A conversation with James Gosling," *ACM Queue*, vol. 2, no. 5, pp. 24–33, July/Aug. 2004.

S. W. Ambler, *The Elements of UML™ 2.0 Style*, Cambridge University Press, New York, NY, 2005.

G. R. Andrews, *Concurrent Programming: Principles and Practice*, Benjamin/Cummings, Menlo Park, CA, 1991.

K. R. Apt, and E.-R. Olderog, *Verification of Sequential and Concurrent Programs*, Springer-Verlag, New York, NY, 1991.

J. Armstrong, *Programming Erlang—Software for a Concurrent World*, Pragmatic Bookshelf, Raleigh, NC, 2007.

J. Armstrong, R. Virding, C. Wikström, and M. Williams, *Concurrent Programming in Erlang*, 2nd ed., Prentice-Hall International, Englewood Cliffs, NJ 1996.

J. Armstrong, "Erlang," *Comm. ACM*, vol. 53, no. 9, pp. 68–75, Sept. 2010.

R. R. Asche, *Multithreading for Rookies*, Microsoft Development Library, Sept. 1993, available: http://msdn.microsoft.com/en-us/library/ms810438.aspx.

B. Asker, "Algol-Genius—An early success for high-level languages," in *History of Nordic Computing: First Working Conference of Nordic Computing (HiNC1), June 16–18 2003, Trondheim, Norway*, J. Bubenko, J. Impagliazzo, and A. Solvberg, Eds., Springer-Verlag, 2005, pp. 251–260.

J. Atlee and J. Gannon, "State-based model checking of event-driven system requirements," *IEEE Transactions on Software Engineering*, vol. 19, no. 1, pp. 24–40, Jan. 1993.

M. Awad, J. Kuusela, and J. Ziegler, *Object-Oriented Technology for Real-Time Systems*, Prentice-Hall, Englewood Cliffs, NJ, 1996.

J. Bacon, *Concurrent Systems*, 2nd ed., Addison-Wesley, Reading, MA, 1997.

J. Banks, J. S. Carson II, B. L. Nelson, and D. M. Nicol, *Discrete-Event System Simulation*, 3rd ed., Prentice-Hall, Upper Saddle River, NJ, 2001.

J. G. P. Barnes, *Programming in Ada 2005*, Addison-Wesley, Reading, MA, 2006.

L. Bass, P. Clements, and R. Kazman, *Software Architecture in Practice*, 2nd ed., Addison-Wesley, Reading, MA, 2003.

P. G. Bassett, "Engineering software for softness," *American Programmer*, pp. 24–38, Mar. 1991.

G. Bate, "MASCOT 3: An informal introductory tutorial," *IEE Software Engineering Journal*, vol. 1, no. 3, pp. 95–102, May 1986.

K. Beck, *Extreme Programming Explained*, Addison-Wesley, Reading, MA, 2000.

B. Beizer, *Software Testing Techniques*, 2nd ed., Thomson Computer Press, 1990.

D. Bell, I. Morrey, and J. Pugh, *The Essence of Program Design*, Prentice-Hall, Upper Saddle River NJ, 1997.

G. D. Bergland, "A guided tour of program design methodologies," *IEEE Computer*, vol. 14, no. 10, pp. 13–37, Oct. 1981.

J. D. Bernal, "The place of speculation in modern technology and science," in *The Scientist Speculates: An Anthology of Partly-Baked Ideas*, I. J. Good, general Ed., Basic Books, New York, 1962, pp. 11–28.

E. H. Bersoff, "Life-cycles: Software, companies & managers," *Colorado Springs Software Engineering Distinguished Speaker Series*, May 12, 2003.

A. Birchenough and J. Cameron, "JSD and object-oriented design," in *JSP and JSD: The Jackson Approach to Software Development*, J. Cameron, Ed., IEEE Press, New York, 1989, pp. 293–304.

G. M. Birthwistle, O.-J. Dahl, B. Myhrhaug, and K. Nygaard, *Simula Begin*, Chartwell-Bratt, 1979.

M. Blaha and J. Rumbaugh, *Object-Oriented Modeling and Design with UML™*, 2nd ed., Prentice-Hall, Upper Saddle River, NJ, 2005.

B. I. Blum, *Software Engineering: A Holistic View*, Oxford University Press, New York, 1992.

B. W. Boehm, "Engineering context [for software architecture]," paper presented at the First International Workshop on Architecture for Software Systems, Seattle, WA, Apr. 1995.

B. W. Boehm, "A spiral model of software development and enhancement," *IEEE Computer*, vol. 21, no. 5, pp. 61–72, May 1998.

C. Böhm and G. Jacopini, "Flow diagrams, Turing machines, and languages with only two formation rules," *Comm. ACM*, vol. 9, no. 5, pp. 366–371, May 1966.

G. Bollella and J. Gosling, "The real-time specification for Java." *IEEE Computer*, vol. 33, no. 6, pp. 47–54, June 2000.

G. Bollella, J. Gosling, B. Brosgol, P. Dibble, S. Furr, and M. Turnbull, *The Real-Time Specification for Java™*, Addison-Wesley, Reading, MA, 2000.

J. G. Bollinger and N. A. Duffe, *Computer Control of Machines and Processes*, Addison-Wesley, Reading, MA, 1988.

T. Bolognesi and E. Brinksma, "Introduction to the ISO specification language LOTOS," *Computer Networks and ISDN Systems*, vol. 14, no. 1, pp. 25–59, Mar. 1987.

G. Booch, "Object-oriented development," *IEEE TSE*, vol. 12, no. 2, pp. 211–221, Feb. 1986.

G. Booch, J. Rumbaugh, and I. Jacobson, *The Unified Modeling Language User Guide*, 2nd ed., Addison-Wesley, Reading, MA, 2005.

J. Bosch and L. Lundberg, "Software architecture—engineering quality attributes," *Journal of Systems and Software*, vol. 66, pp. 183–186, 2003.

P. Brinch Hansen, "Java's insecure parallelism," *ACM SIGPLAN Notices*, vol. 34, no. 4, pp. 38–45, Apr. 1999.

F. P. Brooks, Jr., "No silver bullet: Essence and accidents of software engineering," *IEEE Computer*, vol. 20, no. 4, pp. 10–19, Apr. 1987.

F. P. Brooks, Jr., *The Mythical Man-Month*, anniversary ed., Addison-Wesley, Reading, MA, 1995.

J. G. Brookshear, *Computer Science: An Overview*, 10th ed., Addison-Wesley, Reading, MA, 2009.

B. M. Brosgol, "A comparison of the concurrency features of Ada 95 and Java™," *Proc. SIGAda '98, Ada Letters*, vol. 18, no. 6, pp. 175–192, Nov./Dec. 1998.

B. M. Brosgol, "A comparison of the mutual exclusion features in Ada and the Real-Time Specification for Java™," paper presented at the 10th Ada-Europe International Conference on Reliable Software Technologies, York, UK, June 20–24, 2005, in *Proceedings Series: Lecture Notes in Computer Science*, vol. 3555, T. Vardanega and A. Wellings, Eds., Springer Verlag, Heidelberg, pp. 129–143.

B. M. Brosgol, R. J. Hassan II, and S. Robbins, "Asynchronous transfer of control in the Real-Time Specification for Java™," *Proc. 11th International Real-Time Ada Workshop,* Mount Tremblant, Canada, Apr. 2002, *Ada Letters*, vol. 22, no. 4, pp. 95–112, Dec. 2002.

D. Budgen, *Software Design*, Addison-Wesley, Reading, MA, 1994.

R. J. A. Buhr, "Use case maps as architectural entities for complex systems," *IEEE TSE*, vol. 24, no. 12, pp. 1131–1155, Dec. 1998.

A. Burns and A. J. Wellings, *Concurrent and Real-Time Programming in Ada,* 3rd ed., Cambridge University Press, New York, 2007.

A. Burns and A. J. Wellings, *Real-Time Systems and Programming Languages: Ada, Real-Time Java and C/Real-Time POSIX*, 4th ed., Addison-Wesley, Reading, MA, 2009.

D. R. Butenhof, *Programming with POSIX Threads*, Addison-Wesley, Reading, MA, 1997.

J. R. Cameron, "An overview of JSD," *IEEE TSE*, vol. 12, no. 2, pp. 222–240, Feb. 1986.

J. R. Cameron, *JSP&JSD: The Jackson Approach to Software Development,* 2nd ed., IEEE Computer Society Press, 1989.

D. Caromel, "Toward a method of object-oriented concurrent programming," *Comm. ACM,* vol. 36, no. 9, pp. 90–102, Sept. 1993.

J. R. Carter, "MMAIM: A software development method for Ada," *Ada Letters,* vol. 8, no. 3, pp. 107–114, May/June 1988, and vol. 8, no. 4, pp. 47–60, Aug./Sept. 1988.

J. R. Carter, "Reducing software development costs with Ada," in *Proc. 7th Annual National Conference on Ada Technology,* Atlantic City, NJ, ANCOST Inc., 1989.

J. R. Carter and B. I. Sandén, "Practical uses of Ada-95 concurrency features," *IEEE Concurrency,* vol. 6, no. 4, pp. 47–56, Oct./Dec. 1998.

F. Cesarini and S. Thompson, *Erlang Programming,* O'Reilly, Sebastopol, CA, 2009.

G. Cherry, *PAMELA Designer's Handbook,* TASC, Reston, VA, 1986.

J. Conallen, *Building Web Applications with UML,* 2nd ed., Addison-Wesley, Reading, MA, 2003.

G. Conti, "Why computer scientists should attend hacker conferences," *Comm. ACM,* vol. 48, no. 3, pp. 23–24, Mar. 2005.

A. Cooper, *About Face: The Essentials of User Interface Design,* IDG Books, Boston, MA, 1995.

D. Cooper and M. Clancy, *Oh! Pascal!* W. W. Norton New York, 1982.

G. Coulouris, J. Dollimore, and T. Kindberg, *Distributed Systems Concepts and Design,* 4th ed., Addison-Wesley, Reading, MA, 2005.

O.-J. Dahl, E. W. Dijkstra, and C. A. R. Hoare, *Structured Programming,* Academic, New York, 1972.

O.-J. Dahl and K. Nygaard, "SIMULA: An ALGOL-based simulation language," *Comm. ACM,* vol. 9, no. 9, pp. 671–678, Sept. 1966.

A. M. Davis, *Software Requirements: Objects, Functions, & States,* 2nd ed., Prentice-Hall, Englewood Cliff, NJ, 1993.

A. M. Davis, *201 Principles of Software Development,* McGraw-Hill, New York, 1995.

P. J. Denning and P. A. Freeman, "Computing's paradigm," *Comm. ACM,* vol. 52, no. 12, pp. 28–30, Dec. 2009.

L. P. Deutsch, "Object-oriented software technology," *IEEE Computer,* vol. 24, no. 9, pp. 112–113, Sept. 1991.

M. S. Deutsch, "Focusing real-time system analysis on user operations," *IEEE Software,* vol. 5, no. 5, pp. 39–50, Sept. 1988.

E. W. Dijkstra, "The structure of 'THE' multiprogramming system," *Comm. ACM,* vol. 11, no. 5, pp. 341–346, May 1968.

E. W. Dijkstra, "How do we tell truths that might hurt?" 1975. EWD-498, Burroughs Corporation Records, Edsger W. Dijkstra Papers, 1971–1979, Charles Babbage Institute, University of Minnesota, available: http://www.cbi.umn.edu/collections/inv/burros/ewd498.htm.

E. W. Dijkstra, "The humble programmer" (ACM Turing Lecture), *Comm. ACM,* vol. 15, no. 10, pp. 859–866, Oct. 1972.

E. W. Dijkstra, *A Discipline of Programming,* Prentice-Hall, Englewood Cliffs, NJ, 1976.

E. W. Dijkstra, "Solution of a problem in concurrent programming control," *Comm. ACM,* vol. 8, no. 9, p. 569, Sept. 1965; *Comm. ACM,* vol. 27, no. 1, pp. 21–22, Jan. 1983.

E. W. Dijkstra, "On the cruelty of really teaching computing science," *Comm. ACM,* vol. 32, no. 12, pp. 1398–1404, Dec. 1989.

E. W. Dijkstra, "Go to statement considered harmful," *Comm. ACM,* vol. 11, no. 3, pp. 147–148, Mar. 1968; reprinted in *Comm. ACM,* vol. 51, no. 1, pp. 7–9, Jan. 2008.

B. P. Douglass, *Real-Time UML: Developing Efficient Objects for Embedded Systems,* Addison-Wesley, Reading, MA, 1998.

B. P. Douglass, *Real-Time Agility: The Harmony/ESW Method for Real-Time and Embedded Systems Development,* Addison-Wesley Professional, Reading, MA, 2009.

U. Drepper, "Parallel programming with transactional memory," *Comm. ACM,* vol. 52, no. 2, pp. 38–43, Feb. 2009.

F. Dyson, *From Eros to Gaia,* Pantheon, New York, 1992.

H.-E. Eriksson, M. Penker, B. Lyons, and D. Fado, *UML2 Toolkit,* Wiley, Hoboken, NJ, 2004.

P. Evitts, *A UML Pattern Language,* Macmillan, New York, 2000.

R. E. Fairley, *Software Engineering Concepts,* McGraw-Hill, New York, 1985.

E. S. Ferguson, *Engineering and the Mind's Eye,* reprint ed., MIT Press, Cambridge, MA, 1994.

M. Ferguson, "Karl Pribram's changing reality," in *The Holographic Paradigm and Other Paradoxes,* K. Wilber, Ed., Shambhala, Boston, 1985, pp. 15–26.

R. W. Floyd, "The paradigms of programming," *Comm. ACM*, vol. 22, no. 8, pp. 455–460, Aug. 1979.

M. J. Flynn, J. N. Gray, A. K. Jones, K. Lagally, H. Opderbeck, G. J. Popek, B. Randell, J. H. Saltzer and H. R. Wiehle, *Operating Systems: An Advanced Course*, LNCS 60, Springer-Verlag, 1978.

G. Ford, *Report on Graduate Software Engineering Education*, Software Engineering Institute, Pittsburgh, PA, 1991.

M. Fowler, "Dealing with roles," in *Collected papers from the PLoP '97 and EuroPLoP '97 Conference*, Technical Report #wucs-97–34, Dept. of Computer Science, Washington University, Department of Computer Science, September 1997.

M. Fowler, *UML Distilled*, 3rd ed., Addison-Wesley, Reading, MA, 2004.

M. Fowler, K. Beck, J. Brant, W. Opdyke, and D. Roberts, *Refactoring: Improving the Design of Existing Code*, Addison-Wesley, Reading, MA, 1999.

E. Freeman, E. Freeman, K. Sierra, and B. Bates, *Head First Design Patterns*, O'Reilly Media, Sebastopol, CA, 2004.

E. Gamma, R. Helm, R. Johnson, and J. Vlissides, *Design Patterns: Elements of Reusable Object-Oriented Software*, Addison-Wesley, Reading, MA, 1995.

D. Garlan and D. Perry, "Introduction to the special issue on software architecture," *ACM TSE*, vol. 21, no. 4, pp. 269–274, Apr. 1995.

D. Garlan and M. Shaw, *Software Architecture: Perspectives on an Emerging Discipline*, Prentice-Hall, Englewood Cliffs, NJ, 1996.

J. Gil and D. H. Lorenz, "Design patterns and language design," *IEEE Computer*, vol. 31, no. 3, pp. 118–120, Mar. 1998.

G. L. Glegg, *The Design of Design*, Cambridge University Press, 1969.

J. W. von Goethe, *Faust Parts One and Two*, Trans. G . M. Priest, Knopf, New York, NY, 1967.

B. Goetz, *Java Concurrency in Practice*, Addison-Wesley, Reading, MA, 2006.

H. Gomaa, "A software design method for distributed real-time applications," *Journal of Systems and Software*, vol. 9, no. 2, pp. 81–94, Feb. 1989.

H. Gomaa, *Software Design Methods for Concurrent and Real-Time Systems*, Addison-Wesley, Reading, MA, 1993.

H. Gomaa, "Software design methods for the design of large-scale real-time systems," *Journal of Systems and Software*, vol. 25, no. 2, pp. 127–146, May 1994.

H. Gomaa, *Designing Concurrent, Distributed, and Real-Time Applications with UML*, Addison-Wesley, Reading, MA, 2000.

J. Gosling, B. Joy, G. Steele and G. Bracha, *The Java™ Language Specification*, 3rd ed., Addison-Wesley, Reading, MA, 2005.

D. Gries, *The Science of Programming*, Springer-Verlag, 1981.

A. Gustafsson, "Threads without the pain," *ACM Queue*, vol. 3, no. 9, pp. 42–47, Nov. 2005.

D. Hakim, "Robo-cars make cruise control so last century," *The New York Times* (nytimes.com), Apr. 4, 2004.

D. Harel, "Statecharts: A visual formalism for complex systems," *Science of Computer Programming*, vol. 8, no. 3, pp. 231–274, June 1987.

D. Harel, "Statecharts in the making: A personal account," *Comm. ACM*, vol. 52, no. 3, pp. 67–75, Mar. 2009.

D. Harel, H. Lachover, A. Naamad, A. Pnueli, M. Politi, R. Sherman, A. Shtull-Trauring, and M. Trakhtenbrot, "STATEMATE: A working environment for the development of complex reactive systems," *IEEE Transactions on Software Engineering*, pp. 403–414, Apr. 1990.

D. Harel and A. Pnueli, "On the development of reactive systems," in *Logics and Models of Concurrent Systems*, K. R. Apt, Ed., Springer-Verlag, 1985, pp. 477–498.

D. J. Hatley and I. A. Pirbhai, *Strategies for Real-Time System Specification*, Dorset House, New York, 1987.

C. A. R. Hoare, "Monitors: An operating system structuring concept," *Comm. ACM*, vol. 17, no. 10, pp. 549–557, Oct. 1974.

C. A. R. Hoare, "Communicating sequential processes," *Comm. ACM*, vol. 21, no. 8, pp. 666–677, Aug. 1978.

C. A. R. Hoare, "The emperor's old clothes: The 1980 ACM Turing Award Lecture," *Comm. ACM*, vol. 24, no. 2, pp. 75–83, Feb. 1981.

C. A. R. Hoare, "Programming: Sorcery or science?" *IEEE Software*, vol. 1, no. 2, pp. 5–16, Apr. 1984.

C. A. R. Hoare, *Communicating Sequential Processes*, Prentice-Hall International, Englewood Cliffs, 1985.

C. A. R. Hoare, "Retrospective: An axiomatic basis for computer programming," *Comm. ACM*, vol. 52, no. 10, pp. 30–32, Oct. 2009.

D. R. Hofstadter, *Gödel, Escher, Bach: An Eternal Golden Braid*, Basic Books, New York, 1979.

N. R. Howes, "Toward a real-time Ada design methodology," in *Proc. ACM Tri-Ada Conference*, Baltimore, MD, Dec. 1990, ACM, New York, pp. 189–203.

C. Hughes and T. Hughes, *Professional Multicore Programming: Design and Implementation for C++ Developers*, Wrox Press, Wiley, Hoboken, NJ, 2008.

L. Ingevaldsson, *JSP: A Practical Method of Program Design*, Studentlitteratur and Chartwell-Bratt, 1979.

L. Ingevaldsson, *Software Engineering Fundamentals: The Jackson Approach*, Studentlitteratur and Chartwell-Bratt, 1990.

M. A. Jackson, *Principles of Program Design*, Academic, New York, 1975.

M. A. Jackson, *System Development*, Prentice-Hall International, Englewood Cliffs, NJ, 1983.

M. A. Jackson, "Description is our business," in *VDM'91 Formal Software Development Methods*, Vol. 1: *Conference Contributions*, LNCS 551. Springer-Verlag, 1991, pp. 1–8.

M. A. Jackson, *Software Requirements & Specifications*, Addison-Wesley, Reading, MA, 1995.

M. A. Jackson, "The origins of JSP and JSD: A personal recollection," *IEEE Annals of the History of Computing*, vol. 22, no. 2, pp. 61–63, 66, Apr.–June 2000.

M. A. Jackson, *Problem Frames: Analyzing and Structuring Software Development Problems*, Addison-Wesley and ACM Press, 2001.

M. A. Jackson, "Problem frames and software engineering," *Information and Software Technology*, vol. 47, no. 14, pp. 903–912, 2005.

G. James and R. C. James, *Mathematics Dictionary*, 4th ed., Van Nostrand Reinhold, New York, 1976.

Joint Task Force on Computing Curricula, *Software Engineering 2004*, IEEE and ACM, 2004.

D.-W. Jones, "To task or not to task," *Journal of Pascal, Ada and Modula-2*, vol. 8, no. 5, pp. 61–63, Sept.-Oct. 1989.

D. W. Jones, "A practical cruise control," *Journal of Pascal, Ada and Modula-2*, vol. 9, no. 1, pp. 40–44, Jan.-Feb 1990.

D.-W. Jones, "Cruising with Ada," *Embedded Systems Programming*, vol. 7, no. 11, pp. 18–44, Nov. 1994.

P. C. Jorgensen, *Modeling Software Behavior: A Craftsman's Approach*, CRC Press, Boca Raton, FL, 2009.

L. I. Kahn and R. C. Twombly (Eds.), *Louis Kahn: Essential Texts*, W. W. Norton, New York, 2003.

R. Kazman, G. Abowd, L. Bass, and P. Clements, "Scenario-based analysis of software architecture," *IEEE Software*, vol. 13, no. 6, pp. 47–55, Nov. 1996.

R. Kazman and L. Bass, "Making architecture reviews work in the real world," *IEEE Software*, vol. 19, no. 1, pp. 67–73, Jan. 2002.

A. Kay, "A Conversation with Alan Kay," *ACM Queue*, vol. 2, no. 9, pp. 20–30, Dec./Jan. 2004–2005.

B. W. Kernighan and P. J. Plauger, *The Elements of Programming Style*, 2nd ed., McGraw-Hill, New York, 1978.

M. H. Klein et al., *A Practitioner's Handbook for Real-Time Analysis: Guide to Rate Monotonic Analysis for Real-Time Systems*, Kluwer Academic, 1993.

D. E. Knuth, *The Art of Computer Programming*, Vol. 1: *Fundamental Algorithms*, Addison-Wesley, Reading, MA, 1968.

D. E. Knuth, "Computer programming as an art," 1974 ACM Turing award lecture, *Comm. ACM*, vol. 17, no. 12, pp. 667–673, Dec. 1974a.

D. E. Knuth, "Structured programming with go to statements," *ACM Computing Surveys*, vol. 6, no. 4, pp. 271–301, Dec. 1974b.

D. E. Knuth, *Literate Programming*, Center for the Study of Language and Information, 1992.

A. Koestler and J. R. Smythies (Eds.), *Beyond Reductionism; New Perspectives in the Life Sciences*, Hutchinson, 1969.

P. Kruchten, "The 4+1 view model of architecture," *IEEE Software*, vol. 12, no. 6, pp. 42–50, Nov. 1995.

P. Kruchten, H. Obbink, and J. Stafford, "Guest editors' introduction: The past, present, and future of software architecture," *IEEE Software*, vol. 23, no. 2, pp. 22–30, Mar. 2006.

S. Lammers, *Programmers at Work*, Microsoft Press, Redmond, WA, 1986.

B. Langefors, "Algol-Genius: A programming language for general data processing," *BIT*, vol. 4, no. 3, pp. 162–176, Sept. 1964.

P. A. Laplante, *Real-Time Systems Design and Analysis*, 3rd ed., Wiley-IEEE Press, Hoboken, NJ, 2004.

J. Larson, "Erlang for concurrent programming," *Comm. ACM,* vol. 52, no. 3, pp. 48–56, Mar. 2009.

J. Larus and C. Kozyrakis, "Transactional memory," *Comm. ACM,* vol. 51, no. 7, pp. 80–88, July 2008.

A. M. Law, *Simulation Modeling and Analysis,* 4th ed., McGraw-Hill, New York, 2006.

D. Lea, *Concurrent Programming in Java™,* 2nd ed., Addison-Wesley, Reading, MA, 2000.

E. A. Lee, "The problem with threads," *IEEE Computer,* vol. 39, no. 5, pp. 33–42, May 2006.

P. Leroy, "An invitation to Ada 2005," *Ada Letters,* vol. 23, no. 3, pp. 33–55, Sept. 2003.

B. A. Lieberman, *The Art of Software Modeling,* Auerbach, Boca Raton, FL, 2006.

B. Liskov and J. Guttag, *Abstraction and Specification and Program Development,* MIT Press/ McGraw-Hill, New York, 1986.

K.-P. Löhr, "Concurrency annotations for reusable software," *Comm. ACM,* vol. 36, no. 9, pp. 81–89, Sept. 1993.

A. L. Mackay, *A Dictionary of Scientific Quotations,* Taylor & Francis, 1991.

J. Magee and J. Kramer, *Concurrency: State Models and Java Programming,* 2nd ed., Wiley, Hoboken, NJ, 2006.

B. Magnusson, "Simulating a system of automatically guided vehicles," in *Proc. 13th Simula Users' Conference,* University of Calgary, Aug. 1985, Tech. Report LU-CS-TR: 94-127, Dept. of Computer Science, Lund University, Sweden, 1994.

J. J. Marciniak, *Encyclopedia of Software Engineering,* Wiley, New York, 1994.

S. McConnell, *Rapid Development,* Microsoft Press, Redmond, WA, 1996.

S. McConnell, *Code Complete,* 2nd ed. Microsoft Press, Redmond, WA, 2004.

J. McCormick, "A model railroad for Ada and software engineering," *Comm. ACM,* vol. 35, no. 11, pp. 68–70, Nov. 1992.

J. McCormick, "We've been working on the railroad: A laboratory for real-time embedded systems," *ACM SIGCSE Bulletin,* vol. 37, no. 1, pp. 530–534, Mar. 2005.

W. M. McKeeman, "Graduation talk at Wang Institute," *IEEE Computer,* vol. 22, no. 5, pp. 78–80, May 1989.

A. McQueen, "The importance of naming," *The New Webster Encyclopedic Dictionary of the English Language,* 1980 ed., Consolidated Book Publishers, Chicago, IL, 1977.

S. J. Mellor and P. T. Ward, *Structured Development for Real-Time Systems,* Vol. 3: *Implementation Modeling Techniques,* Yourdon, Englewood Cliffs, NJ, 1986.

Merriam Webster's Collegiate Dictionary, 10th ed., Merriam-Webster, 1993–1996.

B. Meyer, *Object-Oriented Software Construction.* Prentice-Hall, Englewood Cliffs, NJ, 1988.

B. Meyer, "Systematic concurrent object-oriented programming," *Comm. ACM,* vol. 36, no. 9, pp. 56–80, Sept. 1993.

B. Meyer, *Object-Oriented Software Construction,* 2nd ed., Prentice-Hall, Upper Saddle River, NJ, 1997.

R. Milner, *Communication and Concurrency,* Prentice-Hall, Upper Saddle River, NJ, 1989.

K. L. Mills, "Automated Generation of concurrent designs for real-time software," Ph.D. dissertation, George Mason University, 1995.

R. T. Monroe, A. Kompanek, R. Melton, and D. Garlan, "Architectural styles, design patterns, and objects," *IEEE Software,* vol. 14, no. 1, pp. 43–52, Jan. 1997.

R. A. Moran, *Never Confuse a Memo with Reality,* Collins, New York, 1993.

J. Mössinger, "Software in automotive systems," *IEEE Software,* vol. 27, no. 2, pp. 92–94, Mar. 2010.

B. Nichols, D. Buttlar, and J. Proulx Farrell, *Pthreads Programming: A POSIX Standard for Better Multiprocessing,* O'Reilly and Associates, Sebastopol, CA, 1996.

K. W. Nielsen and K. Shumate, "Designing large real-time systems with Ada," *Comm. ACM,* vol. 30, no. 8, pp. 695–715, Aug. 1987. Corrected in *Comm. ACM,* vol. 30, no. 12, p. 1073, Dec. 1987.

E. J. Norman and R. LeFaivre, *LISP Reference Manual: Reference Manual for UNIVAC 1100 Series Computers,* The University of Wisconsin Academic Computing Center, Madison, WI, 1975.

H. R. Pagels, *The Dreams of Reason: The Computer and the Rise of the Sciences of Complexity,* Bantam, New York, 1989.

J. Palme, "Making Simula into a programming language for real time," *Management Informatics,* vol. 4, pp 129–137, 1975.

A. J. Perlis, "The synthesis of algorithmic systems," *JACM,* vol. 14, no. 1, pp. 1–9, Jan. 1967.

A. J. Perlis, "Epigrams in programming," *ACM SIGPLAN Notice,* vol. 17, no. 9, pp. 7–13, Sept. 1982.

D. E. Perry and A. L. Wolf, "Foundations for the study of software architecture," *ACM Software Engineering Notes*, vol. 17, no. 4, pp. 40–52, Oct. 1992.

C. Pescio, "Listen to your tools and materials," *IEEE Software*, vol. 23, no. 5, pp. 74–80, Sept. 2006.

J. Peterson, *Petri Net Theory and the Modeling of Systems*, Prentice-Hall, Englewood Cliffs, NJ, 1982.

K. Peterson, T. Persson, and B. I. Sandén, "A software architecture as a combination of patterns," *Cross-Talk*, vol. 16, no. 10, pp. 25–28, Oct. 2003.

B. C. Pierce, *Types and Programming Languages*, The MIT Press, Cambridge, MA, 2002.

P. J. Plauger, *Programming on Purpose: Essays on Software Design*, Prentice-Hall, Englewood Cliffs, NJ, 1993.

J. H. Poincaré, *Science et Méthode*, Flammarion, Paris, 1908.

G. Pólya, *How to Solve It*, 2nd ed., Princeton University Press, Princeton, NJ, 1957.

B. Randell and J. N. Buxton (Eds.), *Software Engineering Techniques: Report of a Conference Sponsored by the NATO Science Committee*, Scientific Affairs Division, NATO, Brussels, 1970.

L. Rapanotti, J. G. Hall, M. A. Jackson, and B. Nuseibeh, "Architecture-driven problem decomposition," in *Proc. 12th IEEE International Requirements Engineering Conference (RE'04)*, Kyoto, 6–10 Sept. 2004, pp. 80–89.

A. Raybould, "Explanation-oriented design," *IEEE Software*, vol. 23, no. 5, pp. 104–103, Sept. 2006.

E. S. Raymond, *The New Hackers' Dictionary*, 2nd ed., The MIT Press, Cambridge, MA, 1993.

E. S. Raymond, *The New Hackers' Dictionary*, available: http://www.ccil.org/jargon/jargon.html, 2000.

R. Riehle. *Ada Distilled*, available: http://www.adaic.org/docs/distilled/adadistilled.pdf, 2003.

J. Rumbaugh, M. Blaha, W. Premerlani, F. Eddy, and W. Lorenson, *Object-Oriented Modeling and Design*, Prentice-Hall, Englewood Cliffs, NJ, 1991.

J. Rumbaugh, I. Jacobson, and G. Booch, *The Unified Modeling Language Reference Manual*, 2nd ed., Addison-Wesley, Reading, MA, 2005.

B. Russell, "Introduction," in L. Wittgenstein, *Tractatus Logico-Philosophicus*, Transl. C. K. Ogden, Routledge & Kegan Paul, 1922.

M. Samek, *Practical UML Statecharts in C/C++: Event-Driven Programming for Embedded Systems*, 2nd ed., Newnes, Burlington, MA, 2008.

B. I. Sandén, "Restarting a real-time system: A SIMULA model," Tech. Rep. TRITA-CS-7601, Dept. of Telecommunications and Computer Systems, Royal Institute of Technology, Stockholm, 1976.

B. I. Sandén, *Systems Programming with JSP*, Studentlitteratur, Lund, Sweden, 1985a. First published in Swedish by Studentlitteratur, Lund, Sweden, 1983, as *Systemprogrammering med JSP*.

B. I. Sandén, "Systems programming with JSP. Example: A VDU controller," *Comm. ACM*, vol. 28, no. 10, pp. 1059–1067, Oct. 1985b.

B. I. Sandén, "The case for eclectic design of real-time software," *IEEE TSE*, vol. 15, no. 3, pp. 360–362, Mar. 1989a.

B. I. Sandén, "An entity-life modeling approach to the design of concurrent software," *Comm. ACM*, vol. 32, no. 3, pp. 330–343, Mar. 1989b.

B. I. Sandén, "Entity-life modeling and structured analysis in real-time software design: A comparison," *Comm. ACM*, vol. 32, no. 12, pp. 1458–1466, Dec. 1989c.

B. I. Sandén, *Software Systems Construction*, Prentice-Hall, Englewood Cliffs, NJ, 1994.

B. I. Sandén, "Using tasks to capture problem concurrency," *Ada User Journal*, vol. 17, no. 1, pp. 25–36, Mar. 1996.

B. I. Sandén, "Modeling concurrent software," *IEEE Software*, vol. 14, no. 5, pp. 93–100, Sept. 1997a.

B. I. Sandén, "Concurrent design patterns for resource sharing," in *Proc. TRI-Ada*, St. Louis, MO, Nov. 1997b, pp. 173–183.

B. I. Sandén, "Implementation of state machines with tasks and protected objects," *Ada User Journal*, vol. 20, no. 4, pp. 273–288, Jan. 2000. Reprinted in *Ada Letters*, vol. 20, no. 2, pp. 38–56, June 2000.

B. I. Sandén, "A design pattern for state machines and concurrent activities," in *Proc. 6th International Conference on Reliable Software Technologies—Ada-Europe 2001*, Leuven, Belgium, May 14–18, 2001, D. Craeynest and A. Strohmeier, Eds., *Lecture Notes in Computer Science*, vol. 2043, Springer-Verlag, pp. 203–214, 2001.

B. I. Sandén, "Real-time programming safety in Java and Ada," *Ada User Journal*, vol. 23, no. 2, pp. 105–113, June 2002.

B. I. Sandén, "Entity-life modeling: Modeling a thread architecture on the problem environment," *IEEE Software*, vol. 20, no. 4, pp. 70–78, July 2003.

B. I. Sandén, "Coping with Java threads," *IEEE Computer*, vol. 37, no. 4, pp. 20–27, Apr. 2004.

B. I. Sandén, "Intuitive multitasking in Ada 2005," *CrossTalk*, vol. 19, no. 8, pp. 12–15, Aug. 2006.

B. I. Sandén, "Inspired software design: Early Jackson methods to thread architectures," *ACM Software Engineering Notes*, vol. 34, no. 4, July 2009.

B. I. Sandén and J. Zalewski, "Designing state-based systems with entity-life modeling," *Journal of Systems and Software*, vol. 79, no. 1, pp. 69–78, Jan. 2006.

R. W. Sebesta, *Concepts of Programming Languages*, 9th ed., Addison-Wesley, Reading, MA, 2009.

B. Selic and P. T. Ward, "Challenges of real-time software design," *Embedded Systems Programming*, vol. 9, no. 11, pp. 66–82, Oct. 1996.

L. Sha, M. H. Klein, and J. B. Goodenough, "Rate monotonic analysis for real-time systems," Tech. Rep. CMU/SEI-91-TR-6, Software Engineering Institute, Pittsburgh, PA, 1991.

M. Shaw, "Comparing architectural design styles," *IEEE Software*, vol. 12, no. 6, pp. 27–41, Nov. 1995a.

M. Shaw, *Candidate Model Problems in Software Architecture*, Computer Science Dept., Carnegie Mellon University, Pittsburgh, PA, 1995b.

M. Shaw and P. Clements, "The golden age of software architecture," *IEEE Software*, vol. 23, no. 2, pp. 31–39, Mar. 2006.

B. Shneiderman and C. Plaisant, *Designing the User Interface: Strategies for Effective Human-Computer Interaction*, 4th ed., Addison-Wesley, Reading, MA, 2005.

J. E. Shore, *The Sachertorte Algorithm and Other Antidotes to Computer Anxiety*, Viking, New York, 1985.

K. Shumate and M. Keller, *Software Specification and Design: A Disciplined Approach for Real-Time Systems*. Wiley, New York, 1992.

L. Shustek, "An interview with C. A. R. Hoare," *Comm. ACM*, vol. 52, no. 3, pp. 38–41, Mar. 2009.

D. K. Silvasi-Patchin, "Real-time avionics in Ada 83," in *Proc. TRI-Ada 1995*, pp. 118–126.

J. Simpson and E. Weiner (Eds.), *The Oxford English Dictionary*, 2nd ed., Oxford University Press, New York, 1989.

M. Singhal and N. G. Shivaratri, *Advanced Concepts in Operating Systems*, McGraw-Hill, New York, 1994.

C. U. Smith and L. G. Williams, "Software performance engineering: A case study including performance comparison with design alternatives," *IEEE TSE*, vol. 19, no. 7, pp. 720–741, July 1993.

C. U. Smith and L. G. Williams, *Performance Solutions: A Practical Guide to Creating Responsive, Scalable Software*, Addison-Wesley, Reading, MA, 2001.

I. Sommerville, *Software Engineering*, 8th ed., Addison-Wesley, Reading, MA, 2007.

J. Sparkman, "Java threads," Letters, *IEEE Computer*, vol. 37, no. 7, pp. 6–7, July 2004.

Sperry, Sperry Univac 1100 Series Meta-Assembler (MASM) Programmer Reference, Sperry Rand Corporation, 1977.

W. Stallings, *Operating Systems: Internals and Design Principles*, 6th ed., Prentice-Hall, Upper Saddle River, NJ, 2008.

D. B. Stewart, R. A. Volpe, and P. K. Khosla, "Design of dynamically reconfigurable real-time software using port-based objects," *IEEE TSE*, vol. 23, no. 12, pp. 759–776, Dec. 1997.

I. Stewart, *The Problems of Mathematics*, Oxford University Press, New York, 1987.

J.-E. Strömberg, *Styrning av LEGO-bilfabrik. Laboration i digital styrning* (In Swedish), Linköpings Tekniska Högskola, 1991.

W. Strunk, Jr., and E. B. White, *The Elements of Style*, 4th ed., Allyn and Bacon, Newton, MA, 2000.

A. S. Tanenbaum and A. S. Woodhull, *Operating Systems: Design and Implementation*, 3rd ed., Prentice-Hall, Englewood Cliffs, NJ, 2006.

P. Taylor, "Designerly thinking: What software methodology can learn from design theory," in *Proc. International Conference on Software Methods and Tools 2000 (SMT 2000)*, pp. 107–116.

J. R. Trimble, *Writing with Style*, Prentice-Hall, Englewood Cliffs, NJ, 1975.

D. Tsichritzis, "How to surf the technology waves we created," *Comm. ACM*, vol. 40, no. 2, pp. 49–54, Feb. 1997.

S. Turkle, *Life on the Screen: Identity in the Age of the Internet*, Touchstone, 1995.

S. Turkle, *The Second Self: Computers and the Human Spirit*, Simon and Schuster, New York, 1984. Also 20th anniversary ed., MIT Press, Cambridge, MA, 2005.

P. H. J. van Eijk, C. A.Vissers, and M. Diaz, *The Formal Description Technique LOTOS*, North Holland, Amsterdam, 1989.

S. H. Vaughan, "Process migration within a satellite constellation," D.CS. dissertation, Colorado Technical University, Colorado Springs, CO, 1998.

A. Vermeulen, S. W. Ambler, G. Bumgardner, E. Metz, T. Misfeldt, J. Shur, and P. Thompson, *The Elements of Java™ Style*, Cambridge University Press, 2000.

F. Wagner, R. Schmuki, T. Wagner, and P. Wolstenholme, *Modeling Software with Finite State Machines: A Practical Approach*, Auerbach, Boca Raton, FL, 2006.

P. T. Ward and S. J. Mellor, *Structured Development for Real-Time Systems*, Yourdon, vols. 1 and 2, 1985; vol. 3, 1986.

P. T. Ward, "How to integrate object orientation with structured analysis and design," *IEEE Software*, vol. 6, no. 2, pp. 74–82, Mar. 1989.

G. M. Weinberg, *The Psychology of Computer Programming*, Van Nostrand Reinhold, New York, 1971.

J. Weisenbaum, *Computer Power and Human Reason*, W. H. Freeman, New York, 1976.

A. J. Wellings, *Concurrent and Real-Time Programming in Java*, Wiley, Hoboken, NJ, 2004.

A. J. Wellings, R. W. Johnson, B. I. Sandén, J. Kienzle, T. Wolf, and S. Michell, "Integrating object-oriented programming and protected objects in Ada 95," *ACM TOPLAS*, vol. 22, no. 3, pp. 506–539, May 2000. Reprinted in *Ada Letters*, vol. 22, no. 2, pp. 11–44, June 2002.

J. A. Whittaker and S. Atkin, "Software engineering is not enough," *IEEE Software*, vol. 19, no. 4, pp. 108–115, July 2002.

B. Whorf (J. Carroll, Ed.), *Language, Thought, and Reality: Selected Writings of Benjamin Lee Whorf*, MIT Press, Cambridge, MA, 1956.

R. J. Wieringa, *Design Methods for Reactive Systems: Yourdon, Statemate, and the UML*, Morgan Kauffman, Los Altos, CA, 2003.

J. M. Wing, "Computational thinking," *Comm. ACM*, vol. 49, no. 3, pp. 33–35, Mar. 2006.

T. Winograd, *Bringing Design to Software*, ACM Press, Addison-Wesley, 1996.

N. Wirth, "Program development by stepwise refinement," *Comm. ACM*, vol. 14, no. 4, pp. 221–227, Apr. 1971.

W. Yin and M. Tanik, "Reusability in the real-time use of Ada," *International Journal of Computer Applications in Technology*, vol. 4, no. 2, pp. 71–78, 1991.

S. J. Young, *Real-Time Languages: Design and Development*, Ellis Horwood, Chichester, West Sussex, England, 1982.

E. Yourdon, "IT Megatrends—Strategic Planning for the Key IT Trends in the Next Decade," Colorado Springs Software Engineering Distinguished Speaker Series, Feb. 8, 2000.

E. Yourdon and L. L. Constantine, *Structured Design: Fundamentals of a Discipline of Computer Program and Systems Design*, Prentice-Hall, Englewood Cliffs, NJ, 1979.

P. Zave, "A distributed alternative to finite-state-machine specifications," *ACM TOPLAS*, vol. 7, no. 1, pp. 10–36, Jan. 1985.

Index